THE CASES
THAT HAUNT US

From Jack the Ripper to JonBenet Ramsey,
the FBI's Legendary Mindhunter Sheds Light
on the Mysteries That Won't Go Away

JOHN DOUGLAS
AND MARK OLSHAKER

A LISA DREW BOOK

SCRIBNER
New York   London   Toronto   Sydney   Singapore

A LISA DREW BOOK/SCRIBNER
1230 Avenue of the Americas
New York, NY 10020

SCRIBNER and design are trademarks of Macmillan Library Reference USA, Inc.,
used under license by Simon & Schuster, the publisher of this work.
A LISA DREW BOOK is a trademark of Simon & Schuster, Inc.

DESIGNED BY ERICH HOBBING

Set in Bembo

Manufactured in the United States of America

1   3   5   7   9   10   8   6   4   2

Library of Congress Cataloging-in-Publication Data

Douglas, John E.
The cases that haunt us: from Jack the Ripper to JonBenet Ramsey, the FBI's
legendary mindhunter sheds light on the mysteries that won't go away/John Douglas
and Mark Olshaker.
p.   cm.
"A Lisa Drew Book"
1. Murder—Investigation—Case studies. 2. Murderers—Psychology—Case studies.
3. Criminal psychology—Case studies. I. Olshaker, Mark, date. II. Title.

HV8079.H6 D68 2000
364.15'23—dc21   00–063524

ISBN 0-684-84600-4

To the victims
of all the
unsolved violent crimes
this book is dedicated
with respect and love.

They must never be forgotten
nor their cause abandoned.

AUTHORS' NOTE

As usual, we are indebted to many people for making this book possible:

—Our brilliant and insightful editor, Lisa Drew, always there for us.

—Our agent and close friend, Jay Acton, who has shaped our writing careers and everything that goes with them.

—Ann Hennigan, dauntless and intrepid Mindhunters research coordinator, who makes sure we know what we need to.

—Katherine Johnston Ramsland, Ph.D., accomplished author in her own right, who researched and worked up these cases for us and then played the role of local law enforcement agency to John's mindhunting.

—Jake Klisivitch, Lisa's assistant and the one who kept us on track and put together all the pieces.

—Martin Fido, distinguished and prolific author, scholar, criminologist, and now good friend, for his extraordinary contributions to the Jack the Ripper case and our understanding of it, as well as his general good counsel.

—Mark W. Falzini, New Jersey State Police archivist, for his hugely valuable help on the Lindbergh kidnapping case.

—Leonard Rebello, Fall River historian, for equally valuable assistance on the Borden case, photos, and generosity in reviewing the Borden chapter.

—Donald Rumbelow, another of the foremost Ripper experts, for his wonderful book and profound personal insights.

—Paul Cardalucci and the other teachers, staff, and residents of Highfields school, formerly the Lindbergh house, Hopewell, New Jersey, for their gracious hospitality and fascinating tour.

—John Ross, curator of the Museum of Crime, the famous "Black Museum," New Scotland Yard; writer Kris Radish; Martha and Sally McGinn and the staff of the Lizzie Borden Bed and Breakfast, Fall River, Massachusetts, for all of their consideration and kindness.

And, as always,

—Carolyn C. Olshaker, without whose help . . . well, we all know the rest.

—JOHN DOUGLAS AND MARK OLSHAKER
June 2000

CONTENTS

How often have I said to you that when you have eliminated the impossible, whatever remains, *however improbable,* must be the truth?

—Sir Arthur Conan Doyle,
The Sign of Four

INTRODUCTION

On its most essential level, criminology is about why people do the things they do; that is, it is about the human condition. And of all the millions of horrendous crimes that have been committed over the years, certain criminal cases seem to have lives of their own. Despite the passage of time, they continue their hold on our collective imagination, and our collective fears. For some reason, each of these cases and the stories surrounding them touches something deep in that human condition—because of the personalities involved, the senseless depravity of the crime, the nagging and persistent doubts about whether justice was actually done, or the tantalizing fact that no one was caught. In any event, the case remains a fascinating and perplexing mystery and gets to the core of how we see ourselves as human beings and our relationship to society.

Each of the cases we'll be examining in this book has remained extremely controversial. And each of these cases contains some universal truth at its base to which we can all relate. Taken together, they present a panorama of human behavior under extreme stress and an inevitable commentary on good and evil, innocence and guilt, expectation and surprise.

Through the cases we'll examine, we hope to show the uses, benefits, and limitations of modern behavioral profiling and criminal investigative analysis as practiced by the behavioral science units of the National Center for the Analysis of Violent Crime at the FBI Academy in Quantico, Virginia. The operational division that actually does the profiling and case consultations has undergone several changes of name and designation. At the time that I was its chief until my retirement in 1995, it was known as the Investigative Support Unit, or ISU. Sometimes, we can go a long way in determining the identity of an unknown offender. Sometimes, we can only say who it is not. Sometimes, we can't do either. But we've greatly improved our ability to interpret forensic evidence from a behavioral standpoint. Had the discipline been around at the time of the earliest cases in this book, I believe we would have solved them and delivered the offenders to justice.

We will be focusing on several key themes that will be familiar to readers of our previous books. One is motive: why an individual decided to do what he did and how we try to determine that. Another is the evolution and development of the criminal: you don't just wake up one morning and commit any of these crimes without prior behavioral indicators and a specific precipitating stressor. A third is postoffense behavior: how an individual who has committed a serious crime may be expected to act and react afterward. All of these factors will go into our evaluations.

Let's get down to the nitty-gritty. Are we going to be able to "solve" each of these crimes that have tantalized and eluded experts for years, decades, or in two instances, more than a century?

Frankly, that's doubtful.

What we are going to do is to approach each one to some extent differently than it's been approached in the past. We're going to look at and examine each one as I would have as a profiler and criminal investigative analyst for the FBI. We're going to use the crimes and crime-scene evidence to indicate the type of individual we should be looking for. Then we'll evaluate the subjects—those suspected, accused, and/or convicted of the crime—to see how well they fit in.

In much of the revisionist-theory industry surrounding these cases, writers tend to decide what they think and then employ the evidence to support that theory. Then they essentially challenge skeptics to prove a negative. Among the examples of this phenomenon, which will become clear as you read on:

— Why couldn't Mary Kelly's estranged husband have killed four of her friends to scare her into getting back with him, then killed her when she would not, and blamed it all on some mythical Jack the Ripper?

— Why couldn't Emma Borden have secretly come back, snuck into her house, and killed her parents?

—Why couldn't Patsy Ramsey have killed her daughter in a rage if she discovered the child was being molested by Patsy's husband? And why couldn't John Ramsey have been a molester?

Despite absolutely no evidence for any of these suppositions, despite a feeding frenzy of character investigation in all three cases, facts become almost irrelevant to certain "analysts."

"It could have happened that way" is good enough for some theorists. It won't be good enough for us. When there is a discrepancy in the evidence or more than one version of the same set of facts, we'll acknowledge that and see what we can do with it. Whatever we can determine or whatever we fail to determine, we're going to let the evidence lead us, not the other way around.

Okay? Then let's get started.

The Cases
That Haunt Us

CHAPTER ONE

JACK THE RIPPER

In the dark realm of serial killers, this is ground zero: the point from which virtually all history and all discussions begin.

By modern standards, the ghostly predator who haunted the shadowy streets of London's East End between August and November of 1888 was nothing much to write home about. Sadly, many of his successors—people I and my colleagues have had to hunt—have been far more devastatingly productive in the number of lives they took, and even the gruesome creativity with which they took them. But none other has so quickly captured and so long dominated the public's fascination as Jack the Ripper: the Whitechapel Murderer, the personification of mindless brutality, of nameless, motiveless evil.

Why this one? Why him (although some still steadfastly maintain it was a her)? There are several reasons. For one, the crimes—a series of fatal stabbings that escalated into total mutilation—were concentrated in a small geographic area, directed at a specific type of preferred victim. For another, though there had been isolated sexually based killings in England and the European continent in the past, this was the first time most Victorians had ever faced or had to deal emotionally with such a phenomenon. Add to this a social reform movement and a newly energetic and outspoken press eager to call attention to the appalling living conditions in the East End, and you have all the ingredients for what became, literally, one of the biggest crime stories of all time.

The reasons why these murders continue to fascinate above all others, even in this modern age with our seemingly endless succession of "crimes of the century," are equally strong, though, as we will quickly learn, often based on misimpression. In spite of their barbarism, they represent a real-life mystery from the era of Sherlock Holmes—the bygone romantic era of high Victorian society, gaslights and swirling London fog, though where the killings actually took place had little real relationship to

Victorian splendor, and each crime was actually committed on a night without fog. On only one of the nights was it even raining. In fact, at the same time the Ripper murders were terrorizing the desperate East End, a melodrama based on Robert Louis Stevenson's *The Strange Case of Dr. Jekyll and Mr. Hyde* was thrilling audiences at the Lyceum Theatre in the fashionable and comfortable West End. Together these two events, one safely fanciful and the other horrifyingly real, gave many their first dawning awareness of the potential for inherent evil in so-called ordinary or normal people.

And despite a tremendous allocation of manpower and resources on the parts of two police forces at the time, and the efforts of countless "Ripperologists" in the more than 110 years since then, the crimes remain unsolved, tantalizing us with their profound mystery (though if we were working them today, I feel confident we could crack them in relatively short order). Some of the suspects and motives are very "sexy"—far out of the range of the normal serial killer—including not only the royal physician but also the two men in direct line to the throne!

And as important as any other reason for the continuing fascination is that powerfully evocative and terrifying name by which the unknown subject—or UNSUB, as we refer to him in my business—was called. Although here again, I maintain that this was not the identity he chose for himself.

But whatever the misconceptions or qualifications, we have to acknowledge that Jack the Ripper created the myth, the evil archetype, of the serial killer.

As a criminal investigative analyst and the first full-time profiler for the FBI, I'd often speculated about the identity of Jack the Ripper. But it wasn't until 1988, the hundredth anniversary of the Whitechapel murders, that I actually approached the case as I would one that was brought to me at the Investigative Support Unit at Quantico from a local law enforcement agency.

The occasion was a two-hour television program, *The Secret Identity of Jack the Ripper,* set to be broadcast live from Los Angeles in October and hosted by British actor, writer, and director Peter Ustinov, with feeds from experts in London at the crime scenes themselves and at Scotland Yard, the headquarters of London's Metropolitan Police. When the producers approached me about participating in the program and constructing a profile of the killer, I decided it was worth a try for a couple of reasons. First, I thought the profile might be useful in training new agents. Second, it's difficult to resist matching wits, even a century later, with the most famous murderer in history. And third, since it was a hundred years after the fact, no negative consequences were possible other than making a fool of myself on national television, a fear I'd long since gotten over. Unlike with the scores of "real" cases I was dealing with every day, no one was going to die if I was wrong or gave the police bad information. More than a decade later, I still believe in the analysis I did, with an interesting and important addition, which we'll get to later.

I captioned the profile the way I would an actual one that would become part of a case file:

UNSUB; AKA JACK THE RIPPER;
SERIES OF HOMICIDES
LONDON, ENGLAND
1888
NCAVC—HOMICIDE (CRIMINAL INVESTIGATIVE ANALYSIS)

The FBI, like most government agencies, is addicted to acronyms. The one on the last line, NCAVC, stands for National Center for the Analysis of Violent Crime, the overall program established in 1985 and located at the FBI Academy to encompass a bunch of other acronyms including, but not limited to, the BSU, or Behavioral Science Unit (teaching and research); ISU, the Investigative Support Unit, which carries out the actual consulting, profiling, and criminal investigative analysis; and VICAP, the Violent Criminal Apprehension Program computer database on multiple offenders. During my tenure as chief of ISU, we and other operational entities, such as HRT, the Hostage Rescue Team, were pulled in under the umbrella of CIRG, the Critical Incident Response Group. And after I retired in 1995, my unit was, for a time, absorbed into a new group, CASCU, the Child Abduction and Serial Crimes Unit. Anyway, you get the idea.

I cautioned the producers the same way everyone in my unit had been trained to caution the police and law enforcement agencies around the United States and the world with whom we dealt: our work can only be as good as the case information provided to us. Many of the tools we'd have to work with today—fingerprints, DNA and other blood markers, extensive crime-scene photography—were not available in 1888, so I'd have to do without them in developing my analysis. But then, as now, I would still begin with the known facts of the crimes.

Like most serial murders, the case is complicated, with multiple victims and leads that go off in many directions. It is therefore useful to go into the case narrative in some detail, just as we would if we were receiving it from a local law enforcement agency seeking our assistance. So we'll relate the details—anything that might be important to the profile—and analyze each element at the proper point in the decision-making process. In that way, we can see something of how the analytical decisions in mindhunting are made and on what they are based. By the time we present the profile, you should have some background and perspective for understanding the choices and conclusions I've come to. We can then apply this process to all of the subsequent cases we'll consider. The more a profiler knows of the story of *what* happened, the better able he or she will be in putting together the *why* and the *who*.

Whenever we construct a profile or offer analytical or strategic assistance to a local law enforcement agency on a series of unsolved crimes, a critical part of the case materials we request is a map with crime scenes indicated and a description of what each area is like. And in this case, geography is a particularly important consideration because it so carefully defines the type of victim selected and type of offender who would feel comfortable here.

"THE ABYSS"

I always stress the importance of understanding the victimology and social context of the crime. And you can't understand this case without some comprehension of what life was like in the East End of London, specifically Whitechapel and Spitalfields, in the final decades of the Victorian era. Adventure novelist Jack London would characterize this area as "the Abyss" after spending seven weeks living there during the summer of 1902. The nonfiction book that emerged from this experience, *The People of the Abyss,* would become just as much of an instant classic in its own circles as *The Call of the Wild,* published the same year. And the conditions and situation described were little different in 1902 than they had been fourteen years earlier.

The most extreme areas of the East End—the region bordering Whitechapel High Street and Whitechapel Road, just north of the Tower of London and the London Docks—was a strange, distant, and fearful place to those fortunate enough to live elsewhere within the metropolis. Though it was but a short cab or railway journey away from central London, the virtual capital of the Western world when it was true that the "sun never set" on the richest and most economically productive empire in history, this district was a teeming, Dickensian area of factories, sweatshops, and slaughterhouses. Dominated by poor cockneys, it was increasingly populated by immigrants straight off the docks, particularly Eastern

European Jews escaping persecution and pogroms, with their strange languages, insular customs, and wariness of gentiles. Many of them joined their fellow countrymen in the tailoring and leather trades centered around Brick Lane. Middlesex Street, better known as Petticoat Lane, became a bustling Sunday marketplace of Jewish goods and culture.

Here in Whitechapel, skilled jobs were scarce and disease was rampant. Those lucky enough to have a place to live were crammed into dirty and primitive accommodations without even the semblance of privacy. The rest, figured to be about 10 percent of the East End's total population of nine hundred thousand, lived a day-to-day existence—on the streets, in the grim and notorious public workhouses, or in the hundreds of filthy "doss-houses," which offered a bed for around fourpence a night, paid in advance.

Mary Ann Nichols, known as Polly, was a prostitute, one of about twelve hundred in Whitechapel at the time, according to Metropolitan Police estimates. She was five feet two inches tall, forty-five years of age, and had five missing teeth. Many, if not most, of the women like Nichols were not prostitutes by choice. Existence for them (and often, their families) was so desperate that turning cheap tricks might mean the difference between eating and not eating, between having a place to sleep and taking their chances on the dark and dangerous streets. Add to this the chronic alcoholism through which many women tried to forget their hopelessness, and we see a segment of society living on the very fringe.

Polly Nichols was the mother of five children and the survivor of a tempestuous marriage that had finally broken up over her inability to stay away from the bottle, a situation initially caused, she claimed, by her husband William's philandering. He was given custody of the children. At a little after 1:00 in the early morning hours of Friday, August 31, 1888, Polly was attempting to finesse her way into a doss-house on Flower and Dean Street, where she'd been sleeping for about a week. She'd spent most of the last month in another doss-house one block over on Thrawl Street, in a room she shared with four other women. But this evening, she didn't have the required fourpence for her bed, having just spent money she'd earned earlier in the day on liquor at the Frying Pan pub down the block where it intersected with Brick Lane.

The deputy lodging housekeeper would not let her stay without payment. Polly told the man not to give her bed to anyone else and, giddy with drink, declared, "I'll soon get my doss money. See what a jolly bonnet I've got now." Apparently, the hat had been bought for her by a customer and made her feel more attractive.

At about 2:30 A.M., she met up with her friend Ellen Holland, also known as Emily. In the East End, multiple names were apparently common. Holland, who had previously shared the Thrawl Street room with Polly, had come out to watch a large fire, a common form of entertainment for those too poor to afford any other. She reported Polly to be extremely drunk and leaning against a wall for support.

Ellen urged her to go back to Thrawl Street, but Polly confessed, "I've had my lodging money three times today and I've spent it. It won't be long before I'm back." Then she wandered off in the direction of Flower and Dean Street.

That was the last time anyone saw Polly Nichols alive.

About 3:40 that morning, two carmen, or wagon drivers, Charles A. Cross and Robert Paul, were walking to work along Buck's Row, about a block from London Hospital on Whitechapel Road, when Cross thought he saw a tarpaulin on the other side of the street near the entrance to a stable. He went over to examine it more closely and see if it was usable. But when he neared the tarp, he realized it was the body of a woman, her eyes wide open, hands by her side, skirts hiked up to her waist, and legs slightly parted. Next to the body was a black, velvet-trimmed straw bonnet.

Cross called Robert Paul over. He felt the woman's face, which was still warm, leading him to believe she might still be alive. He listened intently and thought maybe he detected a faint heartbeat. But Cross felt her hands, which were cold, and concluded she was dead. The two men left to find a policeman.

They found Metropolitan Police constable Jonas Mizen walking his beat on nearby Hanbury Street and told him what they'd found. Mizen hurried back with them to Buck's Row, where Constable John Neil had just come upon the body on his own. With his lantern, Neil signaled another passing police officer, Constable John Thain. He directed Thain to go find Dr. Rees Ralph Llewellyn, the nearest general practitioner, then told Mizen to secure an ambulance, which in those days meant a two-wheeled wagon long enough to hold a stretcher.

Thain awakened Llewellyn, who arrived on the scene to examine the victim. By this time, two local slaughtermen, Henry Tomkins and James Mumford, were also on scene, though whether they had just happened to show up or had been passing the time with Constable Thain prior to his being called in on the case is unclear. Dr. Llewellyn noted severe lacerations to the victim's throat, but little blood on or around the body. At about ten minutes to 4 A.M., he pronounced the woman dead, estimating that, since the legs were still warm, death had occurred no more than thirty minutes previously and that she had been killed on the spot. The body was taken to the mortuary at the Old Montague Street Workhouse Infirmary. By the time Inspector John Spratling arrived around 4:30 A.M., a crowd was already forming, and the news of the murder started filtering through Whitechapel. Spratling told the other officers to search the scene and surrounding area, then went to join Dr. Llewellyn at the mortuary to record the official description of the corpse.

At the mortuary, Spratling discovered some even more disturbing information than what he'd expect from the "routine" murder of a prostitute—though, strictly speaking, her status had not yet been confirmed since no identification had been made. Still, the circumstances and the fact that she was out on the street at that hour strongly suggested the vocation. Unfortunately, then as now, prostitute murders were not unheard of, often involving simple robbery or a customer who believed he'd contracted a disease. Once clothing had been removed from the body, Spratling could plainly see that in addition to the neck wounds, the abdomen had been ripped open and the intestines exposed.

The following morning Dr. Llewellyn returned to do a complete postmortem. He noted bruising on the face and neck and a circular incision on the neck that completely severed all the tissues down to the vertebrae as well as the major blood vessels of the neck. The deep cuts appeared to have been made with a sharp, long-bladed knife. Llewellyn believed the killer had at least some rough anatomical knowledge and, from a thumb bruise on the right side of the neck, thought he might be left-handed.

BEHAVIORAL CLUES

Looking at this case today with a body of knowledge and experience unavailable to the Victorian investigators (it would be several years before even fingerprinting was available), we could already start putting together some behavioral clues from the wound patterns. The severe bruising about the face suggests to me an initial "blitz-style" attack. In other words, the UNSUB attempted to neutralize his potential victim quickly and unexpectedly before she could put up a defense. This, in turn, suggests an offender who is unsure of himself and has no confidence in his ability to control her or get her where he wants her through any kind of verbal means—an inadequate personality as opposed to one with the confidence to think he can easily dominate women. This, as we'll see, gives us even more clues to his personality and emotional background.

The neck bruising indicates an attempt to choke the victim and further render her incapable of resistance. Then we see the multiple deep stab wounds, which suggest a frenzy of anger and, generally, released sexual tension. That the face suffered no other significant wounds after the initial blitz makes me think that the UNSUB did not know the victim. If this had been a more personally directed attack, I would have expected to see more obliterating wounds to the face, which would represent her persona or humanness. Like just about everything else in profiling and criminal behavioral analysis, this is not a hard and fast rule, as we'll see in the next chapter. But in cases in which the motivation for the crime is essentially power and control—a power and control unavailable to the UNSUB in any other aspect of life, as I would believe it to be here—facial attack is a common phenomenon.

Then we have the deep, circular incision around the neck. This seems clear to me—an attempt to take the head off the victim. Those who have read any of our previous books will know that one of the ways we categorize killers and other sexual predators is according to whether we consider them organized, disorganized, or mixed—that is, a combination of the two types. A killer who wants to decapitate his victim, especially out on the street, which is always a high-risk environment, is someone who I would suggest is "not all there." This is further underscored by the ripping open of the belly and the exposure of the intestines. That doesn't mean he can't mentally form criminal intent, and it doesn't imply that organized killers are normal, socially integrated individuals. It does, however, tell me that this UNSUB's motivations and fantasies are so aberrant that they would interfere with his routine functioning, even his ability to pull off an efficient crime. This is someone who both hates women and has a bizarre and perverse curiosity about the human body that I can only characterize as demented.

While we're on this subject, let's clarify one thing. All killers and sexual predators, in my opinion, have some degree of mental illness. By definition, you can't willingly take another life in this manner and be mentally healthy. However—and this is a big however—though you may be mentally ill, that does not mean that (a) you do not know the difference between right and wrong and (b) you are unable to conform your behavior (not your thoughts necessarily, but your *behavior*) to the rules of society. This is the essence of the M'Naghten Rule, the original codified British legal test of criminal responsibility, which had already been in effect for more than half a century by the time of the Whitechapel murders and which still serves as the basis for the tests of insanity we use today. The rule is named for Daniel M'Naghten, who tried to kill British prime minister Sir Robert Peel, the organizer of London's Metropolitan Police Force.

So someone can be mentally ill but still criminally responsible—they do what they do because they *want to* rather than because they *have to.* Some psychiatrists refer to this problem as a character disorder, a description that I think is pretty accurate.

But are some offenders so far gone that they really do not know what they're doing is wrong? Sure, there are some, and from my experience they also tend to be delusional or hallucinatory. But we can often pick out this type rather quickly, and because they're so disorganized and "crazy," we usually catch them before long. Was the Whitechapel killer one of these? Had he gone over the edge from character disorder to total nutcase? We need more evidence before we can make that determination.

The murder victim was wearing several layers of clothing, which she would have had to do if she was homeless. Her only other personal possessions were a comb, handkerchief, and broken mirror. But on one of her petticoats, police noticed the laundry mark of the Lambeth Workhouse. By process of elimination, the victim was determined to be Mary Ann, or Polly, Nichols, although the initial attempt to have her body identified failed, possibly because of the mutilation. She was eventually identified by Mary Ann Monk, who had been at the Lambeth Workhouse at the same time. On September 6, 1888, she was buried in a pauper's grave in the City of London Cemetery at Little Ilford, Essex.

PATTERN CRIMES?

There was little to go on in solving the crime. Scotland Yard's Chief Inspector Donald Sutherland Swanson admitted that detectives were stumped by the "absence of motives which lead to violence and of any scrap of evidence, either direct or circumstantial." In fact, Swanson and his colleagues just didn't understand the motive. They'd have had no reason to; they'd never seen it before. However, despite the lack of experience with this type of crime, both Dr. Robert Anderson, assistant Metropolitan Police commissioner in charge of the Criminal Investigation Department (CID), and CID assistant chief constable Melville Leslie MacNaghten said that it was obviously the work of a sex maniac.

It was possible, though, that the Nichols killing was related to an earlier prostitute murder in the East End; no one was certain. In fact, they're not sure to this day.

Martha Tabram, also known as Emma Turner, was the estranged wife of a warehouseman, Henry Tabram. After the estrangement, she lived on and off for a number of years with William Turner, who, though a carpenter by training, worked as a street hawker. This accounts for her two surnames. As in the case of Polly Nichols, each man eventually left her because of her excessive drinking.

On the evening of August 6, 1888, a bank holiday, Martha went out with her friend Mary Ann Connolly, known locally as Pearly Poll. Connolly later testified that the two of them had visited several pubs, including the Two Brewers, where they were picked up by two members of the Grenadier Guards, a prestigious unit of the army. They went to other pubs, including the White Swan on Whitechapel High Street, before finally parting company around 11:45 P.M. Poll and her guardsman then went into Angel Alley for stand-up sex against a wall. She saw Martha go into George Yard, presumably with similar intentions.

At around 3:30 the next morning, taxi driver Alfred Crow returned to his tenement flat on the northeast side of George Yard and saw what he thought was a derelict sleeping on the first-floor landing. About an hour and twenty minutes later, another tenant and dockyard laborer, John Saunders Reeves, came downstairs and saw what he realized was a body.

Dr. Timothy Killeen, who examined the body for the police at about 5:30 A.M., estimated that the approximately forty-year-old woman had died about two hours previously, or shortly before Crow first noticed her. Altogether, the victim had suffered thirty-nine stab wounds, with the breasts, abdomen and genitalia being the primary targets. Most of the wounds were unremarkable in terms of the likely weapon used, with the exception of a wound in the center of the sternum, which appeared to have come from a dagger or bayonet. This suggested that perhaps the crime had been committed by the guardsman with whom Martha Tabram had been seen earlier in the evening.

With two unsolved murders in the same area in the same month, uneasiness settled over Scotland Yard. But apart from those who knew either of the unfortunate victims, London as a whole, and even the East End, did not really take notice. After all, homeless prostitutes were the throwaways of society, and even though both crimes were exceedingly brutal and seemed without apparent motive, this was not something with which proper folk had to be overly concerned.

That all changed on the morning of Saturday, September 8, and in a sense, the world of criminology has not been the same since.

ANNIE CHAPMAN

Just before 6 A.M., carman John Davis finally got up after having spent a restless night. He left the third-floor flat he'd occupied for about two weeks with his wife and three sons at 29 Hanbury Street and went downstairs to go to the outside privy. To the left of the back-door steps, he suddenly saw a body. A woman was lying on her back between the steps and the fence of the property's yard. Her dress had been pulled up over her head, her belly had been ripped open, and her intestines were not only visible this time, but pulled out and draped over her left shoulder. Other residents and passersby quickly assembled. Some of them and Davis each went off in search of a policeman. One, Henry Holland, found a constable a couple of blocks away at Spitalfields Market, but the officer told him he could not leave his fixed point. This was but one example of the procedural rigidity of the law enforcement of the day, which would hamper many attempts at bringing the UNSUB to justice.

The first senior police officer on the scene was Inspector Joseph Chandler. He was on duty at the Commercial Street Police Station when he saw men running up Hanbury Street. When he realized what had happened, he rushed to the murder site, covered the body, then sent for Dr. George Bagster Phillips, the police surgeon for H Division, the area where the crime had occurred. Phillips examined the brutally butchered but ritualistically arranged corpse. At the inquest, he described what he had seen:

> The left arm was placed across the left breast. The legs were drawn up, the feet resting on the ground, and the knees turned outwards. The face was swollen and turned on the right side. The tongue protruded between the front teeth, but not beyond the lips. The tongue was evidently much swollen. The front teeth were perfect as far as the first molar, top and bottom, and very fine teeth they were. The body was terribly mutilated. . . . The throat was dissevered deeply; the incisions through the skin were jagged, and reached round the neck. . . . On the wooden paling between the yard in question and the next, smears of blood, corresponding to where the head of the deceased lay, were to be seen.

Phillips went on to observe that all of the wounds appeared to have been made by a sharp knife with a narrow blade and that the evisceration indicated some medical knowledge. He speculated that all of the mutilations may have taken as long as an hour, though with what I've seen from even moderately experienced serial killers, I would suspect less time. As in the case of Polly Nichols, there was no evidence of a struggle. Apparently, the UNSUB had also attacked this one suddenly, neutralizing her before she could fight back.

A message was sent to Inspector Frederick George Abberline of Scotland Yard's H Division, and he quickly showed up on the scene. Abberline, who was forty-five years old and married for the second time (his first wife died of consumption the same year he married her), is something of a legend in police circles, though details of his personal life are rather sketchy. He had risen quickly through the ranks from constable (patrolman) to sergeant, to undercover operative and detective, and then to inspector. Abberline would come to take charge of all the detectives in the Whitechapel investigation.

As he waited for Abberline and other Scotland Yard officials to arrive, Inspector Chandler had the crime scene thoroughly searched. The woman's pocket had been slit open and its contents included such ordinary items as two combs, a piece of muslin, and a folded envelope containing two pills. About two feet away, they found a bloodstained leather apron, of the type worn by slaughterhouse workers or possibly cobblers or leather workers. Since the apron was not wet with blood, it was highly questionable whether it was related to the crime. And since in those days there was no scientific means of typing blood, or even determining for certain whether it was from a human being or an animal, a bloodstained garment from one of the many slaughterhouses in the area would have been easily explainable. Still, any potential clue was likely to have a "life of its own," as this one certainly did.

Dr. Phillips told the inquest he believed the three personal items had been placed with some care—the muslin and the combs at the victim's feet and the envelope by her head. Two farthing coins were also near the body, though this detail was kept secret by the police to help qualify suspects. If this description is accurate, it's another indication of a particular psychosis and mental instability. We often find this in disorganized or mixed offenders—that is, a brutal frenzy of attack, together with careful, ritualistic elements that indicate a need to control or master small, discrete components of the crime scene or victim.

One of my earliest major profiling cases involved the murder of a twenty-six-year-old teacher of handicapped children who was mildly handicapped herself with curvature of the spine. She was found strangled, severely beaten, and sexually abused at the top of the stairwell of the apartment building where she lived with her parents on Pelham Parkway in the Bronx, New York. She had been spread-eagled and tied with her own belt and nylon stockings around her wrists and ankles, though the medical examiner determined she was already dead when that was done. The cause of death was ligature strangulation with the strap of her pocketbook. The NYPD photos showed a scene of appalling gore and cruelty, and this told me a lot about the offender. What told me even more was that her nipples had been cut off after death and placed on her chest, her comb was set in her pubic hair, and her earrings had been placed symmetrically on the ground on either side of her head. This type of compulsiveness and strange ritualism amidst such a frenzy of disorganized mayhem said to me that my prey had some deep and long-term psychological problems. The method of sexual assault, with the victim's umbrella inserted into the vagina, told me that this guy had real problems with normal sexual functioning and, even though he'd be in his twenties, was still very much in the pre- or early adolescent stage of sexual fantasy, experimentation, and curiosity about the female body. Taken together with his obvious sociopathic hostility, it didn't take much imagination to see that we were dealing with a very dangerous individual. I was therefore extremely gratified that we were able to help in hunting down and catching the offender, who, as I'd predicted, lived in the neighborhood, was underemployed, without a car or meaningful job, and had close relatives in the victim's building.

Based at least in part on Dr. Phillips's description of the murder scene at Hanbury Street, I believe the police were dealing with a similar type of offender there, but, of course, they would not have had sufficient comprehension to realize it. Though all the evidence was not yet in, I would have begun honing my profile to reflect a fairly unsophisticated offender, like the killer ninety years later in New York, a combination of a violent and sexually immature and inadequate personality.

Dr. Phillips had the unidentified body removed to the Whitechapel Infirmary Mortuary on Eagle Street, and in the afternoon he conducted a full postmortem, which confirmed some of his earlier observations, including facial bruising as we have discussed previously. Laceration wounds of the neck showed that the killer had tried to separate the various bones of the neck after death, the type of perverse anatomical curiosity I would liken to the attempt to remove Nichols's head.

But there was more. Not only had the intestines been severed from their attachments within the abdomen and placed over the shoulder, the uterus, half of the vagina, and most of the bladder had been entirely removed, apparently cut out with some care. They were not found with the body. The murder of street prostitutes, as we've suggested, was not uncommon. But the postmortem mutilation was essentially unknown to the Victorians.

Not so, unfortunately, to us. What we see here is not only a fevered overkill, but a man who may be taking anatomical souvenirs. The removal of the uterus and vagina suggests to me someone who hates women and probably fears them. By removing the victim's internal sexual organs, he is, in effect, attempting to neuter her, to take away that which he finds sexually threatening. Since, along with this, there is no evidence of traditional rape, the fear of women and their sexual power is a pretty strong bet.

The victim was identified as Annie Chapman by a washerwoman friend named Amelia Palmer. Chapman, born Eliza Anne Smith, was a stout five feet two with brown hair and blue eyes. Of all the victims, she was the most pathetic. In her late forties, her autopsy showed signs of malnutrition and chronic diseases of the lungs and membrane surrounding the brain, which might have killed her before long if the UNSUB hadn't. She had been married to John Chapman, who'd made his living as a coachman for wealthy families in Mayfair. They had three children, one of whom was a girl who died in infancy and another who was physically handicapped. This was not unusual for the poor. Her marriage, like those of Martha Tabram and Polly Nichols, was said to have broken up over her drinking, but since John died four years later of cirrhosis, one might suspect the problem was not one-sided. In any event, she was living by her wits, supplementing whatever small amounts of money she could earn on the streets from selling matches, flowers, and her own crocheting with even smaller amounts from prostitution, working the area right around Spitalfields Market. At the time of her death she was living in Crossingham's Common Lodging House on Dorset Street, where she'd earned a reputation for a violent temper through brawls with other prostitutes. She was also alleged to be a petty thief, and her late former husband had lost at least one job in Mayfair because of her thievery.

Chapman had been wearing three cheap rings, which were not found on her hand. The killer—or some desperate soul—must have taken them, either for their monetary value or as souvenirs.

The accounts of her last night are tragically similar to that of Polly Nichols. Earlier in the afternoon, she had told her friend Amelia Palmer that she was too sick to work but would have to do something to get money for her bed that night. Another resident at Crossingham's saw her in the kitchen, already drunk and taking two pills from a box she kept in her pocket. She dropped the box, which broke, and at that point, she put the remaining pills in a torn piece of envelope lying on the floor. She spent the late night and early-morning hours of Friday, September 7, to Saturday, September 8, drinking, then returned to the lodging house about 1:35 A.M., where John Evans, the night watchman, demanded the fourpence doss money.

She replied, "I haven't got it. I am weak and ill and have been in the infirmary." But, like Nichols, she added, "Don't let the bed. I'll be back soon." She then went upstairs to convey the same message to deputy manager Timothy Donovan, asking him to let her stay on credit. He refused and escorted her off the premises and out to try to make the doss money. As she was leaving, she called out to Evans, "I won't be long, Brummy. See that Tim keeps the bed for me." It's likely that all of the witnesses who reported they saw Chapman drunk that night probably mistook the fact that she was actually very sick. The autopsy showed little alcohol in her body.

From this point on, the narrative gets a little fuzzy. Someone thought he saw her in the Ten Bells pub across from Spitalfields Market soon after it opened at 5 A.M., but this seems to be a case of mistaken identity. A half hour later, Elizabeth Darrell, also known as Elizabeth Long, saw a woman she thought was Annie Chapman on Hanbury Street, talking to a man slightly taller than herself. Darrell characterized the man as foreign-looking, which at the time in the East End was often a euphemism for someone who appeared to be a Jewish immigrant. According to Darrell, the man asked, "Will you?"

Chapman replied, "Yes."

Albert Cadoche, a young carpenter who lived at 27 Hanbury Street, thought he heard a fierce struggle and someone yelling "No!" in the next-door backyard at number 29. But police weren't sure what he'd heard, and like so many other facts about the case, this one remains ambiguous.

Among Inspector Abberline and his colleagues at Scotland Yard, the conclusion was inescapable. The man who had murdered Annie Chapman had also killed Mary Ann Nichols.

Panic spread throughout the East End. Someone was murdering women and the police seemed unable to stop him. Everything was coming together. Did the same fiend who killed Nichols and Chapman also murder Martha Tabram? At first, it had seemed likely that her guardsman escort had done it. But if two other murders had taken place within such a close time and proximity, then that first one could have been done by the same man, too. I would also not discount the possibility that the killer of Polly Nichols was actually attempting to copycat the murder of Martha Tabram.

And some thought maybe that wasn't even the first. On April 2, 1888, another prostitute, Emma Elizabeth Smith, who lived in Spitalfields, had been robbed and raped and a blunt instrument, possibly a bottle, forced into her vagina. Three days later, she died of peritonitis at London Hospital. At the time, police believed she had been the victim of a local gang, though no arrests were ever made. Now, it looked to the terrified residents as if she was merely the Whitechapel killer's first tune-up.

"LEATHER APRON" AND OTHER THEORIES

Suddenly, this forsaken area of London was on everyone's mind. Newspaper reporters flooded in, describing the East Enders as if they were some strange foreign species. The sites of each murder became tourist attractions. The Home Office was advised to offer a reward for information leading to the killer's arrest, but the home secretary decided against it, believing that the locals were so desperate for money that they'd give false information and make the police department's job even more difficult. Though he might have been reacting to his own experience with the local newspapers, for whom playing fast and loose with facts for the sake of a more sensational story was a way of life, he was actually following official Home Office policy. His esteemed predecessor, Sir William Harcourt, had prohibited rewards when he found that they led to false accusations and even deliberately inspired crimes.

The East End was rife with rumors. At least one of the doctors who'd examined the bodies thought the killer showed some medical or anatomical knowledge. Did that mean he was a depraved physician? Perhaps a medical student? London Hospital and its medical college were just across Whitechapel Road from where Polly Nichols was murdered. Were they the killer's training ground and refuge? The poor East Enders were a cynical and mistrustful lot, used to either being ignored or getting the worst of everything. It certainly wasn't beyond the realm of imagination that a healer could be perverted into a brutal taker of lives.

One of the most prevalent suspicions arose from the leather apron found near Annie Chapman's body. When police began questioning Whitechapel street hookers, one of the stories that kept coming up concerned a local bully and hustler known as Leather Apron for the article he was always seen with, supposedly because he was a slipper-maker. According to reports, Leather Apron, who was often seen around Commercial Street, would shake down women and demand money from them. He was generally described as a short, thickset man in his late thirties or early forties, with black hair, a black mustache, and an unusually thick neck. The word on the street was that Leather Apron might well be the Whitechapel killer.

One individual who apparently met this description was a Jewish boot-finisher named John Pizer. A sometime resident of Hanbury Street identified him as the man he had seen threatening a woman with a knife in the early morning hours of September 8. Pizer had a reputation for getting into fights, as well as abusing prostitutes. He was arrested at his residence on Mulberry Street, in the heart of Whitechapel, on Monday morning, September 10. Five long-bladed knives were found there. He was taken to the Leman Street police station and placed in two police line-ups. In one, a female witness was unable to identify him. In the other, a male witness confirmed he was the one seen on September 8, and that Pizer was known around the neighborhood as Leather Apron. Pizer expressed astonishment and outrage at the charge, claiming he didn't know what the police were talking about.

In spite of that, he was a likely suspect, at least for a couple of hours. Then the case began to fall apart. The man who identified him could not identify Annie Chapman's body at the morgue as the woman he had seen being threatened. Then Pizer's alibis for the nights of the Nichols and Chapman murders were checked out and proved ironclad. After a day and a half, he was released.

The John Pizer story provides us with a cautionary tale. Pizer sure looked good for the crimes, and a lot of the surface details fit. Only after police investigated his circumstances was he exonerated. Why am I mentioning this here? Because most of the suspects who've emerged as candidates to be the killer, particularly those who've emerged long after the events, fit with just such convenient circumstantial evidence, as we shall see. Now there's nothing wrong with circumstantial evidence. Sometimes, as we'll further see, it's all we've got and it can be compelling enough for a solid conviction. But the important point to remember here is that anyone we consider as a suspect whom the police at the time could not examine and alibi out in the way they did Pizer is not getting a "fair trial" from us. Of course, no one can, this many years later, but it's something to keep in mind when you hear some of the more interesting, often outlandish, claims.

The police and the press both made a concerted effort to find the "actual" Leather Apron, without any success, while hysteria about the identity of the "Whitechapel fiend" continued to grow.

And a strong undercurrent was emerging as to who he might be. The Jews, emigrating to England to escape persecution in Russia and Eastern Europe, had become a prominent force in the East End. But they spoke a strange language and kept largely to themselves and their own community, maintaining a wary, distrustful distance from gentiles—in other words, "real" Englishmen. When you combine the general resentment of whoever is the most recent immigrant group with the quiet but long-standing strain of anti-Semitism that had been a part of English culture for almost a thousand years, you've got a ready-made scapegoat population. Then add two other factors: Whatever scanty evidence there was suggested that the killer worked in either the local livestock slaughtering industry or shoe and leather trade, both of which were dominated by Jewish immigrants. Just as important, no one believed a true Englishman could do such a horrible thing, so it had to be someone from the largest non-English group evident—the Jews.

And such a horrible thing as what? Who kills and eviscerates just for the hell of it, not for robbery, not for revenge, not even to make a political statement? This was something people hadn't seen before. Was it possible that the character of Mr. Hyde had gone out the stage door of the Lyceum and taken up residence in Whitechapel?

THE LUST MURDERER

In April 1980, my Behavioral Science Unit colleague Roy Hazelwood and I published an article in the *FBI Law Enforcement Bulletin* entitled "The Lust Murderer." We wrote:

> The lust murder is unique and is distinguished from the sadistic homicide by the involvement of a mutilating attack or displacement of the breasts, rectum, or genitals. Further, while there are always exceptions, basically two types of individuals commit the lust murder. These individuals will be labeled as the Organized Nonsocial and the Disorganized Asocial personalities.

We've moved away from such terms as *nonsocial* and *asocial* because they're difficult to understand and differentiate, but it is fair to say that the organized type tends to be someone who may interact well with society; he just has no regard for or interest in the welfare of anyone other than himself. He understands the implications of his crimes and commits them because they give him a feeling of satisfaction and empowerment not present anywhere else in his life. Though he will have a deep-seated sense of personal inadequacy, this sensation will be warring within him with an equally strong sense of grandiosity and entitlement that has nothing to do with his own highly limited accomplishments. He will plan his crimes and is smart enough to commit them some distance from where he lives or works and to take measures to keep them undetected (e.g., hide the body) for as long as possible.

The disorganized offender, on the other hand, is the traditional loner who feels rejected by society. He is not sophisticated enough to commit an organized, well-planned act or to think to hide the body. The crimes, particularly the early ones, will likely be committed close to his home or workplace, where he feels some measure of comfort and familiarity. While we expect some sort of rape or penetration with the organized offender, we often see none from the disorganized one. And as we suggested earlier, while the organized type may mutilate the body as a sign of his contempt or to hinder identification, mutilation by the disorganized type may represent not only his fear, but a basic sexual curiosity about what goes on below the body's surface.

What connects the two types of lust murderers is an obsessive fantasy of the act, beginning long before it is committed. In just about every case of lust murder we've seen or studied, the fantasy comes before the act. Particularly in the case of the disorganized offender, the victim may simply present herself or become available at a time and place at which the subject is ready to act, ready to forcibly draw a human being into his fantasy world. Seldom will the murder weapon be a firearm, because it affords too little interpersonal, psychosexual gratification. More likely, the killer will use his hands, a blade, and/or a club or blunt object of some sort. If an anatomical souvenir is taken, it is often symbolic of wanting to totally possess the victim, even in death.

The term *lust* inevitably brings up the idea of sex, and indeed, sex is a key component of the crime. But as we've already suggested, the motivation for the act, the psychological need it addresses, can be summed up in three words: manipulation, domination, and control. These are the elements that give the perpetrator a heightened satisfaction that he does not achieve from anything else in his life.

So where does the sexual component come in? Clearly, for the lust murderer, sex is joined in his mind and fantasies with power and control. Perhaps the best way to explain it is to use the definition of rape proposed by my friend Linda Fairstein, head of the New York County District Attorney's Office Sex Crimes Unit and one of the great heroes in the constant war against these predators. In the ongoing debate over whether to classify rape as a crime of sex or violence, Linda calls it a crime of violence in which sex is the weapon. Though in the Whitechapel crimes we're not dealing with rape per se, the distinction is still instructive.

In our 1980 article, Roy Hazelwood and I proposed that the formation of a lust murderer personality happens early in life, and subsequent research has given us no reason to alter that opinion. There will be a pattern of behavior leading up to the violence, usually starting with voyeuris-

THE CASES THAT HAUNT US

tic activities or the theft of women's clothing, which serve as a substitute for his inability to deal with women in a mature and confident manner. The organized type will be aggressive during his adolescent years, as if he is trying to get back at society for perceived wrongs or slights. He has trouble dealing with authority and is anxious to exert control over others wherever he can.

If I were examining these cases today, by the Chapman murder I would already be suspecting a lust killer, which will be important when we finally get to our list of possible suspects. Though the crimes largely represent a disorganized UNSUB, mixed aspects suggest a personality somewhere along the continuum.

Did lust murderers exist before the Whitechapel murders? Probably, though for one reason or another they were overlooked as a pattern or misinterpreted as robberies or revenge killings, particularly if the mutilation involved was too extreme. And keep in mind that prior to Victorian London and the Industrial Revolution, cities were smaller and communities more homogeneous. We've speculated that stories and legends about witches, werewolves, and vampires (blood-drinking, or anthropophagy, is a not-uncommon trait of the disorganized offender) may have been a way of explaining outrages so hideous that no one in the small and close-knit towns of Europe and early America could comprehend such perversities.

THE DOUBLE EVENT

The police sent hundreds of extra officers into the East End each evening—one of them reportedly disguised as a woman—trying to catch the killer in the act. This was one of the few effective means of catching a killer of random strangers. If the victim knew the killer, police could follow a trail of relationships and reliable witnesses. If the killer was a robber who followed a pattern in his criminal enterprise, any of a number of casual witnesses or snitches might give him up. But with no precedent for this type of crime, the best strategy seemed to be to use manpower to prevent him from having the opportunity to kill or, if that failed, to have the mechanism in place to stop him as he fled.

About 1:00 in the morning of Sunday, September 30, after a long afternoon and evening of selling, a street jewelry merchant named Louis Diemschutz was returning to the International Workingmen's Educational Club on Berner Street, a fraternal organization founded by immigrant Jewish socialists and intellectuals. He heard Yiddish or Russian singing coming from the open windows of the club. He was driving a small pony cart.

As he turned off Berner Street into the entrance to Dutfield's Yard, the animal suddenly stopped and wouldn't move forward. Diemschutz noticed a bundle against the gate and prodded it with his long-handled whip. He struck a match and saw that it was actually a woman, who appeared to be drunk. This would have been a common sight in this neighborhood at this time of night. Concerned that the drunk might be his wife, he got down from the cart and went into the club, where she worked. It wasn't she, and he soon returned with several club members. They examined the woman more closely and realized her throat had been slashed. Quickly, two of them ran off to find a policeman, on the way meeting another acquaintance, Edward Spooner. He was talking with a woman, probably a prostitute, outside the Beehive pub on Fairclough Street, which intersected Berner at the first corner. The three of them found Constable Henry Lamb on the corner of Fairclough and Grove Street and brought him back with them to the scene.

Lamb sent for Dr. William Blackwell, who arrived at 1:16 A.M. by his own watch. He pronounced her and stated she had been dead for less than twenty minutes, which meant only a few minutes or less before Diemschutz happened upon the body. The time he took to go into the club in search of his wife may have afforded the lurking killer the opportunity to escape. Dr. Blackwell believed she'd been killed standing up, her head forced backward by the silk kerchief around her neck, and her throat cut. A lot of blood was at the scene, and unlike in the previous murders, defense wounds on the victim's hands indicated a struggle.

A hysterical woman, Mary Malcolm, married to a local tailor, was convinced the victim was her sister Elizabeth Watts Stokes and identified the body by an adder bite on the leg. She claimed she'd had a ghostly premonition that Elizabeth would be murdered that night.

At 1:30 the same morning, thirty minutes after Louis Diemschutz had discovered the body, Constable Edward Watkins of the City of London Police Force was passing through Mitre Square on a beat he completed every twelve to fourteen minutes. He found the square empty and peaceful.

You may have noticed that I identified Constable Watkins as belonging to the City Police rather than the Metropolitan Police. In London, they faced (and still face) one of the same problems that dogs American law enforcement agencies today: overlapping jurisdictions. The City of London refers to a one-square-mile area that comprises the traditional business and historic districts, built on the site of the original Roman settlement. The City boundary runs north from the Thames, just to the west of the Tower of London, and includes St. Paul's Cathedral, the

Bank of England, the Royal Courts of Justice, and the Guildhall. It has its own police force, which is separate and distinct from Robert Peel's Metropolitan Police. In the United States, this is a common phenomenon. Beverly Hills and Santa Monica each have their own police forces separate from both the Los Angeles Police Department and the L.A. County Sheriff's Department, even though geographically they are completely within L.A. territory. Various parts of Washington, D.C., are patrolled by the District of Columbia Metropolitan Police Department, the U.S. Park Police, the U.S. Capitol Police, the Secret Service's Executive Protective Division, etc. So who does what, and when, can become problematic. It really gets to be a challenge when an offender is not administratively considerate enough to confine his illicit activities to one jurisdiction.

This is the problem they began facing in London on the night of what became known as the Double Event.

Between 1:40 and 1:42 A.M. Constable James Harvey walked down his beat on Church Passage, one of the three routes into Mitre Square, which fell within the jurisdiction of the City Police. He didn't see anyone and didn't hear anything suspicious. Three minutes later, Constable Watkins began his next tour through the square, approaching from the opposite side. And this time he discovered a body in the southwest corner. A woman was lying on her back in a pool of blood. When Watkins shined his light on the scene, he saw that her throat had been slashed, her dress pulled up above her waist, her abdomen slit open, and her intestines pulled out. Watkins ran to a nearby warehouse to get help, then rushed back to stay with the body. One of the responding officers brought back Dr. George William Sequeira, who said that the woman had been dead only a few minutes. Within another ten minutes, they'd sent for Dr. Frederick Gordon Brown, the City Police surgeon.

Dr. Brown arrived shortly after 2 A.M. and conducted a meticulous examination. A thimble was lying near one of the victim's fingers on the right side. The intestines had been positioned over the right shoulder. The uterus and kidneys had been removed from the body and were not at the scene. The face and right ear had been severely mutilated in what appeared to be a deliberate, ritualistic manner, unlike the seemingly random slashing and cutting of the rest of the body. Dr. Brown determined the death would have been practically immediate, from hemorrhage from the left common carotid artery. All of the mutilations were inflicted postmortem.

THE GOULSTON STREET GRAFFITO

City police fanned throughout the area, hoping to catch a killer whose trail was still hot. At 2:20 A.M. Metropolitan Police Constable Alfred Long, on his first night on the beat, passed down Goulston Street, which came off Whitechapel High Street on the north side and was just over the line (Middlesex Street) from City jurisdiction. Nothing seemed out of the ordinary. Thirty-five minutes later something was there. A bloody piece of cloth, still wet, was lying on the landing of an entryway to 108–119 Goulston Street, a tenement known as the Wentworth Model Dwellings. It turned out to be part of an apron worn by the Mitre Square victim and was probably the only documented piece of physical evidence in the entire case.

On the wall above where the apron fragment was lying, Long saw a message written with white chalk. By his recollection it read: "The Juwes are the men That Will not be Blamed for nothing."

Other officers reported the wording and capitalization as "The Juwes are not The men That Will be Blamed for nothing."

The discrepancy arose because no evidentiary record of what became known as "the Goulston Street graffito" remains. Superintendent Thomas Arnold, head of H Division, arrived at the scene. Alarmed by the implication of the scrawled message and fearing, whether it was related to the killer or not, that it would incite violent anti-Semetic passions already kicked up by the Leather Apron rumors, he sent for an officer with a wet sponge to have it erased. Others, particularly in the competing City Police, argued that it would soon be daylight, at which point the evidence could be photographed before its destruction, but Arnold did not want to take the chance. Police Commissioner Sir Charles Warren arrived on the scene sometime later and confirmed Arnold's order. He thought the graffito was written by someone who wanted to cast general blame on Jewish socialists. The message was wiped out just before sunup, about 5:30 A.M.

Three weeks later, amidst a firestorm of criticism, both personal and as to how the Met was handling the case, Warren would resign his post.

Even if the Goulston Street graffito had been preserved and was known to have come from the killer, it would have been of limited forensic value. Chalk on a wall will not give you the handwriting exemplar of ink or pencil on paper, so attempting to match up the scrawl with any known handwriting would be fairly meaningless. Behaviorally, it might be of some use, but largely, I would think, to say that the writer was unstable, anti-Semitic, or both.

The location where the apron was found, however, is a much more important indicator, because behaviorally, we may reasonably conclude that Goulston Street was along the killer's route between two critical locations: Mitre Square, where the murder took place, and the unknown spot where the killer lived or sought refuge that night. We have to be a little careful about this because, as Scotland Yard pointed out when they retraced the suspected path, a stray dog could have picked up the cloth wherever the killer dropped it and carried it as much as a hundred yards. But I think we can still be confident about the general direction. We should also mention that Mitre Square is only about a twelve-minute walk from Berner Street, where the night's first victim was discovered.

Yet, having said all that, we cannot discount the enormous significance of Arnold's and Warren's decision to erase the message. By doing so, they spawned one of the great conspiracy theories of the case—that of Masonic involvement—and we might as well go into it here.

Most people within the police ranks believed that "Juwes" was merely an illiterate spelling of *Jews*, the people already resented by much of the East End and suspected of involvement with the murders. But there was another interpretation. Juwes, according to some, referred in the secret traditions of Freemasonry to three traitors who had worked on King Solomon's temple and had murdered its architect and master mason, Hiram Abiff. Their names were Jubela, Jubelo, and Jubelum. According to the tradition, the three Juwes had all manner of insidious tortures inflicted on them as punishment and warning, including the removal of their tongues and ritual disembowelment, with the intestines thrown over one shoulder. This, of course, recalls the mutilation of some of the Whitechapel victims, particularly with regard to the intestines. However, with all the mayhem, the tongues were not cut out, which would seem to have been just as symbolic and therefore just as important. As far as the intestines are concerned, there was so much mutilation that you could practically connect any historical mutilating torture with it and not be too far off.

A significant number of those involved with the case, including Warren and for a brief period Dr. Robert Anderson, were Masons. The conspiracy thinking had it that the murders were part of a vast Masonic plot, and that by erasing the graffito, Warren was attempting to protect his fellow Masons, even if it meant destroying evidence and hampering an investigation. Of course, if we accept that it was a warning, why would he then erase it before anyone could be warned? Either way, the logic is just too messy to make much sense from an investigative analysis perspective. It must be said, however, that the Masonic conspiracy theory continued to grow and become more elaborate until finally it even attached itself to already established royal-family theories.

All in all, I tend to agree with the police that the graffito was an incidental finding, not related to the murder. Coincidence that it just happened to be on the wall above the apron? Maybe, maybe not. Graffiti were common in that area, particularly with similar sentiments. The first thing we have to ask is, what the hell does "The Juwes are the men That Will not be Blamed for nothing" or "The Juwes are not The men That Will be Blamed for nothing" mean? For the most logical interpretation, I turn to Martin Fido, the prominent British scholar, author, and crime historian, and among the most knowledgeable and resourceful of Ripper investigators. Fido interprets the syntax of the Goulston Street graffito as being characteristic of the cockney tendency to use double negatives. Fido notes that Goulston Street is right around the corner from Middlesex Street, or Petticoat Lane, the largest Jewish marketplace in London. Connecting the two was Wentworth Street, site of a cheap shoe market. Given anti-Semitism, and that it was well-known that one could obtain inexpensive shoes, clothing, and other goods from Jewish merchants, Fido explains that in cockney dialect the graffito can be "translated" into "The Jews are the men who won't take responsibility for anything" and was probably scrawled by a bigoted and irate (not to mention poor-spelling) East Ender who felt he had been cheated by a Jewish merchant who would not stand behind his product. It would, therefore, be mere happenstance that the angry message was seen right above the bloody apron fragment.

If you accept Fido's double-negative interpretation, which I do, then why couldn't the message just as easily refer to the Juwes of Freemasonry lore? Why couldn't it hearken to a Masonic conspiracy? Well, for one thing, in 1888 London, the "Juwes" reference would have been extremely esoteric. According to Fido's research, all references to Jubelo, Jubela, and Jubelum had disappeared from the already highly secretive English Masonic ritual between 1811 and 1815. Anyone who would know something that obscure was not the type who would scrawl it on a tenement entryway, particularly in flight from a bloody and disorganized murder. And as for its being a Masonic warning about the fate that might befall "traitors," if you're that secretive, why give yourself away in so crude a manner? No, it just doesn't add up.

THE VICTIMS IDENTIFIED

On the evening of October 1, the identity of the Berner Street victim was finally known. Notwithstanding Mary Malcolm's identification of her sister Elizabeth Watts Stokes as the dead woman, Mrs. Stokes turned up very much alive. The actual victim was Elizabeth Stride, a forty-four-year-old émigré from Sweden who was identified by her former husband's nephew, Metropolitan Police Constable Walter Frederick Stride. It is difficult to know what she looked like in life as the only known photograph of her was taken in the mortuary after death. All of the teeth were missing from her left lower jaw, which indicates she seemed to have lived a life of chronic disease and poverty as did the other victims.

And like the other victims, her marriage had broken down at least a few years before. She gravitated from the grim Whitechapel Workhouse to one of the common lodging houses on Flower and Dean Street, then moved to Dorset Street with a laborer named Michael Kidney, who was seven years her junior. Kidney had a criminal record and was said to have beaten her from time to time. She was known in the neighborhood as Long Liz and had repeatedly been arrested for drunkenness.

As closely as the police could reconstruct, Liz Stride was seen at the Queen's Head pub at around 6:30 P.M. on September 29, then returned to Flower and Dean Street at about 7 P.M. Around 11 P.M., two laborers saw her leaving the Bricklayers' Arms pub on Settles Street between Whitechapel Road and Commercial Road. She was with a man who appeared to them to be very properly British, about five feet five. The two men called out teasingly to Liz to be careful in case her escort was Leather Apron. Forty-five minutes later, another laborer saw her with apparently the same man on Berner Street. After the couple kissed, the man said to her, "You would say anything but your prayers." Fifteen minutes after that, fruit merchant Matthew Packer sold a half pound of grapes to a man he believed to be the one others saw with Liz. It was raining, and he noted that the couple stood outside, across Berner Street from his shop, for almost half an hour. They were still there when Metropolitan Police Constable William Smith noted a couple that matched the other descriptions.

Like the previous crimes, this one also gets fuzzy. Dock worker James Brown saw a couple he thought was Liz Stride and her client leaning up against a wall on Fairclough Street. She was saying, "Not tonight. Maybe some other night." When Brown saw Stride's body at the mortuary, he stated he was certain that was the woman he had seen.

Yet at the same time, a Hungarian Jewish immigrant named Israel Schwartz was returning to the International Workingmen's Club on Berner Street when he thought he saw a man throwing Liz Stride to the ground. He crossed the street, at which point the man shouted "Lipski!" at him, an anti-Semitic epithet referring to a Jewish murderer who had recently been hanged. Schwartz said he noticed another man nearby lighting his pipe and, fearful of being mugged, ran away. He gave a complete account to the police, and when he was taken to Stride's body in the mortuary, he also identified her as the woman he had seen.

It was only about fifteen minutes after Schwartz's encounter that Louis Diemschutz encountered the body in approximately the same place. Was it, in fact, Elizabeth Stride that Schwartz had seen? If so, was she killed by the man who threw her down? Or did she get away from him only to be fatally attacked by another? Could this person have been the second man Schwartz saw lighting his pipe? Perhaps that man and the one who threw Liz down had nothing to do with each other. In any event, neither of them matched the description of the man in the couple Constable Smith had seen fifteen minutes earlier.

When you can't resolve conflicting witness statements—and it happens with great regularity—you try to put them all in the back of your mind and move on with other evidence, forensic or behavioral, that seems more solid and reliable. Then, if any other lead opens up, you can go back to what the witnesses thought they saw and see if any of it fits in.

The Mitre Square victim was identified with less difficulty than Elizabeth Stride. She was wearing and carrying all of her worldly possessions, and among them was a mustard tin containing two pawn tickets. One of them was in the name of Anne Kelly, close to the name Mary Anne Kelly given by a woman who had been picked up drunk on the pavement at eight-thirty Saturday night and taken to Bishopsgate police station to sleep it off. The following Tuesday, an unemployed market porter named John Kelly went to the police, fearing that the pawn tickets belonged to his common-law wife, Catherine Kelly, also known as Catherine Conway, whose first husband had been a soldier named Thomas Conway. The victim turned out to be the woman Kelly feared, though the name she was most commonly known by was her nickname Kate and her own maiden name, Eddowes. In a pathetic replay of earlier victims, Conway had left her eight years before over her drinking. She and Kelly, though desperately poor, apparently got on well together.

They had just gotten back on Thursday from a trip to Kent where they had been paid for picking hops, something like migrant farm labor. This was a common activity for East Enders. It got them out into the fresh air while giving them a little money for their efforts. When Kate and Kelly had returned, still nearly broke, they spent a night together at the Shoe Lane Workhouse, where she was well-known. On Friday, Kate gave Kelly a few pennies to stay at a doss-house on Flower and Dean Street while she went to the Mile End Workhouse to try to squeeze out another night before they'd put her to work. On Saturday, she met Kelly back at Shoe Lane and took a pair of his boots to pawn, receiving two shillings and sixpence.

The couple used the money to buy groceries and have breakfast, and then, broke again, Kate went to try to find her daughter to borrow money, but couldn't find her. The next time she was accounted for was that evening, when City Police Constable Louis Robinson found her lying drunk on the pavement. When she couldn't stand up on her own, that's how she ended up at Bishopsgate police station.

She woke up about half past midnight and asked to be released. Constable George Hutt promised to let her go when she was "capable," finally opening the door for her at 1 A.M., when he thought it would be too late for her to get any more to drink.

"I shall get a damned fine hiding when I get home," she said, testifying to the domestic violence that was rampant then.

At about 1:35 A.M., Joseph Lawende, a cigarette salesman, Harry Harris, a furniture dealer, and Joseph Levy, a butcher, believed they saw Kate Eddowes at one of the entrances to Mitre Square, talking amicably to a man. But none of the three of them saw her face, only what she was wearing.

That was the last sighting of Catherine Eddowes alive.

LINKAGE

Now, the first thing we have to ask ourselves as profilers is, were the two murders of the Double Event related? The initial response would be yes, but before we jump to conclusions, let's look at the behavioral evidence.

The crimes were committed within a twelve-minute walk of each other, within about a twenty-to-thirty-minute period. The victimology was similar in both cases. What are the chances that there would be two lust killers operating in the same area at the same time, with virtually the same modus operandi—or MO? I used to get asked that kind of question quite frequently by detectives, and then later on if I testified in court trying to link several cases together to show a pattern of behavior.

We were able to argue this quite successfully in the 1993 trial of Cleophus Prince Jr., accused of murdering six women in San Diego. We felt

Prince was extremely dangerous, and if the prosecution could prove he was guilty of all six murders, rather than merely the one they had solid DNA evidence on, then this would qualify under California law as "special circumstances," which would make it a capital case. If that could be established, then there'd be no chance of Prince's getting out on the street again to wreak more human destruction. By showing the similarity of victimology, modus operandi, signature elements, weapons, and locations, we showed the jury how it was beyond reason that two or more different offenders who happened to have identical behavioral traits could be operating in the same San Diego area at the same time.

But is that what we're talking about here in the Double Event in Whitechapel? What are the chances of two lust killers operating at the same time and place? Well, we have a couple of issues to consider.

In the first place, Stride's throat was cut and there was deep bruising on her face and neck, but she was not mutilated in the same way as Nichols, Chapman, and Eddowes. According to the terminology we would use at Quantico, the MO is the same, but the signature appears to be different. MO and signature are two of the most important terms we deal with. Both are used in evaluating behavior and tracking UNSUBs. But they're two distinct aspects of a crime. MO refers to the techniques the offender employs to commit the crime. Signature refers to the elements not necessary to carry out the crime, but what the offender has to do to satisfy his emotional needs. If a bank robber tapes over the lens of a surveillance camera, that's MO. If he feels a need to tear his clothes off and dance naked before that same camera, that's signature. It doesn't help him commit the crime—in fact, in this case, it hurts him—but it's something he has to do to make the experience emotionally satisfying.

Let's take a more serious example of these two elements, and we can get it right from the Whitechapel murders. The killer blitz-attacked Annie Chapman because that's what he thought he had to do to neutralize her so he could commit murder. But then when the murder's been accomplished, the victim dead, he needs to mutilate her. This is very much what we refer to as a signature crime. The murder is not a means to an end, such as robbery or political statement. It is done so the offender can rip her up to satisfy his psychosexual needs.

Okay then, is there a reasonable way of explaining this divergence of signatures between Stride and the previous three victims? Sure there is. His name is Louis Diemschutz. A logical reason why the UNSUB did not butcher Liz Stride after he'd killed her is that Diemschutz surprised him and he had to flee before his work was completed. But then, his bloodlust was not sated, so he had to go find another woman, a vulnerable prostitute, to mutilate. This next time, with Kate Eddowes, he had his way. In fact, maybe he had so much time that he actually wrote a cryptic message on the wall of Goulston Street for his pursuers to find and interpret.

This is good criminological analysis so far. But we've got another issue, one potentially more serious than the divergence of signature elements. It is clear from the postmortem examination of Elizabeth Stride that she was killed with a short-bladed knife, not a long-bladed one as was obviously used on Nichols and Chapman. Maybe this isn't a problem. The killer would likely own more than one knife, particularly if he was in either the livestock or the leather trade. But from a crime analysis perspective, this is a problem. Why? Because Catherine Eddowes was also killed with a long-bladed knife.

If the short knife had been used on the second victim of the evening, whether or not it was used on the first, we wouldn't have a linkage problem. That would mean either that the UNSUB had simply changed knives for whatever reasons of MO, or that after the first killing, he thought he could be traced by the long knife and had better switch to another one. But as it is, the long knife is used slightly later in the evening on Eddowes, referring us straight back to Nichols and Chapman but not necessarily to Stride.

Could this mean there was another killer out that night? It could. In fact, a number of Ripperologists think that it does.

Maybe it was a copycat. But so close in time and place? Wouldn't it be awfully coincidental that the copycat struck and then less than half an hour later the original killer struck close by? Yes, coincidences do happen in this business, but I think it is highly unlikely. Based on the victimology, the MO, and the location, I would advise the Metropolitan and City Police to link the Stride murder with the three (and possibly four) others.

But then, what's the behavioral answer for the use of the short knife with Stride? I don't know. It doesn't add up. Did the UNSUB take two knives with him on a whim, then, when he killed Elizabeth Stride, decide that the short one didn't work as well? Could be. This is not an exact science. People, criminals included, do all sorts of things for no particular conscious reason, and this is difficult to factor into your analysis. From my experience, every major case seems to have loose ends. If you're a detective or a profiler, you get used to this ambiguity. You don't like it, but you learn to live with it.

"DEAR BOSS"

If the Annie Chapman murder sent the East End into a spasm of terror, the Liz Stride and Kate Eddowes killings sent all of London into paroxysms. And now, the evil finally had a name.

By Monday, October 1, the world became aware of the contents of two communications—a letter and a postcard—mailed four days apart from two separate locations in east London to the Central News Agency and reprinted in the morning *Daily News* and evening *Star.* By that point, they'd already been forwarded to Scotland Yard for analysis, and the police would disseminate them on their own with the expectation that someone would recognize the wording or handwriting and come forward. The letter, written in red ink and crayon, with a flowing, proper-looking handwriting, read:

> 25 Sept 1888
>
> Dear Boss,
> I keep on hearing the police have caught me but they wont fix me just yet. I have laughed when they look so clever and talk about being on the right track. That joke about Leather Apron gave me real fits. I am down on whores and I shant quit ripping them till I do get buckled. Grand work the last job was. I gave the lady no time to squeal. How can they catch me now. I love my work and want to start again. You will soon hear of me with my funny little games. I saved some of the proper red stuff in a ginger beer bottle over the last job to write with but it went thick like glue and I cant use it. Red ink is fit enough I hope ha. ha. The next job I do I shall clip the ladys ears off and send to the police officers just for jolly wouldnt you. Keep this letter back till I do a bit more work, then give it out straight. My knife's so nice and sharp I want to get to work right away if I get a chance.
> Good luck.
>
> > yours truly
> > Jack the Ripper
>
> Don't mind me giving the trade name

There was a second postscript attached sideways, and this was the part written in red crayon:

Wasn't good enough to post this before I get all the red ink off my hands curse it No luck yet. They say I'm a doctor now ha ha.

This became known forever more as the "Dear Boss" letter, and the first appearance of "Jack the Ripper," a name that quickly superseded the "Whitechapel Murderer" in public dialogue and private nightmare.

The other communication, referred to as the "Saucy Jacky" postcard, was also written in crayon and read:

> I was not codding dear old Boss when I gave you the tip, youll hear about saucy Jacky s work tomorrow double event this time number one squealed a bit couldnt finish straight off. had not time to get ears for police thanks for keeping last letter back till I got to work again.
>
> Jack the Ripper

So the phantom monster had finally communicated with the world and given out his bloodcurdling name. Or had he?

Let me say here that although the police were immediately suspicious of the communications, many Ripperologists, after careful consideration, continue to believe that the "Dear Boss" letter and "Saucy Jacky" postcard are authentic. After some analysis of my own, I go with Scotland Yard and believe them to be fakes.

The process we use to evaluate communications from UNSUBs, such as ransom notes and letters to the police, is known as psycholinguistic analysis. It is not a handwriting analysis—we can get other experts to do that for us when we think we need it—but rather stresses the actual use of language, the style, and of course, the underlying message.

Of all the self-styled Jack the Ripper "copycats" over the years, perhaps the most famous and notorious was the so-called Yorkshire Ripper, who bludgeoned and stabbed women, mostly prostitutes, in the north of England from 1975 through 1980. There had been eight deaths, three other women had escaped, and the case had become the largest manhunt in the history of British law enforcement when I happened to be in England to teach a course at the Bramshill police academy, their equivalent to Quantico, about an hour outside London. The police had already conducted literally tens of thousands of interviews.

As might be expected in a case of this enormity, both the police and the media had received a number of letters purporting to be from the Ripper. They were all evaluated, but I don't think the police placed much evidentiary value on any of them. But then a two-minute tape cassette arrived by mail to Chief Inspector George Oldfield, taunting the police and promising to strike again. Just as the "Dear Boss" letter had been reprinted in newspapers throughout England, the Oldfield tape was played everywhere—on television and radio, on toll-free telephone numbers, even over the PA systems at soccer matches—in the hope that someone would recognize the voice and identify the UNSUB.

I'd heard a copy of the tape back at Quantico, and after classes at Bramshill one evening, they asked me what I thought. I asked them to describe the scenes to me. It seemed the UNSUB maneuvered to get his female victims into a vulnerable position, then, like the Whitechapel Murderer, he'd blitz-attack them, in this case with a knife or hammer. And as in Whitechapel, he'd mutilate them after death. I thought the voice on the tape was pretty articulate and sophisticated for someone who got his ultimate satisfaction out of life from killing and mutilating prostitutes, so I said, "Based on the crime scenes you've described and this audiotape I heard back in the States, that's not the Ripper. You're wasting your time with that." In my business, it is extremely important to be able to evaluate any and all behavioral clues so that the police do not waste their time and always limited resources. With a serial offender, wasted time equals wasted lives.

The actual perpetrator of these crimes would not communicate with the police in this fashion. He'd be an almost invisible loner in his late twenties or early thirties with a pathological hatred of women, a school dropout, and possibly a truck driver since he seemed to get around the countryside quite a bit. When thirty-five-year-old truck driver Peter Sutcliffe was arrested on a fluke on January 2, 1981, then admitted and was proved to be the Yorkshire Ripper, he bore little resemblance to the individual who had made and sent the tape. The impostor turned out to be a retired policeman who had a grudge against Inspector Oldfield.

I suspect something similar was going on with the "Dear Boss" letter. But the letter is clever and legitimate enough that it has led on a lot of people for over a hundred years. So, like the Oldfield tape, I believe it had to be forged by someone who knew how the game was played. The most likely candidate would be a reporter, a conclusion we can arrive at from several directions.

First, the boss referred to is not the boss of the police but the boss of the Central News Agency. While it would not be unusual for a certain type of sexually oriented predator to communicate with the press, to blow his own horn and let the world know how he thinks of himself and what he wants to be called, we would expect this communication to be with an individual newspaper. We know, for example, that both the *Star* and *News,* among many other papers, were publishing regular and lurid details of the Whitechapel murders. On the other hand, it takes a fair amount of sophistication for an offender not associated with the business of journalism even to realize that a news agency exists that supplies the various papers. This type of insider information would be particularly beyond the range of the type of largely disorganized, emotionally deficient individual that the behavioral clues had shown this killer to be.

This is further underscored, in my opinion, by the use of language in the letter. Psycholinguistically speaking, the "Dear Boss" letter is a performance, a characterization by a literate, articulate person of what a crazed killer should sound like. It's too organized, too indicative of intelligence and rational thought, and far too "cutesy." I don't believe an offender of this type would ever think of his actions as "funny little games" or say that his "knife's so nice and sharp."

Rather, this all points to someone who knows how to use language and knows the system and wants to get the message out as quickly as possible, rather than giving an individual news organization an exclusive. And when we look at journalism in Victorian England, we find it to be a freewheeling, sensationalistic business in which truth and restraint were often sacrificed in service of a big story.

Everyone had a vested interest in the Whitechapel murders: the people of the East End who were the potential targets; the rest of London who had had their confident, insular world shaken; the police, who had been tested as never before; the government, which was increasingly embarrassed; and of course, the press. The Whitechapel murders sold papers and kept journalists employed. How much more mileage could they get out of the Jack the Ripper murders?

And it wasn't solely a matter of commerce for the press, either. The agenda for some was more complex. As Martin Fido points out, this was the time of the London County Council elections, and the radicals were attempting to take over the East End and make their mark. The year before, on November 13, 1887, the Metropolitan Police under the leadership of Sir Charles Warren had put down a massed demonstration by the unemployed in Trafalgar Square. The event became known as Bloody Sunday. The Whitechapel murders became a ready-made issue for the radical press. The fear generated became a way for them to say, "Look at the conditions here! What is being done? What would be done if this were happening in the West End?" The mainline papers had to pick up the story or be left behind.

So the "Dear Boss" letter, being made public so soon after the Double Event, helped keep the case in the forefront. Yet I remain in agreement with Assistant Metropolitan Police Commissioner Dr. Robert Anderson and Chief Inspector Donald Swanson, who believed the writer to be an enterprising journalist. In fact, they both believed they knew the identity of the man.

And just as significant as any of these considerations is that, like the Yorkshire Ripper almost a century later, this type of UNSUB would not communicate with the police in this manner. Unlike the organized antisocial type, this individual would not want to proclaim himself this way, particularly not talk about future crimes. This type thinks only of what he is doing at the moment. And he would not have come up with a nickname for himself, particularly such a flamboyant one. In my twenty-five years of experience, all of the serial offenders who communicated with the press or police and proposed names and identities for themselves leaned much more to the organized, antisocial side of the continuum than the disorganized, asocial side. I therefore believe that by disseminating the "Dear Boss" and "Saucy Jacky" communications, the police and press were actually hindering the investigation, diverting attention away from the real UNSUB.

Now, if you've been paying attention to the case chronology, another important consideration for any investigator or analyst, you may have noticed that the "Dear Boss" letter was dated September 25 and postmarked September 27. The Double Event took place on the night and morning of September 29 to 30. And the writer does refer to "clip[ping] the ladys ears off and send to the police officers just for jolly."

Catherine Eddowes's right earlobe was, in fact, sliced off. Was this a lucky guess? Probably. So much was done to Eddowes that the writer could have mentioned just about anything and have been right. If it was the real guy, wouldn't he more likely have mentioned some of the major mutilations he intended to inflict? And of course, he did not send the ear to the police.

As far as the timing, arriving just a day before the Double Event, this again may have turned out to be a lucky guess, but not an uneducated one for someone paying close attention, as an enterprising newspaperman would. The Nichols murder had taken place on a Friday. The Chapman murder had occurred a week later on a Saturday. There had been no murders for the next two weekends, so if one was going to happen at all, the weekend of September 28–29 would be a likely time. Also, with no murders in that stretch of time, the story was starting to get cold, so if you wanted to revive it, this would be the moment.

The "Saucy Jacky" postcard then, which was posted on October 1, was an attempt to "catch up" with what had actually happened and authenticate the first communication: the "double event this time number one squealed a bit couldnt finish straight off . . ." People believe what they want to believe, and for a public anxious to know the monster they were dealing with, this was just the kind of authentification they needed.

Of course, in one important sense, the "Dear Boss" letter became a real and self-actualizing part of the case. Because even if the communication was not authentic, it ensured that this series of crimes would be immortalized. Without the Jack the Ripper identity, I doubt whether this offender would have so captured history and the public imagination.

"FROM HELL"

The frenzy was still intense. In addition to the stepped-up police patrols, locals had formed their own protective organizations. The most highly visible was probably the Whitechapel Vigilance Committee, which was headed by George Akin Lusk, a builder who specialized in the restoration of music halls. Lusk attained a high profile for himself by writing about the case in the *Times*.

On October 16, Lusk received a package in the mail: a small cardboard box wrapped in brown paper and bearing a London postmark. In the box was half a kidney, soaked in wine to preserve it. Wrapped around the kidney was a crudely written letter:

> From hell
>
> Mr Lusk
>   Sor
>   I send you half the Kidne I took from one women prasarved it for you tother piece I fried and ate it was very nise I may send you the bloody knif that took it out if you only wate a whil longer
>   signed   Catch me when
>   you can
>   Mishter Lusk.

Lusk assumed the organ and letter to be a hoax, possibly by a medical student or group of students with easy access to an anatomy lab. But he was persuaded by friends to hand it over to authorities for analysis. Dr. Thomas Openshaw of London Hospital believed it to be human, and from an individual of about forty-five and suffering from Bright's disease, not an inconsistent finding in a chronic alcoholic. A number of other experts had a chance to examine the kidney, with mixed opinions as to its authenticity in the Eddowes murder. That authenticity, however, has never been ruled out, and much of the scholarship over the years suggests that the kidney may actually have belonged to the victim.

I can't speak to the forensic likelihood of the kidney's having come from Catherine Eddowes's body, but the accompanying letter is certainly intriguing. Despite the apparent differences in handwriting (possibly attributed to an increasingly fragmented psyche), many of the Ripperologists and other students of the case who believe the "Dear Boss" and "Saucy Jacky" communications to be authentic believe the same of the Lusk letter, and vice versa. I'm not so sure. Handwriting experts are divided on the matter, so I can't rely on them for help.

I think it is highly significant that even after the frenzy created by the Jack the Ripper pseudonym, the writer of the Lusk letter does not use it. Even after he is tagged with such a "glamorous" title, he does not take it on himself. Since I believe the Boss and Jacky letters to be fakes, I'm intrigued by the possibilities for this one. Though I said I didn't believe this type of offender would feel the need to communicate with the public, it is possible that the Boss letter, especially arriving so soon after the Double Event, may have compelled the disorganized killer to come out and "set the record straight," to keep control, as it were. He may have sent the piece of kidney to authenticate himself after the ear mention in "Dear Boss." In other words, he wouldn't have felt a need to communicate until someone else claimed credit and tried to define his personality and identity for him.

His own sense of identity and emotional orientation is more accurately portrayed by where he says the letter is coming from: "From hell." The style of the writing itself is virtually an illiterate parody of the cleverer and more sophisticated style of the first letter, as if the writer is trying unsuccessfully to show himself equal to the wit and flair of the pretender. I might add that Donald Rumbelow, a former police officer, a gifted author, and one of the greatest experts on the case, agrees with the assessment that of all the communications, the Lusk letter is the only one likely to be genuine.

Some of the letter's critics claim that the spelling—"Sor," "prasarved," "Mishter"—suggests "stage Irish" dialect; in other words, an educated person's attempt to sound colloquial. Although that's possible, to me the spelling suggests someone not terribly familiar with English writing, most likely an uneducated immigrant, who is writing it the way he hears it.

That the letter was sent not to the police, not to the press, but to a local ad hoc community leader is also significant, because I believe strongly that this type of disorganized offender is going to be operating only within his own circumscribed zone of comfort. This is a concept we'll develop in more detail shortly.

It's also not beyond the realm of possibility that a disorganized offender who, we've already established, has a perverse sense of curiosity about the inside of the human body, might try to satisfy that curiosity by eating some of it. And as to the closing salutation, "Catch me when you can," that can have two meanings. One would be an obvious taunt to the police from someone who has found that he can repeatedly get away with murder. The other would be a cry for help, similar to the "For heAVens Sake cAtch Me BeFore I Kill More I cannot control myselF" message scrawled on a wall by Chicago murderer William Heirens with his victim's lipstick. One of Heirens's other victims, a six-year-old girl, was found cut up in pieces in a suburban sewer.

Could I be mistaken about the authenticity of the Lusk letter? Sure. A lot of the experts disagree with me. But what I can say is that unlike the communications that came before it, this one is consistent with what I would expect from the type of UNSUB I suspect Jack the Ripper to have been.

PROACTIVE IDEAS

There was much speculation about the best way to catch this elusive and unprecedented killer, some of it from ordinary citizens, some from "experts." Sir Arthur Conan Doyle, whose first Sherlock Holmes novel, *A Study in Scarlet,* had been published the previous year, speculated that the killer might be a man disguised as a woman. A midwife walking around Whitechapel in the early-morning hours with a bloody apron would arouse little suspicion.

A few years later, in 1894, Conan Doyle suggested to an interviewer how Holmes would have attempted to crack the case. One of his techniques would have been to reproduce the "Dear Boss" letter and invite the public to respond. This is a highly legitimate proactive technique, which Special Agent Jana Monroe of my unit used successfully in the Rogers murder case in Florida when a billboard reproduction of the killer's handwriting led to a swift ID. To give the Metropolitan Police their due, however, they did reproduce the "Dear Boss" letter on posters that were placed throughout the East End, but the technique came to nothing. As I don't believe the letter to be authentic, I'm not surprised.

One newspaper reader, as described by Donald Rumbelow in his landmark *Jack the Ripper: The Complete Casebook,* suggested in a letter that police search the "Saucy Jacky" postcard; since "no two persons' thumbs are alike, the impression of one suspected person's thumb should be taken and microscopically examined." Rumbelow reports that the letter was filed away and that it would be seventeen years before the first fingerprint conviction.

When the press began circulating the idea that the killer could be a depraved doctor or medical student, Rumbelow writes how one person suggested placing the following advertisement in newspapers the Ripper might see:

> Medical Man or Assistant Wanted in London, aged between 25 and 40. Must not object to assist in occasional post mortem. Liberal terms.

Although I do not believe the Ripper to have been a medical man, he certainly had the curiosity, and this is the kind of ploy that might just have brought him out.

Dr. Forbes Winslow, a flamboyant physician and amateur detective who believed the killer to be a homicidal maniac goaded on by a religious mania, suggested having wardens from lunatic asylums patrolling with the police since they would be much more likely to recognize such tendencies in an individual. He also proposed a newspaper advertisement reading:

> A gentleman who is strongly opposed to the presence of fallen women in the streets of London would like to cooperate with someone with a view to their suppression.

The police would then gather in hiding at the prearranged meeting place and grab whoever showed up.

"BLACK MARY"

On the morning of Friday, November 9, Thomas Bowyer, an Indian army retiree known to friends and neighbors as Indian Harry, was dispatched by his boss, local merchant John McCarthy, to collect rent at a house he owned at 13 Miller's Court. It was almost right next to Spitalfields Market and a short walk from both Goulston Street to the south and Hanbury Street, site of the Chapman murder, to the northeast. With the kinds of tenants who lived in such buildings as McCarthy's, collecting the rent was a regular ordeal for both landlord and renter.

The entrance to Miller's Court was a narrow, dingy passageway next to McCarthy's candle shop. Bowyer knocked on the door of Mary Jane

Kelly, also said to have been known as Ginger, Fair Emma, and Black Mary to her various friends and clients. She was a streetwise, twenty-four-year-old Irish girl and by most accounts was quite pretty, though no photographs of her are known.

It was about 10:45 in the morning when Bowyer called on her, a good time to find her in. He knocked several times without response and began to suspect she didn't have the rent money and was avoiding him. He tried without success to spring the lock, but there was a long-broken windowpane that had never been fixed. Inside it, an old coat had been hung in place of a proper curtain for some measure of privacy. He pushed aside the coat and peered in. The room was only ten by twelve feet, and the sight that met Thomas Bowyer's eyes was one of such unmitigated horror that he was virtually paralyzed. A body was lying on the bed, but it was so mutilated, so torn apart, with so much of the flesh ripped off and the insides strewn across the bed and onto the floor, that the dimensions of the body, the outlines of its form, could no longer be discerned.

When the hideous sight had finally registered in his brain, Bowyer raced down to McCarthy's shop. McCarthy went back up with Bowyer, glanced in the broken window himself, then immediately dispatched Bowyer to the Commercial Street police station.

He returned with Inspector Walter Beck and Detective Constable Walter Dew. Dew was a tough straight-shooter known as Blue Serge because of the suit he wore habitually. He would go on to fame as the detective who caught the notorious poisoner Dr. Hawley Harvey Crippen. But the image he saw at 13 Miller's Court was so emotionally harrowing that it haunted him the rest of his life. Since this was the first indoor scene, where good evidence could be collected, a conscientious effort not to disturb it was made, and not until 1:30 P.M., when Superintendent Thomas Arnold arrived, was the door finally broken in.

The bed and surrounding area were saturated with blood. The body, as described by Dr. George Bagster Phillips, showed what had to be the final escalation of the killer's homicidal mutilating frenzy. The face was cut apart and the head just about severed. The breasts had been cut off, abdomen ripped open, and the internal organs thrown about the room. Much of the remaining body, including the pubic area, right thigh, and right buttock had had the flesh removed down to the bone. The heart was missing from the scene. Not only had the killer attempted to desex this victim, he'd gone all the way to dehumanize, to depersonalize her. Some of the doctors who either visited the scene or studied the body in autopsy estimated that the mutilation had taken as long as two hours, though the cause of death, the severing of the carotid artery, had taken place far sooner.

It is difficult for normal people to conceive of an act this depraved as a sexual fantasy, but our research shows that it is. Part of the fantasy is destroying the victim to the extent that the offender feels that he becomes her sole possessor. The mutilation murderer James Clayton Lawson Jr., who teamed up with rapist James Russell Odom, whom he met in California's Atascadero State Mental Hospital, explained his 1970s killings of young women whom Odom had just raped with forthright candor: "Then I cut her throat so she would not scream. . . . I wanted to cut her body so she would not look like a person and destroy her so she would not exist. I began to cut on her body. I remember cutting her breasts off. After this, all I remember is that I kept cutting on her body."

When pressed about the details of his involvement with the victim as distinguished from Odom's, Lawson insisted, "I did not rape the girl. I only wanted to destroy her."

This, I think, is what investigators were seeing at 13 Miller's Court.

Inspector Frederick Abberline arrived and inspected the room. He concluded from the smoldering remains in the fireplace that the killer had burned clothing in there, as well as using the flames for illumination for his work.

For about a year before the murder, Mary Jane Kelly had been living on and off with a Billingsgate Market fish porter named Joseph Barnett. Life with him wasn't uniformly harmonious. In July 1888, he'd lost his job because of theft, and at the end of October, he'd moved out of the room they shared because Mary had invited another prostitute to share the premises. He did, however, continue to visit her almost daily, sometimes giving her small amounts of money. There are also stories that he wanted to get her out of the street trade.

He last saw her between about 7:30 and 8:00 on the evening of Thursday, November 8, when he came by the room. Mary was in the company of her friend Lizzie Allbrook. Around eleven, someone thought they saw her in the Britannica pub with a young man. About forty-five minutes later, Mary Cox, another prostitute who lived in Miller's Court, saw Mary with a different man, with a blotchy face, mustache, and hat. She was noticeably drunk. Between twelve and one, several other Miller's Court residents heard her singing.

At two, she approached George Hutchinson, an unemployed laborer whom she knew, and asked for the loan of sixpence. Hutchinson was broke, so had to turn her down. Hutchinson saw her approached by another man as she walked away, and they were both laughing. He thought he heard the man say something like "You will be all right for what I have told you."

Hutchinson couldn't see the man's face, but followed the pair back to Miller's Court. He heard Mary say, "All right, my dear, come along, you will be comfortable."

Approximately 3:45 A.M. on Friday morning, three women in Miller's Court thought they heard a scream of "Oh, murder!" from the direction of number 13. If it was Mary Kelly who uttered that scream, they would have been the last words she ever spoke.

Joseph Barnett was subjected to four hours of intense questioning by the police. They took his clothing and examined it for bloodstains and other clues. They were satisfied he was not the killer. Recently, however, he has again emerged as a suspect, most prominently in the work of Bruce Paley, whose book *Jack the Ripper: The Simple Truth* was published in 1995. The theory is that he murdered the other women to scare Mary into giving up prostitution, and that he finally killed her in a mad frenzy when it became clear that she had tired of him and would not take him back. During his interrogation by police, Barnett admitted that he frequently read Mary newspaper accounts of the Whitechapel murders.

This theory offers an explanation of why the murders stopped, because they did, with Kelly's death. Proponents of Barnett's candidacy also point out that he was skilled with knives, had some rudimentary knowledge of anatomy, was a local who felt comfortable in the area and could therefore probably approach local hookers without alarming them, and generally fits the eyewitness descriptions. Barnett would, obviously, have easy access to Kelly's room, and it could be more than coincidental that the "Dear Boss" letter mentions ginger beer bottles and such bottles were found in the room.

Paley also cites the analysis I did at the time of the 1988 television series, as well as more general research about serial predators that has come out of my unit at Quantico in showing how Barnett fits the profile. This could be true in certain ways—age, race, dysfunctional childhood with no father, comfort zone, triggering emotional event such as the loss of his job, for example—but these are the superficial characteristics, true of a lot of people. They're almost boilerplate for a certain type of offender. You have to get into the specifics to see if it really fits. And I have never seen, nor do I believe someone would, in this manner, brutally kill women he knows, even vaguely, to scare his own partner and "teach her a lesson." Particularly, on the night of the Double Event, a guy of this type would have been scared off by the first one. He would never have gone after Liz Stride.

The motive just doesn't work. Yes, there are sexual sadists who get off by torturing women. But the mutilation here is all postmortem, so that doesn't fit. Also, these are not planned, considered kills; they're frenzied, out-of-control overkills. If the perpetrator were someone with a personal relationship with the victim, we might expect to see some degree of overkill in stabbing or wounds to the face, but not this kind of ritual mutilation. There's no pattern or internal logic to it. No one who has had a relatively normal relationship with a woman, as Barnett evidently did, could perpetrate this kind of crime.

So if it wasn't Joseph Barnett, who would have had no reason to go on killing after Mary Kelly's death and would have been sufficiently scared by the police interrogation to keep his nose clean the rest of his life, why did the Ripper murders stop after Friday, November 9, 1888? That, of course, is one of the most tantalizing mysteries of the case.

Our research and experience in the Bureau shows that serial sexual predators stop for one of several key reasons, and burnout is generally not one of them. On rare occasions, an offender will have "accomplished" what he set out to do emotionally and will cease on his own. One such example would be Edmund Kemper, who abducted and murdered a series of coeds around the campus of the University of California, Santa Cruz, in the early 1970s. His rage against women was actually directed at his domineering, hectoring mother, and eventually he got up the guts to bludgeon her to death in her sleep with a claw hammer, decapitate her, rape her headless corpse, then tear out her larynx and jam it down the garbage disposal. He then called his mother's best friend, and when she arrived at the house, he clubbed and strangled her to death. Having exorcised this demon from his system, he had a good night's sleep in his mother's bed, then drove to Pueblo, Colorado, where he called the Santa Cruz police from a phone booth and told them to come and get him. But as I say, such self-limiting killers are rare.

More often, serial predators stop for one of three reasons: they're caught; they're caught and put on ice for something else such as a break-in or robbery but not linked to their predatory crimes; or they die, while committing a crime, by the hand of an associate or other offender, by suicide, or by some other "natural cause." Or they don't really stop, they merely get scared out of a particular location and move on to another where their previous crimes are not linked.

Were any of these likely in the Ripper case? Let's take a look at the profile to see if it gives us any suggestions.

THE PROFILE

Victimology

All of the victims were street prostitutes with moderate to severe drinking problems. Both of these facts create "high risk" victims, which makes it difficult to develop suspects. If any evidence such as hair and fibers or semen were obtained from the victim, even if such techniques had been available in 1888, investigators would not know for certain if it came from the subject or some other partner or customer. And since these prostitutes were independent, not controlled by pimps as so many are today, there would be little monitoring of their activities and transactions. That is to say that even more so than today, a female prostitute who drank heavily and then plied the already dangerous East End streets was looking for trouble.

Notwithstanding the Barnett theory and certain of the other conspiracy theories, all reasonable evidence suggests that the victims were targeted because they were readily accessible. The offender did not have to initiate the contact. With the exception of the last victim, Mary Kelly, the others were relatively old, beaten down by life and fairly unattractive. They would have initiated the contact. These are all important investigative considerations.

Medical Examination

The critical findings for a behavioral analysis are:

1. No evidence of sexual assault.
2. Subject killed victims swiftly.
3. Subject was able to maintain control of victims during the initial blitz-style attack.
4. Subject removed body organs from some of the victims, indicating some anatomical knowledge or curiosity.
5. No evidence of physical torture prior to death.
6. Severe postmortem mutilation.
7. Evidence of manual strangulation.
8. In most cases, blood was concentrated in small areas.
9. Rings were taken from one of the victims.
10. The last victim was killed indoors and was the most mutilated. Subject spent considerable time at the scene.
11. Time of death in all cases was in the early-morning hours.

CRIME AND CRIME-SCENE ANALYSIS

With the exception of Kelly's murder, all of the crimes were committed outdoors, and all within an easy walk of each other. This makes the crimes high risk for the UNSUB since these are areas that are often populated around the clock, particularly in the warmer weather months before winter. The bodies of the four outside victims were all discovered within minutes with no attempt to hide them. This in itself is indicative of a disorganized killer. All of the homicides occurred either on Friday, Saturday, or Sunday early-morning hours.

After the first homicide on Buck's Row near Whitechapel Station, the subject moved slightly across town to the west. If a line is drawn from crime scenes two, three, four, and five, a triangular configuration is formed. This has been observed in other types of serial crimes, and the triangle is viewed as a secondary comfort zone for the UNSUB. This movement is caused when a subject believes that the investigation is heating up in his primary comfort zone, which in this case would be the location of the first homicide, in the vicinity of Whitechapel Station. It's my opinion that there were other attacks in the Whitechapel area that either went unreported or for some reason were not considered to be crimes of this offender. If, for instance, the Martha Tabram murder (which occurred not on a weekend but a bank-holiday Monday, another nonworkday) is considered a possible Ripper crime, we should note that it occurred just outside this secondary comfort zone, but to the west. I could make the case that the offender then went eastward for his next kill, before moving gradually back to the area in which he felt most comfortable.

Though the modus operandi evolves with the serial predator, the signature, or ritual aspect, remains in place, often becoming more elaborate over time, as was the case with the final victim. Here, the subject had the time and the privacy to fully act out his fantasies. If there were to be further murders, then, particularly if they were outdoors, we would not expect the subject to engage in such elaborate mutilation; he would not have the time.

COMMUNICATIONS ALLEGEDLY RECEIVED
FROM THE SUBJECT

It is unusual for a serial killer of the disorganized asocial type to communicate with the police, media, family, etc. When they do, they generally provide specifics about the crime that are known only by the subject. In addition, they generally provide information about their motive for committing such heinous crimes. In my opinion, this series of homicides was not perpetrated by someone who set up a challenge against law enforcement. While the killer knew he would be receiving national and international publicity, this was not his primary motivation. If time and law enforcement resources were to be expended on the identity of the author or authors of the communications, emphasis should have been placed on the Lusk letter.

OFFENDER TRAITS AND CHARACTERISTICS

As noted earlier, these homicides may be classified as lust murders. This has less to do with the traditional meaning of the word than with the fact that the subject attacks the genital and sexually oriented areas of the body. Generally, when male victims are attacked in this fashion, they have been involved in homosexual relationships. Though it has been speculated that the offender could be a woman ("Jill the Ripper"), I have never experienced a female serial lust murderer either in research or cases we've received at Quantico. We can therefore state with confidence that Jack the Ripper was, in fact, a male. He was white, since these crimes tend to be intraracial, and since a black, Hispanic, or Asian would have stood out at the crime locations.

The age of onset for these types is generally between the mid to late twenties and early thirties. Based upon the high degree of psychopathology exhibited at the scene and his ability to avoid detection despite the high-risk nature of the crimes, the age of the subject is around twenty-eight to thirty-six. However, it should be noted that age is a difficult characteristic to categorize, and consequently we would not eliminate a viable suspect exclusively because of age. For example, though we were correct on all other significant traits, we underestimated the age of a serial killer of prostitutes in Rochester, New York, in the late 1980s. The subject, Arthur Shawcross, had been in prison for fifteen years on charges of child assault and murder. When he got out, he merely picked up where he'd left off.

Jack would not look out of the ordinary. In my initial profile I suggested that the clothing he wore at the time of the assaults would not be his everyday dress, as he would want to project to unsuspecting females that he had money, so he wouldn't have to initiate contact. But experts on the era have since informed me that unlike most of the modern prostitutes that I have encountered in crime investigation, the Victorian East End prostitutes were so desperate they would have approached anyone, regardless of dress. In fact, after the rumors surfaced that Jack might have been a medical doctor, they could have been even warier of a well-dressed and decidedly out-of-place customer.

I would expect this UNSUB to have come from a family with a domineering mother and weak, passive, and/or absent father. In all likelihood, his mother drank heavily and enjoyed the company of many men. As a result, he failed to receive consistent care and contact with stable adult role models and became detached socially with a diminished emotional response toward others. He became asocial, preferring to be alone. His anger became internalized, and in his younger years, he expressed his pent-up destructive emotions by setting fires and mistreating or torturing small animals. By perpetrating these acts, he discovered increased areas of dominance, power, and control and learned how to continue violent destructive acts without detection or punishment.

As he grew older, his fantasy developed a strong component that included domination and mutilation of women, along with a basic curiosity about them, unfulfilled in his real life. For employment, he would have sought a position where he could work alone and vicariously experience his destructive fantasies. If he were capable of such work, this might include employment as a butcher, mortician's helper, hospital or morgue attendant. If employed, he'd have been off work on the weekends and holidays. He was paranoid and carried one or more knives with him in case of attack. This paranoid-type thinking would have been in part justified because of his poor self-image. He might have had some physical abnormality, scarring or speech problem that he perceived as psychologically crippling. He was not adept at meeting people socially, and most of his relationships would have been with prostitutes. Due to the lack of hygiene practices by street prostitutes at the time and the absence of treatment for venereal diseases, he may have been infected, which would have further fueled his hatred and disgust for women.

We would not expect this type of offender to have been married or to have carried on a normal relationship with a woman. If he had been married in the past, it would have been to someone older than himself, and the marriage would have been brief.

He would have been perceived as a quiet, shy loner, slightly withdrawn, obedient, and fairly neat and orderly in appearance. He may have drunk in the local pubs, at which point he may have become more relaxed and found it easier to engage in conversation. He lived or worked in the Whitechapel area, and the first homicide would have been close to either his home or workplace. Note that London Hospital is only one block from the Nichols murder.

The police might well have interviewed him more than once during the investigation. Unfortunately, at this time there is no way to correlate this type of information. Investigators and citizens in the community had a preconceived idea of what Jack the Ripper would look like. Because of the belief that he would appear odd or ghoulish, they could have looked right past this individual.

PRE- AND POSTOFFENSE BEHAVIOR

Prior to each homicide, the subject was in a local pub drinking and lowering his inhibitions. He would have been observed walking all over the Whitechapel area during the early-evening hours. He did not seek a certain look in a woman; however, it was no accident that he killed prostitutes. He had the sense to know when and where to attack his victims. Many other women would have come in contact with this subject but were not assaulted because the location was not secure enough.

Postoffense behavior would have included returning to an area where he could wash his hands of blood and remove his clothing. Unlike more organized offenders, we would not expect him to have injected himself into the police investigation or to have provided bogus information.

Jack hunted nightly for his victims. When he could not find another, he would have returned to the locations of previous kills. If marked grave sites were accessible to him, he might have visited them in the early-morning hours to relive the experience of his crimes.

This subject would not have committed suicide after the last homicide. It would also be surprising for him to suddenly stop on his own without some outside cause.

INVESTIGATIVE AND/OR PROSECUTORIAL TECHNIQUES

If the suspect had been apprehended, I would have recommended interviewing him in the early-morning hours when he would have felt most relaxed and likely to talk or write about his motivation for killing women. He would not have been visibly shaken or upset if directly accused of the homicides because he believed they were justified in removing garbage from the streets. He would, however, have been psychologically and physiologically stressed if confronted with the fact that he became personally soiled by the victims' blood. He would not have tried to outwit interrogators but might have become frustrated by their inability to understand why he took the actions he did.

THE SUSPECTS

It would be at this point in a typical investigation, *after* I'd presented my profile and suggestions, that we'd consider the local investigators' list of suspects.

We've dealt with John Pizer, the alleged Leather Apron, and Joseph Barnett, Mary Kelly's sometime live-in companion. Presented with these two, I could easily have eliminated them—Pizer on alibi and Barnett on motive. So who else was there?

Well, there were plenty, and more and more as the years and decades went by and greater numbers of people from all over the world became interested in, then obsessed by this case. The search for Jack the Ripper's identity has become like the speculation over who "really" wrote Shakespeare's plays—it has become a Rorschach test that often reveals more about the beholder than the subject beheld. But let's take a look.

PRINCE EDDIE

Perhaps the most intriguing suspect is Prince Albert Victor Christian Edward, Duke of Clarence and Avondale, son of Albert Edward, Prince of Wales (later Edward VII), and grandson of Queen Victoria. I mean, what could be more fascinating than a suspect from the highest, most powerful family in the world? I can tell you that having spent twenty-five years investigating and chasing the lowest of the lowlifes, if a local cop brought me a suspect like him, it would sure get my attention. I should point out here, though, that this theory never came up during the actual Ripper investigation. In fact, it didn't surface until the early 1960s, so I'm somewhat skeptical going in.

Known as Prince Eddie, the twenty-eight-year-old was second in the line of succession to the throne. This theory has it that the prince, never known as the brightest light or most upstanding exemplar of the Hanover line, suffered from effects of syphilis on the brain as a result of his debauching and that he used to slum in Whitechapel and pick up lowly women. The dementia caused him to kill some of these women for sport, and as a deer hunter he had the skill to disembowel his victims. Once operatives at Buckingham Palace learned what was going on, they had him put away under the supervision of royal physician Sir William Gull until he died of pneumonia in January of 1892. An alternate theory has Gull either dispatching him himself or supervising his "euthanasia" when it became clear he was too great a liability to the crown. His fiancée, Princess Mary of Teck, was then betrothed to his younger brother. Together, those two went on to become King George V and Queen Mary. Another variation of the story has Prince Eddie frequenting homosexual brothels in the East End and conducting the murders as a manifestation of his mad hatred and fear of women.

Still a third narrative—in many ways the most interesting—suggests that Eddie secretly married Annie Elizabeth Crook and had a baby girl by her. Since Annie was not only a poor, lower-class woman but also a Catholic (by law, members of the royal family could not marry outside the Church of England and still maintain their station and place in the line of succession), this would have been a huge scandal that would have shaken the very foundations of the monarchy. Operatives of the crown picked up Annie, spirited her off to a lunatic asylum (who there could possibly believe such a lowborn girl's claim of marriage to the Prince of Wales' son?), and figured they'd suppressed the problem.

But there was a complication, as there always is. The baby's nursemaid, Mary Jane Kelly, spilled the beans to some of her friends—Polly Nichols, Annie Chapman, Liz Stride, and Kate Eddowes—and tried to blackmail the government with what she knew. It was then necessary to eliminate all of these people to keep the story quiet. This is where Sir William Gull comes in again. It was his responsibility (with his obvious medical knowledge) to venture out into the East End with a driver and henchman, find the women, and kill them. Gull, a Freemason, employed the ritualistic punishment meted out to the Juwes as a warning to others who would interfere.

Okay, there are a number of problems with all of the Prince Eddie theories. For one, and this has nothing to do with profiling, the prince can be alibied for each of the murders by eyewitness accounts and the myriad royal diaries and court circulars. Sure, it's possible for a prince to duck out of sight, but not in situations where he's being seen by scores or hundreds of people.

A second problem, even apart from the fact that absolutely no contemporary or historical evidence supports the claim against the prince, is that no one who could commit these kinds of crimes, particularly the frenzied butchery of Mary Jane Kelly, could continue functioning and interacting with people in a relatively normal way. Someone would have noticed something, and it would not have stayed a secret. These are the crimes of an individual who does not know how to interact with women, and whatever his personal hangups or character flaws, Prince Albert Edward would have been trained to this social grace. Moreover, to me, these crimes are the work of a disorganized, paranoid offender. I cannot conceive of the killer, particularly the prince, planning the crimes to the point of venturing into a foreign neighborhood with great risk of being recognized with the intended purpose of mutilating women he'd never met. The same logic applies to Dr. Gull, who, in addition, was more than seventy years old and had had a stroke.

We face conspiracy theories over and over again in criminology, and the royal conspiracy theory will probably continue to attract attention as long as interest in the Ripper murders remains. Conspiracy theories are attractive. They make sense of the random, the banal. It is much more palatable, for instance, to suppose that the president of the United States—the most powerful man on earth—was murdered and history changed because of some vast and powerful group of evil men than because one lone and inadequate paranoiac didn't feel good about himself and therefore felt the need to make a stab at personal significance.

But if you have to work too hard to get a conspiracy theory to come together so all the pieces and connections fit, it's probably not authentic. Even simple conspiracies are difficult to pull off. People setting out to commit crime do not think in elaborate, step-by-step-by-step ways.

DR. FRANCIS TUMBLETY

Francis Tumblety was born into a poor family in Ireland in the 1830s, the youngest of eleven children. While he was still a child, the family moved to Rochester, New York. From an early age he was an energetic hustler, selling pornographic literature to canal-boat travelers while still in his teens, then learning about medicines from a disreputable Rochester druggist. He ventured out into the world, beginning in Detroit, and set himself up as an "herb doctor." Somehow, he got people to fall for his claims and he became rather well-off. He would move from city to city as authorities recognized him as a charlatan.

He began wearing elaborate uniforms, and during the Civil War, moved to Washington, D.C., where he claimed to be a military surgeon and friend of President Abraham Lincoln and General Ulysses Grant. After the war he traveled widely throughout the United States, getting in and out of trouble with the law. His personal life was shrouded in secrecy, though he was outwardly flamboyant, and at one point he was sued by another man for sexual assault. Many people who knew him believed he disliked and avoided women.

On November 7, 1888, he came to the attention of the Metropolitan Police in London when he was arrested for gross indecency and indecent assault with force and arms against four men, beginning in July. Awaiting trial, he jumped bail and fled to France and then back to the States under the alias Frank Townsend. By the time he returned, American newspapers were already printing the rumor that London police suspected him of being Jack the Ripper. The rumor gained adherents when Inspector Walter Andrews, who was working on the case, was dispatched to New York, at which point Tumblety hastily quit that city, too. It was reported that Scotland Yard had requested samples of his handwriting. He dropped out of sight, then turned back up in Rochester, where he lived with his sister. He died in St. Louis in 1903. His considerable fortune was distributed to various nieces and nephews and several charities. Obituaries mentioned that he had been a suspect in the Ripper murders. A collection of preserved human uteruses was found among his possessions.

In spite of this interesting finding, the fact that the murders stopped when he fled England, and all the contemporaneous speculation about him, I don't find Tumblety a serious suspect. He was apparently homosexual, and I do not believe he would have had the passion and frenzy for such destructive overkills and mutilation of the other sex. I also believe it unlikely that the man who perpetrated the Kelly murder could have gone on to a functioning life afterward without any outward signs of the depraved behavior. Tumblety was a con man, the exact opposite of the UNSUB I'd be looking for. His constant hustles and flights show Tumblety to be an organized, intelligent individual. And as I've mentioned, I believe the actual Ripper to have been someone who would not seek personal publicity—again, just the opposite of Tumblety. There is also every indication that he was still in police custody awaiting bail at the time of the Kelly murder.

SEVERIN KLOSOWSKI AND NEILL CREAM

Severin Klosowski was born in Poland, where he apprenticed in surgery. He came to England in 1887 and worked as a hairdresser and barber, ultimately in a basement shop on the corner of Whitechapel High Street and George Yard, but this was proven to have happened in 1890, after the final murder. He becomes a suspect because of this physical proximity to the murders and the fact that between 1895 and 1901, and now calling himself George Chapman (after the woman he cohabited with, who coincidentally shared the name Annie Chapman with the second Ripper victim), he poisoned three successive women with whom he had lived as husband. He was charged, tried, convicted, and executed by hanging in April 1903. Some contemporaneous evidence suggests that Inspector Abberline believed Klosowski/Chapman to be the Ripper.

We can discount this one relatively quickly, too. He is not a good match for any of the eyewitness accounts. Yes, he was in the area and, from his training, knew his way around the inside of a human body. But he was still hanging around and in business when the murders ceased. And he had relationships with women, which I do not believe the Ripper would have. He was organized enough to marry and dispatch three women in succession, though since he probably wasn't technically married to any of them, the profit motive doesn't really come into play here. Still, there is no way a man hacks apart five or six women, lies low for ten years with no one noticing anything about him, then resumes his homicidal career as a poisoner, who, along with bombers, are the most cowardly and detached of all murderers.

It just doesn't happen that way in real life.

Other poisoners who have been suggested as suspects can be eliminated for similar reasons. Most prominent among these is probably Dr. Neill Cream, whose checkered career also included arson, blackmail, and illegal abortions. He was found guilty of the strychnine poisoning of four London prostitutes in 1892, so you can see why his name comes up.

On the scaffold, as he was about to be hanged, he is reputed to have declared, "I am Jack the—" and then the trapdoor was released.

As tantalizing as this is, we have another real problem with Cream, too. He is known to have been incarcerated at the Illinois State Penitentiary at Joliet from November 1881 into July 1891. So the American correctional system has given him his alibi.

JAMES MAYBRICK

Since 1993, anyone doing investigation into the identity of Jack the Ripper has had to come to grips with the possibility of James Maybrick. Though he had never been considered a suspect before then, in that year a book was published entitled *The Diary of Jack the Ripper*. It purported to show how a successful Liverpool cotton broker led a secret life as the

Whitechapel Murderer. Maybrick is an interesting case for another reason. He was allegedly the victim of murder himself, by arsenic poisoning, for which his beautiful American wife was tried, convicted, and just
barely avoided the gallows.

By 1887, Maybrick's marriage to Southern belle Florence Elizabeth
Chandler had become shaky. He had a mistress and Florrie had a lover.
When his business started going downhill, in supposed punishment for
her infidelities he began beating her. He was also a hypochondriac who
treated himself with arsenic, both for his health and as a sexual stimulant.

In April 1889, Maybrick became ill. He died on May 11. Florrie became
a suspect when a packet of arsenic was found in her room and it was discovered that James had changed his will to cut her out. There were,
indeed, traces of arsenic in Maybrick's corpse, but since he'd been self-
administering the stuff for years, who could tell how it got there? Even so,
Florrie was put on trial.

The judge was Sir James Stephen, whose son James Kenneth Stephen
was a tutor to Prince Eddie at Cambridge and has become a minor Ripper
suspect in his own right, partially due to his poetry demonstrating a
rather severe, paranoid hatred of women. At the time of the trial, Judge
Stephen was practically senile and, by most accounts, completely mis-
handled the proceedings. After Florrie was convicted, he sentenced her to
death. The sentence was commuted, and after she'd served fifteen years,
she was freed. She returned to America in 1904 and lived until 1941.

The evidence against James Maybrick as the Ripper is a sixty-three-
page journal, written on the leaves of a Victorian photo album that was
given to Michael Barrett, a Liverpool scrap-metal dealer in 1991 by his
drinking buddy Tony Devereux. Devereux died sometime after the
transfer and, in any event, according to Barrett, said he knew little of the
journal's provenance.

The writer of the journal does not identify himself as Maybrick, but
many references in the work demonstrate that it is his. The published
book consisted of a photographic copy of the diary along with extensive
background and commentary by Shirley Harrison, an author brought to
the project by the British publisher. When the book hit the stands, it was
hyped as "the day the world's greatest murder mystery will be solved."

Through Harrison and others, the diary has been subjected to a number of tests by handwriting experts, ink and paper specialists, and histori-
ans, with ambiguous results. Some say it is genuinely of the age, and
others claim it to be an elaborate forgery. The handwriting does not
match any of Maybrick's known exemplars, but some supposed experts
have explained this away by saying that since the writer clearly suffered

from multiple personality disorder, he would have had several distinct handwriting styles. I think this is bogus, but let's go on.

The basic thrust of the diary is that the Ripper murders were caused by the writer's grief and rage over the infidelities of his wife, whom he thought of as a whore. He couldn't kill her, so he displaced that rage by killing actual prostitutes. Since a prominent Liverpool businessman couldn't do this in his own neighborhood, he'd go somewhere else during his business travels and do it there. Professionally, he frequented the area around Whitechapel Street in Liverpool, so he would carry out his murderous activities around Whitechapel Street in London. There's also some rather fancy stuff about the name Jack coming from the first two letters of James and the last two of Maybrick.

The final entry reads:

I give my name that all know of me, so history do tell, what love can do to a gentle man born.
    Yours truly

Jack the Ripper

Dated this third day of May 1889.

First of all, take my word for it—love can do a lot of things to a gentle man, but what the Ripper did isn't among them.

A number of forensic factors suggest the diary is fake. There is evidence that much of the writing was done at only a few sittings, rather than episodically, as an actual journal would have been. A Scotland Yard examiner stated that many of the handwriting flourishes appear to have been added after the writing was completed to make it look more authentically Victorian. Martin Fido, one of the experts called in to evaluate the diary before publication, found about twenty anachronisms in the text. Some of the descriptions appear to be based on newspaper accounts, rather than what was later learned to have actually taken place.

Then there are certain crime-scene issues. The writer speaks of a hideout on Middlesex Street, or Petticoat Lane. Yet why would the killer of Catherine Eddowes, clearly on the run from the police, flee from Mitre Square and *past* Middlesex Street to drop the bloody apron in Goulston Street, then return to Middlesex Street? It doesn't make sense.

Even more to the point, how does a fifty-year-old man with a family, children, and no sociopathology suddenly blossom into a disorganized serial killer? He can't, and doesn't. Anyone who thinks his situation through enough to decide that he wants to kill prostitutes to get back at his wife but must do so on trips to another city, where he'll hide out, stalk women of the night, rip them up, and then return to his own world and home, would not exactly be disorganized. In fact, I've never seen one that organized. No one plans that carefully, then goes into such a frenzy of sexual pathology. And as we've said with other suspects such as Joseph Barnett, even if he did, he wouldn't be able to return to normal life after that without someone recognizing something about his postoffense behavior.

I have seen many diaries and writings of serial offenders. This one is noteworthy not so much for what it doesn't get wrong, as for what it fails to reveal. Lee Harvey Oswald, Sirhan Sirhan, and Arthur Bremer, to name but three, all left extensive writings full of specific detail. If this diary were authentic, I would expect it to shed some new light on the crimes or their methodology, which is missing here. In a real killer's diary, I'd expect to see his whole pathological construct laid out, rather than just a simple and breast-beating excuse for why he has to kill these women. All of that is missing from the so-called Maybrick diary, which must be judged an elaborate fake.

WHAT DID THE POLICE KNOW?

We could go into many more suspects here—there are scores of them— but none of the theories has enough going for it to be taken seriously and they don't shed enough light on the investigative process to warrant the space.

Was Jack, then, such an elusive, clever criminal genius? Not by any means. He knew the area and he was lucky. The dark corners and back alleys favored by the lowest rung of prostitutes, who had no place indoors to go with their clients, were the same ones that facilitated a killer like Jack.

Now it's time to review those individuals the police considered suspects. And as we do that, let me profile the police actions themselves, based on the behavioral evidence they collectively left.

Did the police have a good idea in the end of Jack's identity? They may very well have.

The fact is, the major police effort, the tremendous expenditure of resources and manpower, stands down rather quickly after the murder of Mary Jane Kelly—more quickly than after the previous murders. We have already noted that the police were really under the gun, being subjected to massive public and press criticism and condemnation. Would they have risked another murder by easing up on their presence in

Whitechapel? Knowing the way bureaucrats and public servants respond to outside pressure, it is difficult to conceive that they would. So alternatively, we may speculate they had reason to believe that although the killer had not been captured and brought to justice, the reign of terror was over.

So who at Scotland Yard might have known or at least thought he knew?

We have three main sources for this: the MacNaghten Memoranda; Dr.(at this point, Sir) Robert Anderson's 1910 memoir, *The Lighter Side of My Official Life;* and the so-called Swanson Marginalia, actually Scotland Yard Chief Inspector Donald Sutherland Swanson's handwritten commentary in his copy of Anderson's book, which was released by his family after the 1987 publication of Martin Fido's book *The Crimes, Detection and Death of Jack the Ripper.*

Sir Melville Leslie MacNaghten had been assistant commissioner in charge of Scotland Yard's Criminal Investigation Department, having joined as assistant chief constable in 1889. We must therefore point out that his information would not have been firsthand, though he would have had access to all important information. The memorandum was written in 1894 and consisted of seven pages written in his own hand, marked "Confidential" and placed in his files. He names three likely suspects:

(1) A Mr M.J. Druitt, said to be a doctor & of good family, who disappeared at the time of the Miller's Court murder, whose body (which was said to have been upwards of a month in the water) was found in the Thames on 31st Dec.—or about 7 weeks after that murder. He was sexually insane and from private info I have little doubt but that his own family believed him to have been the murderer.

(2) Kosminski, a Polish Jew, & resident in Whitechapel. This man became insane owing to many years indulgence in solitary vices. He had a great hatred of women, specially of the prostitute class, & had strong homicidal tendencies; he was removed to a lunatic asylum about March 1889. There were many circs connected with this man which made him a strong "suspect."

(3) Michael Ostrog, a Russian doctor, and a convict, who was subsequently detained in a lunatic asylum as a homicidal maniac. This man's antecedents were of the worst possible type, and his whereabouts at the time of the murders could never be ascertained.

In his memoirs, Robert Anderson speaks of a lower-class Polish Jew whom he does not name and states that the subject "was caged in an asylum, the only person who had ever had a good view of the murderer at once identified him, but when he learned that the suspect was a fellow-Jew he declined to swear to him."

This witness Anderson mentions is probably Joseph Lawende, the cigarette salesman who was believed to have seen Catherine Eddowes with the Ripper at the entrance to Mitre Square. The Polish Jew in question would be Aaron Kosminski, the second name in the MacNaghten Memoranda.

Kosminski was a hairdresser who moved to England in 1882. The records of the large Colney Hatch Lunatic Asylum, which would have handled most of the patients in and around Whitechapel, listed attacks of mental illness going back to 1885. By the late 1880s, he was known to wander about picking food scraps out of the street and would refuse food offered by anyone else. He would not wash and had at one point threatened his sister with a knife. From 1890 on, he essentially spent the rest of his life in asylums.

In the margin of his personal copy of Anderson's book, where he talks about the Polish Jew and the witness who refused to ID him, Donald Swanson penciled:

> because the suspect was also a Jew and also because his evidence would convict the suspect, and witness would be the means of murderer being hanged, which he did not wish to be left on his mind. D.S.S.

He continues:

> And after this identification which suspect knew, no other murder of this kind took place in London.

On the endpaper he wrote:

> After the suspect had been identified at the Seaside Home [probably the police convalescent home in West Brighton where the suspect and the witness were apparently taken to get them away from the glare of London publicity] where he had been sent by us with difficulty in order to subject him to identification and he knew he was identified.
>
> On suspect's return to his brother's house in Whitechapel he was watched by police (City CID) by day and night. In a very short time the suspect with his hands tied behind his back he was sent to Stepney Workhouse and then to Colney Hatch and died shortly afterwards—Kosminski was the suspect—D.S.S.

THE REMAINING SUSPECTS

When I was asked to participate in Peter Ustinov's television special in 1988 and offer a profile, I agreed with the understanding that I could only analyze the evidence, materials, and suspects presented to me.

The suspects they presented were Robert Donston Stephenson, who often went by the name of Dr. Roslyn D'Onston; Montague John Druitt and Aaron Kosminski, two of MacNaghten's three suspects; Sir William Gull, the royal physician; and Prince Edward Albert, Duke of Clarence.

The only one of these five we haven't mentioned so far is Stephenson, a self-publicizing con man who claimed to be a practitioner of magic. He was in Whitechapel at the right time and was known to be very interested in the Ripper murders, one time acting them out for startled onlookers. Since he was into witchcraft, these elements would surely have shown up in ritualized ways in the crimes. He would also have been able to bring his victims to a secure location rather than risking murdering them on the streets. Though the theory has its supporters, I have found nothing in his murky background that qualifies him as a good suspect.

Prince Eddie and Gull we have already considered. So let's consider the remaining two here, Druitt and Kosminski, plus the third Mac-Naghten suspect, Michael Ostrog.

Ostrog was an immigrant, probably from Russia or Poland, a known criminal and possibly a doctor. He was too old and too tall to match the witness accounts. He was imprisoned in September of 1887 but transferred to Surrey Pauper Lunatic Asylum when he displayed signs of insanity (probably faked), then released in March 1888. Since he was sentenced to prison for theft in Paris on November 18, it's unlikely he was even in London at the time of all of the Ripper murders. He surfaces again in London in 1904, partially crippled and living in the St. Giles Christian Mission.

The police were definitely paying attention to him and were concerned during the murder series when he failed to report to them as directed. That he was in and out of mental institutions also probably had something to do with MacNaghten's interest in him, but again, I find nothing compelling in the facts we know to suggest that he might be the Ripper. Nothing else in his background suggests a propensity toward the type of savage violence we see in these crimes, and despite the mental illness, he seems too organized and "together" to fit the personality I'd be looking for.

Which gets us to Montague John Druitt. Druitt is an interesting suspect primarily because of when he died. He was pulled out of the Thames on December 31, 1888, and police estimated he'd been in there more than a month. His coat was weighted down with stones, and he had cash on him and two checks from the boys' school in Blackheath where he'd taught. They were probably severance checks, and the supposition is that he had gotten into trouble for sexual advances to some of the students. Though he has been described as a doctor, he was, in fact, a schoolteacher who was just beginning to make his way as a junior barrister. There was some mental instability and a history of depression in his family, and after his father died, his mother was placed in an asylum.

I have always been a little surprised by the weight given to Druitt's candidacy as the Ripper. Aside from his untimely but convenient death, nothing really ties him to the crimes, including any known association with Whitechapel. There is no evidence of violence in his background, and a man doesn't just jump full-blown into the kinds of crimes we're talking about.

But Aaron Kosminski looked good for the murders. A Polish Jewish immigrant hairdresser with a history of mental illness and a reported dislike of women, he fit the eyewitness descriptions, the disorganized personality, and the police descriptions. The escalation of mutilation and depravity in the murders was dramatic, and the Mary Jane Kelly kill certainly strikes me as the work of a guy pretty much at the end of his mental rope. That is not to say that he'd turn himself in, as Edmund Kemper did, or kill himself. Rather, it suggests that he might not be able to continue functioning on his own much longer. And a guy who is so paranoid he eats garbage off the streets rather than accept food from anyone would tend to fit the bill.

His is also the only name that comes up in all three of the key documents (though Anderson does not mention him by name). According to Swanson, when Kosminski was placed under surveillance, the killing stopped. Though some have questioned the recollection of all three former cops, there is no compelling reason to think they were wrong in the essence of what they were saying. Martin Fido has extensively researched the lives and writings of all three men, and he states that everything else Robert Anderson wrote, on subjects far diverse from the Ripper murders, is accurate and creditable. So there is no reason to doubt him here.

My subject, it will be noted, was an immigrant Jew, the very type many of the citizens of Whitechapel suspected, feared, and despised. Is his Jewishness a significant factor in either the profile or the commission of the crimes? No. Jack the Ripper had to be a poor East End local. A significant number of poor East End locals at that time were immigrant

Jews. There are sick and murderous individuals in every definable race and ethnic grouping. That's it.

Although Kosminski seemed to fit my profile and evaluation, I cautioned on the show that a hundred years after the fact, I could not prove that he was the actual killer. What I said was that Jack the Ripper would either be Aaron Kosminski or someone like the man I was describing. And I stand by that.

But, as I learned in the years after the airing of the show, there are a couple of problems with Kosminski, information I had not been given at the time. For one thing, Swanson turned out to be wrong on one critical fact: Kosminski did not die shortly after the murders, but actually lived in asylums until 1919! During that time he was often dissociative but not violent and never gave any indication of being the Ripper. I would expect a paranoid individual of this nature to talk frequently of this. Kosminski seems too docile and passive to have been a predatory animal nightly on the hunt for victims of opportunity.

Reenter Martin Fido. He had also believed that the man the police referred to as Kosminski was the answer to the Ripper mystery, but the problems struck him as just as real as they did me. Knowing that the Polish Jew description from Anderson was more reliable than the name, Fido exhaustively checked the records of all the prisons and insane asylums in the area. And of all the names he went through, he came up with one fascinating candidate.

David Cohen was a Polish Jew, twenty-three years of age at the time (exactly the same age as Kosminski), whose incarceration at Colney Hatch fits precisely with the end of the murders. He had originally been brought by police to Whitechapel Infirmary on December 12, 1888, when they "found him wandering at large and unable to take care of himself."

Unlike Kosminski, Cohen was violently antisocial and was kept in restraints. When he was given any clothing, he would rip it off his body. He spoke little, and when he did, it was a foreign language that attendants took to be German. Though we know he was in Whitechapel at the time of the crimes, we don't know where he lived or if he actually had a job.

He became ill on December 28, and while he gradually regained some of his strength during the spring and summer of 1889, he suffered a relapse and died on October 20. The cause of death was put down to "exhaustion of mania." This diagnosis, rather crude by modern standards, still fits in perfectly with the profile. The killer and mutilator of Mary Jane Kelly was at the end of his emotional rope.

His address had been given as 86 Leman Street, an unlikely possibility since this was the address of the Protestant Boys' Club. However, Fido quickly discovered that number 84 was the Temporary Shelter for Poor Homeless Jews, which seemed completely logical. But this home only accepted newly landed immigrants for two weeks. Immigrant Jews taken in by their fellow immigrants in this way were often listed for employment in one of the traditional Jewish trades, either tailor or shoemaker. Cohen is listed as a tailor, but it is certainly possible that he had been a shoemaker. The connection of shoemakers with Leather Apron would have been enough to change the designation for his own protection.

It's easy to see how 84 Leman Street could be mistranscribed as 86, but how do you confuse Kosminski and Cohen? Well, one possible way was explained to Fido. *Cohen* was a John Doe–type surname often given to Jewish immigrants whose actual surnames were difficult for Englishmen to pronounce or spell. It is therefore possible that the City Police were following Kosminski while Scotland Yard was following Cohen. The Yard knew their man had died, but weren't certain of his real name.

The situation is further complicated by another fellow, generally referred to as Nathan Kaminsky, an immigrant Jewish bootmaker, the same age and general description as both Kosminski and Cohen. He was treated for syphilis in a workhouse infirmary shortly before the murders and then suddenly and inexplicably vanishes from the records. He lived right in the heart of the Ripper's comfort zone. There are no death records for him.

So I think there is every chance that these three immigrant Polish Jews with documented emotional problems were combined and confused by the various police officials and agencies. I don't set much store in elaborate conspiracies and cover-ups, but I've seen enough bureaucratic gaffes and fumbles in my time to believe quite heartily in them. And yet, what is the element of truth or consistency that runs throughout the three accounts and also squares with the profile of the Whitechapel Murderer?

As we have seen, it's impossible to be certain of the true identity after all these years, but the behavioral evidence as to the *type* of individual he was is plentiful and compelling. Therefore, I'm now prepared to say that Jack the Ripper was either the man known to the police as David Cohen . . . or someone very much like him.

CHAPTER TWO

LIZZIE BORDEN

Lizzie Borden took an axe
And gave her mother forty whacks;
When she saw what she had done
She gave her father forty-one.

This is the way the most famous and notorious American murder case of the nineteenth century has chiefly been remembered. But if the unnamed authors of this rather cruel ditty were being responsible and accurate, they would have recast their verse into something less tuneful yet somewhat more in line with the established facts of this officially unsolved case:

An unknown subject took a hatchet
And gave Lizzie Borden's stepmother nineteen whacks;
Ninety minutes after that deed was done
He or she gave Borden's father ten plus one.

The one being sufficient to cause death; the other ten constituting out-and-out overkill. But as we'll discover, this was a behaviorally different type of overkill than what we saw in the Whitechapel murders.

What was it about this brutal daytime murder in a small but prosperous New England town at the height of the Industrial Revolution that struck such a nerve, not only in New England but, within days, across the nation and around the globe, just as Jack the Ripper had four years previously? For one thing, proper, well-to-do women just didn't get accused of cold-bloodedly hacking people to death. If the Whitechapel murders were about the potential for random brutality and the loss of public innocence regarding the presence of evil in a confident and complacent world, this case was about the potential for violence lurking within seemingly normal families, and the even more profound and searing loss of innocence that implied.

It's difficult to avoid the interesting, almost uncanny parallels to another instance of officially unsolved, allegedly domestic murder that would take place 102 years later and an entire continent away: the killings of Nicole Brown Simpson and Ronald Goldman outside her condominium in the Brentwood section of Los Angeles in 1994. Both cases involved an upstanding, well-off, community-pillar defendant, represented by the finest legal team money could buy, who vigorously proclaimed innocence of the savage mutilation murders of one male and one female victim by bladed weapons that were not found at the scene. Nor had virtually any blood been found on either defendant. Both offered substantial rewards for information leading to the killer—rewards that were never claimed. And in both cases, the world was riveted to every word uttered in trial, during which each defendant chose not to take the stand to give her or his own account of what had happened. In fact, the only words both defendants uttered in open court were single sentences proclaiming their innocence.

When people all over the world asked if a wealthy, famous, handsome, and charming ex–football star could possibly be capable of savaging his former wife and an innocent bystander in a fit of murderous rage, they were harkening back to a similar question from the century past:

Could a demure, well-mannered, and well-to-do former Sunday-school teacher, active in her church and charities and a prominent member of the Women's Christian Temperance Union, actually be a monster?

It was a question that, with individual variations, would be posed many times in the years between the two cases. It is, in many ways, the essence of criminological behavioral science.

THE BORDENS OF FALL RIVER

Let's begin with the undisputed facts.

At around 11:15 on the warm and humid morning of Thursday, August 4, 1892, Rufus B. Hilliard, the city marshal of Fall River, Massachusetts, received an urgent telephone call at the central police station. It was from John Cunningham, a local newsdealer. Cunningham happened to be at Hall's Livery Stable when he saw Mrs. Adelaide Churchill frantically approach her carriage driver, Tom, telling him to go find a doctor. Her next-door neighbor Andrew Borden, one of the wealthiest and most prominent citizens in town, had been brutally attacked in the sitting room of his house on Second Street. Noticing Cunningham, she suggested that someone call the police.

Which is what Cunningham did. But not before he first called the *Fall River Globe* and gave them the exclusive story.

The Borden family consisted of four members: Andrew Jackson Borden, one of the town's most prominent businessmen, seventy years of age; his second wife, Abby Durfee Grady Borden, sixty-four; and Andrew's two adult, unmarried daughters by his late first wife, Sarah Anthony Morse Borden, forty-one-year-old Emma Lenora and Lizzie Andrew, thirty-two. There was also a live-in maid, a twenty-six-year-old Irish immigrant named Bridget Sullivan, who had been with the family for more than two years.

In 1890, Fall River had a population of eighty thousand and manufactured more cotton textiles than any other city in the world. And if one name could be associated with the economic origins and continued prosperity of the town, that name would be Borden. Though he was related to the family that had established Fall River and was by then enjoying its third generation of wealth, Andrew was only a second cousin of the wealthy Borden branch and had grown up without any of their power or advantages. His grandfather had been a brother of one of the original Bordens who made good, and Andrew's father had never made anything of himself. Everything Andrew had—and he had a lot—he'd earned completely on his own, beginning as a casket maker, then opening his own undertaking business and investing the profits in real estate, banks, and mills. Now tall, thin, white-haired, and bearded, and almost invariably dressed in a heavy black suit regardless of the weather, Andrew Borden was president of the Union Savings Bank; a director of the Merchants Manufacturing Company, the B.M.C. Durfee Safe Deposit and Trust Company, the Globe Yarn Mills, the Troy Cotton and Woolen Manufactory; and the owner of several farms. By 1892 his personal wealth was estimated as high as a half million dollars, a tremendous sum in those days.

Probably as a result of his own struggle, Andrew was known as a fair but tough and hard-nosed bargainer in business, and in his personal life, he was parsimonious in the extreme, eschewing luxuries that were at this point commonly enjoyed by people with far less than he, such as electricity or indoor plumbing. The simple two-story frame house at 92 Second Street was furnished with a water closet in the basement and slop pails in the bedrooms, which had to be emptied every morning. Andrew, who according to all available research had never been accused of a sense of humor, saw no reason for such amenities, much to the dismay of his daughters, who seemed to feel that their father's penurious lifestyle was prohibiting their chances for social success.

On the morning in question, Emma was away from home, visiting friends in Fairhaven, some fifteen miles away. But the household also had an overnight guest, John Vinnicum Morse, fifty-nine years of age, brother of Andrew's late wife. He had lived in Iowa for twenty years, but three years before had returned to the Northeast and resided in South Dartmouth. He arrived on the afternoon of Wednesday, August 3, then he left for one of Andrew's farms in Swansea. Normally, the eggs from the farm were delivered to Andrew by the farmer on Thursdays. But Wednesday night, Morse brought back with him the weekly egg delivery. Then, Morse apparently discussed business details with his former brother-in-law. Though there is some suggestion the two men were talking about Andrew's intention to write a will, there is no documentation on this point.

The Borden household, normally a rather dour place, would have been particularly unpleasant that Wednesday. At 7:00 in the morning, Abby had gone across the street to the home of Dr. Seabury Warren Bowen complaining that both she and Andrew had been violently ill during the night with nausea and vomiting and she was afraid someone was trying to poison them. After a quick exam, Dr. Bowen told her he did not think the illness was serious and sent her home. Later that morning, just to be certain, Bowen paid a call on the Bordens. Andrew ungraciously declared that he was not ill and had no intention of paying for an unsolicited house call. Since Andrew was as excessively thrifty with food as he was with everything else, the gastrointestinal upset had possibly been caused by the mutton stew the family had been having at various meals for several days in a row, despite the warm weather. Bridget, who was suffering some of the same symptoms, was convinced the stew had gone bad, but Andrew would not let her dispose of it.

On Thursday, John Morse had breakfast with Andrew and Abby. Lizzie did not join them, which would have been normal. Despite living in the same small house, Lizzie seldom dined with her father and stepmother. Morse left the house around 8:40 A.M., stopped at the post office, then went across town to see other relatives, the Emerys. Mr. and Mrs. Emery later reported that Morse had been with them between 9:40 and 11:20 A.M., and their impression was that after leaving them, he was headed home by way of New Bedford.

Abby had directed Bridget to wash all of the windows, inside and out. This would have been a formidable task on any hot summer day, but it was particularly taxing this morning when she had already prepared and cleaned up after breakfast and was still feeling so ill. Around 9 A.M. she had to interrupt her work to rush outside to the yard to vomit.

A few minutes later, Andrew left for his business rounds. Mrs. Churchill, the next-door neighbor on the north side, saw him leave. Bridget was still in the backyard being sick, and Abby was upstairs straightening out the guest room that John Morse had occupied. When Bridget came back in the house, she overheard Abby and Lizzie talking in the dining room.

At a store he owned that was being remodeled, Andrew Borden told carpenters he didn't feel well and was going home, where he arrived around 10:40 A.M. He tried to open the front door with his key, but found it bolted from the inside with an additional lock, unusual during the day. So he knocked and Bridget came over to open it. She had trouble springing the bolt, and according to Bridget, Lizzie was standing at the top of the stairs and laughed at her brief struggle.

Andrew was carrying a small package wrapped in white paper. We do not know what was in this package. Since a burglary in the house the year before, he had kept his and Abby's bedroom locked, so he took the key from its place on the mantel and went up the back stairs. When Andrew returned downstairs, Lizzie told him that Mrs. Borden—she had some time ago stopped calling Abby "Mother"—had received a note from a sick friend and had gone out. Still characteristically dressed in his tie and jacket, Andrew lay down for a nap on the couch in the sitting room with his feet resting on the carpet.

So as not to disturb him, Bridget moved into the dining room and began on the windows there. Lizzie came into the room carrying an ironing board, which she set up and began ironing handkerchiefs.

"Maggie, are you going out today?" Lizzie asked. Interestingly, Maggie was what Lizzie and Emma called Bridget, since that had been the name of the previous Borden maid. Apparently, the habit was too hard to break. Andrew and Abby called her by her actual name.

Bridget replied, "I don't know. I might and I might not. I don't feel very well."

"If you go out, be sure and lock the door, for Mrs. Borden has gone out on a sick call and I might go out, too."

"Miss Lizzie, who is sick?" Bridget asked.

"I don't know. She had a note this morning. It must be in town."

Bridget found this odd, since Abby, who was shy, plain, short and overweight, normally told her when she was planning to leave the house, which didn't happen all that often. But Bridget accepted Lizzie's story.

As Bridget was finishing up the dining room windows, Lizzie said to her, "There is a cheap sale of dress goods at Sargent's this afternoon at eight cents a yard."

This elicited a more enthusiastic response from the young woman, who declared, "I'm going to have one!" She left Lizzie ironing in the dining room and went upstairs to her own room in the attic to rest for a little while, hoping to feel better. She lay down on top of the bedspread without taking off her shoes. It was too hot for a deep sleep, but she fell into a doze until she heard the city-hall clock strike 11 A.M. She lay on the bed for another few minutes.

At that point she heard Lizzie calling urgently from downstairs, "Maggie, come down!"

"What is the matter?" Bridget called back.

"Come down quick! Father's dead! Somebody came in and killed him!"

Bridget rose quickly and rushed down two flights of stairs. As she was about to head into the sitting room where Andrew had been napping, Lizzie said, "Oh, Maggie, don't go in!" She then instructed her to go find Dr. Bowen.

THE CRIME SCENE

Mrs. Adelaide Churchill had been returning home after buying groceries when she saw Bridget Sullivan darting back in vain from Dr. Seabury Bowen's house across the street. She set her parcels down, then rushed over to the Bordens', fearing from Bridget's actions that someone was gravely ill. Lizzie was standing just inside the screen door on the side of the house, looking dazed. Mrs. Churchill called out to her, "Lizzie, what is the matter?"

"Oh, Mrs. Churchill," Lizzie responded, "do come over! Someone has killed Father!"

The neighbor went around the fence and up to Lizzie. "Where is your father?" She had to ask several times before Lizzie finally responded:

"In the sitting room."

Mrs. Churchill went into the sitting room and beheld the carnage for herself. When she emerged moments later, she asked Lizzie where she had been when this happened.

Lizzie replied that she had been in the barn behind the house, where she'd gone to find some iron to use as fishing weights for an upcoming trip. When she'd heard a noise, she had come out and noticed that the screen door was open.

"Where is your mother?" Mrs. Churchill asked.

Lizzie replied, "I don't know. She had got a note to go see someone who is sick. But I don't know but she is killed, too, for I thought I heard her come in." Then she offered, "Father must have an enemy, for we have all been sick, and we think the milk has been poisoned. I must have a doctor."

At that point, Adelaide Churchill went out in search of Dr. Bowen herself, setting in motion the chain of events that summoned law enforcement authorities.

As it happened, most of the Fall River Police Department was out at their annual picnic and clambake at Rocky Point, Rhode Island. Hilliard dispatched George W. Allen, a young and relatively inexperienced officer, one of the few he had on hand.

Meanwhile, Dr. Bowen had arrived, followed shortly thereafter by Bridget's return with Lizzie's best friend, Alice Russell. Bowen quickly went to the sitting room and came upon Andrew Borden's body. The corpse was half-sitting, half-lying on the sofa, the head resting on Borden's carefully folded coat, used as a pillow. His boots were still on his feet. The face was essentially unrecognizable. Blood spots were on the floor, on the wall over the sofa, and on the picture hanging on that wall. But the clothing was not disturbed, and there was no apparent injury to any part of his body other than the face.

The most immediate concern of those in the house was Abby's whereabouts. Lizzie had reported her outing to a sick friend. With Abby's limited circle, the only one Bridget could imagine her going to see was her younger half-sister, Mrs. Sarah Whitehead. Bridget suggested that she go try to find Mrs. Whitehead, and if Abby was with her, to tell her only that Mr. Borden was very sick and she needed to hurry home. Then they could give her the horrible truth.

Lizzie brought up again her suspicion that Abby had returned home, but if she had, then why hadn't she come downstairs when she heard the commotion? "Maggie," she said, "I am almost positive I heard her coming in. Won't you go upstairs to see?"

That was the last thing Bridget wanted to do, fearing what she might find. "I am not going upstairs alone," she insisted.

Mrs. Churchill said she would go with her, so together the two women climbed the stairs.

When they got to the top, they could see her, lying facedown in the guest room, propped on her knees as she had fallen. They raced back downstairs, where they found Lizzie now lying down.

Alice Russell asked, "Is there another?"

"Yes, she is up there," Adelaide Churchill replied.

By this time Officer George Allen had arrived at the Borden home, finding a housepainter named Charles Sawyer on the street near the house. He enlisted Sawyer to guard the house while he went in to investigate. The front door was locked, so Allen moved around to the back, but was able to get in through the screen door on the left side near the rear of the house. When he got there, Dr. Bowen had already left to send a telegram summoning Emma home.

Shaken by the grisly sight in the sitting room, Allen quickly searched the remainder of the first floor, then raced back to the police station and reported his findings to Marshal Hilliard, leaving Charles Sawyer guarding the residence. Other officers had returned to the station house, and Hilliard sent them out with Allen. By 11:45 A.M., seven police officers were in the Borden residence, along with Bristol County medical examiner William Dolan.

Based on the comparative temperatures of the bodies, the condition of the blood on each, and an examination of the contents of the digestive systems, Dolan determined that Andrew had died at least one hour after Abby.

Andrew Borden had been struck in the face. One eye was cut in half. His nose was severed, and eleven distinct cuts extended from the eye and nose to the ear. Fresh blood was still seeping from the wounds when he was found. Despite the severity of the attack, the clothing was not disturbed. The wounds were inflicted by a sharp, heavy weapon. He had been struck from above the head while he slept.

The postmortem exam on Abby Borden revealed that her head had been crushed, apparently by the same weapon that would kill her husband. One misdirected blow had struck the back of her head, almost at the neck, cutting off a chunk of scalp. When her body was discovered, the blood was already dark and congealed.

Abby Durfee Borden had also been hacked to death, suffering a total of nineteen blows from a sharp-bladed instrument. As with her husband, the first blow was probably sufficient to cause death.

Officer Michael Mullaly asked Lizzie if there were any hatchets in the house.

"Yes," she said. "They are everywhere." Later, at the coroner's inquest, she testified that she did not know if there were any hatchets in the house. This was only the first of a number of troubling inconsistencies in Lizzie's responses.

Bridget accompanied Mullaly down to the basement, where he found four hatchets. One was a rusty claw-headed hatchet. A second was dusty and appeared little used. The blade of a third one was covered in ashes and had all but a few inches of the handle broken off. From the condition of the wood fiber, the break appeared to be recent. A fourth bore the residue of dried blood and hair.

About this time, John Morse came back, having been asked by Andrew to return for the noon meal. He strolled into the backyard, where he picked some pears from the trees beyond the barn and spent several minutes eating them, apparently unaware of what was going on inside the house.

Officer William Medley went to the barn and climbed up to the loft where Lizzie said she had been looking for lead to make sinkers for her planned fishing trip after she joined Emma in Fairhaven. He found the loft floor thick with dust and no evidence that anyone had been there recently. By this time, Dr. Bowen was back. He took Lizzie upstairs and gave her bromo caffeine for her headache and to calm her nerves. (The next night he administered the first of what would be a series of injections of sulfate of morphine as a tranquilizer.) Alice Russell noted that while Lizzie was upstairs, she changed from the light blue dress she had been wearing to a pink and white outfit.

Police found a small spot of blood on the sole of one of Lizzie's shoes and another small spot on one of her underskirts, about a sixteenth of an inch in diameter. It was consistent with human blood, and later laboratory examination determined that the saturation was more concentrated on the outside of the fabric than on the inside. This is important because Lizzie explained the spot as a flea bite, a euphemism at the time for menstrual blood, which was not discussed in polite society, even when speaking with the police.

At 3 P.M. the bodies of Andrew and Abby Borden were carried into the dining room and placed on undertaker's boards, like a folding table. Dr. Dolan performed autopsies there, where just that morning the two victims had had their breakfast. He removed and tied off the stomachs, which were sent by special messenger to Dr. Edward S. Wood, professor of chemistry at Harvard.

Upstairs, Deputy Marshal John Fleet questioned Lizzie, asking her if she had any idea who could have committed the murders. She said that a few weeks ago, her father had had an argument with a man she didn't know, but other than him, she couldn't think of anyone. Fleet then asked directly whether her uncle John Morse or Bridget Sullivan could have killed her father and mother. She pointedly reminded Fleet that Abby was not her mother but her stepmother, then said it would have been impossible for either Uncle John or Bridget to have committed the crimes.

Emma returned from Fairhaven just before 6:00 that evening. The bodies of the Bordens were still in the dining room, awaiting the arrival of the undertaker. Sergeant Philip Harrington continued questioning Lizzie. Finally, the police left, cordoning off the house to keep away the curious, who had assembled en masse. Bridget left to stay with Dr. Bowen's maid while Emma and Lizzie remained in the house. Uncle John slept in the guest room where Abby had been killed, and Alice Russell slept in the Bordens' bedroom.

Officer Joseph Hyde, on guard that night, reported that he saw Lizzie and Alice go down to the cellar with a kerosene lamp and carrying a slop pail. A few minutes later, Lizzie went down again by herself. He could see her bent over a sink but couldn't tell what she was doing.

LIZZIE'S STORY

On August 5, an interview appeared in the *Fall River Globe* with another of Lizzie's uncles, Hiram Harrington, married to Andrew's only sister, Luana. The interview claimed that Harrington had spoken with his niece the previous evening and that the reason she had not shown any emotion or grief was because "she is not naturally emotional."

This became a key issue. Lizzie had seemed to many observers to be emotionally flat—not the type of response one would expect from someone grieving for her beloved father, if not her stepmother. Now, we certainly look closely at this factor in criminal behavioral analysis, but I am always wary of considering this subject in a vacuum; that is, strictly in and of itself. My several decades of experience in dealing with perpetrators, victims, and their families has told me that responses to horrible emotional trauma are very individual. It is true here, and it will be equally true when we consider the Charles Lindbergh Jr. and JonBenet Ramsey cases.

It is in the nature of my work that I have been around many people who have lost loved ones to violent crime. Some of them, such as Jack, Trudy, and Stephen Collins and Gene, Peggy, and Jeni Schmidt, will be familiar to our readers and have remained close friends. I have spoken with and spent time with others in the national spotlight who have suffered such loss, people such as John Walsh and Marc Klaas. And I can tell you that the way a person responds to the unspeakable and unimaginable—whether it is by screaming to the heavens or essentially shutting down—is so private, so interior, that until you really know the individual in question, it is extremely risky to make judgments based on that response. So if I were handling the Borden murder case, I would not, at this point, have been placing much store in Lizzie's emotional reaction, one way or the other.

But from a forensic perspective, there were a couple of highly problematic areas. The first was the time line. Abby would have been killed around 9:30 in the morning. Andrew died a couple of minutes after 11 A.M. Did the killer hang around the house for an hour and a half, waiting for Andrew to return home? If so, where did he hide? The house was old-fashioned in design, without hallways and only a few tiny closets. To get from one room to another, you went directly through a door to that room. Doors that the family did not want to be opened for privacy were kept locked with furniture up against them. So did the intruder listen for Bridget and Lizzie and whoever else might be home and manage to stay out of their way for ninety minutes? If it was his plan to kill the elder Bordens—and no other motive is apparent—wouldn't he have staked out the home for a time when they would be there without Lizzie, Emma, and Bridget? Did he leave and then return when he saw Andrew coming home and manage to get into the house a second time undetected? There was no sign of forced entry. In fact, Andrew himself couldn't get in until Bridget unbolted the door.

Andrew Borden was wearing a gold ring, a silver watch, and had more than $80 in his pocket, all of which was undisturbed, nor was there evidence of anything having been taken from the house. Robbery or burglary were therefore unlikely scenarios.

The most logical way around these problems, of course, was that there was no intruder at all. That made Lizzie and Bridget the prime suspects.

Bridget's account was pretty straightforward; there was nothing much for the police to sink their teeth into. But Lizzie's story had some interesting details, holes, and inconsistencies, even if you discounted her supposedly inappropriate affect on learning of her father's and stepmother's murders.

There was no indication that Abby had left the house at all that morning. Her half-sister Sarah Whitehead, the only one Bridget could figure she might go visit, turned out not to be ill or even out of town that day and had not sent Abby a note. In fact, no one who knew Abby was ill and none knew anything about a note. Police searched the Borden house but could never find one.

Lizzie had told the police she had gone out to the barn shortly after her father returned home, which would account for why she hadn't seen the murder or become a victim herself. But depending on whom she spoke to, she had differing versions as to why she was there. One had to do with the lead sinkers she'd need for her planned fishing trip. She told Alice Russell she needed lead for a broken window screen she wanted to repair. Neither statement squares with Officer Medley's observation that the loft was so thick with dust that any footprint would have left a lasting impression.

A corollary detail was equally troubling. The day before the murders, Lizzie had gone to Smith's Drug Store, minutes from where she lived, according to the clerk, Eli Bence. She wanted Bence to sell her ten cents' worth of prussic acid—hydrogen cyanide in solution—saying she needed it to kill insects in a sealskin cape. Bence explained that he couldn't sell it to her without a prescription, at which point he said she became visibly annoyed and claimed she'd had no trouble purchasing it in the past. Lizzie denied having been at Smith's, though another clerk and a customer each identified her there between 10:00 and 11:30 in the morning. Later, another witness stated that Lizzie had tried to buy the poison from a different pharmacy on an earlier date.

Saturday, August 6, was the day of the funerals for Andrew and Abby Durfee Borden. The service was conducted by the Reverends Edwin Augustus Buck and William Walker Jubb, both representing the town's central Congregational church. However, the burial at Oak Grove Cemetery did not take place as scheduled. The police had been informed that Dr. Wood wanted to conduct an examination of his own. So after the mourners had left the graveside, the undertaker brought the bodies back, after which the heads were removed and defleshed. Plaster casts were made of the skulls.

(Though untrue, it has long been said that for reasons undetermined, Andrew's skull was never returned to his coffin and that its whereabouts are unknown to this day. Actually, it was later reburied at the grave site at his feet, as Abby's was buried at her feat. Another grisly sidelight to this grisly case.)

That day, Emma and Lizzie published their offer of a reward of the then enormous sum of $5,000 to "any one who may secure the arrest and conviction of the person or persons, who occasioned the death of Mr. Andrew J. Borden and Wife."

That same day, after the funeral, Fall River mayor John W. Coughlin and Marshal Rufus Hilliard informed Lizzie that she was officially a suspect.

On Sunday morning, Miss Russell and Emma observed Lizzie burning a dress of blue cotton Bedford cord in the kitchen stove. "What are you going to do?" Emma asked.

"I am going to burn this old thing up," Lizzie replied. "It is covered with paint."

Alice said, "If I were you, I wouldn't let anybody see me do that, Lizzie," then added, "I am afraid the burning of the dress was the worst thing you could have done, Lizzie."

Lizzie replied curiously, "Oh, what made you let me do it?" and "Why did you let me burn the dress?"

The dress probably was, in fact, stained with paint. This was corroborated by others. But burning it was still odd at best. The Borden family was so frugal that they made rags out of clothing that could no longer be worn. Perhaps this was Lizzie's first conscious or subconscious act of defiance against that frugality.

An inquest was held before Judge Josiah Coleman Blaisdell of the Second District Court, during which Lizzie testified. All testimony was kept secret. At this time she was not yet represented by counsel, and as we shall see, this became a critical factor in her subsequent defense.

She was formally arraigned, according to a warrant drawn up by Marshal Hilliard. The grand jury indictment relating to her father asserted:

> That Lizzie Andrew Borden of Fall River, in the county of Bristol, at Fall River in the county of Bristol, on the fourth day of August, in the year eighteen hundred and ninety-two, in and upon one Andrew Jackson Borden, feloniously, willfully and of her malice aforethought, an assault did make, and with a certain weapon, to wit, a sharp cutting instrument, the name and a more particular description of which is to the Jurors unknown, him, the said Andrew Jackson Borden feloniously, willfully and of her malice aforethought did strike, cutting, beating and bruising, in and upon the head of him, the said Andrew Jackson Borden, divers, to wit, ten mortal wounds, of which said mortal wounds the said Andrew Jackson Borden then and there instantly died.
>
> And so the Jurors aforesaid, upon their oath aforesaid, do say, that the said Lizzie Andrew Borden, the said Andrew Jackson Borden, in manner and form aforesaid, then and there feloniously, wilfully and of her malice aforethought did kill and murder; against the peace of said Commonwealth and contrary to the form of the statute in such case made and provided.

On Friday, August 12, her prominent attorney, Andrew J. Jennings, declared before the court held at the police station, "The prisoner pleads not guilty."

She was taken to the jail in Taunton, Massachusetts, eight miles to the north, because Fall River had no facilities for long-term female prisoners. They'd never had the need.

On August 16, the bodies of Mr. and Mrs. Borden, minus their heads, were finally interred in Oak Grove Cemetery.

And on August 22, six days of preliminary—or probable cause—hearings were held before Judge Blaisdell. Lizzie didn't testify at these hearings, though the record of her secret testimony for the inquest was offered into evidence.

The murder weapon was still a problem and remains one. After completing his examination, Dr. Edward Wood testified that he could find no human blood or tissue on any of the hatchets from the Borden basement, and that the blood and hairs noted on one ax were from a cow.

That fact notwithstanding, at the end of the hearings, on September 1, Judge Blaisdell rendered his judgment, which is worth examining for its pained but resolute logic:

> The long examination is now concluded, and there remains but for the magistrate to perform what he believes to be his duty. It would be a pleasure for him, and he would doubtless receive much sympathy if he could say, "Lizzie, I judge you probably not guilty. You may go home." But upon the character of the evidence presented through the witnesses who have been so closely and thoroughly examined, there is but one thing to be done. Suppose for a single moment a man was standing there. He was found close by that guest chamber which, to Mrs. Borden, was a chamber of death. Suppose a man had been found in the vicinity of Mr. Borden, was the first to find the body, and the only account he could give of himself was the unreasonable one that he was out in the barn looking for sinkers, then he was out in the yard, then he was out for something else. Would there be any question in the minds of men what should be done with such a man? So there is only one thing to do, painful as it may be—the judgment of the Court is that you are probably guilty, and you are ordered committed to await the action of the Superior Court.

On November 7, the grand jury began three weeks of consideration of the case of Lizzie Andrew Borden. When prosecutor Hosea M. Knowlton completed his presentation, he invited Jennings to present a case for the defense. This was a great surprise, unheard of in Massachusetts. In effect, the two attorneys were conducting a trial before the grand jury.

For a time, it looked as if charges against Lizzie would be dismissed. There were no eyewitnesses, no clearly identified murder weapon, and questionable motive. The key circumstantial piece of the case against her was that she had the proximity and best opportunity to have committed both murders, and no other scenario was nearly as intellectually satisfying.

Then, on December 1, Alice Russell testified about the burning of the dress. The next day, Lizzie was charged with three counts of murder: of her father, of her stepmother, and of both of them together. The trial was set for June 5, 1893. Altogether, Lizzie was in Taunton Jail for nine months before that date arrived.

THE TRIAL

Emma and Lizzie Borden had inherited their father's estate. So together they had plenty of money and lined up the best defense that money could buy. In addition to Andrew Jennings, they hired a forty-two-year-old Boston attorney named Melvin Ohio Adams. Adams had been an assistant district attorney and was a specialist in criminal prosecution. And the key to the defense team was the Honorable George Dexter Robinson, fifty-nine, former senator, congressman, and governor of Massachusetts. In the "small world" department—or possibly the "conflict of interest" department, depending on your point of view—while governor, Robinson had appointed Justin Dewey, one of the trial's three presiding judges, to the Massachusetts superior court. Emma and Lizzie paid Robinson the monumental sum of $25,000 for her defense, roughly five times what judges were paid annually. It has been asserted that Robinson would not agree to take the case until he was convinced of Lizzie's innocence. At their first meeting, he advised Lizzie to start wearing black. If convicted, he informed her, she could face a sentence of death by hanging, although no woman had been executed in Massachusetts since 1778.

This is just one of many precursors to other cases and trials we see acted out with Lizzie Borden. I can't tell you how many times I've seen a suspect right after his arrest and then compared that to the way he looked in court months later. He's cleaned up, cut his hair, wearing a conservative suit, with an intense, pensive, and vulnerable look in his eyes that says to the jury, this fine young man couldn't possibly have done the hideous things you've heard described. Sometimes, when I'd walk into court and glance over at the defense table, I couldn't tell which was the defendant and which the attorney.

To assist Hosea Knowlton for the prosecution, Massachusetts attorney general Arthur E. Pillsbury appointed forty-year-old William Henry Moody, the district attorney for Essex County, who would be appearing in his first murder trial. Moody would go on to a career as a congressman, secretary of the navy, U.S. attorney general, and Supreme Court justice. Shortly after the trial, Knowlton replaced Pillsbury as Massachusetts attorney general.

On May 31, 1893—five days before the scheduled start of the trial—an unexpected event, astounding in its proximity to the trial and profound in its implications, occurred in Fall River.

Stephen Manchester, a dairy farmer, came home from his milk deliveries to find his twenty-two-year-old daughter, Bertha, lying beside the black iron stove in the kitchen, hacked to death. Defense wounds and rips in her clothing suggested she had put up a fierce struggle with her assailant. Stephen and Bertha had lived alone in the farmhouse, both of his previous wives having left him, reportedly because he was both cheap and mean.

Dr. William Dolan again conducted the autopsy and described "twenty-three distinct and separate axe wounds on the back of the skull and its base." Very similar to the wounds inflicted upon the back of Abby Borden's head.

The crime took place in the morning, at the same time as Abby's murder. There was little blood. Nothing of value was taken. It was likely that the killer had spent considerable time in the Manchester house.

The implications were clear to everyone in Fall River. An almost identical crime had taken place while the accused murderess was safely locked away in Taunton Jail—one of the best alibis I've ever heard. Attorney Andrew Jennings commented to the press almost gleefully, "Well, are they going to claim that Lizzie Borden did this too?" Suddenly, there was an alternative theory of the case based on an UNSUB with similar MO who could not possibly have been Lizzie. What could create more "reasonable doubt"? The prosecution knew what had to be on the mind of every prospective member of the jury pool.

Then, on the very day Lizzie's trial was to commence, a Portuguese immigrant in his late teens or early twenties named Jose Correira was arrested. He had worked as an itinerant laborer for Stephen Manchester and had gotten into a bitter argument with him over severance pay. Apparently, he had returned to the farm to have it out with Stephen, but when he wasn't there, Correira confronted Bertha instead, murdering her in an overkill frenzy. He waited around the house for a while for his main target to return home, but after some time had passed, he reconsidered the situation and left.

The fact that Correira was Portuguese, and a Portuguese from the Azores at that, had the same effect on Fall River residents as the Jewish rumors surrounding Leather Apron had had on the East Enders of London during the Whitechapel murders. Poor and illiterate Portuguese immigrants were the lowest and most maligned caste in that part of Massachusetts, so if anyone was capable of such a ghastly crime as the murder of Andrew Borden and his wife, it would probably be "one of them." A proper American certainly wouldn't be capable of that.

It was later documented that Correira had not entered the United States from the Azores until April 1893, eight months after the Borden murders. But by the time this information became public, the Borden jury had already been chosen and sequestered. Of course, for everyone else, another subtext remained, almost as powerful: if one violent Portuguese immigrant could break in, attack Bertha Manchester with an ax or hatchet in a frenzy of overkill, then wait around for the man of the house to return, another one certainly could have done the same to the Bordens.

The trial of Lizzie Borden began on the morning of June 5, 1893, in the Superior Court for the County of Bristol. This was arguably the most celebrated criminal case of the century—rivaling the trials of Dred Scott, John Brown, the Haymarket bombers, even the impeachment of President Andrew Johnson—such was the interest and hoopla this spectacle created. The murders had long since become the prime topic of conversation not only in Fall River, but throughout New England, just as the Simpson-Goldman murders would rivet Los Angeles and the rest of the nation 102 years later. And as would happen with the Simpson trial, the national and world press converged upon the courthouse. Wealthy, prominent people just didn't get hacked to death, and their children didn't get accused of doing it. If this kind of thing could happen to a man like Andrew Borden and his wife, it could happen to anyone.

Knowlton, the district attorney of Fall River, was a reluctant prosecutor, forced into the role by Attorney General Arthur Pillsbury, who, at the time, would have been expected to try capital cases himself. But as the trial date approached, Pillsbury sensed pressure building from Lizzie's supporters, particularly women's groups and religious organizations. The Women's Christian Temperance Union, of which Lizzie was a member, publicly proclaimed its "unshaken faith in her, as a fellow worker and sister tenderly beloved." Likewise, Lizzie's ministers and fellow congregants at the Central Congregational Church—the most socially prominent church in Fall River—thought it impossible that the kind, demure, and dignified woman they knew could have committed such a pair of unthinkable acts.

The first day was devoted to selecting a jury—all white male—and then the prosecution presented its case. William Moody made the opening statements for the prosecution, presenting three essential arguments that were to represent the body of his case: that Lizzie Borden was predisposed to murder her father and stepmother and planned to do so; that the evidence would show that she did, in fact, murder them; and that her behavior and contradictory accounts were not consistent with innocence. Equally important, Moody made clear, was that the defendant had had the time to kill her stepmother while Bridget was washing the outside windows and was not in the house to hear anything. Then, when Andrew Borden came home, Bridget was up in her room in the attic lying down and, Moody contended, Lizzie was not in the barn but alone on the first floor of the house with her father.

Since there was no sign of struggle, the killer was logically someone well-known to both victims, who would not elicit any alarm. The only one who fit this criterion, the prosecution maintained, was Lizzie Borden herself.

The prosecution called Thomas Kieran, an architect and engineer who was sent in by the government to take full measurements of the Borden house. On cross-examination, he acknowledged that someone could have hidden in the closet in the front hall and not been seen by anyone inside the house. That afternoon, the judges had the jury visit the house to examine the crime scene for themselves.

John Morse testified that he had not seen Lizzie from the time he arrived at the Borden house on Wednesday until he returned after the murders on Thursday. He had been an early suspect, but convinced the police his alibi was sound and that he knew nothing about the crime. Interestingly, he was able to give a full and complete account of his own whereabouts at the time of the murders, down to the number of the streetcar he had ridden, the number on the conductor's cap, and the names of everyone he had encountered. It is almost as if he knew he would need to have this corroborating information and so made careful note of all of it.

Bridget Sullivan testified that she had no knowledge of the communication from Abby's sick friend that Lizzie had mentioned. When Robinson asked her if anyone could have entered the house while she was washing the outside windows, she admitted she had spent some time in a corner of the yard talking over the fence to the maid of the neighbors, Dr. and Mrs. Michael Kelly.

Crucial to the case was the evidence suggesting a motive. Knowlton and Moody called witnesses to establish that Andrew Borden was intending to write a new will. An old will was never found, nor its existence proven, although John Morse had testified that his brother-in-law had told him he had a will, but then later testified that Andrew had not mentioned one. The "new" will, according to Morse, was to leave Emma and Lizzie each $25,000, with the remainder of Andrew's $500,000 estate going to Abby. Further, Knowlton developed the additional motive of Andrew's intent to dispose of his farm to Abby, just as he had already transferred ownership of a house occupied by Abby's half-sister Sarah Whitehead to her. This was apparently a sore point between the Borden sisters and their stepmother, and they feared it might be "handwriting on the wall" as to their father's future intentions.

Hannah Gifford, a local dressmaker, recalled a conversation with Lizzie in March 1892, in which she had referred to Abby as Lizzie's mother.

Lizzie had rebuked her for referring to Abby this way, calling her "a mean good-for-nothing."

"Oh, Lizzie, you don't mean that," Gifford said she replied.

"Yes," Lizzie countered, "I don't have much to do with her."

Bridget testified that in the two years she'd been with the Bordens, she'd never heard "any trouble with the family, no quarreling or anything of that kind."

All in all, however, the testimony about Lizzie's predisposition was ambiguous and contradictory. The relationship between Lizzie and her father could be proven neither cold and flinty nor warm and fuzzy. As is so often the case with human behavior, it depended on who was observing.

However, two rulings by the court became crucial to the eventual outcome of the trial.

On Saturday, June 10, the prosecution moved to enter Lizzie's testimony at the inquest. George Robinson objected, since Lizzie had not been formally charged and was therefore not represented by counsel at the time. On Monday, when court resumed, the justices disallowed the introduction of Lizzie's contradicting testimony. Although today the absence of counsel would weigh quite heavily in the defendant's favor, many legal scholars were mystified by the decision.

Of the other contradictions that crept into the record, the defense got Dr. Bowen to acknowledge that the morphine he had prescribed for Lizzie could have left her thinking fuzzy and confused.

The most dramatic moment of the trial took place on the seventh day. Dr. Edward Wood testified about his examination of the victims' stomach contents and said that he had found no evidence of poisoning. He had examined the hatchet head broken off from its handle—the one police felt most likely to have been the murder weapon—and could find no traces of blood. He said that the killer ought to have had considerable blood on his or her person. (Remember that Lizzie was seen by Mrs. Churchill within ten minutes of Andrew's murder.) Told he would produce the actual skulls of the victims to show how the blade would have penetrated them, Lizzie fainted. A true lady, too sensitive to countenance such raw displays, she was allowed to leave the room. Certainly the men of the jury would not have held it against her.

But that this particular blade had been the murder weapon was only a theory. If the police and prosecution couldn't definitively identify the weapon, then it might have been taken from the house by whoever committed the crimes, leaving a vast gulf of reasonable doubt in one of the key points of the case.

On Wednesday, June 14, the prosecution called Eli Bence, the drugstore clerk. The defense objected. After hearing arguments from both sides as to the relevance of Lizzie's attempt to purchase prussic acid, the justices ruled that Bence's testimony—and the entire issue of Lizzie's alleged attempt to secure poison—was irrelevant and inadmissable.

There was, however, a chilling account from Alice Russell about a visit Lizzie had made to her on Wednesday, August 3, the evening before the murders. She quoted Lizzie as telling her, "I feel depressed. I feel as if something was hanging over me that I cannot throw off, and it comes over me at times, no matter where I am."

After telling her friend about the sickness of her father and stepmother, she confided, "Sometimes I think our milk might be poisoned."

When Russell had related that comment to the police on the day of the murders, they had seized the Borden milk supply and had it tested. Nothing unusual turned up.

Lizzie also mentioned a previous break-in to the house and two break-ins to the barn. She even said she had seen a "strange man run around the house."

"I feel afraid sometimes that father has an enemy," she said.

Another item was Anna Howland Borden's statement recalling Lizzie's unhappy description of her home life as the two women returned (along with Anna's sister Carrie Lindley Borden) from a nineteen-week trip through Europe that Andrew had given Lizzie as a thirtieth birthday gift. Some accounts have referred to Anna and Carrie as Lizzie's cousins, but the trial record states that they were not related (though, of course, Borden was a prominent name through this part of New England). Anna Borden's statement said that Lizzie did not want to return to her stifling home life after the freedom and stimulation of the grand European tour.

When the defense objected to the introduction of the statement, the judges ruled that the testimony was too ambiguous and did not point directly to ill will against either Lizzie's father or stepmother, so it, too, was excluded.

The defense used only two days to present its case. Essentially, they called witnesses to verify the presence of a mysterious young man in the vicinity of the Borden home. The intruder scenario was their alternative theory of the case. They explained away the missing note by suggesting that women did not like publicity and therefore it was natural that no one would come forward to say she had requested Abby's presence on the fateful morning. The defense emphasized that no blood was found on Lizzie, ignoring testimony that the way the murders were committed—the killer's position relative to the victims'—the offender easily could have avoided being spattered.

Andrew Jennings tried to get across several points to the jury: Lizzie must be presumed innocent unless she could not be proved guilty beyond a reasonable doubt. There was no direct evidence against Lizzie, and some of the circumstantial links were weak. There was no weapon identified. There was no well-established motive, and nothing in the defendant's character or previous behavior indicated she was capable of violence. Others had the opportunity to enter the house during the crucial time.

To counteract the effects of Alice Russell's testimony regarding the burning of the dress, Emma took the stand and said that she had urged Lizzie to burn the dress, a family custom when clothes were irredeemably soiled. This sounded odd from the household of a man as obsessively thrifty as Andrew Borden, actually known to make rags out of old clothes.

Emma testified that Lizzie deeply loved her father, that Andrew had worn a ring Lizzie had given him every day for the rest of his life. She insisted that she and Lizzie had been completely cooperative with the police during their examination of the house and had amply demonstrated they had nothing to hide.

To most observers, Emma remained something of an enigma. So retiring was she, few photographs are known to exist. She was described as shy, small, plain-looking, thin-faced, and bony—altogether an unremarkable forty-one-year-old spinster. She was strongly supportive of Lizzie during the trial, although one witness, Hannah Reagan, a day matron at the Central Police Station who had responsibility for Lizzie during the preliminary hearing, had testified to overhearing an argument between the sisters while Emma was visiting Lizzie on August 24.

"Emma, you have given me away, haven't you?" Lizzie charged.

"No, Lizzie, I have not," Emma responded.

"You have and I will let you see I won't give in one inch."

"Oh, Lizzie, I didn't," Emma insisted.

Lizzie did not take the stand in her own defense.

On Monday, June 19, defense attorney Robinson delivered his closing arguments, reiterating the points Jennings had made and dismissing the possibility that Lizzie could have kept changing out of blood-soaked dresses without anyone noticing and getting rid of them without a trace, as would have had to have happened if she had been the killer.

Then Knowlton began his own closing arguments, completing them the next day. He painted a word picture for the jury of what he considered the most likely scenario. He had Lizzie killing her hated stepmother, then knowing she could not face her father, she had no choice but to kill him, too.

After both sides were done, chief justice Mason asked Lizzie if she wanted to say anything. For the only time during the trial she spoke in open court, saying just, "I am innocent. I leave it to my counsel to speak for me."

THE VERDICT

Justice Dewey's charge to the jury remains one of the most controversial aspects of the entire trial. He instructed them to take into account her fine character and devotion to charitable organizations and to keep in mind that any single unprovable element in the prosecution's chain of logic "is fatal to the government's case," or as he restated even more sharply, "if there is a fact established—whether in that line of proof or outside of it— which cannot reasonably be reconciled with her guilt, then guilt cannot be said to be established."

At 3:24 on Tuesday, June 20, 1893, the jury was sworn and given the case. At 4:32 that same afternoon they announced that their deliberations were completed. Yet another way in which this trial prefigured the O. J. Simpson trial a century later.

The verdict was not guilty on all counts.

The case remains officially unsolved to this day.

Many commentators have stated that the trial and the verdict represented the triumph of law over popular emotion, and if one reviews the actual record of the case, this may well be true. But from every perspective other than the strictly jurisprudential one, the case remains troubling and unsettled, with the more than nagging feeling lingering that in the Lizzie Borden case, justice has not been served.

So how would we on the behavioral analysis side evaluate these crimes? And then, once that evaluation is complete, what could we have come up with of a proactive nature that might have gotten us closer to justice?

THE NATURE OF THE CRIME

If we were consulting on a case such as this today, the first thing we'd try to do is to define the crime according to several standard criteria and classifications. Some of this might seem self-evident as we go along, but it is important in all criminal investigations to proceed in a logical, step-by-step manner in which each step makes us more confident of the direction in which we're heading. A good, experienced detective takes nothing for granted. It's almost like a pilot's preflight checklist. He may have gone over each item a million times, but if he happens to ignore one and that turns out to be the weak link, then he and his passengers could be headed for disaster. It is too easy—and I have seen this many times—to come to one simple, but wrong, conclusion and then proceed off logically from there. You will then, of course, come up with a logical and well-reasoned, but wrong, answer.

First of all, these murders are what we would term personal-cause homicides, which simply means acts ensuing from interpersonal aggression. Before we can be secure with this, though, we have to examine the other possibilities.

Nothing of value was taken from the victims or the house, which would tend to rule out the felony murder—that is, a murder during the commission of another crime, such as burglary—or the normal criminal-enterprise type of homicide. However, we'd have to say that since the victim was a man of considerable means, we must consider that this could have been a contract—or third-party—killing, or an insurance/inheritance-related death. Sometimes there will be a mixed motive, and we should keep both of these in mind as we proceed.

Nor does this scenario fit the other two general categories for murder. It does not suggest itself to be a sexual homicide as we saw with the Whitechapel murders. And there is no evidence of a group-cause homicide, which would include cult and extremist murders, hostage situations, or what we refer to as group-excitement homicides, in which two or more people commit murder as a result of the spontaneous excitement of the moment.

Because of where the crimes took place, we have to strongly consider that they may be domestic homicides, a subcategory of personal-cause homicides. And within this subcategory, we have the further refinements of spontaneous domestic homicide and staged domestic homicide. The prime difference between the two is that the latter involves some degree of planning and follow-through.

The first killing, determined by both direct forensic and circumstantial evidence, was of Abby. This might have been either a spontaneous or a planned crime. The subsequent killing of Andrew had to have been planned. The prosecution's theory notwithstanding, this gives us some reason to believe the first killing may have been planned as well.

In any case, the sustained aggression of the repeated hatchet cuts to the face of both victims, much more than was necessary to cause nearly instant death, is commonly seen in domestic homicides. We believe this to be not only a manifestation of deep-seated and often long-standing anger by the offender against the victim, but also an attempt to depersonalize him or her. In the Whitechapel murders we could interpret the mutilation of the genitalia and evisceration of the vagina, uterus, and ovaries as an attempt to strip the victim of her sexual identity and power. Here, the facial battery indicates an attempt to strip the victim of actual identity and familiar power.

Significantly, Andrew was attacked as he slept. The first blow would have been sufficient to cause death and would have prevented him from crying out and alerting anyone. From the wound patterns on Abby's body, however, it is clear that the killer straddled her during the attack, which means he or she would have had to look straight into the victim's eyes.

VICTIMOLOGY

We have examined Andrew Borden's business prominence and his seemingly obsessive, almost ostentatious frugality. There is no indication he was a likable man. But from what we can gather, despite the frugal nature of the daily lives he imposed on himself and his family, he was moderately generous with his wife and daughters. He did, after all, give Lizzie an expensive trip to Europe for her thirtieth birthday. He was tidy, reserved, and brusque, but we have to keep in mind that it was the social ethos of the day that males worked hard to support the family and, in turn, were expected to rule that family. This was especially true in New England.

Ever since the house had been robbed in the summer of 1891, Andrew had kept his own bedroom locked, although he left the key in plain sight on the downstairs mantel. This may seem strange until we look further into the family dynamics. Though it was never proven, Andrew suspected Lizzie of having been the burglar. This wasn't just an idle speculation. For some years, Lizzie had had a quiet reputation around town as a kleptomaniac. The local merchants would discreetly present invoices to Andrew for what she had taken and he would discreetly pay them, avoiding any taint of public scandal. As far as we can tell, this habit was never mentioned in the Borden household. It is likely that locking the bedroom door but leaving the key in plain sight was a silent communication to Lizzie.

How much of Lizzie's behavior was acting out to get her father's attention is open to psychological interpretation. Andrew had married his first wife, Sarah Anthony Morse, in 1845. Sarah died in 1862. Emma had just turned twelve. Lizzie was two and a half. Two years later, Andrew married Abby Durfee Grady, a shy, squat, heavy, and humorless woman from a family nearly as prominent as the Bordens. Abby was thirty-six years of age and had never been married.

Andrew was a rigid obsessive-compulsive and together with Lizzie's behavior, there has been speculation that his traits match those of a sexual abuser and hers match those of a woman victimized. Certainly he kept his family socially isolated, and his driving force seemed to be having power and control over others. His choice of a second wife is significant in that it was as pragmatic as everything else in his life. He opted for a socially prominent but unattractive woman without other prospects who he could be assured would be grateful and subservient to him, rather than a younger woman who might give him the son he had always wanted.

Abby was devoted to her much younger half-sister Sarah Whitehead, and Abby's generous, eager-to-please personality came out only in the home of her sister. Other than with Sarah and Sarah's daughter, Abby appeared to have no real close relationships. Since the squabble over the ownership transfer of some of Andrew's properties, Lizzie had stopped calling Abby her mother and now called her Mrs. Borden. She wasn't shy about telling friends how oppressive she found her home life with Abby.

PRIME SUSPECTS AND MOTIVES

Okay, so where do we go from here?

The next factor to consider is the relative risk level of the crime. It took place in broad daylight, in a low-crime area, on a street with frequent pedestrian and vehicular traffic of both a personal and business nature. And since this was before the days of automobiles, such traffic would be relatively slow. Moreover, we know from Bridget Sullivan's account that the door Andrew Borden used to gain entry to the house had been locked and bolted. Is it possible that an intruder gained entry through an unlocked door and then locked it behind him to keep others away? Highly doubtful, because an intruder's primary concern is going to be how to get quickly out of the premises. Bridget herself had trouble with the bolt. This would not have allowed for a quick getaway.

Since we've ruled out professional or amateur burglary, what other type of offender might take the kind of risk this crime entailed?

If the stakes were high enough or the payoff sufficiently worthwhile, a contract killer might take such a risk. We could, off the tops of our heads, come up with a scenario in which any of the numerous parties with whom Andrew Borden had business might have a reason to want him "out of business." But there are two problems with this. First, investigators found no such animosity. Andrew was a hard-driving, tightfisted businessman, but no one was out to get him or found to have profited significantly from his death. Second, a contract killer would have had no conceivable reason to kill Abby. So if the UNSUB got to the Borden home expecting Andrew to be there and found he was not, he would simply have gotten the hell out and waited for another opportunity.

There is, of course, one exception to this logic. And that is if the reason for the murders had to do with insurance and/or inheritance. In that case, Abby is a critical target. And in that case, who would have had reason to put up the contract? The suspect population is small: Emma, Lizzie, and possibly Abby's half-sister, Sarah Whitehead.

We can reasonably eliminate Sarah. Not only did she and Abby have a close relationship, she had no problem with the Bordens. Andrew had deeded over some of his property to her already and there were indications of more, a fact that the Borden sisters were said to have resented deeply. Also, even if Mrs. Whitehead had decided to do in her sister for her inheritance, she would have needed Andrew to die *first*, so that according to law, Abby would have first inherited her husband's estate. As it was, with Abby dying first, the estate would go to his heirs, namely Emma and Lizzie.

And this is exactly what happened. It cannot be by chance that Abby was killed first.

Which leaves the two sisters and a believable motive. But if Emma and/or Lizzie was going to hire a contract killer, wouldn't the trained professional have made the crime look like a robbery, or at least the clear work of an intruder? What would be the point of hiring a contract killer but then having the crime scene and circumstantial evidence point right back to Lizzie? Unless it was Emma who hired the killer and her intention was to set up Lizzie so that Emma would get the entire estate. But that's really getting excessively complicated. There is nothing in Emma's personality to suggest she could be this Machiavellian, and more to the point, when she had the perfect opportunity to cut her sister loose after she was arrested and indicted, Emma stood by her and insisted Lizzie did not commit the heinous killings.

Given all of the foregoing, I'm ready to eliminate the contract killer scenario and move on. Okay, so no robber-burglar, no hit man. What about a disorganized offender? The rumors about a crazed madman were rife. Maybe he broke in and could even have hidden himself in the downstairs closet for the hour and a half between the murders. But not after the rage and overkill demonstrated with Abby's murder and not before the rage and overkill that would be demonstrated again on Andrew. Nobody with that kind of seething turmoil inside is going to be able to control himself to that extent for that long. I've never seen or read about anything like it. Even waiting out in the open for Stephen Manchester to return home after the killing of Bertha, Jose Correira gave up and left. And this was someone with a discernible grudge. Given the physical setting, too, I would be extremely surprised to see a disorganized offender leave no blood trail between the upstairs murder site and the one downstairs. Certainly there would have been blood traces in the closet in which he would have hidden.

So what I'd be telling local police is the same conclusion they came to themselves: This is probably the work of someone close to the family, with knowledge of their comings and goings, with knowledge of the layout of the inside of the house. Someone whose presence would not arouse suspicion.

So is there anyone of this description who had motive for the murders? We could make cases for Emma, Lizzie, and Bridget. And of those, who had access and opportunity between 9:30 and 11:00 A.M. on August 4, 1892? Because of Emma's trip to Fairhaven, we're down to Lizzie and Bridget.

What was Bridget's possible motive? What was the precipitating stressor? She wasn't feeling well that warm and humid morning; she'd been vomiting and was weak from her ordeal. And yet Abby insisted she clean all the windows in the house, inside and out. Maybe she just cracked . . . lost it. The two years of domestic oppression caught up with her and she took out all of her frustration and rage on the hapless Abby. She could then either run away or stick around and complete the job on Andrew when he returned home and make it look like an intruder. But then wouldn't she have killed Lizzie, too? Leaving her alive would have been more dangerous than leaving Andrew alive.

And we have another problem with this. Bridget liked her job. She wanted to be able to keep it. There is no indication that she ever had a serious disagreement with her employers. They got along well, and Mr. and Mrs. Borden treated her with respect and consideration. They even called her by her proper name, something Emma and Lizzie couldn't be bothered with, calling her Maggie rather than Bridget.

What about Lizzie and Bridget in collusion? One or both of them kills the Bordens, Lizzie inherits a fortune and pays Bridget off for her troubles.

Again, we have to deal with personality, and there didn't seem to be anything in Bridget's that would allow her to take that bold a step. She would have been too scared. The police found her quite timid. Nothing indicates that she would have been motivated to commit such a crime for any amount of money. If Bridget had been involved, a vulnerable young servant with her personality would have broken under interrogation, particularly with the intimidation tactics the police would have used back then. That said, Bridget had to have suspected Lizzie. She was the only other one there, and Lizzie had pointedly brought up the cloth sale, likely in an attempt to get Bridget out of the house.

Although Emma seems to have been out of town during the murders, she has not avoided suspicion. After she received the telegram from Dr. Bowen, she did not take the first train back from Fairhaven. She did not take the second, nor the third. The fourth train did not get her back until the evening. This does not indicate conspiracy to me, but I sure wouldn't discount it as a possible indication that as soon as she heard about the murders, Emma had at least a vague fear about what had really happened. The same could be said for Uncle John, who strolls back and, despite the activity on the street, stands around the backyard eating pears that have fallen from the trees.

Frank Spiering, who in *Prince Jack* proposed Prince Eddie, the Duke of Clarence, as Jack the Ripper, weaves a scenario for Emma as the killer of her father and stepmother in *Lizzie*. He has her establish her alibi fifteen miles away in Fairhaven, then surreptitiously driving her buggy back to Fall River, hiding upstairs in the house, committing the murders, then driving back to Fairhaven. Once Lizzie is accused, the sisters work together to protect each other. However, at one point it seems that Emma is trying to double-cross Lizzie, and Lizzie forces her to share the inheritance equally.

The problem with this scenario is that there is absolutely no evidence to support it—only that it *could* have happened. To me, this is a perfect example of the common tendency to make the facts fit the theory, rather than the other way around. All of the behavioral evidence concerning Emma—all of it—suggests she was shy, self-effacing, timid, and dominated by Lizzie. There is no way she could have come up with such an elaborate plan to kill her father and stepmother.

Another theory concerns Andrew's alleged disturbed, illegitimate son, William Borden, by a local woman named Phebe Hathaway. Author Arnold R. Brown makes a case for William as the killer in his interesting and provocative 1991 book, *Lizzie Borden: The Legend, the Truth, the Final Chapter.*

According to the William Borden theory, he was making demands of his father, who was drawing up his will. These demands were rejected by Andrew. William, in a fit of rage, killed Abby first, hid in the house with Lizzie's knowledge, then killed his father. Because of his illegitimate status and a possible claim he might have to Andrew's estate, Lizzie, Emma, Uncle John, Dr. Bowen, and attorney Jennings conspired to keep his crime hidden. The conspirators then either paid William off, threatened him, or both. They decided that Lizzie would allow herself to be a suspect and be tried for the murders, knowing she could always identify the actual killer, should that become necessary. William apparently was fascinated with hatchets and may have had a connection to the Bertha Manchester murder. Arnold Brown questions whether it might have been a contract murder to divert guilt away from Lizzie. As intriguing as this theory may be, there doesn't seem to be any evidence to support it. In fact, Leonard Rebello, author of the comprehensive and exhaustively researched *Lizzie Borden Past & Present,* writes, "No information was located to substantiate Mr. Brown's allegation." The behavioral evidence regarding Lizzie, on the other hand, has been well documented.

LIZZIE

Let's take a look at Lizzie's situation. From photographs, she had been rather cute as a child and teenager. But by the time in question, she had matured into what can be most delicately described as a rather plain, round-faced, robust woman—not exactly like the late actress Elizabeth Montgomery, the talented beauty I remember from the TV movie about Lizzie. She was an unmarried spinster living in her father's house, not getting along with her stepmother, with no real prospects of getting out or changing things. The same can be said for Emma, but Emma was not the kind of outgoing woman with high social expectations that Lizzie was. Since their mother's death, Emma had essentially dedicated herself to caring for Lizzie, a promise she had made to her mother on her deathbed.

Lizzie was willful and stubborn and liked to be noticed, which would almost surely have put her into conflict with her father. At the inquest, she often displayed a belligerent temper. She dropped out of school in the tenth grade, was subject to black moods, and indulged in numerous remedies to deal with them. She desperately wanted to live in the style to which she felt her family's social station entitled her, and that began with a house on "the Hill," by far the best neighborhood in town. The people Lizzie envied there were largely her rich cousins who had inherited their wealth for two generations running and had no compunction about spending it. Her father, who had scraped for every penny, however, had no interest in such pretensions. He gave Lizzie a generous allowance, and Lizzie had all the fine dresses she wanted, but Andrew thought the house at 92 Second Street was perfectly adequate for their needs. If he wouldn't go for electricity and modern plumbing, he certainly wasn't going to relocate his family to a grand house on the Hill.

Lizzie was in a bind. She yearned to move out and live in a socially prominent manner. But she certainly couldn't afford to do that on her own, and even if she could, it was so socially improper for a single woman of her class not to live at home while her parents remained alive that had she moved out, she would not have been accepted by the society she so craved to join. The real hope would be marriage to a well-to-do gentleman. But she was thirty-two, so that didn't look likely. She had had a few beaux over the years, but all of the relationships had been short-lived. The men in her neighborhood were all working class, and she couldn't very well have the young men who lived on the Hill come calling in her embarrassing house.

And the situation might have been getting desperate. Andrew had already turned over real estate holdings to Abby and her half-sister as early as 1887—five years before—and Lizzie and Emma both feared they would increasingly be cut out of their father's estate. If that was the case, then they would be at Abby's mercy when the already seventy-year-old Andrew passed on.

We know that the night before the murders, Andrew and John Morse discussed business with each other in the first-floor sitting room. There is some indication Andrew was seeking advice about his will. So whether or not Lizzie had been gradually trying to poison her parents, this discussion with Uncle John could have been the precipitating stressor that made the act urgent. Once there was a will bequeathing everything to Abby, it would be too late.

Did a will actually exist? We'll never know. None was ever found, though it is difficult to imagine a man as meticulous as Andrew Borden not having one. Perhaps the stained dress was not the only thing burned.

Strong evidence suggests that at least at one time, Lizzie and Andrew were close, though his marriage to Abby would have made their relationship emotionally complicated at best. He constantly wore the ring Lizzie had given him as a sign of her love and devotion. Father and daughter had gone on frequent fishing trips together while she was growing up, and she maintained a passion for fishing, though she had not been in five years. This fact made her story about going into the barn to make sinkers somewhat suspect.

Another story believed by case scholars to be apocryphal offers an interesting possible precipitating incident in May 1892. Some say Lizzie kept pigeons roosting in the barn, which had recently been broken into. Andrew surmised that the culprits were boys wanting to steal the pigeons, so to thwart them, he went into the barn with a hatchet and killed all of the birds, leaving a bloody hatchet for all, including Lizzie, to see.

The symmetry with the murders three months later seems almost too neat and facile, but we certainly can't ignore the possible influence if the first event occurred. At the very least, it would show two people apparently unable to deal with each other's emotional needs or sensibilities.

I don't think it is going too far to say that in many ways Lizzie saw herself as a victim. Under the section on Staged Domestic Homicide in the *Crime Classification Manual,* we wrote: "Post-offense interviews of close friends or family members often reveal that the victim had expressed concerns or fears regarding his or her safety or even a sense of foreboding." If Lizzie had somehow transposed the roles of attacker and victim in her mind, then the anguished visit to Alice Russell the night before the murders fits perfectly into this emotional context.

In late July of 1892, Lizzie accompanied Emma to New Bedford, Massachusetts. By some accounts they left home after a family disagreement over a suspected transfer to Abby of one of the Swansea farms they had often visited as girls. They were on their way to see friends—Emma to the Brownells in Fairhaven and Lizzie to some acquaintances in Marion. But in New Bedford, Lizzie decided to spend several days with an old schoolmate before returning home on August 2. By then, Andrew and Abby were complaining of stomach upset, and Abby would then go to Dr. Bowen with the notion that someone was trying to poison them. (Note again the just mentioned passage from the *Crime Classification Manual.*)

It was the next day that Lizzie was seen in the drugstore trying to buy prussic acid (for another try?) and that night that she visited Alice Russell.

THE BEHAVIORAL CASE

The personality and the pre-offense behavioral indicators are there. Let's look at the crime scene indicators.

Lizzie claimed to have discovered her father's freshly slain body, but did not leave the house. Instead, she sent Bridget out and called a neighbor over, even though she would have to presume the killer might still be inside. Mrs. Churchill reported no expressions of fear for their immediate safety by Lizzie at this time.

Likewise with the first murder, Lizzie said she believed her stepmother had just returned home and asked Bridget (ultimately accompanied by Mrs. Churchill) to go look for her upstairs.

With a crazed killer still in the house?

Lizzie made no move to flee the house or to get the others out to safety. Nor did anyone suggest to Dr. Bowen or arriving police officers that maybe the killer was still in the house.

In domestic murders, the killer often sets up someone else to discover the body, rather than having to "find" it him- or herself.

To assume an intruder, we have to deal with all the implications of someone coming into the house, staying there for more than an hour and a half, and not alerting any family members. This guy would have had to have had the stealth and assassin skills of a Navy SEAL. From my experience, there is no way a stranger off the street would have come in and gone straight up to the second floor. He wouldn't have known who was inside, what the environment was. He would have been afraid of being trapped. Even a maniac wouldn't hang around for ninety minutes, and he would have killed Lizzie and Bridget, too. No one is going into that house without some critical information, and this is a subject with which we'll also deal in the next chapter.

As we've said, no note to Abby was ever found, even though Lizzie and Emma offered a substantial reward for it. The story about Abby's going out would have been necessary to keep Andrew from going upstairs to see her when he returned home.

Normally in a domestic homicide we expect to see some effort at staging the crime scene to make it look like a rape or robbery gone bad or something else that would suggest an intruder rather than someone from the house or family. I think the reason we don't have that staging here is because with Bridget in and around the house, Lizzie knew there was too much of a chance she would be seen doing this. Also, to make it look like a robbery, she'd have had to take something, and if she was remaining in the house, what would she do with it? She had to know the house would be thoroughly searched.

The crime scene photograph of Andrew Borden shows his wool overcoat folded on the arm of the sofa, as if he had been using it as a pillow. While it is possible that he did this, it would have been completely out of character. He was as meticulous about his clothing as he was about everything else, and it's unlikely he would have wrinkled a coat he would then wear again on his afternoon business rounds.

Is it possible, we have to wonder, that he had actually hung it up or left it draped over the back of a chair, and that the killer put it on to avoid being spattered with blood? Then, once the deed was done, folded it to appear as if Andrew had been using it as a pillow so that the blood could easily be explained? And who would need to avoid the blood? Only someone who was not planning on getting away from the scene immediately after the murders.

And what of the rest of the blood? There is, of course, the dress Lizzie burned in the stove, which she could have been wearing during one of the murders. It is also possible that she stripped naked to carry out the murders and then quickly washed herself, though I would wonder about a woman of that era with the social pretensions Lizzie had taking off all her clothing in this manner, not to mention the risk of being seen by Bridget. In some ways, that is more difficult to conceive of than the murders themselves.

Bloody water was seen in a washbasin in the house, but when Dr. Albert C. Dedrich, a Fall River physician who also examined the Bordens' bodies, asked about it, he was told that one of the other doctors or police officers had washed his hands in it after touching the crime scene.

That same afternoon, Officer William Medley noticed a pail of water in the wash cellar containing small towels that seemed to be covered with blood. He asked Lizzie about it, and she replied that she had explained it all to Dr. Bowen. Bowen, in turn, assured Medley that it was all right, implying that the pail contained menstrual rags, a subject about which men were exceedingly squeamish. No one was going to examine Lizzie to determine if she was actually having her period, and no one checked the potential evidence of the pail. Lizzie said it had been there for three or four days, although Bridget claimed she had not seen it before that day. It probably would not have been there two days before or Bridget would have noticed it when she did the washing.

When it came to the trial, the idea that the pail contained menstrual rags was accepted as fact. George Robinson reminded the jury "that Professor Wood said he would not undertake to say that that blood was not menstrual blood. . . . You know enough in your own households, you know all about it. You are men and human. You have your own feelings about it. I am not going to drag them up, but you must not lose sight of these things."

And no one did.

STRATEGIES

So if you believe Lizzie Borden to have been the killer of her father and stepmother, is there anything that could have been done in the investigation or trial that might have brought about a verdict to that effect? Based on the experience we've had in many cases within the Investigative Support Unit, I think that there is. Of course, as in the Whitechapel murders, this presupposes an understanding of criminal behavior and practice that hadn't been developed at the time, but if it had, could we have gotten Lizzie to crack?

The first thing I would have tried was to play on the strain in Lizzie and Emma's relationship as perceived by the prison matron. One way to accomplish this would have been to befriend one of the zillions of reporters who were haunting the town and given him an accurate but pretty generic evaluation of the case. I would have told him that it has been our experience that in a crime of this nature, there would have been a primary offender, but also a secondary person, almost a compliant victim, who was dominated by the subject, who knows exactly what happened, and who should now be very concerned for her own well-being.

We would be trying to drive a wedge into a psychological master-slave relationship. The dominant individual will want all of the money and control. The loyalty in the relationship is one-sided. Since this person has shown the capacity to kill twice in cold blood, he or she could easily kill again. And even if she does not resort to violence, she could easily turn on her benefactress and point the finger at her.

I'd make sure my target had seen the newspaper articles before I attempted to interview her. They would confirm a fear that was already in her mind. Important to this strategy would be trying to keep Emma away from Lizzie, since Lizzie's personality was so dominant.

And I would try this not only with Emma, but with Uncle John as well, since we couldn't be sure which or if both of them might have had inside information or harbored fears about Lizzie.

Of course, I would take a shot with Lizzie, too. In situations where the subject is facing a possible capital murder conviction, getting an outright confession is going to be difficult. He's got nothing to gain and everything to lose by telling the truth. So we try to offer some sort of face-saving scenario that the subject can buy into.

As readers of *Mindhunter* will recall, Larry Gene Bell, the brutal and psychologically sadistic abductor and killer of seventeen-year-old Shari Faye Smith and nine-year-old Debra May Helmick in Columbia, South

Carolina, was hunted down and caught through an efficient combination of profiling and first-rate police work. Sheriff Jim Metts and his detectives knew they had the right man, but he was understandably unwilling to confess to these despicable acts that could (and ultimately did) get him an appointment with the South Carolina electric chair.

So they gave me a crack at him. I gave him some background on the serial killer study we'd done in the FBI, how we'd gone around to the penitentiaries and learned from the actual killers what was going on in their minds.

"The problem for us, Larry," I explained, "is that when you go to court, your attorney probably isn't going to want you to take the stand, and you'll never have the opportunity to explain yourself. All they'll know about you is the bad side, nothing good, just that you're a cold-blooded killer. We've found that very often when people do this kind of thing, it is like a nightmare, and when they wake up the next morning, they can't believe they've actually committed this crime."

All the time I was talking, Bell was nodding his head in agreement.

I knew if I asked him outright about the murders, he'd deny it. So I leaned in close and asked, "When did you first start feeling bad about the crime?"

And he said, "When I saw a photograph and read a newspaper article about the family praying at the cemetery."

"Larry, as you're sitting here now, did you do this thing? Could you have done it?"

He looked at me with tears in his eyes and said, "All I know is that the Larry Gene Bell sitting here couldn't have done this, but the bad Larry Gene Bell could have."

I would think a similar tactic might have worked on Lizzie. I'd start by playing on the blood, asking her where it all went. How she washed it off. How she had to burn that dress. She would have been more sophisticated than Bell, so the approach would have to have been commensurate to her intellectual level, but it might have gone something like this:

"Lizzie, we know from our experience and research that this type of act is unlike a woman, certainly unlike a woman of your standing and upbringing. So if you were involved, we know that there must have been strong and compelling factors that drove you, factors over which you had no conscious control. We can only imagine what it must have been like to lose your mother when you did, then having to live with Abby all those years. We know how manipulative she must have been, how she took advantage of your father, how she subtly turned him away from you and Emma. Emma cared for you and protected you, and now you realized the time had come for you to care for and protect her, to assure her future and yours after your father passed on."

I know I'd have her attention. She'd be quiet, listening carefully, evaluating what I was saying, trying to figure where I was coming from and how it would affect her. If I were dealing with an innocent person, I'd expect a series of strong denials to practically every statement I made. But Lizzie would be receptive as I reeled her in.

"And what about your father? We know he tried to love you, as much as he was capable of. But think back, rip off the scar tissue of the old wounds. Is it possible that he loved you too much, or in the wrong way? You were so much like your mother, a woman he adored far more than he could ever care for Abby. And is this something Emma knew about? Something she saw? You may have repressed this. I know how painful it is, but I've seen other cases like this and I know what can happen. I understand. People say you haven't shown enough grief. But when I see this, I know there's a reason. What has he done to you? We can't change the past, Lizzie—the distant past or the recent past. But what we need to do is to get people to understand why you did what you did. I'm going to leave a pad of paper with you, and if and when anything comes to mind, I want you to write it down. Sometimes that's the easiest way."

Then I'd go away and give her time to build her story. But before I left, I'd add something to the effect of, "Lizzie, the person who did this doesn't need punishment, she needs help. She doesn't need to be in a prison, she needs to be in an institution."

She might have been disdainful of this approach to begin with, but if I could keep the dialogue going and get her involved, I'd have confidence something useful might emerge.

Another variation of this technique would be to try to get another newspaper article out. This one would be an interview with me, touting me as the outside expert brought in to consult with the police. But in the interview, I'd concede disagreement with some of the investigators and within the department itself. I'd say that most of the detectives feel this was a well-planned, cold-blooded assassination-style crime. But I believed it was impulsive, that it represented suddenly uncontrolled rage, that the subject was literally out of her mind for those brief moments. I'd say that many of these acts are like a dream, but there will be one aspect that will make the subject say to herself, "My God, maybe I did do this!" This would help plant a defense and build up trust in me and my views for the prospective interview. I'd want her to perceive me as her one possible lifeline: she might not get away with murder, but I might understand.

THE AFTERMATH

Two months after the trial, Lizzie and Emma moved into a fourteen-room light stone house they had purchased at 7 French Street, on the Hill. Lizzie named the house Maplecroft and had the name carved into the top stone step leading up to the front door. Lizzie, who began calling herself Lizbeth, found it impossible to go back to her old church because of the gossip and social ostracism. Emma, on the other hand, remained a churchgoer.

Strangely, prosecutor William Moody received in the mail a package from Lizzie containing official photographs of the trial—including the crime scenes—along with a handwritten note to the effect that she thought he might like them "as souvenirs of an interesting occasion."

As we would expect from someone whose crimes were situational and directed at close family, Lizzie Borden never committed another known act of violence throughout her life. In fact, she became a great friend to animals and was a fervent supporter of the humane movement.

In 1897, Lizzie was charged with the theft of two paintings, valued at less than $100, from the Tilden-Thurber Co. store in Providence. The problem was privately resolved, although a rumor persisted that in exchange for the charges being dropped, she had agreed to sign a confession to the murders of her father and stepmother. The "signature" proved to be fake.

In 1904, Lizzie met a beautiful and glamorous young actress named Nance O'Neil, and for the next two years, the two women were practically inseparable. After Lizzie staged a lavishly catered party at Maplecroft for O'Neil's theatrical company, Emma moved out and went to live in Providence. Sometime around 1923, Emma moved to Newmarket, New Hampshire, where she rented a place and lived quietly and virtually anonymously.

On June 1, 1927, after complications from gallbladder surgery, Lizzie Borden died in Fall River at age sixty-seven. Emma was not included in her will and did not return to Fall River to attend the funeral. Nine days later, Emma succumbed to chronic nephritis. Like Lizzie, she left her estate to a variety of charitable causes.

Both sisters were buried in the family plot at Oak Grove Cemetery in Fall River, along with their father, their mother, their stepmother, and Alice Esther, the sister who had died in infancy.

The day of the murders, Bridget left the house, never to return. She was rumored to have gone back to Ireland, although this story has never been verified. In the late 1890s, she settled in Anaconda, Montana, where she married a man whose surname was also Sullivan. She did not speak of the Borden murders until 1943, when she contracted a severe case of pneumonia and believed she was going to die. She called her closest friend to her bedside, saying she had a secret to confide. But by the time the friend arrived, Bridget was on her way to recovery and said nothing. The only thing she later told the friend about Lizzie was that she had always liked her. She died on March 25, 1948, in Butte, Montana, at age seventy-three.

The house at 92 Second Street in Fall River is still standing. Since 1996, it has been open as a bed-and-breakfast. The curious or morbidly inclined can actually stay in the John Morse Guest Room, the site of Abby Borden's murder. That room and the downstairs sitting room where Andrew was killed have been furnished to look just as they did on that warm, humid day in August of 1892.

CHAPTER THREE

THE LINDBERGH
KIDNAPPING

Lucky Lindy up in the sky,
Fair or windy, he's flying high
Fearless, peerless, knows every cloud,
The kind of a son makes a mother feel proud.

Plucky Lindy rides all alone
In a little plane all his own.
Lucky Lindy showed them the way
And he's the hero of the day!

As these 1927 song lyrics suggest, from a May morning of that year and well into the 1930s, Colonel Charles Augustus Lindbergh was the most famous man in the world. He was in his midtwenties and exceedingly handsome, of solid Midwestern stock, the son of a former U.S. congressman. He was brave, daring, and visionary, yet at the same time modest and shy. And he had done what was supposed to be impossible—flying solo for thirty-three death-defying hours, from New York to Paris in his tiny, silver, single-engine *Spirit of St. Louis*. Instantly he became the Lone Eagle, Lucky Lindy—in short, the ultimate hero, a hero who embodied all of America's best qualities. Then, during of tour of Mexico, this most famous, most eligible bachelor in the world met Anne Spencer Morrow. She was the shy, sensitive, and beautiful daughter of multimillionaire businessman-diplomat and ambassador Dwight Whitney Morrow, the financial whiz who had taken over as senior partner at J. P. Morgan upon the death of its founder. Charles proposed to Anne, and the American public settled down to live vicariously the lives of its new royalty.

The kidnapping of their baby firstborn son instantly became "the crime of the century," unquestionably the biggest news story since Lindy's historic flight five years earlier. And for many, despite the subsequent atom-bomb spy ring, the John and Robert Kennedy and Martin Luther King assassinations, the Manson family murders, the slayings of Nicole Brown Simpson and Ronald Goldman, and so many other cases, this remains the crime of the century.

The facts and the evidence have been so persistently and painstakingly sifted for so many years that there are probably no completely "new" theories left to present. And like the Whitechapel murders, this case is a perfect example of the emotional tendency to come up with a scenario, then arrange and organize facts and evidence to fit it. What we want to do here is start from the opposite side—the only proper side for an investigator—to work our way through those facts and evidence in an attempt to arrive at an explanation that makes sense . . . whether or not it conforms to the official record. There are literally millions of pages of accumulated evidence, reports, and testimony, and no one person could possibly go through it all. Keep in mind as you read along, though, that every element presented is, or may be, significant in determining what happened, and who caused it to happen.

Like the Ripper case, the Lindbergh case is about the potential for random and unexpected evil to appear at any time. Like Lizzie Borden's case, it is about what can happen behind the closed doors of the most proper and upstanding home. And as much as anything, it is also about the potentially malignant consequences of celebrity and fame.

Charles Lindbergh had a complicated and troubled relationship with his own celebrity. He accepted the adulation and the ticker-tape parades, the meetings and receptions with world leaders, the endless testimonial dinners, the appointments and commissions and consultancies. An exhibit of his awards and trophies in St. Louis attracted a million visitors a year. He understood that his opinion on anything was instant news, and each daring new exploit—whether it was opening up a new aviation route or testing a new piece of technology—only further burnished his gleaming image. And yet he was suspicious of it all, wary of any emotional intrusion, resentful that the press just wouldn't leave any aspect of his existence unexamined. In the midst of a life lived under the unrelenting spotlight of a public's interest and attention, privacy became an obsession for Lindbergh.

When they weren't traveling around the world, the Lindberghs lived at Next Day Hill, Dwight and Elizabeth Morrow's palatial estate in Englewood, New Jersey. For their own home, the Lindberghs selected a secluded 425-acre tract of wooded hills in New Jersey's Sourland Mountains a few miles from Hopewell. The property overlapped the Hunterdon and Mercer County lines. Lindbergh had spotted the site from the air and thought it would offer the refuge they sought. He also liked that the land was suitable for a private airfield. The couple built a traditional-style, $80,000, twenty-room, whitewashed fieldstone house with a thick slate roof and all the modern technological advances. It was designed by Chester Aldrich, the architect of Next Day Hill. Here, Charles and Anne hoped to start and then raise their family. During the construction, they rented an old farmhouse between the property and Princeton.

After months of rumors eagerly reported by the press, the world got the news it had been waiting for. On June 22, 1930—Anne's twenty-fourth birthday—she gave birth to a seven-pound-six-ounce baby boy at Next Day Hill. They named him Charles Augustus Lindbergh Jr. and called him Charlie. But in the headlines he soon became "Little Lindy," "Eaglet," or "the Baby Eagle." Telegrams, letters, and gifts poured in from around the world. If his father was the earth's most famous man, Charlie was the most famous baby. Every detail of the baby's day-to-day existence was grist for the papers. In his outstanding 1998 biography, *Lindbergh,* A. Scott Berg reported that there was a standing offer of $2,000 for any "secrets of the household."

So thick were rumors that the reluctant Lindbergh felt himself forced to call a press conference in New York to clarify matters. He had personally barred five newspaper chains, including Hearst, which had published stories speculating that the baby was deformed or somehow imperfect. When he was asked what he hoped his son might grow up to be, Lindbergh replied testily, "I don't want him to be anything or do anything that he himself has no taste or aptitude for. I believe that everybody should have complete freedom in the choice of his life's work. One thing I do hope for him, and that is when he is old enough to go to school, there will be no reporters dogging his footsteps."

THE HOUSE NEAR HOPEWELL

The Lindberghs began staying at the nearly completed Hopewell house on weekends, returning to the Morrow compound fifty miles away on Monday mornings. The Lindbergh's full-time staff consisted of an English butler, Aloysius "Olly" Whateley, and his wife, Elsie. In February, 1931, the Lindberghs hired Betty Gow, a recently emigrated Scottish woman of Anne's age, to be Charlie's nursemaid. She had been highly recommended by another member of the Next Day Hill domestic staff. Charlie had developed a head full of golden curls and had his father's distinctive cleft chin, and Anne was pregnant with a second child. She had also begun to seriously consider her goal of becoming a professional writer and had been recording her experiences of her and Charles's recent trip to the Orient. Her chief domestic concern was that despite their attempts at security, unless the baby was watched every moment of the day, photographers might sneak in and take pictures of him.

The narrative of the few days before the crime is well documented by Scott Berg. As had become their custom, during the afternoon of Saturday, February 27, 1932, the Lindberghs left Next Day Hill and drove from Englewood to Hopewell to spend the weekend at the nearly completed house. But by Sunday, little Charlie, now twenty months old, had developed a cold, which left him sneezing, stuffy, and feeling ill. On Monday, February 29, the baby was still sick, and after lunch Anne called Betty Gow at Next Day Hill and said they'd stay in the Hopewell house until Charlie was feeling better. That evening, Lindbergh called from New York to say that he'd be spending the night in town and planned to return the next night. He had been pursuing his interest in biological research at the Rockefeller Institute.

On Tuesday morning, the baby seemed to be a little better, but Anne herself had come down with the cold. She called Betty Gow again and asked her to come to Hopewell. Gow arrived early in the afternoon and spelled Anne so she could get some rest. A little before 3 P.M., according to Berg, the two women went into the nursery together and found Charlie much improved. He played in the living room until around 5:30, then Gow took him back upstairs to the nursery, which, as you approach the house, was the room in the far left rear of the second floor. Gow fed him some cereal, then around 6:15 Anne came in and they prepared him for bed.

They rubbed his chest with Vicks VapoRub, then Gow quickly made a simple undershirt for him out of some leftover cream-colored cotton flannel. They put on his diapers, a woolen vest-style shirt, and a gray, size-2 Dr. Denton's sleeping suit. Lindbergh did not want him to suck his thumb, so he'd outfitted his son with wire thumb guards at night that clipped onto his sleeves. Betty laid him down in the dark wooden four-poster crib and pulled up the blankets.

Anne tried to close the shutters but found the ones on the corner window too warped. She left the room around 7:30, and Betty Gow stayed another few minutes, opening one window about halfway for some circulation before turning out the light and leaving to wash the baby's clothes. After that, she went in again to check on him and safety-pinned the blanket to the mattress to keep him warm. She then went to the basement to hang up the things she had washed and joined Elsie Whateley for dinner in their sitting room at about 8 P.M.

Twenty-five minutes later, Lindbergh arrived home. Actually, he was supposed to be at a dinner hosted by New York University at the Waldorf-Astoria hotel, but there had been a scheduling mix-up, so he had driven home to Hopewell. He came from the garage through the kitchen. He and Anne sat down for dinner together around 8:35. After dinner, they went into the living room, which occupied the central area of the ground floor on the back side of the house.

Just after 9 P.M., Lindbergh thought he heard a strange sound, which he later described as similar to a wooden orange crate breaking. He thought maybe it had come from the kitchen on the right front side of the house, in line with the dining room in the back. Anne recalled that about fifteen minutes before Charles drove up to the garage, she thought she'd heard the sound of car wheels crunching the gravel of the driveway. But no one had been there. The Lindberghs' dog, Wahgoosh, had not barked at any point, and so Anne had paid little attention.

During this time, Betty Gow got a call from her boyfriend, Henry "Red" Johnson, a Norwegian sailor who was currently working as a deckhand on a yacht. They were supposed to have gone out that evening, but had to cancel the date when Gow was called to Hopewell. Instead, Johnson told her, he was going to drive up to Hartford, Connecticut, to see his brother.

After sitting in the living room for a little while, Anne and Charles went upstairs to their bedroom, which was just above the living room at the rear of the house and connected to the nursery by a short hallway that led past their bathroom. Charles bathed, then dressed again and went downstairs to read in the library, which was next to the living room at the left back corner of the house and directly under Charlie's nursery. Meanwhile, Anne bathed and went to bed around 10 P.M.

At around the same time, Gow went back to the nursery to check on Charlie. She didn't want to disturb his sleeping so she only turned on the light in the bathroom. It was now cold enough outside that she closed the half-open window and plugged in an electric heater.

But as she approached the crib, she was alarmed that she couldn't hear the baby breathing. In the dim light, he didn't look to be in the crib, but she felt all over with her hands to make sure.

She went through the connecting door to the Lindberghs' bedroom and found Anne as she was coming out of the bathroom. "Do you have the baby, Mrs. Lindbergh?" Gow asked anxiously.

"No," Anne replied, confused. Perhaps Colonel Lindbergh had him, she suggested, then went into the nursery while Gow ran downstairs to the library.

"Colonel Lindbergh, have you got the baby?" Gow asked. Then, since Lindbergh was known as a notorious practical jokester, she added, "Please don't fool me."

Lindbergh expressed surprise that Charlie wouldn't be in his crib, getting up quickly to examine the nursery for himself. He strode into his and Anne's bedroom, went to the closet, grabbed his rifle, and loaded it. Then, with Anne, he went back to the nursery.

The crib was empty and the room was surprisingly cold. Lindbergh glanced over and realized the corner window—the one with the warped shutter—was unlatched and slightly open. On top of a radiator enclosure just under the window, Lindbergh noticed a small white envelope. He had the restraint and presence of mind not to touch it before authorities arrived.

"Anne," he said, "they have stolen our baby."

"MY SON HAS JUST BEEN KIDNAPPED"

At about 10:25 P.M., Olly Whateley called the Hopewell Sheriff's Office to report the crime. Lindbergh himself called his attorney and close friend, Henry Breckinridge, in New York City. Then he called the New Jersey State Police in Trenton, where he spoke to Lieutenant Daniel J. Dunn. "This is Charles Lindbergh," he said. "My son has just been kidnapped."

Dunn asked him when it had happened and for a description of the baby and what he was wearing. After hanging up, Dunn described the call to Detective Lewis J. Bornmann. They discussed the matter briefly and, to make sure it wasn't a prank, decided Dunn should call the Lindbergh house to confirm that the voice he had spoken to was, in fact, the colonel's. When Lindbergh answered the phone, Dunn reported that the police were on their way. Meanwhile, Lindbergh went outside, hunting for signs of the intruder, but found nothing.

The first officers on scene, local sheriff's deputies, arrived at 10:40. They looked inside the nursery and outside the corner window, where they noticed impressions in the ground. From there they followed a set of footprints seventy-five feet away from the house toward the southwest, where they found a wooden ladder, obviously homemade, lying on the ground. Light in weight, it was rather crudely constructed in two sections that folded together with the rungs seemingly inconveniently far apart, and the side rail of the upper section had split. About ten feet beyond, they discovered a third section of ladder, designed to fit on top of the other two. When fully unfolded and assembled, the ladder measured about twenty feet but could be collapsed down to six and a half feet.

At 10:46, a Teletype alarm was sent across the state instructing police to stop any car that might be carrying a child dressed in a sleeping suit. By 11:00, the statewide roadblock was in place, and the state police of Delaware, New Jersey, and Connecticut had also been notified.

The first state trooper to arrive at the house was Corporal Joseph A. Wolf from Lambertville, who reached the house at 10:55. A number of other officers and officials followed, including Colonel H. Norman Schwarzkopf, the thirty-seven-year-old chief of the New Jersey State Police, West Point graduate, and World War I army veteran (and father of the commanding general of the Desert Storm campaign against Iraq). He was accompanied by his second-in-command, Major Charles Schoeffel.

Betty Gow searched the house from cellar to attic on her own, opening every closet. Anne went back to her bedroom, opened a window, and leaned out. She heard what sounded like a cry, but Elsie Whateley assured her it was just a cat.

Corporal Wolf noted yellow clumps of mud or clay on a suitcase beneath the corner window of the nursery. He then went outside to investigate and saw footprints in the wet ground below the window. He didn't have a ruler or tape measure, so he compared the impressions to his own size-9 shoe and found the prints larger. No plaster casts were ever made.

By 11:15 other troopers had arrived. They reported seeing two sets of footprints, made by two different people, but later changed their story to say they had only seen one. This is somewhat ambiguous—only one of many ambiguous aspects of this highly troubling case. One explanation is that they concluded the smaller set of prints were actually Anne's. She said she had been outside the nursery earlier in the day and had thrown pebbles up to the window to try to attract the baby's attention. But as reported by Berg and others, beneath the window, near where the ladder had evidently stood, was a clear shoe print with a textile design, suggesting that socks or a bag of some sort had been worn over the shoe. Near the ladder impressions, officers found another potential piece of evidence: a nine-and-a-half-inch-long, wood-handled, three-quarter-inch carpenter's chisel manufactured by Buck Brothers Company.

The investigators wondered why the dog had not alerted the household to a potential intruder, but Lindbergh explained that Wahgoosh had been on the far side of the house, where he slept, and would not have heard anything that far away above the wind noise.

By this time, Lindbergh's lawyer, Henry Breckinridge, had arrived. He accompanied his friend and client and Schwarzkopf and other officers into the nursery. Corporal Frank A. Kelly from the Morristown Barracks, the crime scene technician, dusted for fingerprints. With the exception of one inconclusive smudge, no prints were discovered—not even those of Anne Lindbergh or Betty Gow—a fact that continues to confound and attract controversy to this day. Kelly took photographs and collected samples of the mud on the leather suitcase and the hardwood floor around the window.

Breckinridge called FBI director J. Edgar Hoover. They had met and become friends while Breckinridge served as assistant secretary of war during the Harding administration. Ironically, Hoover had been among the Lindberghs' distinguished houseguests at Hopewell, along with the likes of Amelia Earhart, Will Rogers, Wiley Post, and Albert Einstein. Hoover assured Breckinridge of full cooperation.

The ladder was brought inside before Kelly had a chance to photograph it in a preserved crime scene. He dusted for prints, but found none of any use. Soil on the rungs appeared to be of the same consistency as that found in the nursery. He also dusted the chisel, but found no prints there, either.

Kelly turned his attention to the white envelope in the nursery, carefully slitting it open with his penknife. He removed a single folded sheet of white paper. The note was written in blue ink in a shaky hand. He handed it over to Lindbergh:

> Dear Sir!
> Have 50.000 $ redy 25 000 $ in
> 20 $ bills 1.5000 $ in 10 $ bills and
> 10000 $ in 5 $ bills. After 2–4 days
> we will inform you were to deliver
> the Mony.
> We warn you for making
> anyding public or for notify the Police
> the child is in gut care.
> Indication for all letters are
> singnature
> and 3 holes.

This last statement referred to the bottom right-hand corner of the sheet. There were two interlocking blue-circle outlines, each a little more than an inch in diameter. The area where the two overlapped had been colored red, and three small holes had been punched into the design about an inch apart at the left, center and right. No prints were on the letter.

By the time it was light, scores of reporters had found their way to the estate, tramping over the property. Schwarzkopf had established a police command post in the three-car garage on the side of the house opposite the nursery, but he found it impossible to protect the area from contamination.

Stories began surfacing of strange people in the area. Olly Whateley said he had seen a man and a woman in a green automobile drive up to the estate to take photographs. He had sent them away, but later saw the woman behind a bush taking photos and focusing on the nursery window.

Two men in a blue-black sedan were reportedly asking around on Tuesday how to find the Lindbergh estate. The car was traced to a resident of Brooklyn, who said it had been stolen that day.

In Trenton, police were told that at midnight, railroad brakemen had seen two men and a woman with a child on the platform, waiting for the New York–bound train and appearing nervous and agitated. These people were never identified.

Schwarzkopf requested a list of everyone who had worked on the house, all to be checked out. He also asked for the names of all servants both in Hopewell and at Next Day Hill, to follow up the possibility of an inside job. No one could understand why the kidnapper or kidnappers had taken such risks rather than wait until everyone in the house would likely be asleep and the child's disappearance would go unnoticed longer. That, and the fact that the dog had not barked, helped focus the chief's attention on the domestic staff.

Yet at the same time, he had to acknowledge that the Lindbergh home was far from unknown outside the family. Its construction had been featured in magazines all over the country, with elaborate photos and floor plans. The house sat on one of the highest points in the state and would have been fairly visible, especially at night, to anyone secluded in the woods. And with only one road leading in and out, the family's movements were easily monitored. That the offender had brought a chisel with him suggested he didn't know the shutter could not be completely closed. Since the baby's blanket was still essentially in place in the crib, it appeared that he had been pulled out by the head and therefore possibly handled roughly. There were no odors of chloroform, but that did not rule out the use of some chemical or drug to quiet or neutralize the child.

TAKING CHARGE

Lindbergh had built his career and reputation on controlling himself and whatever situation in which he found himself. With the life of his son at stake, he was not about to give up control here. And with his fame and influence, he had the clout to exert control and take charge, even in the face of a police investigation. Schwarzkopf, who deeply admired the aviation hero, essentially had to work around him.

In consultation with Breckinridge, Lindbergh decided that the best chance of securing the return of the baby was to do what the kidnappers asked. But this was not an easy task. In the first few days after the abduction, thousands of pieces of mail were received at Hopewell. Three state police officers worked full-time sorting through it all looking for clues.

It's important to remember that during those Depression years, kidnapping had become a common criminal enterprise. There were even kidnapping syndicates in some of the major cities. Going back only two years—to 1930—four hundred abductions had been reported in Chicago alone. The day after Charlie Lindbergh disappeared, a boy in Niles, Ohio, was taken. That March, sixteen kidnappers were convicted and sent to prison. In fact, Anne's younger sister had come close to being abducted in 1929.

During the wait for further word from the kidnappers, several working theories were evolving. Lindbergh believed the offenders were professionals because of the absence of prints and the apparent knowledge of the house and the baby's room. He suspected a gang was involved and wanted to get in touch with the underworld to see if a deal could be worked out.

Because of the kidnappers' apparent familiarity with the house and the location of the nursery, the construction of the ladder, and the relatively modest ransom request, Norman Schwarzkopf believed the offenders were local and nonprofessional.

Lieutenant Arthur T. Keaton, Schwarzkopf's principal detective, wanted to pursue the possibility that the kidnapping had been an inside job, the work of domestic employees, since somehow the offenders knew that the family was not returning to the Morrow estate right after the weekend, as was their established custom, since the baby was ill. They had never before spent a Tuesday night in Hopewell.

Charles and Anne expressed total faith in the family servants from the very beginning and never wavered in that faith.

As with Lizzie Borden forty years earlier, Lindbergh raised some eyebrows by his seemingly overly stoic reaction to Charlie's abduction. He was so unemotional, it was said, that either (a) he did not really love his son in the normal, human way, or (b) he had to have had something to do with the crime. The rumors began to resurface about the little boy being somehow defective, either mentally or physically, and that the perfectionist colonel couldn't deal with this.

I bring this up here primarily to shoot it down. First of all, there was absolutely no remotely creditable evidence to suggest anything was abnormal about the child. But more to the point, I have seen enough parents in times of terrible grief to know that emotional reaction to such horror is very individual. Some people let the floodgates open up; others maintain a quiet and icy control. Most are somewhere in the middle. But no reaction is "right" or "wrong." Everyone who faces what must be the worst thing that can happen to a person copes as he or she must.

One time when I was on the television program *America's Most Wanted*, I was talking to host John Walsh about this subject as it related to a case they were currently featuring. Walsh, whose career as a pursuer of predators had its origins with the horrible murder of his young son Adam, put it succinctly: "Who are any of us to say how a person is supposed to react to something like this?"

In the case of Lizzie Borden, the detachment reflected the mind-set of a calculating murderess. In the case of Charles Lindbergh, it reflected the personality of a man who had regularly faced death and gotten through the experience by not going to pieces. So each reaction means something different. If surface behavior were that easy to interpret, it would take little or no training and anyone could be a profiler.

Anne did whatever she could to cope, relying heavily on the emotional support of her mother and confessing her fears to her own diary. Her father, Dwight, always a source of strength, had died in his sleep of a cerebral hemorrhage the previous October 31. Those around Anne worried that the stress and sleeplessness might threaten her pregnancy. In an attempt to do something constructive, on the morning after the abduction she wrote out the baby's diet and offered it to the press. The diet appeared the following day on the front page of virtually every newspaper in America. Anne and Charles also published a statement in those same newspapers expressing their desire to make personal contact with the kidnappers or to communicate with them through any intermediaries they might designate. They said they would keep all pledges of secrecy and were only interested in getting their child back; that they would "not try to injure in any way those connected with the return of the child."

New Jersey attorney general William A. Stevens issued his own statement, empathizing with the Lindberghs' anguish and desire to get their child back, but making it clear that the kidnappers were in no way being offered immunity.

On March 2, a postcard arrived that said, "Baby safe. Instructions later. Act accordingly." No red and blue circles were present, and the handwriting was different from that of the note found in the nursery, but police certainly took it seriously. However they were able to trace it to a mentally disturbed seventeen-year-old boy who wanted to see if it would get into the newspapers.

THE DEMANDS

On March 4, a second ransom communication arrived, scolding Lindbergh for involving the police, and upping the monetary demand to $70,000 because of the additional security and "administrative concerns" this imposed on the offenders. The same signature of interlocking circles appeared at the bottom of the note. It was handwritten in ink on both sides of the paper and had been mailed from Brooklyn, New York.

> Dear Sir. We have warned you note to make anyding public also notify the police now you have to take consequences—means we will holt the baby until everyding is quite. We can note make any appointments just now. We know very well what it means to us. It is rely necessary to make a world affair out of this, or to get your baby back as sun as possible to settle those affair in a quick way will be better for both seits. Don't by afraid about the baby two ladys keeping care of its day and night. She also will fed him according to the diet. Sintuere on all letters
>
> We are interested to send him back in gut health. And ransom was made aus for 50000 $ but now we have to take another person to it and probably have to keep the 25000 $ in 20$ bill 15000 $ in 10$ bills and 10000 in 5$ bills Don't mark any bills or take them from one serial normer. We will form you latter were to deliver the mony. But we will note do so until the Police is out of the cace and the pappers are qute. The kidnaping we prepared for years so we are preparet for everyding.

Thinking that this note might have been intercepted by the police, the offender sent another letter to Breckinridge's office to be delivered to Lindbergh.

Dear Sir: Dit you receive ouer letter from March 4.we sent the mail on one off the letter—near Boro Hall, Brooklyn. We know Police interfer with your privatmail. How can we come to any arrangements this way. in the future we will send ouer letters to Mr. Breckenbridge at 25 Broadway. We believe polise captured our letter and let note forwarded to you. We will note accept any go-between from your seid. We will arrangh theas later. There is no worry about the boy. He is very well and will be feed according to the diet. Best dank for information about it. We are interested to send your boy back in gut health.

It is necessary to make a world-affair out of it, or to get your boy back as soon as possible. Why did you ignore ouer letter which we left in the room the baby would be back long ago. You would not get any result from Polise becace our kidnaping was planet for a year allredy. But we were afraid the boy would not be strong enough.

Ouer ransom was made out for 50000 but now we have to put another to it as propperly have to hold the baby longer as we expected so it will be 70000$ 20000 in 50$ bills 25000 in 25$ bills 12000$ in 10$ bills and 10000 in 5$ bills. We warn you again not to mark any bills or take them from one ser.No. We will inform you latter how to deliver the mony but not before the polise is out of this cace and the pappers are quite.

Now, despite what I just said about not everyone being able to be a profiler, I think you'll agree that a couple of things come across loud and clear in these notes. The letter writer's first language is not English; he is not American-born, even American-born illiterate. Though many of the basic words are badly misspelled, he got a lot of the hard ones right, which suggests he was using a dictionary. Rather than an illiterate American, the communications suggest a Germanic language speaker, as evidenced by such spellings as *gut* for *good,* and phonetic spellings such as *ding* instead of *thing.*

So Lindbergh had to be wrong from the get-go—this was not the work of any organized crime organization in the United States. They wouldn't be so sloppy on communicating something so directly related to their business. It's just too "unprofessional." Also, they would have asked for far more money and would have made a direct threat if their demand was not met.

Could it be that more than one person was involved? Maybe, maybe not; we wouldn't know that from the letters. The notes certainly appeared to have been written by one person, and none of the myriad of handwriting experts eventually brought into the case disagreed with that presumption. However, kidnappers often communicate as "we" even if there is only one to project more strength and organization than they actually have, and this one was clearly doing that in claiming that the crime had been "planet for a year allredy."

Despite what appears obvious from this perspective, Lindbergh decided to deal with the criminal underworld. Al Capone, who had been the king of organized crime in Chicago until brought down on tax evasion charges, was at the moment residing in Cook County Jail in preparation for transfer to the federal penitentiary in Atlanta. Capone—who had ruthlessly stamped out his competition, such as Hymie Weiss, and then had seven men in a North Side garage massacred on St. Valentine's Day, 1929, while searching unsuccessfully for Weiss's successor, George "Bugs" Moran—expressed himself outraged and morally offended that such a crime had taken place and personally offered a $10,000 reward for information leading to the safe recovery of the child. He also told Hearst newspaper columnist Arthur Brisbane that he was pretty sure the mob had done it and he thought he could get the baby back—if he could be let out of jail long enough to accomplish the mission. Not surprisingly, the feds would have none of it.

But Lindbergh believed in the mob connection and announced that a pair of bootleggers, Salvatore Spitale and Irving Bitz, would be authorized by him to deal with the kidnappers. Their associate Morris Rosner took over as Lindbergh's "secretary" and on March 12 claimed that the baby was alive and negotiations were progressing well. He asked for $2,500 in personal expenses, which Lindbergh gave him. A little later, Spitale and Bitz unintentionally proved their underworld bona fides by getting arrested and charged with criminal conspiracy by federal Prohibition agents for a shipload of bootlegged booze that had come into a dock in Brooklyn. Their connection with Lindbergh, however, was enough to have the charges summarily dropped.

Meanwhile, perhaps the strangest and most enigmatic figure of all entered the case.

ENTER JAFSIE

John F. Condon, seventy-two years of age with a distinguished white mustache and always neatly turned out in a dark suit and vest, was a retired physical education teacher and principal in the Bronx, a place he considered the most beautiful in the world. Though he was almost universally referred to as "Doctor," we have found no specific reference to a Ph.D., and he was certainly not a medical doctor. Jim Fisher, an FBI special agent during my early years with the Bureau and now a professor and writer, describes Condon in his important book, *The Lindbergh Case,* as perceiving himself as a scholar-athlete. I would surmise from Condon's subsequent behavior with both the media and law enforcement authorities that he must have been the kind of teacher who liked to stand up in front of the class and hear himself talk. He would pontificate at the drop of a hat. He was also deeply patriotic in an ingenuous, almost mawkish way. He was appalled by this crime against America's greatest hero, thought it was a national disgrace, and wanted to do something to help. Just as likely, I think, he wanted to have some personal connection and self-importance in what was shaping up as the biggest story of the age.

After reading about the role these cheap thugs Spitale and Bitz were playing, Condon wrote a letter to the *Bronx Home News,* which appeared in the March 8 edition, offering his own services as intermediary with the kidnappers and pledging $1,000 of his own hard-earned savings to add to the ransom. I think this one fact says a lot about that sense of self-importance.

Since the paper was hardly known outside the Bronx, no one in the investigation gave Condon's offer much attention, if they knew of it at all. Certainly Lindbergh did not.

The day after his letter appeared in print, Condon was out of his house until around ten in the evening. When he returned home, the first thing he did, as was his habit, was to sort through the day's mail. One envelope was in a primitive handwriting. Inside was the following hand-written letter:

dear Sir: If you are willing to act as go-between in the Lindbergh case please follow strictly instruction. Handel incloced letter *personaly* to Mr. Lindbergh. It will explain everyding. don't tell anyone about it as soon we find out the press or Police is notifyd everyding are cancell and it will be a further delay. Affter you gett the mony from Mr. Lindbergh put these 3 words in the *New-York American*
MONY IS REDY
Affter notise we will give you further instruction. don't be affrait we are not out fore your 1000$ keep it. Only act stricly. Be at home every night between 6-12 by this time you will hear from us.

Inside the envelope was a smaller one bearing two lines in the same handwriting:

Dear Sir: Please handel incloced letter to Colonel Lindbergh. It is in Mr. Lindbergh interest not to notify the Police.

Despite the warning not to tell anyone, Condon didn't feel he could exactly keep quiet about so momentous a development. For one thing, he concluded, he would have to get this communication to his hero Colonel Lindbergh and he didn't have a car. He decided to confide in his friend Al Reich, who did.

Reich was a former prizefighter who now worked in real estate and was known to hang out at Max Rosenhain's restaurant at 188th Street and the Grand Concourse. Condon took a trolley, but when he got to the restaurant, Reich wasn't there. Not able to contain himself, Condon showed the letter to Rosenhain, who suggested he show it also to another friend of both men, Milton Gaglio, a clothing salesman who happened to be there at the time. Gaglio did have a car and agreed to drive Condon to Hopewell. The three discussed exactly how they should go about this, finally concluding that it would be best for Condon to call first and establish his credibility.

Condon got through but was handed off from voice to voice until he got to someone who said he took all of Colonel Lindbergh's calls. This was his personal secretary, Robert Thayer. Condon explained who he was, spewing out a long list of his academic credentials and teaching positions. At this point, accounts diverge. Thayer stated that he alone spoke with Condon. Condon, who was much given to pomposity and self-aggrandizement, claimed that he then spoke directly to Lindbergh. I tend to doubt this version, but in any event, Condon did read the letter, then was asked to open the accompanying envelope and read its contents aloud.

Dear Sir, Mr. Condon may act as go-between. You may give him the 70000 $. make one packet the size will bee about—

Condon explained that a drawing of a box indicated the size should be seven inches by six inches by fourteen inches, then continued reading:

we have notify your already in what kind of bills. We warn you not to set any trapp in any way. If you or someone els will notify the Police ther will be a further delay. Afffter we have the mony in hand we will tell you where to find your boy You may have a airplane redy it is about 150 mil awy. But befor telling you the adr. a delay of 8 houers will be between.

"Is that all?" the listener (whether Lindbergh or Thayer) asked.

Condon said it was, but then added the two interlocking circles at the bottom of the note. That got the listener's attention. It was agreed that Lindbergh should have the letter right away, so Condon, Rosenhain, and Gaglio set out for Hopewell shortly after midnight in Gaglio's car. They arrived around 2 A.M. and were met by Henry Breckinridge in the kitchen.

Condon was taken to an upstairs bedroom to meet with Lindbergh. As soon as he saw the handwriting, the misspellings, and the signature circles, Lindbergh knew the note was authentic. None of that had been made public. The sketch of the box was rendered in perspective and looked like something a carpenter might draw, which might also then tie in with the obviously homemade ladder.

Condon's account of that night is so flatulent it's almost stomach-turning. When he was introduced to Anne, he writes:

> . . . she stretched out her arms towards me instinctively in the age-old appeal of motherhood.
>
> "Will you help me get my baby back?"
>
> "I shall do everything in my power to bring him back to you."
>
> As I came closer to her I saw the gleam of tears in her soft dark eyes. I smiled at her, shook a thick reproving forefinger at her. With mock brusqueness I threatened Anne Lindbergh:
>
> "If one of those tears drops, I shall go off the case immediately."
>
> She brushed away the tears. When her hands left her face, she was smiling, sweetly, bravely.
>
> "You see, Doctor, I am not crying."
>
> "That is better," I said. "That is much, much better."

Not only is this reminiscence just plain icky, it also goes against the far deeper and genuinely sensitive portrait of Anne that comes across in her own writings. But it does give us an important insight into John Condon's personality and perspective.

Rosenhain and Gaglio drove back to the Bronx, but Lindbergh invited Condon to spend the night, an invitation Condon readily accepted. He went even further than that. Early in the morning, he strolled into the baby's nursery, looked around, then went into, as he called it, "the Lone Eaglet's crib" and removed the two safety pins that still fastened the baby's blanket to the mattress. At the toy chest he took out some carved wooden animals. He then asked Lindbergh if he could take the toys and safety pins with him so that if and when he did meet up with the kidnapper, he could identify the baby by his reaction to his animals and qualify the kidnapper by asking where he had seen them before. Lindbergh agreed, and after breakfast, he, Breckinridge, and Condon went upstairs and drafted a short note: "We hereby authorize Dr. John F. Condon to act as go-between for us." The note was dated March 10, 1932, and signed by both Charles and Anne.

The problem of the press came up again. Breckinridge was prepared to place the "Money is Ready" notice in the *New York American* according to the instructions in the note, but if Condon signed it, reporters would immediately know he was the intermediary and besiege him. That would be the end of the negotiations.

So Condon suggested using his initials—JFC—to come up with the name "Jafsie." The kidnappers would recognize it, but no one else would.

Before being driven home to the Bronx by Breckinridge, Condon spent more than an hour studying family photographs of Charlie so he'd recognize the child on sight. Breckinridge would spend evenings at Condon's home at 2974 Decatur Avenue until they heard from the kidnappers.

VIOLET

That same day, detectives from the Newark Police Department set about the routine interviewing of all twenty-nine domestic servants in Mrs. Morrow's employ at Next Day Hill. Betty Gow was an obvious potential suspect in Schwarzkopf's mind; she had both knowledge of the baby's whereabouts and direct access to him. She had also worked in Detroit, where a mobster called Scotty Gow operated, sometimes dabbling in kidnapping for profit. But no connection could be established between him and Betty, and all of her responses to investigators seemed genuine and appropriate.

The New Jersey State Police also had the Hartford, Connecticut, department pick up Gow's boyfriend Red Johnson for questioning. In addition to having knowledge of the child's whereabouts on March 1, he also drove a green Chrysler coupe, and one local resident had reported a green automobile in the vicinity of the Lindbergh house. Close to four hundred green cars had already been checked out, but when detectives examined Johnson's Chrysler, they found an empty milk bottle in the rumble seat. Johnson explained forthrightly that he drank a lot of milk and tossed the containers in the backseat while he was driving. Police held him for more than a week, but could never shake his story, and nothing in his background suggested he could be involved with the crime. Ultimately, the investigation of Johnson led nowhere, and two weeks after the kidnapping, Schwarzkopf made a public statement exonerating Johnson. Unfortunately for him, however, he turned out to be an illegal alien, and Schwarzkopf was ultimately able to dispense with him completely by turning him over to the immigration service.

As a group, the Morrow and Lindbergh servants were cooperative and matter-of-fact in their responses, with one surprise exception.

Violet Sharpe, twenty-eight years of age, was a maid who had left her rural village in Bradfield, England, in 1929 for Toronto, where she worked for nine months before moving to New York City to look for a better position. Shortly after registering with an employment agency, she was hired to work for the Morrows. Her sister Emily worked for Constance Chilton, who was the partner of Anne Lindbergh's sister Elizabeth in a private school. Photographs show Violet to be plain but pleasant-looking, slightly on the heavy side with short dark hair and large brown eyes. From all accounts, she was friendly, a good worker, and liked by everyone on the staff. She was thought to be romantically involved with Septimus Banks, the butler and head of the Next Day Hill household staff. Banks had previously served as butler to British aristocracy and to industrialist Andrew Carnegie. The other servants believed that someday Violet and Septimus would get married. The only thing that might stand in their way was the butler's alcoholism, a problem that had gotten him fired several times, but each time Mrs. Morrow had relented and welcomed him back. Violet got him to promise to stay off the bottle for a year.

On the day of the kidnapping, Violet had been the one who had received Anne's telephone call to Next Day Hill asking for Betty Gow. Before Betty left, she told Violet the baby was sick, so instead of the Lindberghs coming back here, she'd be going there.

When they spoke to Violet, the detectives were expecting another routine interview, but it didn't go exactly that way. She seemed nervous and agitated, and in accounting for her whereabouts on March 1, she told a convoluted story that didn't seem to go anywhere. At around 8 P.M., she had gotten a call from a man she'd met the previous Sunday while she was walking with her sister Emily in Englewood. A man drove by and waved; she assumed she knew him so she waved back. He stopped and offered them a ride home. She didn't know him, as it turned out, but he seemed friendly and said he would call her to take her out—this despite the fact that she had an understanding with Septimus Banks.

Violet and this man went out together with another couple on the evening of March 1. The four of them went to a movie. After the movie, he drove her back to Next Day Hill, walked her to the servants' entrance, and they said good-night. She agreed to see him again on March 6, but then broke the date.

So who was this man? What was his name? Violet didn't remember. What about the other couple? She couldn't recall their names, either.

What movie did they see? She didn't remember. Well, then, what was it about? Nothing came to her. What was the name of the theater? It was in Englewood, but she didn't know the name.

The detectives told her they knew this was trying and that she must be nervous. She snapped back that she wasn't nervous, but they had no business prying into her private life. They asked her to tell them *anything* else about her actions or whereabouts on the first of March, but she had nothing else to say.

While she was being interviewed, other officers went through Violet's room. While no clues or direct evidence of anything was found, a deposit book from a New York City bank indicated a balance of around $1,600. Considering that this was in the midst of the Depression, that Violet's salary was $100 a month, that she had been working for the Morrows less than two years, and that she was regularly sending money home to her family in England, this sum called attention to itself. As she had no room or board expenses, it was technically possible for her to have saved so much if she was extremely frugal. But together with the hostility and evasiveness of the interview, it made police look at her far more closely than they would have if she'd reacted to their inquiries as the other servants had.

"CEMETERY JOHN"

The ad signed "Jafsie" appeared in the *New York American* on March 11. That same afternoon, Mrs. Condon answered the telephone to a voice she later described as having a "thick, deep, guttural accent." The caller asked for her husband. She said he was at Fordham University, but would be back by 6 P.M. The caller said he would call again at 7:00 and suggested that Dr. Condon stay home and wait.

By the time the mysterious man called again, Condon and Breckinridge had both returned home.

"Did you gottit my letter with the singnature?" he asked. Condon immediately picked up on the Germanic verb form and the pronunciation of *signature* as it had been spelled in the letter.

"Where are you calling from?" Condon asked.

"Westchester," the man said, before asking Condon a few more qualifying questions. Condon distinctly heard him speaking to someone in
the background.

Then Condon heard a background voice saying, *"Statti citto!"* Condon
took that to be Italian, roughly for "Shut up!"

"You will hear from us," the caller promised, then hung up.

Colonel Schwarzkopf had wanted to set up a trace on Condon's telephone, but Lindbergh had overruled him. The fact that Lindbergh could
overrule the chief of the lead law enforcement agency on the case spoke
directly to the aviator's enormous and unique power. Lindbergh had
gotten where he was by exerting total control, both in his professional
and personal lives. He believed that the best chance of getting his son
back alive lay in "playing straight" with the kidnappers. And so the police
had no way of using this call to Condon to help locate the offenders.

Some of the people Lindbergh had chosen to work with, though,
were difficult to control. On March 12, Morris Rosner, Lindbergh's
newly appointed "personal secretary" and liaison to organized crime,
announced to the press that he knew that the baby was alive and well and
would soon be returned to his parents. That same day, New York City
police commissioner Edward Mulrooney announced that Rosner had
just been indicted for land fraud. He was later acquitted; some say it was
because of the Lindbergh connection.

On Saturday, March 12, Condon went to a cabinetmaker in the Bronx
to have a wooden box constructed to the kidnappers' specifications. He
had the design based on an old ballot box he had received years ago as a
gift so that it could easily be identified if it turned up in anyone's possession. He paid the cabinetmaker $3.

By 6:00 that evening, Condon was back at his house with his friend Al
Reich and Henry Breckinridge when the doorbell rang. This had to be the
communication they were waiting for. But it was just Milton Gaglio and
Max Rosenhain. Breckinridge was worried that their visit might have
scared off the kidnappers. Then around 8:30 the doorbell rang again. It
was a taxi driver named Joseph Perrone, who explained that he had been
given the envelope he was carrying by a man wearing a brown overcoat
and brown felt hat who had hailed him on Gun Hill Road and Knox Place
and asked him to deliver it to Dr. Condon. Upon further questioning
from Breckinridge and Gaglio, Perrone said that the man spoke with a
thick German accent and wrote down the license plate number of Perrone's cab before leaving.

Condon opened the envelope and they all read:

Mr. Condon
We trust you, but we will note come in your haus it is to danger.
even you can note know if Police or secret servise is watching you
> follow this instruction.

Take a car and drive to the last supway station from jerome Ave here. 100 feet from this last station on the left seide is a empty frankfurther stand with a big open Porch around, you will find a notise in senter of the porch underneath a stone.

> this notise will tell
>
> you were to find us.
>
> act accordingly.

After 3/4 of a houer be on the place. bring the mony with you.

The now familiar signature circles were at the bottom of the note.

The box wasn't ready and neither was the cash, but Condon felt it was important to follow the instructions to the letter. When he arrived at his destination, he would explain to whoever met him. Al Reich would drive him to the location in his Ford coupe.

At the closed hot dog stand Condon got out of the car. On the porch he found an envelope under a rock. He went back to the car and opened it.

> Cross the street and follow the fence from the cemetery direction to 233rd Street. I will meet you.

The cemetery in question was Woodlawn, a four-hundred-acre burial ground separated from Van Cortlandt Park by a wrought-iron fence. Condon waited at the front gate. Someone walked by and stared at Condon but kept on walking. Later, Reich stated he felt strongly that this individual was there as a lookout. Condon continued waiting about fifteen or twenty more minutes, until he saw someone inside the fence waving a white handkerchief at him. Condon looked closely; he was wearing a brown coat and fedora, just like the man Perrone had described. As he held the handkerchief in front of his face, he asked in a thick accent, "Did you gotted my note? Have you gotted the money with you?"

It was the same voice Condon had heard on the telephone.

"No," Condon responded. "I can't bring the money until I see the baby."

They heard footsteps. The shadowy man accused Condon of bringing in the police. Condon insisted he wouldn't do that. The man hoisted himself up on the cemetery gate and jumped over, landing near Condon. "It's too dangerous," he said, then took off north on Jerome Avenue. Condon noted that the footsteps they had heard belonged to a cemetery guard. After assuring the guard that everything was all right, Condon took off after the man, not an easy task for a seventy-two-year-old, even one who paid as much attention to his physical condition as Condon did.

He finally caught up with the man about a half mile later at the southern tip of the lake in Van Cortlandt Park, when he stopped running. "You should be ashamed of yourself," Condon chided him in his pompous professorial tone. "No one will hurt you."

"It was too much risk," the man countered, still doing his best to pull his hat down and his collar up to protect his identity. "It would mean thirty years."

The two men walked to a shack near the tennis courts. Condon pointed to the nearby bench. He estimated the man to be in his midthirties, about five nine, 160 pounds, with a small mouth, high cheekbones, and deep-set, almond-shaped eyes. No longer assertive, the man now seemed preoccupied. He said again that he could get thirty years if he was caught. "And I am only go-between. I might even burn."

"What was that you said about burning?" Condon asked.

"What if the baby is dead? Would I burn if the baby is dead?" It was unclear whether he meant burning in hell or the New Jersey electric chair. Either way, Condon was distressed by the reference.

No one had yet made any public reference to the possibility that the baby might already be dead, but though they hadn't addressed it with the Lindberghs, Schwarzkopf and his officers must have been considering it. Almost two weeks had gone by. Kidnapping is one of the riskiest major crimes, because it involves extended and ongoing dealing with the victims, who will almost always be in contact with the police. In the case of a well-publicized crime, everyone will be looking for the kidnapped child as well. It is therefore incumbent on the offender to get in and out of the crime as quickly as possible. The longer the ordeal drags on, the less chance he's kept the abductee alive.

Condon confronted the stranger, asking what he meant. He said there was no point in this negotiation if the baby was dead.

"The baby is not dead," the man insisted. "The baby is better than it was. We give more to him to eat than we heard in the paper from Mrs. Lindbergh. Tell her not to worry. Tell the colonel not to worry. The baby is all right."

Wanting to make certain the man with whom he was dealing was authentic, Condon asked several qualifying questions, then pulled out the safety pins he had taken from Charlie's crib. The man correctly identified them. "What is your name?" Condon demanded.

"John." Further questioning elicited that he was a Scandinavian sailor from Boston. The two men talked for more than an hour, during which time John said the baby was on a "boad" about six hours away by air and that he was being well cared for by two women. He said further that the kidnapping gang consisted of four men, the leader of whom he said was a high-level government employee, that neither Betty Gow nor Red Johnson were involved, and that the crime had been planned for a year, waiting until the baby was old enough that they could keep him alive away from home. He said that on Monday he would send proof that his gang was actually holding the baby.

What would it be? Condon wanted to know. The man replied he would send the baby's sleeping suit. When the cash was ready, Condon was to place an ad in the *Bronx Home News*. The man then rose, walked away, and disappeared into the darkness. It was about 10:45 P.M.

Condon found Reich and together they drove back to the house, where Breckinridge was waiting for a thorough debriefing. Condon said he was sure he could identify "Cemetery John" if he saw him again. Breckinridge called Lindbergh. Condon had not seen the communication referring to the crime having been planned for a year, so when he reported this detail, taken with everything else such as the accent and pronunciations, Breckinridge and Lindbergh felt confident that Cemetery John was actually part of the kidnapping rather than simply an opportunistic extortionist.

Condon and Breckinridge composed an ad for the *Bronx Home News:*

> Money is ready. No cops. No Secret Service. No press. I come alone, like last time. Jafsie.

On Sunday, March 13, police brought Dr. Erastus Mead Hudson, physician and independent fingerprint expert, to see if he could do any better than the police had done. After meticulously working the crime scene, he was able to lift thirteen prints from the baby's toys, which was important since Charlie, having been born at home rather than in a hospital, had never been fingerprinted. Hudson also found an astounding five hundred or so partial prints on the ladder. Most of them were unusable, but this demonstrated how many individuals had been handling this crucial piece of evidence in this most publicized of all cases.

The next day, Monday, Condon got a call from Cemetery John. "There has been a delay sending the sleeping suit," he reported. "It will come. You will have it soon." Then he hung up.

On Tuesday morning, March 15, a brown-paper-wrapped package turned up in Condon's mail. Condon recognized the printing of the address and immediately called Breckinridge at his office. In less than an hour, Breckinridge was at Condon's house, where the two men opened the parcel. It was a carefully folded gray wool, one-piece, size-2 Dr. Denton's sleeping suit with feet and appeared to be authentic. A one-page note was enclosed, with writing on both sides. On the front it said:

Dear Sir: Ouer man fail to collect the mony. There are no more confidential conference after we meeting from March 12. Those arrangemts to hazardous for us. We will note allow ouer man to confer in a way like befor. circumstances will note allow us to make transfare like you wish. It is impossibly for us. wy shuld we move the baby and face danger. to take another person to the place is entirely out of question. It seems you are afraid if we are the rigth party and if the boy is allright. Well you have ouer singnature. It is always the same as the first one specialy them 3 holes.

This note did, indeed, bear the now familiar signature. On the back was written:

Now we will send you the sleepingsuit from the baby besides it means 3 $ extra expenses because we have to pay another one. please tell Mrs. Lindbergh note to worry the baby is well. we only have to give him more food as the diet says.
    You are willing to pay the 70000 note 50000 $ without seeing the baby first or note. let us know about that in the New York-American. We can't do it other ways because we don't like to give up ouer safty plase or to move the baby. If you are willing to accept this deal put these in paper.
    I accept mony is redy
    ouer program is:
After 8 houers we have the mony received we will notify you where to find the baby. If there is any trapp, you will be
    responsible what
    will follows.

If there was any remaining doubt about the possibility of organized crime involvement—and there shouldn't have been, though several leads were still being followed up—this note should have squelched them. The idea of suddenly upping by $20,000 a ransom demand that had supposedly been planned for a year was ludicrous enough. But grousing that sending the sleeping suit as proof was costing them another $3 for a new one clearly demonstrated the level on which the offender or offenders were operating. By this time Condon had met with Cemetery John and heard his accent, which tied right in with the spellings and syntax of the written communications. In certain respects, at least one of the offenders had profiled himself.

At 1:30 the following morning, Lindbergh himself arrived at Condon's house. He had come in disguise to evade reporters. Lindbergh studied the suit for several minutes before proclaiming it authentic. Then he noted that it had been laundered since Charlie had worn it. He and Anne both felt the return of the suit was a good sign and didn't want the negotiations to drag on any longer than necessary. He also knew that Jafsie's identity would not stay secret for long. He instructed Breckinridge and Condon to do exactly what the kidnappers demanded. They ran the "Money is ready" notice, adding, "John, your package is delivered and is O.K. Direct me. Jafsie."

But nothing happened. Breckinridge placed another Jafsie ad. Condon received a reply on Monday, March 21. The letter was postmarked two days earlier from the Bronx. It again bore the interlocking circles.

Dear Sir: You and Mrs, Lindbergh know ouer Program. If you don't accept den we will wait until you agree with ouer deal. we know you have to come to us anyway But why should Mrs. and Mr. Lindbergh suffer longer as necessary we will note communicate with you or Mr. Lindbergh until you write so in the paper.

we will tell you again; this kidnapping cace whas prepared for a year already so the Police won't have any luck to find us or the child. You only puch everything farther out did you send that little package to
Mrs. Lindbergh? it contains
the sleepingsuit for the baby.
the baby is well.

The reverse side of the page bore a single line: "Mr. Lindbergh only wasting time with his search."

Breckinridge was troubled by the note. It suggested that John had not seen the previous ads they had run. Things could be falling apart. They ran another ad in the *Bronx Home News* on Tuesday, March 22. It acknowledged again receipt of the sleeping suit evidence but asserted the need to see the baby before the cash was handed over.

There were obvious reasons for this and not so obvious ones. In addition to the Jafsie angle, Lindbergh was pursuing several other avenues, hoping that one would lead to Charlie's return. There was the Rosner-Spitale-Bitz connection, which, despite all of Rosner's blustering, had turned up nothing. There was also an industrialist in Norfolk, Virginia, named John Hughes Curtis, head of a boatbuilding company. He had gone to his Episcopal minister, Harold Dobson-Peacock, with a story about repairing a boat for a rumrunner who said he had been asked by the kidnappers to have Curtis act as go-between. Dobson-Peacock had known the Morrows in Mexico City. Lindbergh didn't know what to make of Curtis's story, particularly after the Condon connection surfaced, but he was unwilling to completely dismiss it, either.

And then there was Gaston Bullock Means, a thirty-two-year-old investigator who had been both a veteran of the Bureau of Investigation, the FBI's predecessor agency, and the defendant in a murder trial. He was acquitted, but his reputation continued to be somewhat shady, and when J. Edgar Hoover took over in 1924, he immediately got rid of Means. Means then got involved in a series of hustles that did get him thrown into the federal pen in Atlanta. When the Lindbergh kidnapping broke, Means got in touch with one of his former clients, Evalyn Walsh McLean, the wealthy Washington socialite, current owner of the Hope Diamond, and estranged wife of the publisher of the *Washington Post.* Means said that the kidnappers had asked him to take part in the crime, but upstanding soul that he was, he'd refused. However, this put him in a unique position to negotiate with them. He'd met the head of the gang while in the Atlanta Penitentiary, and if Mrs. McLean would fork over $100,000, he was confident he could get the baby back safely. The heiress willingly put up the money, along with additional funds for Means's expenses.

In the end, neither the Means nor the Curtis gambit proved to be real, and both men ended up being tried for fraud, convicted, and sentenced to jail time. Curtis's sentence was suspended.

There was never any question in Charles Lindbergh's mind that he would pay the ransom. He sold much of his stock to raise the cash. The one agency he did call for help with the logistics was the Treasury Department, which put him in touch with the Internal Revenue Service's chief law enforcement officer, Elmer Irey. Irey had become something of a legend as the one who had developed the strategy to get Al Capone behind bars for income tax evasion. The Lone Eagle was still trying to play it completely straight with the kidnappers, but when Irey heard that Lindbergh intended to have the J. P. Morgan Company assemble seventy grand without even recording the serial numbers, he said he'd have nothing to do with the case unless it was handled in a more sensible way. Tracing ransom money can be one of the most effective ways of catching up with a kidnapper, and if Lindbergh was going to prevent this, Irey felt the investigation would be too hamstrung to be effective. Finally, Lindbergh agreed to do it Irey's way, after being convinced that this tactic could not endanger the baby. The kidnappers would have no way of knowing whether serial numbers had been recorded or not.

Not only did Irey get the serial numbers of the ransom cash recorded, he came up with a highly creative nuance. The Treasury Department was already planning for the United States to go off the gold standard, which would take place in about a year. As part of the transition, remaining gold coins and gold certificate paper currency would be called. The bills would be replaced by silver certificates, which would not carry the characteristic round yellow seal of the gold notes. Irey's idea was to stack the ransom bills with gold certificates, which would be easy to spot once the nation was off the gold standard. He had his agents arrange the money into two packages that corresponded in denomination to what the ransom note had demanded. The first package was $50,000, all but $14,000 in gold notes. The second, $20,000 package, consisted of four hundred $50 gold notes, which would be easy to spot when passed. All serial numbers were nonsequential.

What Lindbergh wouldn't go for, however, was to have the police anywhere near the money exchange or to have Condon tailed until he met up with Cemetery John or an associate. Lindbergh and Breckinridge were concerned John was getting spooked and then placed another Jafsie ad in the *Home News* edition of Sunday, March 27: "Money is ready. Furnish simple code for us to use in paper. Jafsie."

On Tuesday Condon found a response in his mailbox:

Dear Sir: It is note necessary to furnish any code. You and Mr. Lindbergh know ouer Program very well. We will keep th child in ouer same plase until we have the money in hand, but if the deal is note closed until the 8 of April we will ask for 30000 more. Also note 70000–100000.

How can Mr. Lindbergh follow so many false clues he knows we are the right party ouer singnature is still the same as in the ransom note. But if Mr. Lindbergh likes to fool around for another month, we can help it.

Once he has come to us anyway but if he keeps on waiting we will double ouer amount. There is absolutely no fear aboud the child is well.

Lindbergh and Breckinridge took from this letter that they were running out of time; the kidnapper was annoyed by what he had heard about John Curtis claiming to be in touch with the gang and fed up with what he perceived as the family's screwing around with him. I and my unit would have read it as increasing desperation on the offender's part that we could have exploited. Of course, the hands of everyone involved with the investigation were tied by Lindbergh's own management of the case, so it would have been difficult or impossible to get permission to set up a trap, something we've done in other kidnapping cases and could have done here, had we been around yet. Since then, of course, the FBI has been involved in countless kidnapping investigations, and one of things on which they pride themselves is virtually never losing the "package"—the ransom money.

Breckinridge placed a "Money is ready" ad in both the *Home News* and *New York Journal* editions of March 31. On April 1, Condon received the letter they'd been waiting for. Postmarked from Fordham Station, it instructed Lindbergh to have the money ready Saturday evening, to place an ad to that effect, and eight hours after the money had been received, the location of the child would be revealed. Condon lobbied for a "cash and carry" arrangement—the money for the child—but Lindbergh was unwilling to take the chance of upsetting John.

Lindbergh accompanied Breckinridge to Condon's house, where they turned over the ransom money to him to be placed in the specially constructed ballot box. They managed to get the first package in, but the additional $20,000 wouldn't fit, so Condon decided to carry it separately.

On the afternoon of Saturday, April 2—the day the latest Jafsie ad had run—Lindbergh and Breckinridge waited with Condon and Al Reich in Condon's living room for word from John. Knowing the situation would be dangerous, Lindbergh told Condon he would be perfectly understanding if the old professor wanted to back out from the actual money exchange. Condon assured him he had no intention of backing out now. Colonel Schwarzkopf had reluctantly given his word that law enforcement would stay away.

THE MONEY DROP

At about 7:45 in the evening, a taxi driver rang the doorbell and left an envelope on the front steps. With Lindbergh and Breckinridge looking over his shoulder, Condon tore it open.

Dear Sir: take a care and follow east tremont Ave to the east until you reach the number 325 east tremont ave.

It is a nursery.

Bergen

Greenauses florist

ther is a table standing outside right on the door, you find a letter undernead the table covert with a stone, read and follow instruction.

On the reverse side the offender warned:

don't speak to anyone on the way. If there is a ratio alarm for policecar, we warn you, we have the same equipment. have the money in one bundel.

we give you 3/4 houer to reach the place.

The plan was for Lindbergh to drive Condon to the meeting point and wait there for him. At the last minute, Reich suggested that Lindbergh take his Ford coupe. John had seen it and so he wouldn't think a new or unexpected element had been added to the equation.

The place they had been directed to was another cemetery, St. Raymond's. Tremont Avenue ran along its north side. The Bergen Greenhouses referred to in the note were near the intersection of Tremont and Whittemore Avenues. Near the door to Bergen's flower shop they saw the table. Lindbergh stopped the car in front. Condon got out and spotted the note held down by a rock. He brought it back to the car and together the two men read it.

Cross the street and walk to the next corner and follow whittemore Ave to the soud

take the money with you.   Come alone and walk

I will meet you

Lindbergh said he was coming, too, but Condon reminded him that the note said to come alone. Lindbergh reluctantly agreed, handing him the ballot box. Condon said he'd come back for it after he'd met with John.

Instead of walking south on Whittemore, which was a dark, poorly lit dirt road, Condon headed east on Tremont, where the light was better and he felt safer. But he couldn't see anyone, so he headed back to the car to report to Lindbergh. But before Lindbergh could answer, Condon heard a voice from the direction of the tombstones.

"Hey, Doctor!" It sounded like Cemetery John.

There is a minor discrepancy in the stories at this point, one of many. According to some accounts, Condon answered, "All right," then the man called out, "Hey, Doctor. Over here! Over here!" According to other accounts, Condon didn't respond until the man had called to him for the second time. This may be significant as to how much of the exchange Lindbergh himself heard, since he remained in the car, and years later he was called upon to identify the voice. Had he allowed police surveillance of the scene, it would not have been so great an issue.

Condon strode down Whittemore Avenue and into the cemetery, the direction from which the voice came. Inside, he saw a figure moving parallel to him through the gravestones. He began following the man down the hill and to an access road bounded by a five-foot-high cement wall. The man climbed over the wall, crossed the access road, scaled a low fence on the other side of the road, then crouched down below a hedge just to the left of where Condon was now standing.

The man called out to him. Condon boldly told him to stand up. He recognized the man as Cemetery John. He was wearing a black suit and the same felt fedora. "Did you gottit the money?" he asked.

"No," Condon replied. "It's up in the car."

"Who is up there?"

"Colonel Lindbergh."

"Is he armed?"

"No, he is not." This was a lie. Condon knew Lindbergh was carrying a revolver. He demanded the baby. John said he could not get the baby back for about eight hours after the money was received. The two men went back and forth over this for several minutes, with Condon ultimately demanding a receipt for the money and a note telling exactly where the baby was before he would go back to get the money. John said he didn't have those items with him. They both agreed to get what the other asked and return in a few minutes.

Then Condon had a stroke of inspiration, a way to do one more favor for the man he admired so much. These were hard times, he explained to John. Lindbergh was not nearly so rich as many believed. All he'd been able to raise was the original $50,000, not the additional $20,000. But if John would accept that amount, he'd go right to the car and get it.

John shrugged. "Well, all right. I suppose if we can't get seventy we'll take fifty."

It was 9:16. Condon went back to the car and reported to Lindbergh, who handed him the box and the other package from his pocket. Condon told him to put it away, that he'd talked him out of the other twenty.

When Condon and John met up again just before 9:30, John asked, "Have you gottit the money?"

"Yes," Condon answered. "Have you got the note?"

"Yes."

Condon handed over the box. John opened it and briefly examined the contents. He instructed Condon not to open the envelope he'd given him for six hours. They shook hands. Condon made another vain plea to be taken directly to the child.

John turned and disappeared back into the cemetery. Condon made his way back to the car, disappointed that he didn't have Charlie in his arms, but optimistic that he soon would and pleased that he'd saved Lindbergh twenty grand of his money.

In fact, this was much more a problem than a slick maneuver on Condon's part. The $20,000 package contained the $50 gold certificates—the easiest bills to spot and trace. Elmer Irey was crestfallen when he found out. Condon's initiative had removed four hundred potential "red flags" from the investigation.

Back at the car, Condon told Lindbergh of his agreement not to open the note for six hours. Surprisingly to him, the superstraight aviator said he would uphold the bargain. But on the way home, Condon asked Lindbergh to stop the car. He pointed out that only he had made the pledge, not Lindbergh, so he should feel no obligation to wait.

Lindbergh opened the envelope and read:

the boy is on Boad Nelly. it is a small Boad 28 feet long. two person are on the Boad. the are innosent. you will find the Boad between Horseneck Beach and Gay Head near Elizabeth Island.

Finally, they had something to go on.

THE SEARCH

Lindbergh knew the waters described in the note, where he might find the "boad" *Nelly*. The area was around Martha's Vineyard, where he and Anne had spent their honeymoon.

After stopping off at Condon's house to pick up Breckinridge and Reich and to send a coded message to the Hopewell house that the money had been delivered, they proceeded to the town house the Morrows owned on Seventy-second Street in Manhattan. There they were met by the IRS team, including Irey. They put together a sketch based on Condon's description of John.

Following his own instincts and taking matters once again into his own hands, Lindbergh took to the air, searching up and down the Massachusetts coast with navy planes and coast guard cutters to assist him. Meanwhile, the Treasury Department distributed a fifty-seven-page list of all the ransom bill serial numbers to every bank and financial institution in the country. And Condon led an FBI team back to St. Raymond's Cemetery, where they searched for evidence and took plaster casts of footprints where Condon said John had been standing.

After a full day of searching, no sign of the *Nelly* or any other suspicious boat had turned up, and Lindbergh returned to Hopewell exhausted and finally beginning to believe the kidnappers had double-crossed him. The next day, he and Breckinridge set out in Lindbergh's own Lockheed Vega, working down the coast as far as Virginia. But still nothing. At this point, more than a month after the abduction, Scott Berg reports, Anne finally seemed to lose hope.

Charles continued his search, but the press was catching up with the facts. On April 8, a bank teller tipped off journalists that the ransom money had been paid but the Lindberghs had not gotten their child back. The next day, Schwarzkopf confirmed the story. Then on Monday, April 11, the *New York Times* broke the news that Dr. John F. Condon was Jafsie. Reporters immediately beat a path to his doorstep. His effectiveness as an intermediary, if there was ever a possibility of further contact with Cemetery John, was gone.

But he became an instant celebrity, his every strut picked up by the media. He had to change to an unlisted phone number. When the press and total strangers didn't keep him busy, the police did, having him go over countless mug shots and view endless lineups. He was the only one who had seen the kidnapper face-to-face. Eventually he went on the vaudeville circuit and published a book entitled *Jafsie Tells All!*

On April 13, Harry Walsh, an inspector with the Jersey City Police Department on loan to the state police and a personal friend of Schwarzkopf's, went to interview Violet Sharpe at Next Day Hill. It was the first time police had questioned her since Newark police officers had conducted their routine questioning of all the servants on March 10. With full knowledge of her edginess and evasiveness during the previous interview, Walsh was careful to be cordial and nonthreatening. Still, Violet was no more relaxed or comfortable. This time she said she now remembered that she hadn't gone to the movies on March 1, which would account for why she couldn't remember the name of the film, who was in it, anything about the story or the theater where it was showing. In fact, she said, she and her date and the other couple had gone to a roadside restaurant called the Peanut Grill, about an hour's drive from Englewood. Since the last interview, she had recalled that her date's name was Ernie, because he had called the Morrow house. Ernie was in his midtwenties, tall and thin with light hair. There was passing conversation regarding the Lindbergh baby, but nothing more than pleasantries. That was still all the information she could provide.

Walsh wasn't any more satisfied with Violet Sharpe's responses than the Newark police had been. He discussed the matter with Captain John Lamb of the state police. Violet's story just didn't ring true. She was practically engaged to Septimus Banks, she was very proper and grateful for her job in the midst of this crippling depression, and yet she would risk scandalizing her employer by going to a roadside hangout and probable speakeasy with a guy whose last name she didn't even know? Then there was another troubling detail: on April 6, Violet's sister Emily had left the country for home without informing the police. She had applied for her return visa to England on March 1, the day of the kidnapping.

By this time Evalyn Walsh McLean had realized that Gaston Means was taking her for an expensive ride and turned the matter over to her attorney, who got in touch with J. Edgar Hoover. But one of the other dead-end hustles was still playing itself out. On Saturday, April 16, John Curtis proclaimed that the baby was safe. Lindbergh agreed to meet with him in Hopewell the following Monday, where he heard more details about a five-man Scandinavian gang—led by Cemetery John. A German nurse was also involved, and she had written all the ransom notes.

Curtis described how the gang had neutralized the baby with chloroform (though no telltale odor was detected in the nursery), then taken him down the steps and left by the front door because the ladder was too unstable. They had a floor plan of the house. They had told Curtis a key was still inside a door they had used, and when Lindbergh checked, the key was there. The baby had been taken directly to Cape May, New Jersey, and from there by boat to the area around Martha's Vineyard. Oh, and the gang wanted an additonal twenty-five large because another underworld organization was bidding for the child, too.

Though Schwarzkopf placed no faith in this tale, just enough fit in with other pieces of the puzzle that Charles and Anne regarded it seriously. Lindbergh made a trip to Cape May, and things went back and forth with Curtis for several weeks with no noticeable progress. By the second week in May, Lindbergh was going out with Curtis on Curtis's friend's boat, the *Cachalot,* from which they were supposed to establish contact with the gang in the waters off the New Jersey coast. For several days they stayed on the *Cachalot* because Curtis's intelligence had told him they needed to meet up with the gang on a fishing boat called the *Mary B. Moss.*

Lindbergh was still in Cape May the afternoon of May 12, when a forty-six-year-old truck driver named William Allen, heading in the direction of Hopewell with a load of timber, stopped on the Princeton–Hopewell Road about a half mile outside Mount Rose, to relieve himself. He walked about seventy feet from the roadside into the woods. There he saw what looked to be the skull of a child and one leg sticking out of the ground. He called his fellow driver, Orville Wilson, over to see. Then they went into town looking for a police officer. They found Patrolman Charles Williamson at the barbershop. He went back to the site with them, which was about four miles from the Lindbergh house, whose lights were clearly visible from the spot at night.

The baby's corpse lay in a shallow depression that appeared to have been made by someone's foot. The rain-saturated, blackened body was facedown, covered with leaves and insects. It was little more than a skeleton, the outline of a form in a dark, murky heap of rotting vegetation. The left leg was missing from the knee down, as were the left hand and right arm. Most of the organs and some of the lower part of the body were gone, scavenged by animals. The body had decomposed to such an extent that it wasn't possible at first to determine its sex. Poignantly, the eyes, nose, and cleft chin were Charlie's. While trying to reposition the head with a stick to remove some of the clothing, one of the investigators pierced the fragile skull.

Though the body was in terrible shape, the clothing was substantially intact. Two of the officers drove to the Lindbergh house, where Betty Gow described what Charlie had been wearing, then gave them samples of the cotton flannel and the spool of thread she'd used to make his undershirt that night.

Norman Schwarzkopf himself came to inspect the site. Not only did the flannel material and thread match up, the label on the T-shirt the baby was wearing was the same as the nine others in the package Anne had bought. Schwarzkopf then broke the news to Betty Gow, then to Elizabeth Morrow. Together they told Anne, Elizabeth saying simply to her daughter, "The baby is with Daddy." Anne then called her mother-in-law in Detroit.

The corpse was removed to the Swayze & Margerum Funeral Home at 415 Greenwood Avenue in Trenton. In addition to being a mortician, Walter Swayze served as the Mercer County coroner. Betty Gow went to officially identify the remains and did so from clothing, hair, facial features, teeth, and Charlie's characteristic overlapping toes.

A postmortem exam was conducted, officially by Dr. Charles H. Mitchell, but the actual dissection and physical examination was handled by Walter Swayze since Mitchell was elderly and had severe arthritis. That Swayze did the actual hands-on work of the autopsy was not revealed until 1977. The baby's pediatrician, Dr. Philip Van Ingen, was there to compare measurements from his own examination records. There was no evidence of strangulation or gunshot. The cause of death appeared to be a massive skull fracture as evidenced by a decomposing blood clot. It had occurred the night of the kidnapping, probably when the ladder had broken and a burlap bag, found along the road and containing blond hairs consistent with Charlie's, had been dropped. The extra weight of the baby could have caused the ladder failure, and he probably hit the concrete footer of the house in the fall.

The finding of Charlie's remains should have quieted once and for all the persistent and ugly rumor that Lindbergh himself had killed the child because of some defect. Of course, it did not. Some people, fueled by the least responsible members of the media, seem to revel in these ideas. But in my unit, we've seen over and over that the method of disposal of a child's body tells us a lot about the personality and motive of the murderer. It is a sad fact that parents do kill children, but as we will see in chapter 6, there are ways they do and ways they do not.

By the same token, there are ways they treat the body after death. Of course, in some instances, such as the Susan Smith case in South Carolina in which a desperate and distraught single mother got rid of her two young sons by plunging her automobile into a lake and letting them drown, there is no body disposal at all. But wherever we see postmortem handling of a child by a parent, we almost always see some attempt at careful or "protective" treatment. The body will be wrapped, buried with dignity or tenderness.

In the Lindbergh case, we have a body casually dumped by the side of the road when it is of no further use to the offender. A rudimentary attempt is made to bury it, but only to avoid detection. Nor is there a conscious attempt to degrade the body or symbolically pose it. This is the work of someone who just doesn't care about anything beyond himself.

One more small point: In case you think I'm giving away trade secrets here—letting parents know how they can murder their children and avoid suspicion by treating the body in a certain manner—let me assure you in the plainest terms that any individual who thinks he or she can outsmart the law that way will make so many behavioral errors, leave so many other inadvertent behavioral clues in the commission of the crime and its aftermath, it will be easier rather than more difficult for us to crack the case.

As soon as they learned of the discovery of the Lindbergh baby's body, state police officers drove to Cape May, where they found Charles on board the *Cachalot,* waiting for the next act of that drama. He rushed home to comfort his wife, saying that the examination showed Charlie hadn't suffered long, and that since he was dead from the beginning, nothing they had done, no decision they had made, would have changed the outcome. Charles went to Swayze's and identified the body for a second time. For him, the search was finally over.

THE POLICE TAKE CHARGE

Even in death, the media would not leave the Lindberghs alone. A photographer had snuck into the funeral home and taken photos of Charlie's remains. The photos were going on the street for $5 each. Fearing that a grave site would turn into a similar circus, Lindbergh had Charlie's remains cremated, then he took them up in his plane and scattered them among the clouds where he felt most comfortable and secure.

Now, his need for control of the case was over. The police could do whatever they needed so as to find the monster or monsters who had changed his and Anne's life so horribly and profoundly.

Anne and Charles moved back to Next Day Hill, abandoning the nearly completed Hopewell house forever. They never spent another night there. Their ultimate desire, once Anne gave birth, was to get as far away as they could—from the press, from the police, from the memories.

President Herbert Hoover announced that the federal law enforcement establishment would be thrown behind the case to aid Schwarzkopf's department, saying, "We will move heaven and earth to find out who is this criminal that had the audacity to commit a crime like this."

In spite of the effective involvement of the IRS and the Treasury Department, especially Elmer Irey, the president named FBI director J. Edgar Hoover to lead the federal investigative effort. As became his rather notorious custom over the decades of his reign, Hoover threw the other U.S. government agencies off the case. But that still left the various New Jersey and New York police departments, as well as district attorneys' offices. Altogether, plenty of people were working the case with plenty of opportunity for toes to get stepped on. The crime was now months old, the trails cold, and Schwarzkopf the target of widespread criticism that would never really go away.

To test the theory of how the baby was abducted and then killed, Schwarzkopf had a duplicate ladder constructed and, in Lindbergh's presence, reenacted the abduction himself at the scene. On his way back down the ladder, the 165-pound chief carried a sandbag weighing the same as the child. When he stepped down on the highest rung of the base section of the ladder, the side rail split, just where it had on the real ladder. When that happened, Schwarzkopf dropped the bag and it struck the cement windowsill of the library.

He also sent the written communications out to independent handwriting experts, most notably seventy-four-year-old Albert Sherman Osborn, considered by many at the time to be the dean of American forensic graphologists. As others had before him, Osborn concluded that one person had written all of the notes, and that certain misspellings, letter transpositions, and handwriting anomalies were consistent throughout. And he said that the writer was German. Even the convoluted sentences made syntactical sense when translated into German. Osborn composed a sample paragraph including many key words from the notes that investigators could get suspects to write without connecting it to the Lindbergh communications.

At the same time that Osborn and his associates were evaluating the notes, Schwarzkopf had pieces of the ladder analyzed by other experts. The critical man here was Arthur Koehler, a wood technologist with the Department of Agriculture's Forest Service Lab in Madison, Wisconsin. According to author and professor Jim Fisher, Koehler was able to identify at least four types of wood in the construction: North Carolina pine, ponderosa pine, western Douglas fir, and birch.

But despite the impressive work of the experts Schwarzkopf had arrayed, despite the NYPD's relentless trotting of John Condon from one police station, prison, or mug book to the next, despite the supposed connections of John Curtis, Gaston Means, and Morris Rosner to the kidnapper or kidnappers, all trace of Cemetery John had evaporated. All that was left of him was Condon's account of his meetings and a few words Lindbergh had heard more than a hundred feet away.

VIOLET REVISITED

On the investigative side, Inspector Harry Walsh believed the kidnapping must have been an inside job. Whoever took the child not only knew the precise location of the nursery, he also knew that the Lindberghs had not returned to Englewood after the weekend. The first piece of knowledge might be explained by publicity about the house, but the Lindberghs themselves didn't know they were staying on in Hopewell until essentially the last minute.

The most suspicious of those with established knowledge, Walsh felt, was Violet Sharpe, and Schwarzkopf was anxious to follow up with her. But on Monday, May 9, she had come down with acute tonsillitis and needed to be hospitalized. While she was in the hospital recovering from surgery, Charlie's remains were found. The day after Lindbergh identified his son and had the body cremated, Violet checked herself out of the hospital against doctor's advice. Schwarzkopf waited a week, then sent the state police surgeon, Dr. Leo Haggerty, to Next Day Hill to examine her and determine if she was up to renewed questioning. Haggerty and a local physician, Dr. Harry D. Williams, found her still weak and advised against proceeding. Nonetheless, Walsh came to interview her on the evening of Monday, May 23. He was accompanied by Schwarzkopf and Lieutenant Arthur Keaton. Lindbergh was there, too.

With her employer present, Sharpe was more docile and cooperative than she had been in previous encounters with the police, but her story was still full of holes and contradictions. For example, she couldn't explain why she had first mentioned a movie and then changed her story to a restaurant. She couldn't even explain why she'd agreed to go out with Ernie since she never went out with people she hardly knew. And it now came out that her mysterious date Ernie had called about an hour and a half *after* Violet learned that Betty Gow was going to Hopewell instead of Charlie and his parents returning to Next Day Hill.

Walsh returned for another round with Sharpe on Thursday, June 9. He had a theory that a cheap crook and former taxi company operator named Ernest Brinkert from White Plains, New York, may have been the Ernie whose last name she couldn't recall. When they'd searched her room back in March, they'd found six of Brinkert's business cards. Violet looked even weaker and more sickly than when she'd gotten out of the hospital.

Walsh showed her a mug shot of Brinkert and asked if he had been her date on March 1.

"That's the man," she confirmed.

Then how come she didn't know his last name since she'd had his cards in her room? She knew nothing about the cards.

She was growing hysterical. A doctor was called in. Walsh agreed to suspend the interview, but said he wanted to resume the following day at his office. Laura Hughes, Mrs. Morrow's secretary, was present to record the interview. When Violet left the room, she flashed Hughes what has

157

been described as a sly smile, then gave her a wink. Walsh and the doctor were unaware of this.

That night, Sharpe again became hysterical, this time in the presence of Betty Gow and other servants, swearing the police would not take her away and that she would answer no more questions. The next morning, Walsh phoned the estate to let Violet know a state police car would be by to bring her in for another interview.

Before the car arrived, Violet Sharpe was dead. She had mixed cyanide chloride, a powdered silver polish, with water, drunk it, come downstairs, and collapsed in the pantry.

Later than night, Ernest Brinkert surfaced, getting in touch with the White Plains police. He told them he didn't know Violet Sharpe, had nothing to do with the Lindberghs or the kidnapping, and had no idea why his name had been connected with the case in any way or how his cards had ended up in Sharpe's room. On the night of March 1, he was visiting a friend in Bridgeport, Connecticut. Dr. Condon was brought in to see if Brinkert could be Cemetery John, and as soon as he saw him, Condon said he was not.

The New York police handed him over to New Jersey, where the questioning continued, and he gave handwriting samples according to Osborn's sample paragraph. Brinkert's wife could also alibi him for the night in question.

Then on Saturday, June 11, a twenty-three-year-old bus driver named Ernest Miller told detectives of the Closter, New Jersey, police department that *he* was the Ernie who was out with Violet Sharpe on March 1. The police were left scratching their heads. He named the other couple, and his story matched up with the revised one Violet had given.

But why didn't Violet identify him? Miller had no idea. He'd certainly given her his name. And why did she identify the photo of Ernest Brinkert, who looked nothing like Miller? Again, Miller was in the dark. Police rounded up the other couple. Their stories squared with Miller's. Now there were more questions and fewer answers.

Since Violet Sharpe's suicide, Lindbergh case scholars and aficionados have wrangled over what significance, if any, it had beyond her personal tragedy. Some have accused Schwarzkopf and Walsh of harassing her to death. Violet's sister Emily essentially said as much after Scotland Yard investigated and cleared her back in England. Others have suggested Violet was afraid the police interest in her and her small improprieties might have lost Septimus Banks's affection and caused Elizabeth Morrow to sack her and leave her jobless. It was suggested that she had been married years ago in England and the close police scrutiny would reveal this "scandal." But further investigation proved this claim to be without foundation.

To me, Sharpe's suicide calls to mind the case of Leonard Lake, thirty-eight years of age, who was picked up by South San Francisco police in June of 1985 for stealing a $75 vise from a lumberyard. Police found the vise and a silencer-equipped .22-caliber pistol in his trunk, took him to the station house, and booked him on theft and weapons charges. He was carrying a driver's license that identified him as Robin Stapley, but the photograph looked nothing like him. After a couple of hours in the station, he asked for a drink of water, and before the cops knew what was happening, he'd swallowed a cyanide capsule from a secret compartment in his belt buckle. He went comatose and died after several days on life support.

When we in the behavioral business see something like this, it raises some instant questions. Why does a guy up for petty and routine charges take his life so dramatically? Well, it turned out these insignificant details had nothing to do with it. Leonard Lake was a rapist-torturer-murderer of young women who, with his younger partner, Charles Ng, had captured multiple victims and videotaped their hideous activities in what amounted to snuff films. They would replay these tapes over and over to get off. When Lake was picked up on unrelated charges, he figured his real crimes would soon come out and the game would be up.

I'm not suggesting that Violet Sharpe took the Lindbergh baby—Miller and his companions could pretty well alibi her—or even that she was part of the kidnapping ring. But her suicide for the stated reasons of being overwrought by the questioning and the general trauma of the events rings false to me.

It may be a cliché to say that when those of us in law enforcement hear incomplete, evasive, and hostile responses in a routine interview, we tend to get suspicious, but it's true and true for good reason. During the initial interviews of the Morrow servants, Sharpe had to know how serious the police were on such a high-profile case, so it defies all logic that she would have been so cavalier in her answers simply because she felt annoyed and put out. If she were so concerned about her reputation with Mrs. Morrow as some have said, she would have gone out of her way to be cooperative if she had nothing to hide. And you don't suddenly up and kill yourself in so agonizing a manner simply because you've had enough of perceived police harassment. As with Leonard Lake, something else has to be going on behind the scenes.

Among the documents and pieces of evidence Mark Olshaker and I examined at the voluminous Lindbergh case archives at New Jersey State Police headquarters in Trenton was Violet Sharpe's small red diary.

In it we found poems, commentaries, and various brief accounts of her life. What struck us particularly was her ongoing sense that there was more to life than being a servant, that even though that's what the outside world saw her to be, inside she strove for a higher, grander, more poetic existence. Someday, she would be able to break out of her circumscribed world into the life she dreamed of.

Do I think she saw the ticket into this finer world as participation in a hideous crime? No. Was she part of this yearlong planning to which the notes and Cemetery John referred? No, again. Nothing in her background or makeup suggests that she ever considered illegal activity for solving problems or achieving what she desired.

But Violet Sharpe's personality suggests a young woman desperate to improve herself and be liked and appreciated by others, and I think it possible, even likely, that somewhere along the line, culminating on March 1, 1932, she had been giving information about the Lindbergh family's activities, their comings and goings, to one or more other persons. This may have been completely innocent on her part. But when she learned that the baby had been taken, I believe she must have started completing the picture in her mind and realized her unwitting complicity in the act. Now maybe the offender didn't actually obtain his information from Sharpe; maybe it came from someone or someplace else. But for Violet to have behaved as she did with the authorities—despite Lindbergh's consistent stated belief in her and her fellow servants' complete innocence—she had to have been worried that she had inadvertently betrayed her employer and enhanced the offenders' ability to pull off the crime. Was she the "missing link"?

An FBI file we found in the police archives states:

> Under direct questioning she indicated that she had never had a boy friend prior to this date with Ernie, however, when asked directly if she had not been friendly with a newspaper reporter or photographer by the name of McKelvie employed by the Daily News, New York City, she admitted that she had been out several times with McKelvie. (According to Inspector Walsh, McKelvie had made the statement that Violet Sharpe furnished him the first information from the Morrow home as to the sex of the Lindbergh baby when all newspapers were clamoring for this information, and that this tip from Violet enabled McKelvie to score a beat in that he furnished the desired information to his paper five hours before any of the other newspapers. . . .)
>
> Violet Sharpe would not answer questions as to whether she had furnished McKelvie the above information.

We do see here that though it may have been innocent, Violet was willing to talk to outsiders about what happened within the household and the family.

With Violet's suicide and Emily Sharpe's clearance by Scotland Yard, this aspect of the case quickly dropped below the horizon. But I don't believe we can dismiss Violet that easily or what I suspect was her link in the chain of intelligence information that made the kidnapping possible. This is something that should be kept in mind as we examine the subsequent occurrences in the case.

THE TRAIL GOES COLD

With Violet Sharpe dead, the other names floating around all cleared, and no trace of Cemetery John, the kidnapper's trail was growing cold.

As some consolation, on June 22 Congress passed what became known as the Lindbergh Law, the most famous provision of which was that after one week from the abduction, if the case had not yet been solved, the kidnapper was presumed to have crossed state lines and the FBI could then be given primary jurisdiction. The law is still in effect, and in later years the presumption period was considerably shortened. The law also called for a federal maximum penalty of life imprisonment.

On Tuesday, August 16, Anne gave birth to another baby boy, this time in her mother's apartment at 4 East Sixty-sixth Street in Manhattan. She and Charles named him Jon, and Charles once again appealed to the press to leave him and his family alone. Once again the request went unheeded.

A few of the bills from the ransom money had begun turning up in and around New York City, but by the time anyone at a bank noted the serial number, there was no way to track who had passed the bill. Did this mean Cemetery John and his cohorts, if any, were still in the area? Or were these bills showing up as the result of secondary or tertiary passing, with the original holders long since out of the picture? Detective James Finn maintained a pin map with each location where a bill turned up.

That fall, a New York psychiatrist named Dudley D. Schoenfeld got in touch with the NYPD, who in turn contacted New Jersey State Police, about having him study the notes. Schwarzkopf didn't have much to go on, so he took a shot on Schoenfeld.

According to Jim Fisher in *The Lindbergh Case,* Schoenfeld believed "the kidnapper had a mental disease called dementia paralytica (today considered a form of schizophrenia). Although the kidnapper felt omnipotent or all-powerful, he was, in reality, a powerless man who occupied a low station in life. Angered and frustrated by his status, he blamed others for his inadequacies, laboring under the illusion that certain forces in society were preventing him from realizing his grandiose goals in life.

"Colonel Lindbergh was everything this man wasn't and wanted to be—powerful, wealthy and universally revered. The kidnapper saw him as a rival, someone to defeat, outsmart and humiliate. This was the unconscious motive for the crime. Schoenfeld said that such a man would work alone and take great personal risks."

Fisher goes on to say, "Schoenfeld concluded that the kidnapper was a forty-year-old German who had served time in prison. He had homosexual tendencies, was mechanically inclined, secretive, and not prone to confess. The psychiatrist speculated that the kidnapper was physically similar to Lindbergh, and if married, would be tyrannical. He would have female friends but his life would revolve around men. Because he was secretive, cautious and untrusting, the kidnapper would be very difficult to catch."

It is certainly common for violent offenders, particularly sexual predators, to feel a strong conflict between inadequacy and powerlessness, and omnipotence and entitlement. Such a person would be jealous of someone like Lindbergh who really was a success and seemed to have everything he wanted. Such a person might want to bring a world hero down to normal size by making him suffer the most basic of griefs. The German nationality isn't much of a stretch.

If you accept that the man worked alone—and I'm not saying I do—then some of the other traits have to follow from that. He had to be secretive and control-oriented for no one else to know about the crime. He had to be mechanically inclined, because if he worked alone, then he had to have built the ladder. Perpetrators of major crimes don't suddenly blossom from nowhere, fully skilled in their craft, so it is likely he would have done some time in prison. Snatching the baby right out of his crib with one parent in the next room and the other one a floor below is an extremely daring, high-risk crime, so of course he would be someone who took great personal risks. And no one who pulls off a notorious crime that has the FBI and half the law enforcement establishment in three states looking for him is going to be prone to confess. Still, this was a good example of early profiling, and Schoenfeld earned himself a respected place in the history and development of the discipline.

In August of 1934, Condon did think he spotted Cemetery John. While on a bus in the Bronx, he thought he saw John dressed in workman's clothes, walking along the road. In true Condon fashion, he shouted to the driver, "I am Jafsie! Stop the bus!" But by the time Condon began his pursuit, the man had vanished.

DECONSTRUCTING THE LADDER

By early 1933, Arthur Koehler had given each component of the ladder an individual designation. He numbered the rungs one through eleven and the six side rails of the three-section ladder twelve through seventeen, starting with the lowest section. The key piece of the puzzle was rail sixteen, the left-side support of the top section. It piqued Koehler's interest because it alone had four extra square-nail holes, indicating to him that it had previously been used for something else. In other words, as the builder got to the final section, he likely ran out of lumber and had to cannibalize a piece from something else.

Koehler further determined that eight of the rungs made of ponderosa pine had been cut from a single board and planed by a defective tool that left characteristic marks on the wood. Of the five side rails made of southern pine, the planing marks were so distinctive that he believed they might be used to isolate and identify a single mill. Altogether, he sent inquiries to more than fifteen hundred mills along the Atlantic seaboard, giving the specs of the kind of lumber plane he was looking for, how fast it would feed boards through, and how many cutting blades it would employ.

Though laborious investigation, Koehler finally traced characteristic boards from a mill in McCormick, South Carolina, to the Halligan and McClelland Company in New York, and from there to the National Lumber and Millwork Company on White Plains Avenue in the Bronx. There, on November 19, 1933, in one of the storage bins, Koehler found what he considered the perfect match. He was convinced that side rails twelve through fifteen had been dressed by the same cutting machine.

But the lumberyard said they would have no records for anyone who paid cash for their wood and took it with them, so Koehler's brilliant deduction was only a partial victory. Handwriting samples were taken from all of National's employees, but nothing of promise turned up.

THE MONEY TRAIL

On April 5, 1933, the new president, Franklin D. Roosevelt, announced that the United States would be going off the gold standard and, to prevent hoarding of gold, directed that all gold coins and gold certificates over $100 in total value had to be turned in for equivalent value of new currency by May 1. As a side benefit, investigators hoped that when the gold notes started flooding in, bank personnel would be more mindful of ransom-money serial numbers as listed in the fifty-seven-page document they'd distributed shortly after the payoff to Cemetery John.

In fact, on May 1, a packet of $2,980 in gold notes was given in for exchange to the Federal Reserve Bank in New York City. Each one was a ransom bill. The deposit slip accompanying the bills was made out by a J. J. Faulkner of 537 West 149th Street. It turned out to be a fake. To this day, this was the last anyone ever heard of J. J. Faulkner, and the trail of this money was as cold as every other lead to Cemetery John or other kidnappers.

A few individual notes were continuing to turn up, most of them characteristically folded into eight sections. Recollections of clerks and tellers who encountered these notes were sketchy, but generally centered around a white male of medium height with blue eyes, high cheekbones, and a pointed chin. No surprise, the man spoke with a foreign accent and tended to be seen with a soft felt hat pulled down over his forehead. Though vague, the descriptions fit in with Condon's description of Cemetery John and cabdriver Joseph Perrone's of the man who had him deliver an envelope to Condon.

By the time Arthur Koehler had located the National Lumber and Millwork Company, a pattern had emerged to the passing of the smaller bills—fives and tens—from the ransom money. They were turning up around Lexington and Third Avenues in upper Manhattan and the German areas of Yorkville. And shortly after Koehler completed that phase of his work, Cecile Barr, a cashier at Loew's Sheridan movie theater in Greenwich Village, took in a $5 gold note, creased into eight sections, that caught her attention. It turned out to be Lindbergh ransom money, and the description she gave matched the previous ones, down to the suit and dark felt hat. But that was it. The crime of the century remained unsolved.

By January of 1934, the ransom money was turning up at a higher rate—about $40 a week, all in tens. The kidnapper must have used up all the fives, so he would soon be getting to the twenties. But by the summer, the trail of bills had dried up again. It might have been connected to another round of newspaper stories on the ransom, this time related to a standing $5 reward from NYPD every time someone turned in a ransom bill. According to Schoenfeld's profile, the kidnapper would be cautious.

Then in September, some tens started turning up again, then a twenty in the Fordham Road area of the Bronx. More tens and twenties surfaced, again in upper Manhattan, Yorkville, and the Bronx.

FINALLY, A SUSPECT

The break occurred on September 18, 1934. The head teller of the Corn Exchange Bank in the Bronx was sorting bills and came across two $10 gold certificates. Both were listed as ransom bills. One of the bills had "4U-13-14 N.Y." penciled at the edge. It looked like a license plate number, and police had asked service station attendants and anyone associated with automobiles to record license numbers of cars whose drivers paid with gold notes. Three gas stations near the Corn Exchange cleared receipts through the bank. One of these was the Warren-Quinlan Service Station at 127th Street and Lexington Avenue in Manhattan. When Detective James Finn came over to interview them, both the manager, Walter Lyle, and his assistant, John Lyons, recalled taking in the cash. It had come from a white male of average height, speaking with a German accent and driving a blue 1930 Dodge sedan. He had bought 98¢ worth of gas (remember, this was at 1934 prices!) and paid with the $10 bill, which he took from a white envelope in his pocket.

Lyle looked hard at the note. "What's wrong?" the man asked. "That's good money." The manager commented that one didn't see many of these around anymore and the man agreed. "I have only about one hundred left," he said.

Lyle's main concern at this point was that the bill was counterfeit, so he took down the license number and wrote it on the bill before putting it in his cash drawer.

From the New York Bureau of Motor Vehicles, Finn found out that the license number was assigned to a blue 1930 Dodge sedan that was registered to a thirty-five-year-old, German-born carpenter named Richard Hauptmann who lived at 1279 East 222nd Street, at the intersection with Needham Avenue, in the Williamsbridge section of the Bronx. This was close to Woodlawn Cemetery, ten blocks from National Lumber and Millwork, four miles from St. Raymond's Cemetery, and about ten miles from the Warren-Quinlan Service Station.

Instantly, all the mental lightbulbs started popping in the minds of Finn and his fellow detectives. They immediately put the two-story house where Hauptmann and his wife rented a five-room flat on the second floor under surveillance. A little before 9:00 in the morning on Wednesday, September 19, Hauptmann came out, walked back to the detached, ramshackle single-car garage, unlocked a padlock, and went inside. Hauptmann had built the garage for his landlord in exchange for its exclusive use while he lived there. A few moments later his car emerged onto Needham Avenue. Hauptmann, of medium height, was a reasonable fit for the physical descriptions.

Had I been around and working the case in 1934, I would have been equally thrilled with Hauptmann as a suspect, even knowing little else about him. With the exception of the crime scene site itself, over which the offender had no control, every other venue associated with the case—the original meeting site, the money-exchange site, the lumber supply, the bill-passing locations, even John Condon's house—were all within what we would characterize as Richard Hauptmann's comfort zone, based on where he lived. If he was the kidnapper, if he was Cemetery John, he could reasonably be expected to have all of these events take place exactly where they did. Add to that the guy was German, fit the description, and was a carpenter, and you've got one of the greatest initial suspects in history!

Within a few minutes the detectives had arrested Hauptmann, got him out of his car, frisked and handcuffed him. They looked in his wallet. Among the bills was a $20 gold note, folded into eight sections. He said he had several hundred more at home, which he was holding as a hedge against inflation. In Germany after the World War, inflation had run rampant.

They got some basic information from him. Hauptmann's first name was Bruno, though everyone in America, including his wife, knew him by his middle name, Richard. During the World War, he had served twenty months with the 103rd Infantry, drafted into the German army when he was only fourteen. The war had taken the lives of two of his older brothers. He had come to America initially as a twenty-three-year-old stowaway on the German liner *Hanover.* He was discovered when the ship docked in America, and he was sent back to Germany. A month later, he snuck aboard the same ship but was discovered before it pulled out to sea. He escaped arrest by diving overboard. Two months after that he stowed away on the S.S. *George Washington,* and this time he made it. Hauptmann was nothing if not determined. He got a job as a dishwasher, worked his way up to mechanic, and finally to carpenter. On October 10, 1925, he married a waitress named Anna Schoeffler. Eight years later she gave birth to a son, Manfred, nicknamed Bubi. Anna Hauptmann had worked at a bakery and restaurant on Dyre Avenue, but had left the job in December of 1932 to take care of Bubi and the house full-time.

When police searched Hauptmann's apartment, much to Anna's shock when she returned home, they were surprised by how nice and expensive-looking his furniture was. Most impressive was a late-model floor radio that cost about $300, quite a sum in those days, particularly during the Depression. Anna had no idea why so many police officers and detectives were swarming through her place, and they didn't offer her an explanation. When she got to the master bedroom, she found her husband near the bed, handcuffed to a police officer. In German, Hauptmann told his wife they were here because of a gambling problem he'd had the other night.

The detectives asked him where he had hidden the ransom money from the Lindbergh case. He insisted he knew nothing about it. Pointing out the window to the garage, FBI special agent Thomas H. Sisk asked him if that was where he kept the money. Hauptmann replied that he had no money other than whatever was in his apartment. When asked if he had a police record in Germany, he said he did not.

Police seized seventeen notebooks that they intended to use as exemplars of his writing. In one, they found a sketch of a ladder detail similar to the kidnap ladder.

Bruno Richard Hauptmann was taken to the NYPD Second Precinct Station in lower Manhattan. He was printed and a crime scene team scoured his car for blood and hair and fibers. Nothing turned up, and his prints matched none on the ladder. In addition to the notebooks, police also made Hauptmann produce seemingly endless handwriting samples. Many of those displayed similar handwriting to the ransom notes.

During this initial incarceration, police roughed him up, slapped him around, and deprived him of food and sleep for many hours. That this was fairly common practice in those days makes it no less deplorable and a blatant abuse of the prisoner's rights.

During the long hours of interrogation, detectives got more personal details of Hauptmann's life. He had worked as a carpenter at the decent wage of a dollar an hour until April or May of 1932, at which time he'd given up most of his jobs to devote himself to the stock market, in which he said he'd begun successfully investing the previous year. Keep in mind that this was the depth of the Great Depression and Hauptmann was a poorly educated immigrant. At the time of the Lindbergh baby kidnapping, Hauptmann said he was doing carpentry for the Majestic Apartments in Manhattan. He also acknowledged that he had, in the past, purchased lumber from National Lumber and Millwork. He admitted to having saved $300 in gold certificates and had no explanation as to how he could have come in possession of Lindbergh ransom currency.

Police got Hauptmann into a rather perfunctory lineup. All the other men were tall, strong-looking police officers. Joseph Perrone, the cabdriver, identified Hauptmann. John Condon, much to the annoyance of the police, said he could—or would—not at this time. They felt he was playing some more of his games.

On Thursday, September 20, while Hauptmann was still being interrogated, police went through the garage behind his house. Prying off a board that had been nailed between two joists, a detective uncovered a shelf of a hundred neatly wrapped $10 gold notes. Another package contained eighty-three more. A second detective found a hidden one-gallon shellac can containing twelve more packages of gold notes in tens and twenties. Altogether, police discovered $11,930 in the garage, all of it Lindbergh ransom money. This certainly explained why Hauptmann kept the garage locked up so tight.

When confronted by this evidence, Hauptmann admitted he had lied about having the cash but insisted he'd told the truth about everything else and still disavowed any knowledge of the Lindbergh kidnapping. The money, he said, had been left with him by his friend and partner in a fur import business, a fellow German immigrant named Isidor Fisch.

Fisch would quickly become the most mysterious name associated with the case. In December of 1933, suffering from tuberculosis, Fisch had left New York and set sail for Germany. He returned to his hometown of Leipzig, where he died on March 29, 1934. According to Hauptmann, Fisch left some of his possessions with his friend and partner for safekeeping, including several suitcases and trunks and a shoe box tied with string. Hauptmann was not particularly curious about the contents, and he placed the shoe box on the top shelf of the broom closet in his kitchen, where it remained until a strong rain leaked water into the closet. Removing the soaked items from the upper shelves, Hauptmann came upon the shoe box, opened it, and to his astonishment found fifteen grand in soggy gold certificates. Without saying anything to Anna, he dried out the money and hid it in the garage. He started using some of the money in August 1934. He felt entitled to spend $7,000 of it, because that's how much Isidor owed him from their partnership when he left America.

Fisch's German relatives described him as being penniless, and his American associates claimed he left the country owing them sizable debts. Interestingly, after Fisch died and Hauptmann wrote to the family to tell them about the belongings Isidor had left in his care, he made no mention of the shoe box.

Then some new information surfaced that made things even worse for Hauptmann. It turned out he'd lied about his past in Germany, too. Far from the clean police record of which he'd assured his interrogators, he'd been convicted of grand larceny, petty theft, armed robbery, and receiving stolen property in 1919 when he was twenty. There were nine cases on the record of the County Court at Bautzen, according to a police memo dated November 2, 1934. In one case, he'd broken into the house of the mayor of Bernhbruch, Germany, by climbing a ladder to a second-story window! The armed robbery charge was for stealing groceries from two women at gunpoint. He'd ended up serving more than three years in Bentzin Prison in Seconsen, Germany. He'd tried to get to America because he was about to be arrested for another series of burglaries.

Hauptmann had also escaped from custody several times, once breaking out of jail and jumping out of a police van on another occasion.

During the summer of 1932, about four months after the kidnapping, Bruno had sent Anna on a visit back to Germany. The main purpose of this trip was to try to find out whether he was still wanted by the law over there, or if he could safely return. She was told that if he came back, he'd be thrown in the slammer as soon as they found him. So that ended that hope.

Despite the threats and rough treatment from New York police, Hauptmann wouldn't confess or admit that he knew anything. And there was the sticky matter of Dr. Condon refusing to commit himself. In spite of those obstacles, the New York and New Jersey police knew what they had on their hands. After more than two years of coming up empty-handed, they were now staring at one hell of a great suspect.

THE PUBLIC RECORD

On October 8, 1934, Bruno Richard Hauptmann was indicted by a Hunterdon County, New Jersey, grand jury for the murder of Charles Augustus Lindbergh Jr. A week later, he was placed in the Hunterdon County Jail in Flemington to await trial. William Randolph Hearst's *New York Journal* hired and paid for the services of prominent Brooklyn defense attorney Edward J. Reilly in exchange for Anna Hauptmann's exclusive story. Reilly, near the end of a long career, drinking heavily, and to paraphrase Shakespeare's King Lear, "to deal plainly . . . not in [his] perfect mind," strongly believed in his client's guilt and purposely had few meetings with him prior to trial. Reilly was assisted by three New Jersey attorneys—C. Lloyd Fisher, Frederick A. Pope, and Egbert Rosecrans—who believed more strongly in Hauptmann's innocence and offered a much more spirited defense, particularly Fisher, who stood by Hauptmann until the very end.

On January 2, 1935, the trial began in the Hunterdon County Courthouse in Flemington, New Jersey, presided over by Judge Thomas W.

Trenchard. David T. Wilentz headed up the prosecution team. If the kidnapping was the crime of the century, this was the trial of the century, with the world's press descending on Flemington. Hundreds of extra telephone lines were installed in the courthouse, and the street in front soon resembled an ongoing carnival. H. L. Mencken called the trial "the biggest story since the Resurrection." This was the first time sound cameras had been used in court. As a result of their effect, they were banned for a half century thereafter.

Like the overwhelming majority of the public, the press had already decided Hauptmann was guilty. It certainly couldn't have been an American who would do such a ghastly thing—this despite the fact that Americans were doing such ghastly things all the time, just not to such famous victims.

Though he had failed to do so at the police station, at the trial, during his two days on the witness stand, Dr. John Condon identified Bruno Richard Hauptmann as Cemetery John. Lindbergh also identified him from his voice. During five days of testimony, eight document examiners, including Albert S. Osborn and his son, Albert D., stated their professional opinions that Hauptmann was the writer of all of the ransom notes. One defense handwriting expert, John Trendley, differed from this conclusion.

Arthur Koehler testified that rail sixteen of the kidnap ladder had come directly from a floorboard in Hauptmann's attic.

On January 24, Hauptmann took the stand in his own defense, beginning five days of grueling testimony, including eleven hours of brutal cross-examination by David Wilentz.

On February 13, after twenty-nine court sessions, 162 witnesses, and 381 exhibits, the jury retired to consider the case. Eleven and a half hours of deliberation later, they returned a verdict of guilty of murder in the first degree without a recommendation for mercy, which under New Jersey law meant death in the electric chair.

During a period of appeals, several people, including Edward Reilly, approached Hauptmann in prison with the hope that he would confess in return for a commutation of his death sentence to life. He refused all entreaties, including a last-minute one from famed defense lawyer Samuel Leibowitz and another from New Jersey governor Harold G. Hoffman, who was troubled by the investigation and trial and did not believe that Hauptmann's conviction told the entire story.

After all appeals were exhausted, Bruno Richard Hauptmann steadfastly maintained his complete innocence. He died in the electric chair of the New Jersey State Prison at Trenton on April 3, 1936. The controversy surrounding his guilt or innocence has refused to die.

With minor exceptions, everything we've covered in this chapter up to now is generally considered fact or reasonably accepted interpretation. Nearly everything that follows remains in dispute. That is one of the overwhelming problems with the Lindbergh case, and also one of the prime reasons it has continued to intrigue and remain so controversial after almost seventy years: so much of it comes down to which evidence—*or whose evidence*—you believe.

Countless millions of words have been written about this case, and each succeeding generation has seen formidable and impressive advocates on both sides. At present, among the most staunch, most articulate, and best-researched proponents that Hauptmann was guilty of the kidnapping and acted alone is Jim Fisher. To my knowledge, he has read and studied as much of the record as anyone in preparing his 1987 book, *The Lindbergh Case,* and its follow-up volume, *The Ghosts of Hopewell.* A. Scott Berg, among the best and most respected biographers writing today, came away from his own research for *Lindbergh* with the belief that Hauptmann had acted alone in kidnapping the baby. On the other side we have Anthony Scaduto's 1976 book, *Scapegoat,* and Ludovic Kennedy's 1985 book, *The Airman and the Carpenter: The Lindbergh Kidnapping and the Framing of Richard Hauptmann.* The titles are self-explanatory.

Each author accepts a differing set of facts. If you go with one set, Hauptmann's guilt appears highly questionable. If you go with the other, it's virtually a no-brainer.

Let us consider the major pieces of evidence that slammed the lid on Bruno Richard Hauptmann.

THE RANSOM MONEY

This is a pretty tough one to challenge. Not only was Hauptmann in possession of almost a third of the ransom, he lied about it to police. At the least, he was dealing directly or indirectly with the kidnappers. As mentioned earlier, there was so much kidnapping for hire in the late 1920s and early 1930s that a subindustry grew up in laundering ransom money. It was not uncommon for a kidnapper (or other professional criminal, for that matter) to sell his illegally gotten cash to another party at a discount to prevent authorities from tracing it back to him. Hauptmann might have bought the money, or the mysterious Isidor Fisch, or maybe it had already been laundered by another associate by the time it reached either of them.

I have to say, though, the notion that Hauptmann accepted the shoe box from Fisch and stashed it in his kitchen pantry without even wondering what was in it strikes me as rather ingenuous. Are we to believe that if the ceiling hadn't leaked into that closet, he would never have looked?

More important is the timing of Hauptmann's essential retirement from the carpentry business. It coincides almost exactly with the payment of the ransom. Investigators found that as of April 1, 1932, he had no cash assets. Yet he would have us believe that an immigrant tradesman who had never shown a previous ability to make big bucks in the investment world is suddenly, while professional investors are losing their shirts, able to support his family comfortably enough in the stock market to afford fine new furniture and an expensive radio? You have to look at the background of the individual under suspicion, and in this instance, it doesn't add up.

After Hauptmann's arrest, ransom bills stopped turning up. On the other hand, let us remember that more than half of the ransom money was never found.

THE RANSOM NOTES

Altogether there were fifteen ransom notes. The expert firepower the prosecution arrayed on this point during the trial was impressive. There was little question that Hauptmann spoke in much the same way that the notes were constructed, and many of his letters and word formations taken from random samples of his writing were extremely close. For example, Hauptmann both said and wrote *signature* as *singnature,* as was repeatedly seen in the notes.

Hauptmann's defenders have made the case that what the experts were really saying was that he wrote in the same European style as the actual writer and that any number of people from Hauptmann's background would have compared as closely as he did. I am not a graphologist, though I have worked with a number of them over the years. While it is not an exact science, the evidence suggests to me a pretty close connection between the ransom notes and Bruno Hauptmann's handwriting, style, syntax, and spelling.

At one point fairly early in the investigation, an analyst at Scotland Yard concluded that the interlocking-circles signature suggested a writer with the initials BRH. *B* came from the blue circle, *R* from the red, and *H* from the holes punched in the paper. I would wonder about this, since by the time of the kidnapping Hauptmann was thinking of himself as Richard rather than Bruno, but, hey, if this story is true, it's pretty impressive. With all of my experience in criminal personality profiling and psycholinguistic analysis, I freely admit it's not something I would ever have come up with.

THE EYE AND EAR WITNESSES

The prosecution made a big deal about all of the people who could identify Bruno Hauptmann at various stages of the case. These included Lindbergh neighbors who saw him cruising around the area before the crime, the taxi driver who came to Condon's house, Condon himself, Lindbergh, the cashier at the movie theater in Greenwich Village, and the gas station attendant who wrote the license number on the gold note that led to Hauptmann.

Of all of these, Condon's ID is the most important. He was the only one who spent extended time with Cemetery John and had two real conversations with him. Condon was unwilling to identify Hauptmann in a police lineup. Yet by the time the case got to trial, he stated in no uncertain terms that this was the man he had seen. What happened between those two events?

What probably happened is that the police and/or prosecutors got to him. Hauptmann was a pretty good match for the description of Cemetery John. A pile of evidence had been assembled against him and the police were confident they had the right man. But Condon wasn't completely sure the man in the station lineup was the one he had dealt with and he took his role as a witness seriously enough that he neither wanted to condemn a possibly innocent man nor divert a police investigation by giving an iffy ID. But by the time of the trial, someone must have appealed to him with a variation of the following:

"Dr. Condon, we know that Hauptmann is our guy. He even matches up with your physical description. All we need is for you to confirm that in court. If you do, we've got him. If you don't, it's going to confuse the jury, give the defense something to run with, the brutal killer of that dear little baby is going to go free, and the Lindbergh family you admire so much will never be able to heal."

Condon was just the kind of narcissistic personality to whom this kind of appeal would be effective. You let someone sit with this awhile and he gets surer and surer. That's why I always want eyewitness testimony corroborated with some other type of more objective evidence.

The same scenario could have occurred with Lindbergh: "Colonel, we've got the right guy, the one who took your child from you. You said yourself he had a German accent. All you have to say is that this is the German accent you heard."

Each of the other witnesses had his own motivations. One of the neighbors had been promised reward money. The other encounters were so casual that even a probable ID would have been impressive to a jury. And aside from a few highly questionable witnesses, the police and prosecution were unable to place Hauptmann at the crime scene.

I'm not saying these identifications were erroneous. All of these people may have seen and/or heard Bruno Richard Hauptmann. Or they may not have. I'm only saying that none of these identifications, including Condon's and Lindbergh's, seems sufficiently reliable to me to be authoritative. I don't count them one way or another in our search for what really happened.

One interesting note, though. If the ID by Cecile Barr, the movie theater cashier, was accurate, then Hauptmann was in possession of Lindbergh ransom bills substantially earlier than he claimed he received the shoe box of money from Fisch.

THE CHISEL

Along with the ladder, a three-quarter-inch Buck Brothers chisel was found at the crime scene. Presumably, it was to be used to pry open the window or shutters if necessary. When Hauptmann's carpenter's toolbox was examined, the three-quarter-inch chisel, and only that chisel, was missing. This isn't a smoking gun, but it's pretty damning circumstantial evidence, especially when taken with everything else.

In *The Airman and the Carpenter,* Ludovic Kennedy claims that two three-quarter-inch chisels were actually found in Hauptmann's garage—one a Buck Brothers and the other a Stanley—and that they remained in police custody until Anthony Scaduto came across them. We asked Mark W. Falzini, the New Jersey State Police archivist, about this. Falzini has a comprehensive knowledge of the case and the evidence, but no personal opinion on Hauptmann's guilt or innocence. He told us that he has no idea where Kennedy's and Scaduto's information comes from. No such chisels were ever in police custody.

Yet another example of whose information you want to go with.

THE NUMBERS BEHIND THE DOOR

On Monday, September 24, 1934, four days after the discovery of ransom currency in Hauptmann's garage, NYPD inspector Henry D. Bruckman discovered an address and a telephone number written in pencil on a piece of wooden door molding inside a closet in Hauptmann's son's bedroom. The number turned out to be Dr. Condon's old telephone number before he had it changed to an unlisted one; in other words, it was Condon's number at the time of the encounter with Cemetery John. The address was Condon's as well. Bruckman also found two serial numbers written on the molding, one for a $500 bill and another for a $1,000 bill.

When questioned about it by Bronx County district attorney Samuel J. Foley, Hauptmann conceded that the handwriting looked like his, but didn't specifically recall writing it and continued to maintain that he had nothing to do with the kidnapping. As to why he might have written the telephone number where it was found, he could only suggest that he must have been reacting to news reports of the kidnapping.

"I must have read it in the paper about the story," he told Foley. "I was a little bit interest, and keep a little record of it, and maybe I was just in the closet and was reading the paper and put down the address."

What?

Ludovic Kennedy suggests that the evidence was probably planted as a joke by one of the newspaper men who had access to the apartment; in fact he even proposes a name. And then why would Hauptmann write down a telephone number when he didn't even have a telephone?

Let's take the second part first. You write down a phone number even if you don't have a phone at home because you have to call the go-between, even if it's from a public phone booth. And if you're going to call this person, you have to know his number. If this is part of an illegal activity, you're going to want to hide the number, and the inside of your son's closet is as good a place as any.

As to the possibility of a plant: sure, very possible in those days when crime scenes were not as carefully protected as they are today (and still they're often not protected as well as they should be). But what I can't get past is, why would someone as careful as Hauptmann admit that this was his handwriting if he wasn't certain it was?

I would have expected him say, "I have no idea what it is or how it got there, and this is the first time I've seen it in my life. If you say it's a piece of evidence, then someone planted it!"

175

But that isn't what he said. So either he wrote it there or had strong reason to believe that he did and didn't want to get caught up in any more lies.

THE MAJESTIC ALIBI

One of the more controversial aspects of the Hauptmann defense was when he actually started work at the Majestic Apartments. He claimed that on March 1, 1932, the day of the kidnapping, he was working there until 5 P.M., which would have made it difficult for him to have been at the Hopewell house at the right time. The prosecution claimed that time and pay records indicated Hauptmann had not started working at the Majestic until March 16.

Ludovic Kennedy puts forth evidence that worksheets showing Hauptmann was on the job as a carpenter in Manhattan on March 1 were tampered with to make it look as if he had not started until after March 15, the next pay period. Prosecutor David Wilentz and the Bronx district attorney had seen these records and had them handed over to NYPD for "safekeeping." The payroll records were never seen again. The sheets showing that Hauptmann quit on April 2 appear to have been tampered with. The defense subpoenaed the Majestic timekeeper, Edward Morton, to bring his time sheets to an extradition hearing, but Morton failed to show up. Enough muddiness exists on this issue to throw serious doubt on the prosecution's contention about where Hauptmann was—or wasn't—on March 1.

RAIL SIXTEEN

This is the single most important piece of evidence upon which the case against Bruno Richard Hauptmann hinges. It remains one of the most famous pieces of evidence in the history of modern criminology, right up there with the JFK "magic bullet" and the Simpson case glove.

First, let us consider the ladder itself. It has often been described as "crude" and "homemade," but when you actually look at it closely, it is pretty ingenious. It seems crude because it is so light and the rungs are so much farther apart than on a normal ladder. Well, it had to be light to carry easily, and when Mark Olshaker and I examined it, we thought that whoever built it knew exactly how far apart the rungs could be spaced and still allow climbing; in other words, no more than absolutely necessary.

The sectional structure is equally ingenious. The first two sections fold together on hinges, and the third section fits onto the second section if it is needed. This ladder had been thought through and designed by someone who could visualize the finished product.

Someone like a carpenter.

And don't forget the ladder sketches found in Hauptmann's notebook.

Then we get to the two prongs of Arthur Koehler's research. The first used wood samples and cutting-blade patterns to pinpoint the most likely location where the lumber was prepared, shipped, and sold. Can it be just an amazing coincidence that the place he came up with was right there in the Bronx? Even more amazing, Hauptmann once worked for National Lumber and Millwork. Of course, like everything else about this case, some have questioned Koehler's research methods, techniques, and assumptions, but I have seen no compelling argument that his analysis was incorrect.

And now we come to the heart of the ladder case. On Wednesday, September 26, 1934, two days after Henry Bruckman had found the phone number and address on the molding inside Manfred's closet, police were once again looking around Hauptmann's attic for clues. According to the official account, they noticed a gap in the floor; one floorboard about eight feet long in the southwest corner had been removed. Where the board was missing, there were empty nail holes in four successive joists where it would have been hammered down. Koehler determined by matching grain patterns and nail holes that rail sixteen of the kidnap ladder had been the board removed from the attic. It could have been, based on the prosecution's theory, that Hauptmann ran out of lumber at the last minute and so had to use what was on hand.

But like everything else, this theory has also been disputed. Hauptmann's defenders point out that the police had been poking around the attic several times before they noticed the gap. Is this the kind of thing you miss? Then they also point out that the police had exclusive access to the apartment for several days after the arrest. They wouldn't even let in the FBI. The matter was "cleared up" as a misunderstanding about jurisdiction according to a memorandum of September 28, 1934, from J. Edgar Hoover, who, though annoyed, seemed to accept the police explanation. But technically speaking, if you're going to plant evidence, this would be the time.

The opportunity was there and so was the motivation. But let's look at the big picture. We've examined the ladder and Arthur Koehler's analysis of the matching grain patterns and find it compelling, despite a several inch gap between the end of rail sixteen and the rest of the board still in place in the attic.

What this means is that if police did plant evidence, they would have had to remove the actual rail sixteen from the ladder and replace it with a substitute cut from a certain piece of board. They would have then have had to remove a board from Hauptmann's attic floor and replace it with the remainder of the board from which the substitute rail sixteen had been fashioned, being careful to create new nail holes that lined up with the existing nail holes in the four joists underneath. They would have had to destroy the original rail sixteen but make sure that the substitute looked enough like it in terms of grain, coloration, contour, and distress marks so that if anyone happened to compare it with one of the original photographs taken just after the crime, they couldn't tell the difference.

And then, on top of all that, the men who pulled off this switcheroo would have had to be awfully damn sure than anyone and everyone involved in the conspiracy was completely reliable and that no one would spill. Because if even one person did, not only would the case against Hauptmann be in terrible jeopardy, but each of them would be out of a job and facing serious penitentiary time for tampering with evidence. It's one thing to try to influence witnesses to be a little more authoritative in their identifications. It's quite another to out-and-out falsify evidence, especially when the FBI already has its nose out of joint and would like nothing better than to slam the police. Making a payroll book that almost no one's seen before disappear is one thing if you want to tamper with evidence. Making a piece of the ladder disappear is quite another.

Though I do wonder why a carpenter who had access to plenty of lumber would have to cannibalize his own attic for a piece of wood, for these reasons, I find it extremely difficult to believe that rail sixteen did not actually come from the spot the police and prosecution said it did.

PUTTING TOGETHER THE PIECES

I think there has to be serious question as to whether Bruno Richard Hauptmann got a fair trial. Forgetting even the circus atmosphere and the nation's call for blood, particularly against a foreigner whose country had been on the opposite side in the Great War, other factors stood strongly against him. His own lead counsel, Edward Reilly, privately thought his client guilty and stated that he hoped Hauptmann would get the chair. Reilly was at odds with the rest of the defense team for his poor handling of several aspects of the case and spent a total of thirty-eight minutes with Hauptmann before the trial. Reilly came up with only one handwriting expert, whose testimony was lackluster, and drove away another expert who was convinced she could prove the handwriting on the notes was not Hauptmann's. Reilly's five-hour summation was chaotic and lame, delivered after a drinking bout at lunch. Most people there thought he was intoxicated.

If we take into account not only Hauptmann's lead attorney making a mess of the case, but also the strong possibility that witnesses were swayed and that Hauptmann was abused by the police while in custody, what can we still say about the case against him? Not whether he got a perfect trial or even a fair trial, but whether or not he was the right guy.

You may have noticed something curious in the way this narrative unfolded. In relating the events following the night of March 1, 1932, I generally referred to the kidnappers in the plural. In fact, the existence of multiple offenders was the working assumption of both the New Jersey State Police and the FBI. Yet once Bruno Hauptmann was arrested, all thought of more than one person's involvement seems to have evaporated. In fact, once Hauptmann was identified, most, if not all, serious work to uncover any other suspects ceased.

Does this make sense? I don't think so.

A couple of evidentiary items suggest more than one person. The first is Dr. Condon's belief that he heard some discussion between Cemetery John and another individual during his telephone conversation. The second is the impression by both Lindbergh and Al Reich that John had lookouts at the cemetery observing the car and looking for police.

Then there are the details in the notes themselves. I don't pay serious attention to whether a ransom note speaks of *I* or *we*. In itself, that's meaningless in determining if more than one person is involved. What I tell my people is to stand back and look at what the entire communication is saying. And in this case, an elaborate story was presented about how the baby was being cared for by two nurses on board a boat. Clearly, this did not happen. The baby was dead and discarded the very night of the abduction.

But this story is too elaborate for an otherwise unsophisticated offender to have made up just to get the money. In my opinion, the story of how the baby was being cared for, and by whom, represents the plan of what was *supposed to happen*. The baby's accidental death in the fall to the window ledge or foundation footings canceled all that, but you can't very well admit that and expect to get the money. So you stick with your original story, even down to stripping the sleeping suit off the corpse before you get rid of it. This all suggests to me more than one offender.

As does the crime scene itself. Mark and I and our researcher Katherine Johnston Ramsland spent several hours in the Hopewell house. It is now a state-run school for teenaged boys, but the building is still very much as the Lindberghs left it, down to the original wood paneling in the library and the mantel and Delft tiles imported from Holland above the fireplace in the baby's nursery.

Examining the house and the surrounding countryside, and analyzing the logistics, it is virtually inconceivable to us that one man alone could have pulled off this kidnapping. The easiest and most efficient way to place the ladder would have been directly in front of the nursery window, yet that would have put it directly in front of the library window on the first floor, where there was a good chance Colonel Lindbergh would have been sitting. So the ladder had to be positioned to the side. This corresponds with the impressions left in the ground, but makes access into the window and back out again extremely awkward. It would be nearly impossible for the intruder to maneuver from the ladder to the narrow window, pry it open, climb through, snatch the child, carry him in a bag back out the window and to the ladder without falling, never mind without dropping the bag. The only efficient way to get the child from the nursery window to the ladder is through a handoff.

Was this a handoff of one intruder to another or of a household staff member to an intruder? Could be either, but the dual-intruder theory makes more sense because there is no good reason to suspect any of the servants in the house that night of direct complicity in the crime. But someone had the time to wipe down the room for prints, and this would have been someone sufficiently familiar with the room not to waste time. I just do not believe it was possible for one person to do all that: to drive close enough to the house at night, carry the ladder, the bag, and chisel up to the wall, climb up, climb in, and take the child all by himself. More than one individual took part in the crime that night.

Add to this logistical issue the matter of intelligence. The criminals had up-to-the-minute knowledge. The baby was not supposed to be in Hopewell that night. Only a few people knew that. Was Bruno Hauptmann so unaware of the Lindberghs' habits that he just lucked into going to kidnap the baby on the one Tuesday of his life that he slept at Hopewell? Those are pretty long odds.

Or did Hauptmann drive to Englewood, pull up at Next Day Hill, discover that the child was not there, then get back in his car with his ladder and drive for more than an hour almost halfway across the state to Hopewell to carry out his mission? Once he got to Next Day Hill, how would he have found out? Did he sneak into this huge estate, not find the baby, then leave? Did he knock on the door and casually ask where he could find the Lindbergh baby? Was he able to accomplish this without anyone seeing him? It just doesn't make any sense, and it doesn't match with the timing of the kidnapping as it took place in Hopewell.

Whoever took the baby that night had to have inside information. This doesn't mean one of the servants was consciously in on the crime, only that someone—likely Violet Sharpe—let the information slip to someone else to whom the kidnappers had a direct line. Though he was meticulously investigated, nothing turned up to suggest any direct link between Hauptmann and anyone who would have had this information.

WHODUNIT?

So did Bruno Richard Hauptmann do it?

I think he did *something*. If not, he is the victim of the most incredible, almost indescribable bad luck in the annals of law enforcement: that he was a semiliterate German immigrant when all indications pointed to a semiliterate German immigrant as the writer of the ransom notes; that his handwriting and usage were close enough to the notes for a series of experts to declare it a match; that he resembled the eyewitness descriptions; that he had maps of the area near Hopewell because he said he used to hunt there; that he had come to the United States illegally after a series of crimes that included armed robbery and breaking and entering using a ladder; that he was a skilled carpenter with drawings of ladders in his notebooks when the key to the crime was an individually designed and constructed ladder; that there was another sketch of the money box in one of the ransom notes that looked like something a carpenter would draw; that he had purchased lumber and once worked for the establishment where some of the wood for the ladder had been purchased; that he had about a third of the ransom cash hidden in his garage and he lied about it; that he had come into money and was able to start living a better lifestyle at exactly the same time as the ransom was passed; that he lived close to the cemetery where the original meeting with Cemetery John took place, and the cemetery where the ransom was handed over; that through a lapse of memory he forgot that he hadn't actually written Jafsie's address and phone number inside his son's closet. This string of bad luck would have extended so far as to include having bought a keg of nails from the same batch as those that were used in the kidnap ladder!

We could go on, but I think you get the idea.

Hauptmann had a compulsive, controlling personality. Like many men of his generation, he controlled his household, he controlled the money, he made the decisions. His wife went along docilely and willingly. He kept many secrets from her, and no one has suggested she knew anything of the kidnapping or the presence of the ransom money in the garage. She didn't even know his first name was Bruno until the police told her. She believed in him, and it is understandable that he didn't want to disappoint that belief, even at the cost of his life.

So I have to conclude that Bruno Richard Hauptmann was involved in the Lindbergh kidnapping, though he did not work alone and was not necessarily the leader. His background showed him to be a risk-taker, both in terms of criminal record and in his means of getting to America. Moreover, that record suggested that when he did become involved with crime, it would be with others rather than alone.

I suspect that he was approached by one or more others in the German immigrant community because of his background and his skills as a carpenter. The unrecovered money would have gone to them, some of which may have been laundered in the J. J. Faulkner bank deposit. Since kidnapping was rampant, this would have been perceived as a get-rich-quick scheme. And who better to try than the most famous man in the world? Hauptmann may or may not have actually been at the crime scene. He might have driven the car and taken the handoff. At this late date, absent physical evidence or the possibility of interviewing him, there is no way to know.

If Hauptmann was Cemetery John, then he was probably not in the baby's room, because in the first meeting with Condon, John referred to the ransom note with "singnature" as being left in the crib—perhaps the original plan—when, in fact, it was left on the windowsill.

Could a shady group of German immigrants have had sufficient knowledge of the inside of the house to pull off the crime? Yes. For one thing, plans had been published. This is no substitute for firsthand experience in so "delicate" a crime as kidnapping. But even this we can account for.

Mark Falzini came across an astounding document in the case archives that he called to our attention. It is from FBI New York Field Office File 62-3057, a 1932 summary of the case. Under a section headed "ALOYSIUS WHATELY, commonly referred to as OLLY WHATELY," it reads in part:

> Whately entered the employ of Colonel and Mrs. Charles A. Lindbergh October 15, 1930, and with his wife acted as caretaker of the Lindbergh estate at Hopewell, N.J. and resided there continuously after the house was completed. *Frequently in the absence of the Lindberghs,*

he acted as guide to tourists and other curious visitors showing them through the house and about the adjoining grounds. [Italics added]

There you have it! Anyone could have conducted a reconnaissance run beforehand. This would have been impossible at Next Day Hill, the baby's normal place of residence, which was actually much closer and more convenient to the Bronx, practically just across the Hudson. But Hopewell was the more vulnerable location, so that was where the crime had to take place. And that required specific information.

Whately died in May 1933 at fifty years of age after several months of illness, so this aspect was never followed up.

Was the kidnap ringleader the mysterious Isidor Fisch? Quite possibly, though little is known about him other than that he was a hustler who had bilked friends and other investors out of thousands of dollars in dubious schemes, including a pie-baking company. He was said by his family to be broke, and he departed the States owing a lot of money, yet Hauptmann said he left all this cash with him. One thing that is known is that Fisch applied for his visa on May 12, 1932—the day the baby's corpse was found.

Fisch did not match the physical description of Cemetery John, which meant John either had to be Hauptmann or still another man was involved.

I've come out many times publicly in support of the death penalty. I've stated that I'd be more than willing personally to pull the switch on some of the monsters I've hunted in my career with the FBI. But Bruno Hauptmann just doesn't fit into this category—the evidence just wasn't, and isn't, there to have confidently sent him to the electric chair. To impose the one sentence for which there is no retroactive correction requires a far higher standard of proof than was seen here. Blaming him for the entire crime was, to my mind, an expedient and simpleminded solution to a private horror that had become a national obsession.

I am troubled, for instance, that even after he was convicted and sentenced to death and appeals were denied, when Hauptmann was thrown a lifeline that would have spared him, he refused to grasp it. A number of people in authority came to his cell, including the governor of New Jersey, saying that the death sentence would be set aside if only he would confess—to something. All he had to do to save his life and spare his wife and son all that anguish was to say who else had been involved in the crime and what their roles had been.

And yet he refused, saying simply that he was innocent and therefore had no knowledge of who might have done it.

Not having had the opportunity to interview him myself, it is difficult to say for sure what his motive was. Based on my knowledge of other sociopathic offenders, I suspect this was probably stubbornness, arrogance, the "honor among thieves" of not ratting out a fellow comrade, and an unwillingness to disgrace his family and his name. Perhaps he was afraid for his family's safety if he spilled. As we've seen, there is enough evidence of high-risk behavior in Hauptmann's background to make this likely.

But not certain. I have to say that this refusal to trade his life for any verbal concession inevitably complicates the assessment. It is also a matter of record that Hauptmann asked repeatedly for a lie detector test and that one be administered to Dr. Condon. My colleagues and associates know I have never set much store in the polygraph and am always wary of the results, but it is unreasonable to think that Hauptmann had such a knowledgeable or jaundiced view. If he asked for such a test, unless this was a clever ploy he knew would never be followed up, he must have believed he could pass.

We can say that throughout her long life (she died on October 10, 1994, the sixty-ninth anniversary of her marriage, at age ninety-five), Anna Hauptmann believed fervently in her husband's innocence and did everything in her power to convince others and have the case reopened.

Was a better and more satisfying solution to this infamous case possible? Yes, but not once certain key bridges were crossed.

The greatest single mistake, though it was made for understandable reasons, was allowing Colonel Lindbergh to dictate limitations on the police. In any kidnapping, the major risk for the offender is picking up the package. Had police been allowed to cover the money drop, the chances are great they would have picked up Cemetery John. It wouldn't have saved the baby, but the case would have been cracked.

You cannot lose control of a case. If you do, it's going to be difficult to get it back.

After the first meeting with Cemetery John, we would have wanted to debrief Condon and would have gleaned valuable information from him. For example, the passing reference to burning if the baby were dead could have been used during the second encounter, playing on his fears and sense of guilt to get to the others.

Likewise, Schwarzkopf could have been more proactive in his assumptions regarding an inside job. If we were working this case today, we would have assessed each household servant, then tried to show each one how we didn't think he or she had purposely aided the kidnappers, but that someone had been tricked or duped and we had to have that information. I would have done everything in my power to get the Lindberghs themselves involved with this tactic so the staff would regard it seriously.

During the first encounter with Cemetery John, the offender went to some lengths to convince Dr. Condon that both Betty Gow and her boyfriend Red Johnson were innocent. Why even bother bringing up information about the servants and their friends if this wasn't an avenue they wanted the investigators to avoid?

This was just one area that could have been better explored to get vital information when it would still have been useful. And there are so many other strategies that could have been tried but were not.

Instead, what we are left with is a classic American tragedy.

CHAPTER FOUR

THE ZODIAC

One thing that motivates many serial offenders is the desire to create and sustain their own mythology. The press is often a willing collaborator, giving them such names as the Freeway Phantom, the Hillside Strangler, the Green River Killer. When the media is not so cooperative, they often insist upon their own designations, such as the Son of Sam or the BTK (for bind, torture, and kill) Strangler.

The reasons they feel a need to do this are obvious to those of us in criminal investigative analysis. These are insignificant nobodies whose only "accomplishment" in life, the only time when they feel in control and fulfilled, is when they are causing suffering or fear in others.

Among the most successful in establishing and preserving his mythology was the UNSUB known as the Zodiac. The Zodiac crimes remain unsolved, the offender never identified or caught. And of all the cases about which I am frequently asked, this one comes up as much as any. Particularly on the West Coast, this is one that continues to haunt.

THE FIRST SHALL BE LAST

It was the day before Halloween—Sunday, October 30, 1966— in Riverside, California, about sixty miles southeast of Los Angeles. Joseph Bates and his eighteen-year-old daughter, Cheri Jo, began their day together, going to mass at St. Catherine's Church, then having breakfast at Sandy's Restaurant. After that, they split up, with Joseph heading for the beach and Cheri Jo planning to do some schoolwork. A cheerleader at Riverside City College and at Ramona High before that, Cheri Jo was the all-American, California dream girl: blond hair, blue eyes, attractive tan, five feet three, and 110 pounds. A freshman at RCC, she was an honor student who held down a job at a local bank and aspired to a career as a flight attendant. Since her mother's departure a year earlier, and with her brother serving in the navy across the country in Florida, Cheri Jo lived alone with her father, who worked at Corona Naval Ordnance Laboratory as a machinist.

Around midafternoon, Cheri Jo decided to go to the college library. She called a friend to see if she wanted to go along, but her friend was busy so Cheri Jo went on her own. She was gone by the time Joseph returned home, but had left her father a note. When he went back out, he left a note for his daughter in return.

Joseph Bates wasn't worried when he came back around midnight and saw that the note he had left his daughter hadn't been touched. After all, she was old enough to socialize that late and take care of herself. Thinking she was probably with a few of her girlfriends, he went to sleep.

But by the next morning she still hadn't returned. He called a friend to see if Cheri Jo was at her house and, when she wasn't, reported his daughter missing to the police.

Within the hour, Cheri Jo Bates was no longer a missing person. Her body was found by a college groundskeeper, lying facedown on the gravel path to the library parking lot. She had been stabbed in the chest and left shoulder and slashed in the face and neck, her jugular vein and larynx both severed. The assault was so violent that she was nearly decapitated.

Riverside police tried to reconstruct Cheri Jo's final hours. A coworker at the Riverside National Bank had received a call from her around 5:30 P.M., asking if she'd seen the bibliography for a term paper Cheri Jo was writing. That was the last time anyone reported talking to her. A little after 6 P.M., one of her friends said she saw Cheri Jo driving toward the library in her light green Volkswagen. Someone else reported seeing a blond woman in a car like Cheri Jo's and also noticed a bronze-colored Oldsmobile that followed closely behind.

This detail became important in the context of Cheri Jo's assault. When investigators examined her VW, still parked at the library with newly checked-out books on the front seat, they found it had been tampered with, a wire to the distributor disconnected among other actions. Police, who conducted an impressive, exhaustive investigation, theorized that her assailant followed her to the library, disabled her car, then waited for his prey. He likely watched as she tried to start the car several times unsuccessfully, then offered her help or a ride. Whether he was a stranger or known to her, she trusted him enough that she went with him down the dark path, where he attacked.

Cheri Jo was small but athletic, and she put up a hell of a fight. One report compared the area where she died to "a freshly plowed field." She had human hair and skin under her fingernails. A wristwatch, thought to belong to the UNSUB, was found ten feet from her body. The band had been completely torn away from the face on one side, ripped off in Cheri Jo's desperate struggle.

The timing of the murder, however, was confusing. Two people in the area that night reported hearing screams between 10:15 and 10:45 P.M., but the library closed at 9 P.M. on Sunday nights. Did Cheri Jo and her murderer talk for more than an hour before he killed her?

Even more important, there was no apparent motive. The victim's purse was found next to her body, with her identification intact and less than a dollar in change. The MO—disabling her car and lying in wait—was too complicated for a robbery, and a young college student off for an afternoon or evening of studying hardly made a worthy target for that. There was no sign of sexual assault, and nothing in the young woman's background suggested she was a high-risk victim. At Cheri Jo's funeral five days later, investigators scanned the crowd as her bereaved father collapsed in his grief. Like Joseph Bates, they were no closer to understanding why she had died.

An answer of sorts arrived by mail the next month in a letter to the Riverside police. The author was clever, typing the document in all-caps through perhaps a dozen or so pages of carbon paper, then mailing one taken from the bottom of the stack, rendering it so full of smudges that while its message was legible, it would be next to impossible to trace it to a specific typewriter. Of course, there were no fingerprints. And the writer was not only cunning in avoiding identification, he knew to include enough details of Cheri Jo's murder to gain credibility as her killer.

He began with a taunting lead-in: the word *BY* with nothing but empty space following. The document read:

SHE WAS YOUNG AND BEAUTIFUL
BUT NOW SHE IS BATTERED AND
DEAD. SHE IS NOT THE FIRST
AND SHE WILL NOT BE THE LAST
I LAY AWAKE NIGHTS THINKING ABOUT MY
NEXT VICTIM. MAYBE SHE WILL BE THE
BEAUTIFUL BLOND THAT BABYSITS NEAR
THE LITTLE STORE AND WALKS DOWN THE
DARK ALLEY EACH EVENING ABOUT SEVEN.
OR MAYBE SHE WILL BE THE SHAPELY BLUE
EYED BRUNETT THAT SAID NO WHEN I

ASKED HER FOR A DATE IN HIGH SCHOOL.
BUT MAYBE IT WILL NOT BE EITHER. BUT I
SHALL CUT OFF HER FEMALE PARTS AND
DEPOSIT THEM FOR THE WHOLE CITY TO SEE.
SO DON'T MAKE IT SO EASY FOR ME. KEEP
YOUR SISTERS, DAUGHTERS, AND WIVES OFF
THE STREETS AND ALLEYS . . .

The author went on to describe in precise detail how he removed "THE MIDDLE WIRE FROM THE DISTRIBUTOR." The police had not released this information publicly. The next section of the letter was a grotesque description of Cheri Jo's death, including the moment the UNSUB abruptly turned from Good Samaritan to ruthless killer:

. . . WHEN WE WERE AWAY FROM
THE LIBRARY WALKING, I SAID IT WAS ABOUT
TIME. SHE ASKED ME, 'ABOUT TIME FOR WHAT?'
I SAID IT WAS ABOUT TIME FOR YOU TO
DIE. I GRABBED HER AROUND THE NECK WITH
MY HAND OVER HER MOUTH AND MY OTHER HAND
WITH A SMALL KNIFE AT HER THROAT . . .

At one point, the author alluded to a possible motive: "ONLY ONE THING WAS ON MY MIND. MAKING HER PAY FOR THE BRUSH OFFS THAT SHE HAD GIVEN ME DURING THE YEARS PRIOR."

Police did find a young man who knew Cheri Jo and could be linked circumstantially to the crime. Even years later some investigators considered him the strongest suspect, but there was never enough to bring him to trial.

From my experience, I would suggest that this citation, like the one to the "SHAPELY BLUE EYED BRUNETT" before it, refers more to what the killer sees as female rejection in general than to a specific woman. I say this because of the letter's larger theme, echoed in his closing section:

. . . I AM NOT SICK.
I AM INSANE. BUT THAT WILL NOT STOP
THE GAME. THIS LETTER SHOULD BE PUBLISHED
FOR ALL TO READ IT. IT JUST MIGHT SAVE THAT
GIRL IN THE ALLEY. BUT THAT'S UP TO YOU.

IT WILL BE ON YOUR CONSCIENCE. NOT
MINE . . .
BEWARE . . . I
AM STALKING YOUR GIRLS NOW.

It was probably at least somewhat truthful when the killer wrote of his next possible victim. Despite his reference to the brush-offs, Cheri Jo's killer was probably out on the hunt that night, spotted the pretty young girl in her car and followed her, then set his trap and waited. She could have been a blond in a dark alley; any victim would do. With this letter, her killer set in motion what he really wanted: to put the fear of God in the community that any woman or girl could be next. It was all a game to him. What further supports this as his motive is that, while police remained fearful of another attack, none came. The UNSUB was happy with what he'd accomplished; he didn't need to kill again in the near future. He could just watch and wait.

This ability to wait for the right time to strike again was clear from the crime, which bore the marks of a highly organized offender. Despite what he wrote, this crime was not the work of an insane person, but a methodical and cunning one, capable of hunting for just the right victim, preferably a stranger. This UNSUB was able to set his trap (the disabled automobile), seem normal and helpful enough in behavior and appearance to win his victim's trust, lure her into an area where it would be safe for him to attack, and then get away without attracting attention.

There are a few disorganized elements, such as that Cheri Jo was left where she was killed, with no real effort to hide her body. Also, the UNSUB appeared to have more trouble controlling his victim than he expected, as shown by the presence of the watch as well as the physical evidence under her nails. But these seem to be the marks of a youthful and/or criminally unsophisticated offender, rather than an indication that a true disorganized personality is involved. And certainly we have no indication that more than one UNSUB committed this crime. Indeed, this is the type of offender we'd expect to learn from this experience and "correct" the disorganized elements his next time out.

Months went by and police found no evidence the killer had made good on his threats against another woman. Unfortunately, there was also no real progress in the investigation. The only development in the case was the discovery by a custodian of vandalism on the top of a desk that had been in the RCC library at the time of Cheri Jo's murder. Five months had passed, but the words, etched into the wood in blue pen, stood out for their disturbing message. It was a poem of sorts:

Sick of living/unwilling to die

cut.
clean.
if red/
clean.
blood spurting,
  dripping,
    spilling;
all over her new
dress.
oh well,
it was red
anyway.
life draining into an
uncertain death.
she won't
die.
this time
someone ll find her.
just wait till
next time.
  rh

The police could not conclusively link the strange writings to the murder, but they filed away a photocopy of the desktop along with the rest of the Bates materials.

I've often found that anniversaries are good opportunities to lay traps for offenders of unsolved crimes; these dates are important to them for a variety of reasons. The local paper, the *Riverside Press-Enterprise,* carried a story on the unsolved crime on April 30, 1967, the six-month anniversary of the murder.

Someone made contact the next day. This time there were three recipients: the police, the *Press-Enterprise,* and Joseph Bates. Each received a short, penciled message on a piece of loose-leaf paper that read simply, "BATES HAD TO DIE THERE WILL BE MORE." The notes were signed with what looked like the letter *Z* or the number 2. Since there was nothing to compare the handwriting to (the earlier letter had been typed), and no credibility-sealing details, police considered these notes a hoax generated by publicity from the newspaper article.

"Stranger crimes"—those with no known connection between the

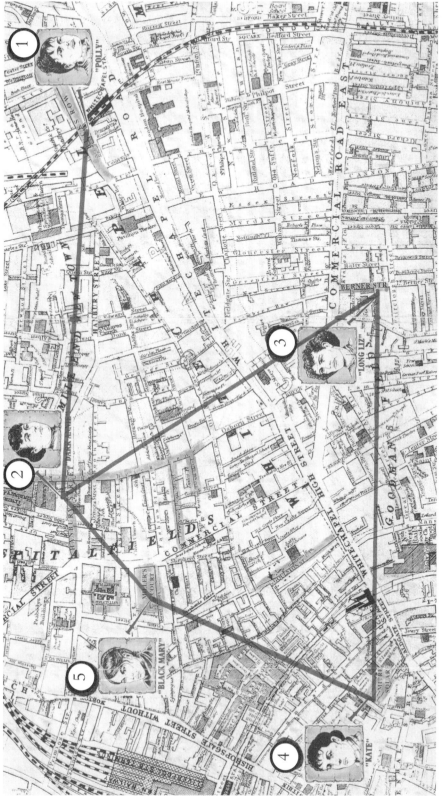

Whitechapel and London's East End, showing the location of each of the five murders commonly ascribed to Jack the Ripper. Note the lines we have added—drawn from one murder site to the next. Sites two through five form an approximate triangle, which represents the UNSUB's secondary comfort zone, as explained in "Crime and Crime Scene Analysis." Map detail copyright © NRSC, Ltd. Reproduced with their kind permission.

> 25. Sept. 1888.
>
> Dear Boss
>
> I keep on hearing the police have caught me. but they wont fix me just yet. I have laughed when they look so clever and talk about being on the right track. That joke about Leather apron gave me real fits. I am down on whores and I shant quit ripping them till I do get buckled. Grand work the last job was. I gave the lady no time to squeal. How can they catch me now. I love my work and want to start again. you will soon hear of me with my funny little games. I saved some of the proper red stuff in a ginger beer bottle over the last job to write with but it went thick like glue and I cant use it. Red ink is fit enough I hope ha. ha. The next job I do I shall clip the ladys ears off and send to the police officers just for jolly wouldnt you. Keep this letter back till I do a bit more work. then give it out straight My knife's so nice and sharp I want to get to work right away if I get a chance. Good luck.
>
> yours truly
>
> Jack the Ripper
>
> Dont mind me giving the trade name

The "Dear Boss" letter, sent to London's Central News Agency on September 27, 1888. This communication, written in red ink, is the first usage of the name "Jack the Ripper" in connection with the Whitechapel murders, and increased the high level of terror. Ironically we, and many experts, believe this letter and the "Saucy Jacky" postcard which followed to be fakes.

> From hell
>
> Mr Lusk
>
> Sor I send you half the Kidne I took from one women prasarved it for you tother piece I fried and ate it was very nise I may send you the bloody knif that took it out if you only wate a whil longer.
>
> Signed Catch me when you Can Mishter Lusk.

The "Lusk Letter," received by George Lusk, chairman of the Whitechapel Vigilance Committee on October 16, 1888, along with a small cardboard box containing part of a kidney, which may or may not have been human, and may or may not have come from the body of Ripper victim Catharine Eddowes. Addressed "From hell," this communication makes no mention of "Jack the Ripper" despite the earlier appearance of the "Dear Boss" letter. It is also far less literate and coherent. Though the authenticity cannot be proven one way or the other, we believe this communication to be genuine.

92 Second Street, Fall River, Massachusetts. Lizzie Borden lived here with her father, Andrew, her sister, Emma, and her stepmother, Abby. Despite Andrew's wealth and standing, the house was simple and unpretentious, boasting few modern conveniences. It was here that Andrew and Abby met their grisly deaths on the morning of August 4, 1892. Photo courtesy of Leonard Rebello, *Lizzie Borden: Past and Present* (1999).

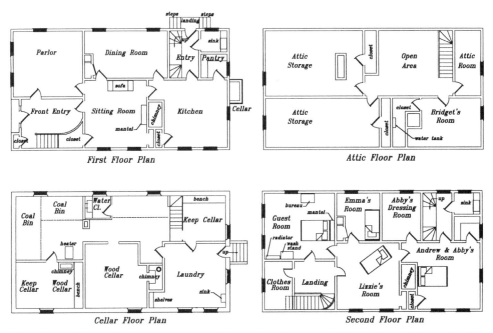

Floor plans of the Borden home at 92 Second Street, based on research by Borden scholar and author Leonard Rebello. It would have been difficult and risky for a stranger to enter the house in broad daylight, murder Abby, then, with Lizzie and the maid, Bridget, on or around the premises, hide out and wait another hour and a half for Andrew to come home and slay him, too, before escaping undetected. Photo courtesy of Leonard Rebello, *Lizzie Borden: Past and Present* (1999).

Aerial view of the Lindbergh home near Hopewell, New Jersey, taken shortly after the kidnapping. The house was secluded but well known. The nursery window is the last one on the second floor on the left side. AP/Wide World Photos.

The Lindbergh kidnapping ransom note, discovered by Charles Lindbergh in his son's nursery on the night of March 1, 1932. Note the interlocking circles and holes at the lower right. The signature would appear on a number of subsequent notes from the kidnapper or kidnappers.

Two views of the homemade ladder—which became the key piece of physical evidence in the Lindbergh kidnapping case—during a New Jersey State Police recreation of the crime. The ladder, with widely spaced rungs to save weight, was made up of two sections which folded together and a third which could be added on top for additional height. In both photos—one showing the full extension and the other the two sections that were used to gain access—the ladder is leaning against the side of the house with access to the nursery window. Photo courtesy of New Jersey State Police Museum.

A section of Zodiac cryptogram which, when deciphered, the killer claimed would reveal his identity. A different section was sent to each of three San Francisco area newspapers in August 1969, along with letters threatening retaliation if the papers did not publish the offender's work. *San Francisco Chronicle*

> Dear Editor
>   This is the Zodiac speaking I am back with you. Tell herb caen I am here, I have always been here. That city pig toschi is good · but I am ~~bu~~ smarter and better he will get tired then leave me alone. I am waiting for a good movie about me. who will play me. I am now in control of all things.
>   Yours truly :
>
>   ⊕— - guess
>
>   SFPD - O

This is considered the last verifiable Zodiac communication to the *San Francisco Chronicle,* received in April 1978. Note the characteristic elements: "This is the Zodiac speaking" opening; circle and crosshairs signature; police "scorecard." *San Francisco Chronicle*

Mr. Ramsey,

Listen carefully! We are a group of individuals that represent a small foreign faction. We do respect your bussiness but not the country that it serves. At this time we have your daughter in our posession. She is safe and unharmed and if you want her to see 1997, you must follow our instructions to the letter.

You will withdraw $118,000.00 from your account. $100,000 will be in $100 bills and the remaining $18,000 in $20 bills. Make sure that you bring an adequate size attache to the bank. When you get home you will put the money in a brown paper bag. I will call you between 8 and 10 am tomorrow to instruct you on delivery. The delivery will be exhausting so I advise you to be rested. If we monitor you getting the money early, we might call you early to arrange an earlier delivery of the

money and hence a earlier pick-up of your daughter.

Any deviation of my instructions will result in the immediate execution of your daughter. You will also be denied her remains for proper burial. The two gentlemen watching over your daughter do particularly like you so I advise you not to provoke them. Speaking to anyone about your situation, such as Police, F.B.I.,etc., will result in your daughter being beheaded. If we catch you talking to a stray dog, she dies. If you alert bank authorities, she dies. If the money is in any way marked or tampered with, she dies. You will be scanned for electronic devices and if any are found, she dies. You can try to deceive us but be warned that we are familiar with law enforcement countermeasures and tactics. You stand a 99% chance of killing your daughter if you try to out smart us. Follow our instructions

and you stand a 100% chance of getting her back. You and your family are under constant scrutiny as well as the authorities. Don't try to grow a brain John. You are not the only fat cat around so don't think that killing will be difficult. Don't underestimate us John. Use that good southern common sense of yours. It is up to you now John!

Victory!

S.B.T.C

The Ramsey ransom note, written on pages from Patricia Ramsey's pad, quickly became the most important and most confounding piece of physical evidence in the case.

The large Tudor style house at 755 15th Street in Boulder, Colorado's University Hill neighborhood, where six-year-old JonBenet Ramsey died sometime between the late evening of December 25 and the early morning of December 26, 1996. AP/Wide World Photos.

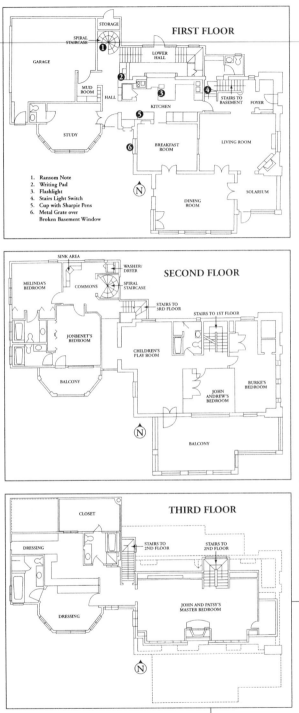

FIRST FLOOR

STORAGE
SPIRAL STAIRCASE ❶
GARAGE
LOWER HALL
MUD ROOM ❷
HALL
❸ KITCHEN
❹ STAIRS TO BASEMENT
FOYER
STUDY
❺
BREAKFAST ROOM ❻
LIVING ROOM
N
DINING ROOM
SOLARIUM

1. Ransom Note
2. Writing Pad
3. Flashlight
4. Stairs Light Switch
5. Cup with Sharpie Pens
6. Metal Grate over
   Broken Basement Window

SECOND FLOOR

SINK AREA
WASHER/DRYER
MELINDA'S BEDROOM
COMMONS
SPIRAL STAIRCASE
STAIRS TO 3RD FLOOR
STAIRS TO 1ST FLOOR
JONBENET'S BEDROOM
CHILDREN'S PLAY ROOM
BALCONY
BURKE'S BEDROOM
JOHN ANDREW'S BEDROOM
N
BALCONY

THIRD FLOOR

CLOSET
DRESSING
STAIRS TO 2ND FLOOR
STAIRS TO 2ND FLOOR
JOHN AND PATSY'S MASTER BEDROOM
DRESSING
N

Floor plans for the Ramsey house. The logistics of the crime made much more sense to me when I actually saw and understood the complexity of the physical layout of the house. Copyright © 1999 by KLS Communications, Inc. Reprinted with permission of HarperCollins Publishers, Inc.

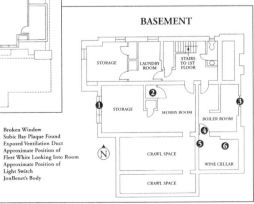

BASEMENT

STORAGE
LAUNDRY ROOM
STAIRS TO 1ST FLOOR
❶ STORAGE
❷
HOBBY ROOM
❸
BOILER ROOM
❹
❺ ❻
N
CRAWL SPACE
WINE CELLAR
CRAWL SPACE

1. Broken Window
2. Subic Bay Plaque Found
3. Exposed Ventilation Duct
4. Approximate Position of
   Fleet White Looking Into Room
5. Approximate Position of
   Light Switch
6. JonBenet's Body

victim and the offender—are the most difficult to solve, because unless there is a witness or the UNSUB leaves some evidence to link himself to his victim, forensic or behavioral, police have no reason to look in his direction.

It would be four years before this terrible crime was seen in the context of an even greater horror.

LOVERS' LANE

December 20, 1968, was a Friday, and teenagers David Arthur Faraday and Betty Lou Jensen had plans for a date that night. Faraday, seventeen years of age, was an excellent student and athlete at Vallejo High School in Vallejo, California, and an Eagle Scout. Because she lived on another side of town, Jensen attended a different school, Hogan High, where the pretty sixteen-year-old was also known as a good student. Although they apparently misled their parents about where they were going—her parents thought they were going to a concert at school and then to a party, but they skipped the concert altogether—they were known as good kids. Neither would be considered a high-risk victim.

David picked up Betty Lou in his mother's 1961 Rambler station wagon, and they left her parents' house around 8:30 P.M. The two first went to visit a friend until about 9:00, then to Mr. Ed's drive-in for a Coke before heading out to Lake Herman Road, known as a local lovers' lane. They parked off the road in a gravel strip just outside an entrance to the Lake Herman pumping station. It was an ideal place for young lovers to spend some time alone, but its isolation also proved dangerous.

Around 11:15, a woman who lived on Lake Herman Road a couple of miles from where the teens had parked came upon the site while going to pick up her son from a show. The passenger door of Faraday's car was open. David lay on his back in a pool of blood, his feet toward the rear wheel. Betty Lou Jensen was nearly thirty feet from the back of the car, apparently as far as she could run before someone shot her dead. The horrified woman drove off for help and flagged down a Benicia police car. Captain Daniel Pitta and Officer William T. Warner rushed to the scene. When they got there, Faraday was still breathing. They summoned an ambulance.

The Rambler's motor was warm, the ignition still on, presumably to keep the car's heater running. Although the front passenger door was open, the three other doors and tailgate were locked. This, plus the location of the bodies, seemed to indicate that the killer somehow herded his victims out the one door so they couldn't flee in different directions. A trail of blood led from the car to where Betty Lou had fallen, and more blood from her nose and mouth pooled around her body. She had been shot five times in her upper back. All the shots were on the right side in a close pattern, quite a feat of marksmanship given that the girl was running for her life in the darkness. David had been shot in the head at closer range, the bullet traveling forward from behind his left ear. Betty Lou was dead at the scene. David was rushed by ambulance to Vallejo General Hospital.

We've discussed in earlier chapters how investigations can get complicated, even, in some instances, compromised, when multiple jurisdictions are involved. In this case, the two Benicia officers were there first because the woman who'd found the crime scene had spotted them. The crime actually occurred, however, outside Benicia's jurisdiction. So when Captain Pitta called in the county coroner, he also got in touch with the Solano County's Sheriff's Office so they could send investigators out to the scene. Around midnight, representatives from both jurisdictions were present to investigate. They were joined by Detective Sergeant Les Lundblad of the sheriff's office. Ultimately, all the work Benicia police did on the case was handed over to the sheriff's office.

While Lundblad investigated the crime scene, he sent two of his officers to get a statement from the surviving victim, but when they got to the ICU, they learned David Faraday had been declared DOA at 12:05.

So what had happened?

A number of witnesses had seen David's car parked at what would later become the crime scene, including a couple who passed by twice between 10:15 and 10:30 P.M., and two hunters who noticed the Rambler just after 11:00. Although David apparently turned the car around after parking it, possibly to provide more privacy, there was nothing inherently suspicious about the scene.

But investigators uncovered one odd, possibly related incident in the area that night. Two other young people on a date had stopped on the side of the road to check their vehicle's engine. They reported being passed by a car, described tentatively as a blue Plymouth Valiant, which first slowed and then backed up toward them. Something about the situation spooked the couple, and they hurriedly drove off, only to be followed by the mysterious car until they exited to head toward Benicia. This occurred around 9:30 P.M. Several of the people who'd seen David's car also reported seeing a white, four-door Chevrolet Impala at the entrance to the pumping station around the same time. These vehicles could provide clues to what had happened or they could be red herrings. The only witnesses to the crime, other than the UNSUB, were dead.

There was also little in the way of physical evidence: no fingerprints, no tire tracks, no signs of a struggle. There were light shoe prints in front of the car, and one heel print nearby. The offender did expend ammunition in his rampage and investigators gathered that evidence: empty shell casings from a .22 were found in the car on the floorboard and outside, and several slugs were recovered from the car and the victims' bodies. The murder weapon was gauged to be a J.C. Higgins, model 80 automatic, or a High Standard model 101 semiautomatic, using a type of copper-coated Super-X bullet produced by Winchester since October 1967.

With no signs of robbery or sexual assault, police looked to victimology, hoping for a clue as to the UNSUB's motive. The Jensens told investigators that Betty Lou had been bothered by a boy whose romantic intentions she did not return. They said he even threatened David at one point. When the sheriff's office followed up on these leads, however, they found the boy had a solid alibi for the night of the murder. Betty Lou had also told her sister she thought someone was spying on her, and her mother found the side yard gate open a couple of times, but nothing was found to connect these incidents to the murders.

This type of crime is emotionally difficult to investigate. Nothing in the victimology indicated why these two young people had been killed and the motive was unclear.

"I WANT TO REPORT A DOUBLE MURDER"

Darlene Ferrin was a gregarious, sociable young lady, twenty-two, who lived in Vallejo with her husband, Dean, and their baby daughter, Dena. Shortly after the murders at the pumping station, she told one of her coworkers at Terry's Restaurant that she knew the victims—or at least knew of them—from having attended Hogan High School, located about a block from where Betty Lou Jensen lived. Darlene found their murders so frightening she said she wouldn't be going back to that area again.

About six months after the Jensen-Faraday murders, on the afternoon of the Fourth of July, Darlene called a friend, Mike Mageau, to see about getting together that evening. Then, leaving Dena at home with baby-sitters, Darlene stopped by the Italian restaurant where Dean worked (not the same one where Darlene was employed) to tell him that she and a younger sister, Christina, were heading off to a parade of boats at nearby Mare Island. Dean told her he'd invited some of his coworkers over for a party after work and asked her to pick up fireworks on her way home. She and Christina went to Terry's Restaurant to invite friends to the party before going to the parade. She also called Mike again. After the parade, they stopped by Dean's work. By now it was after 10:00 P.M. Darlene called to check on her daughter and was told someone at Terry's was trying to get in touch with her, so she went back to the restaurant. Then she drove Christina home and returned to her own house.

Originally, her plan was to take her baby-sitters home and then clean up her house for the party, but after a phone call she instead asked the sitters, two young girls, if they could stay while she went out to get fireworks. They agreed, and Darlene drove to Mike Mageau's house, where Mike was so anxious to see her that he ran out of the house without turning off the TV or lights, leaving the door open. As they left his house, they quickly realized they were being followed by another car, light in color. They tried to lose it and ended up on Columbus Parkway, a route that headed away from town. They turned into Blue Rock Springs Golf Course, not quite as isolated as the Lake Herman Road pumping station but also known as a lovers' lane. As Darlene pulled into the parking lot, her Chevy Corvair stalled out as the other vehicle pulled up. It parked nearby before speeding off, only to return minutes later. As Mike would later recall, the other car pulled into position behind them almost as a police car would, cutting them off and shining its lights into Darlene's car. The next thing he knew, he heard something against the car window, then saw a flash of light as he was shot. The bullets kept coming. Darlene fell onto the steering wheel, struck nine times altogether: two in each arm and five in the back, hitting a lung and her heart.

Mike tried to escape but was unable to find the door handle. As he struggled, he saw the shooter returning to his car. At one point the man turned and Mike got a good look at him: in his late twenties, he was stocky—maybe two hundred pounds, about five feet eight—with light brown hair, curly, cut in a crew cut. He wore a windbreaker, like those worn by people in the navy, and pleated pants, which didn't hide a slight paunch. As his attacker seemed to be leaving, Mike let out a cry of pain, and the man changed direction, going back to Darlene's car. He shot Mike twice more as his desperate victim jumped into the backseat. Then he shot twice more at Darlene, walked back to his car, and left.

Mike made his way out of Darlene's car by opening the door from the outside and falling out. He was bleeding from his face, neck, right arm, and left leg. One of the bullets had cut through his jawbone and tongue, so he couldn't even scream. Fortunately, three other young people were out that night looking for a friend of theirs. They drove into the parking lot and discovered Mageau, writhing on the ground. They raced off to summon help.

Just ten minutes after midnight, the call came in to the Vallejo police switchboard. The two officers first-on-scene were quickly followed by Detective Sergeant John Lynch and Sergeant Ed Rust. And the scene was horrible: Mike Mageau, bleeding profusely, was in a lot of pain, and Darlene was barely alive behind the wheel. Lynch laid Darlene out on the parking lot as they waited for an ambulance. She seemed to try to tell them something, but it was unintelligible. Lynch and Rust had actually heard a report of shots being fired. It had been called in by the son of the groundskeeper at the golf course, who heard the gunfire and the sound of a car leaving quickly. But it was the Fourth of July and the police figured it was fireworks. According to an interview Lynch gave Robert Graysmith, journalist and author of the comprehensive book *Zodiac,* he and his partner felt terrible later, wondering if had they responded more quickly would they have passed the suspect vehicle as it fled the scene. On top of that, when they arrived, they realized they knew one of the victims. Darlene knew a lot of the local police from the restaurant where she worked. She'd even dated them. And she and Dean lived next door to the Vallejo Sheriff's Office. She was pronounced DOA at 12:30 A.M. at Kaiser Foundation Hospital. Mike Mageau was critical and faced surgery to his jaw, arm, and leg, but would recover from his physical injuries.

At the crime scene, detectives found the Corvair's windows were open on both sides with the ignition on. The car was still in low gear, the radio on, and Darlene hadn't applied the parking brake. All of this was consistent with Mike Mageau's description of how the car had stalled; the subject had caught up to them before she had a chance to either properly park or get going again.

Inside the bloody car, along with Darlene's purse and Mike's wallet, investigators found spent nine-millimeter shell casings. Mageau's description of the events made no mention of the UNSUB stopping to reload, and at least nine shots had been fired, so the weapon was thought to be a Browning semiautomatic.

Comparisons between this and the shootings at Lake Herman Road just two miles away seemed inevitable. In both instances, the subject approached young couples as they sat in a car in an isolated location at night. Both times a gun was used. But in this case, according to the surviving witness, the subject actively and aggressively pursued the victim's car, almost herding it to the crime scene. And in this case, the victimology yielded clues that this was not a stranger crime and that perhaps more easily discernible motives applied.

As police looked into the victims' backgrounds, they discovered that Darlene Ferrin may not have been a random target. According to friends and associates, she liked to go out and was often in the company of men other than her husband—Mike Mageau, for example. But this seemed to irk Dean's friends and coworkers more than it bothered him. When they brought it up, he would defend his wife, reminding them she was still young and free-spirited. It was all innocent fun, he insisted, not as if she were having affairs. (This was also the California of 1969.) And he had an airtight alibi that night: he was with his coworkers.

But there were other men in Darlene's life to investigate, including her first husband, Jim, who'd owned a gun. Darlene was said to be afraid of him. But he didn't match the physical description of her killer, and police ruled him out as a suspect. Another man, described as a persistent, frustrated suitor, was ruled out when police found he was home with his wife when the murder occurred.

Witnesses say another man spied on Darlene at home from a white, American car parked in front of her house. One baby-sitter reported that when she had told Darlene about the man in the car, Darlene had said she'd seen him kill someone. Darlene's sister Pam also described a man in a white car who had delivered mysterious packages to the Ferrins' home, including a package he warned Pam not to open. She'd seen him several times and described him as dark-haired and well-dressed. Sometimes he wore horn-rimmed glasses.

Another sister, Linda, also saw this man at Darlene's house. He showed up at a party she threw to get the place painted. According to Linda, Darlene told her to steer clear of him. The baby-sitter and Darlene's sisters all reported Darlene seemed afraid of this man, who'd also been spotted watching her at work at Terry's. On the night she was killed, Darlene had a tense conversation in the parking lot of the restaurant with a man who drove a white car, as witnessed by her sister Christina.

Around the end of June, just before she was murdered, Darlene predicted to Christina that something big was going to happen. Darlene couldn't or wouldn't give her any details, but it would be big enough to get in the papers. People close to Darlene theorized that when she'd gone to the Virgin Islands with her first husband on their honeymoon, they might have fallen in with a rough crowd. Had she seen or heard about a murder there? Were drugs involved? But in the end, all of this speculation led no closer to the identity of her killer.

Mike Mageau was also an interesting character. He and Darlene had met at Terry's, when he was there with his twin brother, David. The nineteen-year-olds were said to have a competition going, vying desperately for Darlene's attentions, fighting over who would get to do favors for her. On the Fourth of July, Mike was wearing several layers of clothing, which stunned police until he explained to Detective Lynch that he was self-conscious about his slight build and wore more clothes to try to fill out his appearance. According to several people who talked to Robert Graysmith, Mageau also gave different versions of the events of that night depending on who asked the questions and when they asked. Variations included how the two ended up at Blue Rock Springs, whether they were randomly followed or whether they met up with someone who argued with Darlene first and were then followed to the parking lot, the physical description of the UNSUB and his vehicle, and so on. Darlene's sister Pam thought Mike believed Darlene knew their assailant and Mike was trying to protect her because he loved her. In any event, after he recovered, he moved away.

At 12:40 A.M. on July 5, a call came in to the Vallejo police switchboard. A man's voice told operator Nancy Slover that there had been a double murder. He gave such precise directions to the scene that it sounded to her as if he'd either rehearsed it or was reading from a script. He did not allow her to interrupt him with questions, and he continued speaking until he was done. For credibility, in addition to the exact description of where the crime scene was, he told her he'd shot his victims with a nine-millimeter Luger. Then he claimed credit for killing "those kids last year," said good-bye, and hung up.

I have no doubt that the caller was working from a script. This was a highly organized offender. He knew the call would be traced, and he had only a brief time to establish credibility and say his piece before getting off. If the police were able to develop a suspect shortly after this shooting, I would have advised them to include notes with directions or drafts of a full script on a scrap of paper in their search warrant, just as we often do in extortion or kidnapping cases.

It took seven minutes for Pacific Telephone to trace the call to a pay phone in front of a service station right near both the Vallejo Sheriff's Office and the home Darlene shared with her husband and daughter. A witness who'd been walking by the phone booth at the time had seen a man inside described as stocky, matching Mike Mageau's first description of the shooter. About an hour later, around 1:30 A.M., "crank" calls were received at Darlene's home, at Dean Ferrin's brother's house, and Dean's parents' house. In each instance, the caller said nothing, and the person answering just heard the sound of someone breathing.

The phone calls, and the location of the phone booth from which the killer reported his work, made it seem that the UNSUB knew at least one of his recent victims. For one thing, the calls were made before news of the shootings, much less the identities of the victims, had been made public. I know from experience that many offenders derive great satisfaction from calling in a report of their crime while looking into the home of their victim, waiting to see the effects of their work. But Darlene and Dean had only lived in the home by the sheriff's office for a few months before her murder; their old address was the one in the phone book. If this offender chose that pay phone so he could gloat over the experience, he'd need to know not only her name, but be familiar enough with her life to know that she'd recently moved.

Was it the mysterious man in the white car Darlene feared? Of course, it's also possible the UNSUB didn't know whom he'd shot and simply picked the pay phone by the Sheriff's Office to taunt authorities.

It makes sense that in looking for a suspect with a connection to these victims the emphasis would be on Darlene. In addition to the victimology, the crime scene itself tells us she was the focus of the offender's rage. She overwhelmingly bore the brunt of the attack, with many more—and more serious—gunshot wounds than her companion. In an attack of this nature, it would make more sense for the male, who normally represents the greater physical threat to the offender, to be the more seriously injured. Also, since the killer took his shots from Mageau's side of the car, one would expect Darlene to be more likely to survive the attack.

But assuming the UNSUB did not know his victim or victims, the focus of the attack on the female is still telling. We saw this in the Son of Sam crimes in New York when David Berkowitz intentionally went to the woman's side of the car with his .44 magnum. The male companions were only secondary considerations.

According to Mageau, the killer doubled back to fire more shots at both of his victims before he left. Given that Mageau was already wounded and vulnerable, we might have expected the shooter to make sure to finish him off this time, but instead he expended two of the four additional bullets at Ferrin, who he could see was already mortally wounded. The male victim was not only left alive, but was able to describe the UNSUB.

Less than a month after Darlene's murder, the self-proclaimed killer made contact once again, but this time to the press instead of the police, and this time by mail. The *San Francisco Chronicle, San Francisco Examiner,* and *Vallejo Times-Herald* all received nearly identical letters from an author claiming to be the serial killer. The letter to the *Chronicle* began:

Dear Editor
This is the murderer of the
2 teenagers last Christmass
at Lake Herman & the girl

on the 4th of July near
the golf course in Vallejo
To prove I killed them I
shall state some facts which
only I & the police know . . .

The letters went on to provide details for each of the two cases, including ammunition used and the position of the victims' bodies. Enclosed with each communication was a section of a long, complicated coded message—made up of neatly printed symbols—each newspaper had received one-third. According to the letters, when solved, the cryptogram would reveal the identity of the killer.

I don't imagine most in the law enforcement community actually believed the murderer was giving us his name. But I've always said that when a subject starts communicating with us, that's a good sign. Compare this with a case like UNABOM, where we also had few solid leads. You'd much rather get your behavioral clues from a letter than a murder scene.

When he makes contact, this is when you start to feel you can catch the guy. His arrogance and feelings of power lead him to reveal more of himself, giving us the means to help someone in the public recognize him (as in the case of the Unabomber, Theodore Kaczynski), and enlightening us as to his motives so we can design effective proactive techniques to flush him out. When you have a series of cases where traditional motives such as greed, anger, or revenge don't apply, the information you get from his communiqués is invaluable in elucidating his motives.

In this instance, the killer didn't stop in taking credit for his crimes and taunting police with his coded puzzle. It wasn't enough for police to know he was the real deal. He wanted every reader of all the local newspapers to know of and fear him.

I want you to print this cipher
on the front page of your
paper . . .
If you do not print this cipher
by the afternoon of Fry. 1st of
Aug 69, I will go on a kill ram-
Page Fry. night. I will cruse
around all weekend killing lone
people in the night then move
on to kill again, untill I end

up with a dozen people over
the weekend.

The papers, in cooperation with the police, published part of the letters without reproducing the entire text. As with other aspects of their investigations, authorities wanted some things held back so that there would still be details only the UNSUB would know. For him, knowledge of these would provide a means for him to establish credibility in later communications. And for law enforcement, ideally, it would set the stage for future identification and prosecution.

Ironically, while the cryptogram would not prove to contain the author's identity explicitly stated, it did provide valuable clues in ways likely unintended by the UNSUB. For one thing, when an UNSUB goes to the trouble of putting something like that together, you know you're not dealing with your average jerk murderer. Not only is this guy meticulous and obviously proud of proving his intellectual superiority to the police (to compensate for his general feelings of inadequacy), but he also enjoys these incredibly detail-oriented tasks. Think of how much time it would take just to painstakingly write out each of those cryptogram characters, all the while trying to mask your natural handwriting. One misguided stroke and you'd have to start over. It's almost the patience of a bomb-maker.

Then there are the symbols themselves. The average reader of a local newspaper would not be familiar with most of the characters in the cryptogram's text, which included meteorological and astrological symbols, Morse and navy semaphore code, and various Greek symbols. We're dealing with someone with exposure to, if not extensive training in, some highly specialized areas. Even if he was not well-versed in these areas, he'd need reference books with the symbols to copy. Although we'd expect this UNSUB to be a loner, family members or associates would know that along with that trait, he'd have this type of educational or work background.

Like the bomb-maker, this subject would view his letters and this code—like the murders—as his art. We would expect him to have a work area set aside where he would do his meticulous printing and keep his reference materials: books on codes, code-breaking, symbols, as well as media coverage of his crimes and communications. It's not as easy to notice as a locked garage or basement room that sometimes emits smoke or strange noises, but it's a sacred, organized work space about which this subject would be compulsively protective.

Let's try to relate these character traits specifically to one of the crimes.

Whether you assume that Darlene Ferrin knew her killer or not, her murder was not the act of an enraged boyfriend-wanna-be, or someone looking to cover his ass on an earlier crime. This UNSUB was on an intellectual campaign of terror, and his target was much greater than any single individual.

It seems fitting, then, that although the police enlisted assistance from experts including those at Naval Intelligence, the National Security Agency, the CIA, and the FBI, in the end it was a couple of newspaper-reading, concerned citizens who finally deciphered the killer's writings. The newspapers printed their sections of the code in different editions on different days, but by Sunday, August 3, all three parts were available to the public.

Donald Gene Harden, a forty-one-year-old high school history and economics teacher, and his wife, Bettye June, spent the next couple of days working to crack the code. All of the consulted experts agreed with their solution:

> I LIKE KILLING PEOPLE
> BECAUSE IT IS SO MUCH
> FUN IT IS MORE FUN THAN
> KILLING WILD GAME IN
> THE FORREST BECAUSE
> MAN IS THE MOST DANGEROUE
> ANAMAL OF ALL TO KILL
> SOMETHING GIVES ME THE
> MOST THRILLING EXPERENCE
> IT IS EVEN BETTER THAN GETTING
> YOUR ROCKS OFF WITH A GIRL
> THE BEST PART OF IT IS THAE
> WHEN I DIE I WILL BE REBORN
> IN PARADICE AND THEI HAVE
> KILLED WILL BECOME MY SLAVES
> I WILL NOT GIVE YOU MY NAME
> BECAUSE YOU WILL TRY TO SLOI
> DOWN OR ATOP MY COLLECTIOG OF
> SLAVES FOR AFTERLIFE
> EBEORIETEMETHHPITI

The solution only provided more proof of the author's cunning. For example, in their analysis of such messages, code breakers try to apply some basic rules. The letter *e* is typically the most commonly used. To cover his tracks, this cryptogram's designer used a total of seven symbols to stand for the letter *e*. As you can see from reading it, there were numerous misspellings, but it is not obvious which were true mistakes on the part of the author and which were planted.

In analyzing the message, much has been made of the reference to the author's rebirth in "paradice" and his use of his victims as slaves. I would argue that this is less telling as an indicator of our UNSUB's religious beliefs and more revealing in the context of other parts of the message, such as his reference to man as "the most dangeroue anamal of all," which sounds a lot like the title of the famous Richard Connell short story "The Most Dangerous Game." The story, which has been made into a movie several times, is about a wealthy madman who lives on his own island and lures passing sailors to dangerous reefs close to his shores with phony navigational lights. He rescues them from their shipwrecks, only to release and hunt them like wild animals in his compound.

Now, this doesn't mean that the serial killer is a literary genius or even particularly well-read, since the 1924 story has been required reading in many high schools, or the killer could have seen a movie rendition. But it does seem highly coincidental that he would use that turn of phrase, given the awkwardness of other parts of his message. I would suggest this shows a fair degree of education. I would also suggest that the author was being truthful when he said that killing was "even better than getting your rocks off with a girl," since I don't think he had much experience with that. As discussed earlier, men with successful, fulfilling relationships with women don't generally gun them down.

It is worth noting, too, that the UNSUB didn't go on a killing rampage the weekend the letters were received, despite the fact that the *San Francisco Examiner* missed the Friday publication deadline, publishing their section of the cryptogram on Sunday. This doesn't surprise me. The Unabomber threatened to blow up an airliner out of Los Angeles over a holiday weekend. He didn't actually do it, but reveled in the attention and fear it generated. Another thing that's better to this subject than getting his rocks off with a girl is watching the public, police, and media sit in fear, waiting for him to do something. Every girl unattainable to him knew of his threat; all the guys who got those girls heard about him on the news; law enforcement from all over the country worked all weekend trying to crack his code. That was exciting to him. That was real power.

Finally, there was the matter of the leftover letters at the end of the cryptogram. When the solution was published, the public rushed to interpret the last line as an anagram for the author's name. Police followed up as names emerged, but as you might imagine, were unable to find a suspect this way.

In the meantime, Vallejo chief of police Jack E. Stiltz went public expressing doubts that the letters and cryptogram were even from the real killer. Although they contained information that had not been released, someone who'd seen the crime scenes would have been able to write them. Stiltz publicly asked the UNSUB to send another letter with even more details that only the killer would know. His challenge worked, yielding not only a letter, but an identity of sorts: the elusive subject gave himself a name that would soon become synonymous with terror in the northern-California region—the Zodiac. Despite the allure and "sexiness" of this appellation, the UNSUB never really explained why or how he'd chosen it. One would expect some sort of mystical, astrological connection. In none of the subject's future communications was this convincing, although Robert Graysmith uncovered a "Zodiac alphabet" dating back to the thirteenth century. The twentieth-century Zodiac may have copied and/or modified some of the symbols in that alphabet to use in his coded message.

The three-page letter was sent to the *Vallejo Times-Herald* just days after Stiltz's request. It began:

> Dear Editor
> This is the Zodiac speaking.
> In answer to your asking for
> more details about the good
> times I have had in Vallejo,
> I shall be very happy to
> supply even more material.
> By the way, are the police
> haveing a good time with the
> code . . . ?

The whimsical, quasi-helpful tone of the opening of the letter underscores the UNSUB's delight in mocking the police. Many people likened the Zodiac's taunting letters to Jack the Ripper's "Dear Boss" communications, though as noted in chapter 1, I believe the Ripper notes to have been fakes. Still, we can't rule out the possibility that the UNSUB was taking his lead from the popular image of the Whitechapel killer. Remember, this guy alluded to a classic short story in his cryptogram; studying the Ripper murders would be even more right up his alley, so to speak. At any rate, he felt superior to the police and press just as the actual author of the "Dear Boss" letters wanted us to think of the East End murderer.

The Zodiac went on to provide explicit, moment-by-moment details of the murder of Darlene Ferrin and the attempted murder of Michael Mageau. Certainly, descriptions such as the following would prove to Chief Stiltz that the author and the killer were one and the same.

> On the 4th of July . . .
> The boy was originally sitting in
> the front seat when I began
> fireing. When I fired the first
> shot at his head, he leaped
> backwards at the same time
> thus spoiling my aim. He end-
> ed up on the back seat then
> the floor in back thrashing out
> very violent with his legs;
> that's how I shot him in the
> knee . . .

He even described the witness who saw him in the phone booth after the murders, "haveing some fun with the Vallejo cop," thus proving he was also the one who placed at least that call. The Zodiac also included an extensive section on the Jensen/Faraday murders.

> Last Christmass
> In that epasode the police were
> wondering as to how I could
> shoot & hit my victims in the
> dark. They did not openly state this,
> but implied this by saying it was a
> well lit night & I could see
> silowets on the horizon.
> Bullshit that area is srounded
> by high hills & trees. What
> I did was tape a small pencel flash
> light to the barrel of my gun. . . .
> When taped to a gun barrel, the
> bullet will strike exactly in the
> center of the black dot in the light.
> All I had to do was spray them . . .

With this, the subject provided proof not only that he was on the scene the night Jensen and Faraday were killed, but that he actively followed his own press. You can see why I say the way facts are presented has an impact on the offender. In this case, the Zodiac had obviously been peeved for months by how the police made it seem that striking his targets that night was easier than it had been. This perception would fuel his general frustration at being misunderstood, that his skills were underappreciated, and his sense of inferiority. He had to make sure the planning, thought, and marksmanship that went into the crime would be fully appreciated. Thus, so many months later, he felt the need to include this information in a letter sent to answer questions about the more recent murders. Again, this speaks to the subject's self-conscious compulsiveness. It also tells us that in conversations with others, he may have been complaining about the police and press coverage of the earlier killings. In the days after the Christmastime murders, I can imagine him grousing to a crony—another loner, less intelligent than he and one of his few confidants—that the police didn't know what they were talking about. Look how dark it was that night, for example.

LAKE BERRYESSA

Saturday, September 27, 1969, was a sunny, warm day—a day to be spent out of doors. And if you knew where to hunt, it was a perfect day for a killer to find new targets. Thirty-five miles north of Vallejo, Lake Berryessa Park was just such a location, with woods and secluded beaches around a man-made lake more than twenty-five miles long.

Cecelia Ann Shepard, twenty-two, was spending time with a friend of hers from Pacific Union College, twenty-year-old Bryan Hartnell, before she went off to continue her studies in music at the University of California, Riverside. After a morning of worship and packing, they spent the afternoon seeing friends and running errands around the Napa Valley wine country before stopping by the park in late afternoon. It was just after 4 P.M. when they walked out onto a peninsula on the western side of the lake and put down a blanket. Every so often, a boat would pass by, but for the most part they were completely alone.

At some point, Cecelia noticed a man approaching them. Because of the topography and foliage, he would disappear from view behind a slope in the hill or a tree, only to reappear much closer. When he was finally in front of them, the couple realized he had a gun. He had also put on a bizarre, elaborate costume, with a hooded mask and a symbol sewn onto his chest. The mask resembled a paper grocery bag in shape, flat on top, with the corners standing out. It was black, with slits cut for eyes and mouth. Over the eye holes, the mysterious man wore clip-on sunglasses. The mask draped down over his chest and back, with the symbol sewn onto it: a circle with a cross, like the crosshairs of a gun sight. The hood was worn over a dark-colored windbreaker, and this, in turn, over a rusty-black shirt. His sleeves were tight around his wrists and he wore black gloves. Under the costume, he had on baggy pleated pants, tucked into boots. He wore a belt with a wooden holder for a long knife. The knife resembled a bayonet and had a wooden handle with brass rivets, wrapped up in surgical tape.

One of his victims would later describe the man as five feet ten to six two, 225–250 pounds, stocky in build. At one point, a glimpse into the space behind his sunglasses revealed brown hair and a glimmer, suggesting he might have worn glasses under the hood. When he spoke, he sounded in his twenties.

He demanded the couple's money and car keys, explaining that he wanted the car to drive to Mexico. When Bryan handed over his money and keys to his VW Karmann Ghia, the man holstered his gun. He explained that he'd escaped from prison in Deer Lodge, Montana, where he'd killed a prison guard. He said he had no money and was driving a stolen car and warned Bryan not to try to be a hero.

For his part, the prelaw student was trying to keep the man calm, offering to help him any way he could. But the man pulled out some clothesline and ordered Cecelia to tie up Bryan. As she did, she pulled his wallet out of his pocket and tossed it to the man. He seemed to ignore this gesture and bound her when she'd finished with Bryan. Then he double-checked her work, retying Bryan's knots when he decided they were too loose. He announced he was going to stab them, and Bryan requested he be the first victim, arguing he couldn't bear to see the man stab Cecelia. The assailant complied, stabbing him repeatedly in the back. He then turned his attention to the girl, who'd been screaming at him to stop. As she squirmed to get away, he stabbed her over and over, hitting her in the back, chest, abdomen, and groin. When he was done, the attacker left the money and keys on the blanket and simply walked off.

His victims were still alive, and although Cecelia was mortally wounded, stabbed twenty-four times and her aorta slashed, the two were able to untie each other's bindings. But they'd lost so much blood neither was in any shape to go for help. A fisherman and his son passing by rushed to contact park rangers from Rancho Monticello Resort two miles from the scene. Ranger Dennis Land responded by patrol car, finding

Bryan several hundred yards from the scene, as far as he could crawl. Ranger Sergeant William White covered the distance by boat. There was no ambulance at Lake Berryessa and the nearest medical help was nearly an hour away in Napa at Queen of the Valley Hospital. Although both survived the long, painful wait, Cecelia eventually succumbed to her injuries and died in the hospital the next afternoon. Bryan was placed under constant guard.

At around 7:40 P.M., a little more than an hour after the attack, as the couple were still awaiting the ambulance, a call came in to the Napa County Police Department. The officer on duty listened as the male caller reported a double murder at the park, giving a description of the victims' car and their location. The caller sounded young, maybe early twenties. In a quiet voice, he ended the call by announcing he was the killer. When he finished talking, he simply left the phone off the hook, and the officer could hear sounds of traffic, people talking in the background. The call was traced to a pay phone at a car wash less than five miles from the police station, twenty-seven miles from the crime scene. Did the caller drive that far because he liked the feeling of being close to the police without them realizing who he was? Was it on his way home? Or both? Based on the timing of the phone call and that the caller said the victims were dead, police figured he must have left Lake Berryessa immediately after the attack. A palm print was pulled off the phone receiver, but there was nothing to compare it to.

A lone man was reported hanging around the lake that day. Three female students from Pacific Union College told police that a man in a car described as a light blue or silver Chevy, California tags, seemed to be watching them that afternoon. When they parked, he parked next to them and just sat in his car, smoking cigarettes. This was shortly before 3 P.M. About 4:00, they were sunbathing at the lake when they spotted the same guy looking at them. They described him as tall—six feet or more, 200–230 pounds, midtwenties to midthirties, with straight dark hair worn with a side part. They thought he looked clean-cut, wearing a black sweatshirt with short sleeves and dark blue slacks, although he had a T-shirt hanging out of his pants in the back. The girls worked with a police sketch artist to develop a composite. Police released the drawing, but Napa Sheriff's Captain Don Townsend stressed that this was not necessarily a sketch of the suspect, but of someone police would like to interview.

A man matching the girls' description was also seen by a dentist out with his son. He estimated the man to be about five ten, stocky, wearing a dark, long-sleeved shirt with some red, and dark pants. When the man realized he'd been spotted, he left, and when the dentist and his son returned to their car, they could tell from tire tracks that a car had been parked right behind theirs.

Near Bryan's car investigators found tire tracks and made plaster cases in hopes they'd soon have a suspect vehicle for comparison. They measured the distance between the tires and noted that the front of the car seemed to have tires that were not only worn, but of two different sizes. Footprints led to the crime scene and back and to the door of the Karmann Ghia. The shoe size was 10½, and based on how deep the prints went into the sand (compared to prints left by a police officer), the subject was estimated to weigh at least 220 pounds. And he was a cool customer—the heels of the man's prints were clearly defined, which told police he wasn't running but walking away as he left his victims to die. The prints also had an identifying mark, which investigators were able to trace to the manufacturer. They were from a Wing Walker, a type of boot produced under government contract and distributed on the West Coast to navy and air force installations.

This was but one indication that law enforcement was looking for a subject with a military background. He was obviously familiar with weapons, was an excellent shot, was not afraid to kill up close and personal with a knife, and had at least been exposed to symbols used by the military and had possibly been trained in codes. He had been described as clean-cut, with short hair. And certainly northern California had no lack of military installations.

I would have advised police to look into medical discharges, or discharges with no reason given, because the subject probably couldn't cut it in such a structured, disciplined environment long-term. He would be highly intelligent and skillful, but would have trouble with authority and resent the intrusions of others.

The UNSUB had also given another clue to his identity by his reference to Deer Lodge, Montana. There is—and was—a prison there, and while the story of his breakout and murder of a guard proved false, connections to that place should not have been ruled out. For one thing, you don't just pull a location like Deer Lodge, Montana, out of a hat. I spent some time as a student at Montana State in Bozeman, and I didn't recognize the name, so I can assure you that most people outside of Big Sky country wouldn't have heard of the place.

This guy fully expected both Cecelia and Bryan would end up dead. In fact, when he misspoke in his call to police to report the crime as a murder, he corrected himself to clarify it was actually a *double* murder. If both victims were to die, there'd be no risk in mentioning a place that held some significance to him. I think this information can be used to law enforcement's advantage.

Here's a scenario: Cooperate with an investigative reporter writing about the cases locally in Deer Lodge. With the facts of the murders, release general profile information on the suspect, indicating that police in California have reason to believe the killer has links to the area without leaking why they believe this. Along with the elements garnered from witnesses—white male, midtwenties to early thirties, etc.—the profile would include the following behavioral traits: suspect is a loner, paranoid, nocturnal, and intelligent. He has an extreme interest in weapons and may have left the area for military reasons, if, for example, he was to be stationed in California, and he may have had a medical discharge from the military since then. He may also have communicated with someone in Deer Lodge in a position of authority in a scornful way (as a precursor to his taunting letters to police and the press in California).

A little later, we'll get into a more detailed discussion of proactive techniques I'd try in this case, but I have to stress now that this is the type of investigation where that approach is most helpful. The offender is communicating with the police and the newspapers, so you know he's following his press. This makes him vulnerable because he can't help but react to what is said (and printed) about him. Look how quickly he responded to Chief Stiltz, for example. On the other side of the coin, he's a white-male, paranoid loner who likes guns and isn't real successful with women. A lot of social misfits out there meet that general description. In this case, then, profiling is only going to be so helpful in narrowing the field of suspects. You have to flush this guy out, do something to make him come forward. I think in large part this is why the Zodiac was never apprehended. In the late sixties and early seventies, he was a modern serial killer being pursued by old-fashioned, tried-and-true investigative techniques. He slaughtered people who were either unknown to him or could not be traced back to him. His motives were nontraditional and undecipherable. He evolved, using different MOs and different weapons at each crime scene. He moved from one jurisdiction to another, manipulating public and press everywhere he went.

Like the Jensen-Faraday case, the Berryessa attacks occurred on a site with overlapping jurisdictions. So while park rangers rushed to the scene and stayed with the victims, the Napa County Sheriff's Office spearheaded the investigation. Detective Sergeant Kenneth Narlow arrived to find someone had already "cleaned up" the crime scene, packing away for him the couple's blanket and the clothesline used to tie them. We've made the case in other chapters, too, that the more people you have working a crime scene, the more confusing it is for the people who end up with ultimate responsibility for the case.

One aspect of the scene, however, was completely undisturbed, although highly disturbing to Narlow. Before he'd left, the UNSUB left a message on the door of Bryan Hartnell's car in black marker:

Vallejo
12-20-68
7-4-69
Sept 27-69-6:30
by knife

The first two dates marked the murders of Jensen/Faraday and Ferrin. Above the words appeared the crossed-circle symbol the Zodiac used as his signature in the letters mailed to the press in early August. This UNSUB wanted to make sure the police realized they were dealing with a serial killer.

At first glance, it might seem obvious that these attacks were related. After all, we're dealing with a subject who targets young couples in remote areas at night or evening and for whom typical motives such as robbery or sexual assault do not apply. But there are critical differences between this case and the others, and I don't mean just the bizarre, apparently homemade costume. Without his hint, given the change in jurisdiction and location, investigators might not have immediately linked this case to the ones in Vallejo. In a sense, the subject was almost giving police a break by telling them to look for one offender.

Back at Quantico, my unit saw many cases of linkage blindness. That is, a serial offender would change and perfect his MO, move to other jurisdictions, or escalate in violence as a typical progression, so police would think several criminals were at work when it was really all done by the same one. Here's an example: A rapist-murderer starts out assaulting and strangling a prostitute, leaving her body in the alley where the crime took place. He realizes afterward that next time it'll be less risky if he transports his victim to another location where he won't face the danger of someone walking in on him. So he picks up his next victim and takes her out to a remote site and leaves her body there. And since he has more time with her, he doesn't have to rape and kill her as quickly, so maybe this time he'll torture her a little. With practice, this same guy could be picking up lonely, vulnerable women in bars, holding them for a few days of torture before killing them, and disposing of their bodies in places where they might never be found. Without behavioral or forensic clues to link the crimes, especially if they're committed in different jurisdictions so investigators in one place never hear about the others, police might never make the connection. And my example isn't such a stretch. I testified as an expert witness to help secure the conviction of serial murderer George Russell Jr., where the linkage was based on the signature element of posing.

Now let's consider the differences between the Lake Berryessa attack and the previous ones in Vallejo. First, there's a big difference between shooting at people in a car and stabbing them. In the first case, you get away clean. You're watching it unfold before you, but you're not really coming in contact with your victims. And at Lake Berryessa, we're talking about spending time talking to the victims, hearing their voices, developing something of a rapport with them. Then, after the subject gets what he is ostensibly after—the victims freely complied with his demands for their money and car keys, remember—he brutally attacks anyway. With each thrust of his knife, he was getting more and more of their blood on him, hearing them screaming and moaning in pain. Remember, too, that he had a gun with him, meaning he didn't have to use his knife. If it was fear or control he was after, he could have used the knife and his words effectively for that, resorting to the gun when it came time to finish them off. He chose to use the knife. And since it was dusk, rather than midnight, he got a good look at the horrible scene before him.

This brings us to the next point: the earlier timing and location of the attack indicates the subject's willingness to take greater risks. It was midafternoon when the three college students and the dentist and his son spotted the suspicious man. The self-styled killing uniform Bryan Hartnell described was good for hiding the killer's face and hair, but would only have attracted attention if he had tried to wear it the whole time he was in the park. Although no one was likely to stumble upon the scene as the killer stabbed Bryan and Cecelia, it was possible. And although a knife makes no noise compared to a gunshot, the victims' screams could certainly attract attention. If someone had seen them from a boat, the UNSUB had no way to keep them from reporting the attack. The best he'd be able to do would be to beat a hasty retreat, possibly leaving several witnesses able to give police a description. He furthered his risks by spending so much time talking to the victims; and murder by stabbing takes longer than a couple of quick gunshots.

There was also the disturbing trend of the shortening time between the murders. Seven months had passed between the Jensen/Faraday murders and the assault on Darlene Ferrin and Michael Mageau. The Lake Berryessa attack came less than three months later. In all aspects, then, this crime clearly represented a progression from the other murders. Successful offenders such as this don't just stop committing crimes, and as they continue, they only get bolder and, typically, more violent and deadly. One could only expect the Zodiac to continue on this course.

TAXI DRIVER

It was 9:30 P.M., October 11, when cabdriver Paul Lee Stine picked up a fare on Geary Street in San Francisco. Stine was actually already answering a call from a fare on Ninth Avenue, but was stuck in the crush of people milling about the theater district on a foggy Saturday night. When the lone man approached his cab for a ride, he requested a location that was on the way to the Ninth Avenue call, so Stine picked him up. He wrote the destination, Washington and Maple, in his log and headed west toward the residential area near the Presidio.

Although Stine's trip sheet said Washington and Maple, the cab eventually stopped one block farther at Washington and Cherry. At this location, instead of paying his fare and exiting the cab, the rider shot Paul Stine in the right side of his face at close range. He then moved into the front seat and took the cabbie's wallet. He also ripped off part of Stine's shirt. He left Stine's Timex watch, checkbook, a ring, and a little over $4 in change in the cabdriver's pocket. When he was done, he got out of the cab and wiped down sections of the driver's door and the left rear passenger door. He then leaned against the divider between the front and back windows of the car as he opened the driver's door and wiped off the dashboard before he closed the door and walked off into the night.

What he didn't know was that virtually the entire event had been witnessed by a fourteen-year-old girl at a party just across the street. She was looking out a second-story window about fifty feet from the cab. When she realized what she was seeing, she summoned her two brothers to the window. By the time the stocky, white man was wiping down the cab, a crowd of people were gathered around, with a clear view out the window. They didn't stop watching until he'd disappeared from their view, turning the corner. He simply walked from the scene.

While this was unfolding, people at the party called the police. At 9:58 P.M., the operator taking details of the crime in progress somehow ended up describing the suspect as a black man. So when the dispatcher put out the all points bulletin, units on the street were given the proper direction the suspect was headed, but an incorrect physical description.

What happened next has been subject to different interpretations. By several accounts—including the Zodiac's, given in a later letter—the first officers responding to the call in a patrol car got to the intersection of Cherry Street and Jackson within minutes and saw a stocky white man walking in the direction of the Presidio. Had there been more light, they might have seen blood on his dark clothing. And had they known the UNSUB was white, this story might have gone in any of a number of different directions. But since they were looking for a black man, they just asked him if he'd seen anything suspicious. He reported seeing a man with a gun running along Washington Street, heading east. So off they went. The patrolmen realized about a week later that they'd likely seen the killer and worked with an artist to develop a composite sketch. When Robert Graysmith researched this miscommunication, he found their report had been filed away as confidential, and the official statement from the San Francisco police was that none of their officers had ever seen the suspect. But that position does not explain the existence of the composite sketch, which was actually the second one prepared, since a police artist drew one the morning after the murder with input from the witnesses at the party.

This near miss could have afforded a great opportunity, unrecognized at the time, to get the Zodiac to come forward. A statement could have been released stating that the police were seeking assistance from the community following this heinous crime. The announcement would make it clear that several people other than the suspect had been seen in the area at the time and were now being identified. Police would like to speak to anyone who was there to see if they'd seen anything. If it worked, the subject would come forward with a story that would legitimately place him in the area and cover his butt in case anyone else had seen him.

When they arrived, police found Paul Stine slumped over onto the passenger side of the front seat, with his head on the floor of the cab. There was much blood, and although the keys were missing, the meter, eerily, was still running. The officers summoned an ambulance and also put out word that the suspect in question was actually a white male. In addition to the first two officers who responded, Inspector Walter Kracke, a homicide detective on his way home, heard the call and got quickly to the crime scene. His experience would prove valuable as he helped the other officers secure the scene. By the time homicide inspectors Dave Toschi and partner Bill Armstrong, the team on duty that night, got there, the ambulance had already arrived and Stine been declared dead. Kracke had notified the coroner and requested all available canine units and a spotlight vehicle from the fire department to assist in the search.

While investigators worked the scene, the search fanned out using dogs, patrolmen on foot, and military police from the nearby base. The Presidio was just a couple of blocks from where the murder took place, and neighbors told police they'd seen a person matching the general description of the UNSUB rushing across a nearby playground and into the wooded base. For the next few hours, it must have seemed almost daylight as floodlights and flashlights illuminated the area. The search was called off at 2 A.M., about four hours after Stine was declared dead from a gunshot wound to the brain. A badly damaged, copper-covered bullet from a nine-millimeter was recovered at autopsy. The killer had fired only the one shot from his semiautomatic pistol. It was an uncommon type—under 150 were sold in the entire Bay Area over the previous three years. Damage to the skin of Stine's right cheek indicated the gun had been held right up to his head. Defense wounds were on the cabdriver's left hand.

Looking at the victimology, Paul Stine, twenty-nine, was married and working toward a doctorate in English from San Francisco State College. To pay for school, in addition to driving the cab at night he worked as an insurance salesman. At five feet nine and 180 pounds, he wasn't a small man. In his personal life, with his interests, nothing would have labeled him a possible victim of violent crime, except that cabdrivers are high-risk victims by profession. Their job calls for them to pick up strangers and take them wherever they want to go at all hours of the day and night. Because they carry cash, they are frequent targets of robberies . . . and worse. Not even two weeks before Stine's murder, another driver from his cab company was robbed, and just over a month earlier Stine himself had been held up by two gunmen.

Indeed, at first this looked like a botched robbery committed by a criminally unsophisticated subject. The offender would have fled with blood all over him, and he left valuables behind. When police reconstructed Stine's earlier fares, they estimated the most the killer could have walked away with was about $25. On top of that, he left evidence: on the side of the car where the UNSUB rested his right hand to balance as he reached in to wipe off the dash, he'd left two fingerprints in blood.

And then there were the witnesses. The kids at the party described Paul Stine's killer as white, in his midtwenties to thirty years of age, with reddish blond hair cut short, like a crew cut. He wore glasses and dark-colored pants and a parka. He was stocky, maybe five foot eight. The description and the composite sketch were circulated among cab companies throughout San Francisco, warning of the killer's MO.

Almost as quickly as the police bulletin made its rounds, a development in the case proved Stine's murder was more than the standard cab robbery gone bad. In October, the *San Francisco Chronicle* received a letter on which the return address was simply a symbol: a circle with extended cross-hairs. It began as another had before it: "This is the Zodiac speaking . . ."

The author claimed credit for Stine's murder and offered graphic evidence as proof, actually enclosing a piece of the victim's bloody shirt. Then he referenced "the people in the north bay area," taking credit for them as well. The lab confirmed that the swatch was from the cabdriver's shirt, and when Toschi and Armstrong met with Detective Sergeant Narlow in Napa, he thought the handwriting matched their guy's, a finding later confirmed by Sherwood Morrill, head of California's questioned documents department in Sacramento.

The police were getting no credit for their hard work from the Zodiac, however. In this latest letter, he mocked their efforts to find him following Stine's murder.

> The S.F. Police could have caught
> me last night if they had
> searched the park properly
> instead of holding road races
> with their motorcicles seeing who
> could make the most noise. The
> car drivers should have just
> parked their cars & sat there
> quietly waiting for me to come
> out of cover . . .

His message seemed to have an effect. San Francisco's Chief of Inspectors Marty Lee put up a brave face before the press, saying that if the Zodiac had really been just outside police grasp that night, he would have mentioned the dogs and the floodlights used in the search. I suggest that if the killer had been the man the patrolmen spoke to, that would explain the level of scorn here. He almost got caught and he got scared, but he couldn't admit that to law enforcement or himself. So he had to get cocky. We expect an offender like this to overcompensate for his feelings of inferiority by putting down those he actually secretly envies. He got lucky, but he had to perceive that he had outsmarted the police.

Another way for this type to prove his superiority is to once again find a way to get more control, more power. This one accomplished that by closing his letter with a terrifying threat:

217

School children make nice targets, I think I shall wipe out
a school bus some morning. Just
shoot out the front tire & then
pick off the kiddies as they come
bouncing out.

In cooperation with SFPD, the *Chronicle* did not release news of this threat for several days, after having released other portions of the letter and the composite sketch. This resulted only in a slight delay of the ensuing panic. Throughout San Francisco, Napa, and surrounding jurisdictions, steps were taken to protect schoolchildren: extra drivers were assigned to buses to watch for trouble and to take over in case a driver was shot; in some cases, armed police guards were on the buses. Pickup trucks from the forestry department and ranger stations at Lake Berryessa were put into service. Airplanes even monitored bus routes from the sky.

You have to be careful with a threat like this. Obviously, this guy is capable of killing people and you have to take precautions. But I find the actual threat more designed to, once again, put the fear of God in the community and manipulate public emotions. If the Lake Berryessa and San Francisco attacks were high risk, you really couldn't get much riskier than shooting at a bus full of kids in broad daylight. From the offender's point of view, this would be almost a suicide mission. But all the police activity generated by this threat becomes the ideal face-saving scenario: he would have carried out his threat, but the heat was just too great.

Some attempts were made to proactively reach the Zodiac via the media. California attorney general Thomas Lynch issued a formal statement in which he assured the killer he would receive help and his legal rights would be fully protected if he turned himself in. Lynch tried to appeal to the Zodiac's vanity, saying that as an "intelligent individual" the killer realized he would eventually be caught and would recognize surrender as the best course. The *Examiner* also tried, but neither approach brought the killer to the police.

In another approach, Dr. D. C. B. Marsh, who headed the American Cryptogram Association, issued a challenge to the killer. Using the Zodiac's own code, Marsh composed a message providing a phone number for the Zodiac to call when he had a coded message that did actually contain his identity. Dr. Marsh's challenge, published in the *San Francisco Examiner,* went unanswered. Despite this, I would still consider it a great idea and the type of technique I advise, as it was tailored to the personality of the UNSUB.

Less than two weeks after the Stine murder, a major meeting was convened at the San Francisco Hall of Justice. Investigators from Vallejo, Napa, Benicia, Solano, San Mateo, and Marin met with representatives of the FBI, the state Bureau of Criminal Identification and Investigation, Naval Intelligence, the California Highway Patrol, U.S. Postal Inspectors, anyone who had a hand in the case. The seminar covered each crime known to be linked thus far and a comparison of all the evidence available.

If I'd been involved, along with interjurisdictional cooperation, I would have been stressing the need to be proactive. Ironically, one approach I counsel police to try in cases like this was initiated . . . but by the offender.

I can imagine the Zodiac in late October 1969, seeing that the news programs and papers were devoting less and less coverage to the school bus threat, wondering how in the hell to top that. While I would not necessarily have been able to predict exactly what shape it would take, I would have been able to tell you that the UNSUB was going to need to do something to get himself back in the limelight. He was probably still reeling from his close call after he killed Stine (although he wouldn't have admitted it), so he wasn't ready for another murder. And since he hadn't carried out his last written threat, he probably sensed that anything he put in another letter would have muted impact. What he needed was a publicity stunt.

Now, one technique I used to recommend was to identify someone in the public eye as a sympathetic character. We know most subjects follow their own press, so depending on the dynamics of the case and the type of offender, I'd advise police to establish someone the offender would feel comfortable contacting in some way. So, for example, at the same time that a local law enforcement bigwig was branding the UNSUB a crazed maniac, you could offer newspaper reporters access to a leading psychiatrist whose message would be 180 degrees in opposition: "This man isn't crazy. In fact, he's highly intelligent, which is why the police haven't caught him. But he is misunderstood . . ." You could photograph the shrink at his office, conveniently mentioning where the office is located and making sure the number and address are in the book. Then you sit back and hope the UNSUB makes contact with the one person he sees as capable of understanding his message, of serving as his voice to correct misperceptions.

What the Zodiac did was bypass the setup. At 2 A.M., a call came in to the Oakland Police Department, across the Bay from San Francisco. The caller identified himself as the Zodiac and requested a phone conversation with high-profile criminal attorney F. Lee Bailey or, if he was unavailable, famed local attorney Melvin Belli. The caller said he wanted one of these two to appear on a local morning talk show. I find the

Zodiac's choices interesting. F. Lee Bailey had a reputation as a master of acquittal, after successfully defending all but three of the more than one hundred killers he had represented, and Belli had made headlines by defending infamous characters such as Jack Ruby and Mickey Cohen. As the years since then have proved, both attorneys had a flair for attracting media attention. And clearly this was what the Zodiac sought.

As it turned out, first-choice Bailey couldn't make it, but Belli appeared that morning on Channel 7, next to host Jim Dunbar. They began the show one half hour earlier than normal. As they anxiously waited and viewers watched, the first of many calls came in a little after 7 A.M. The caller kept hanging up and calling back, identifying himself as "Sam" and giving Belli and Dunbar details of his headaches and loneliness. A dozen of the thirty-five phone calls were actually broadcast, and a meeting was arranged. Belli led a parade of police and media to the appointed spot at 10:30 that morning. You can probably guess the rest: "Sam" never showed. Later phone calls to Belli from this caller were eventually traced to a mental patient at Napa State Hospital. The police officer who had answered the phone when the call first came in to the Oakland PD thought the caller to the TV show sounded different from the one he had talked to. But it really didn't matter who called Belli that morning as far as the Zodiac was concerned. He'd gotten his press, live. He'd succeeded in manipulating everyone in the viewing area, had a whole region on the edge of its seat, and had a famous personality at his beck and call with just a few hours' notice. On top of that, precautions were still being taken to make sure he didn't take out a school bus. And police were no closer to identifying him.

He still had to keep his hand in, though. In early November he sent two communications to the *San Francisco Chronicle,* consisting of a greeting card ("This is the Zodiac speaking"), another cryptogram, a seven-page letter, and a hand-drawn diagram of a bomb designed to destroy a school bus. To establish credibility, another swatch of Paul Stine's bloody shirt was enclosed in one envelope, although by now the Zodiac's handwriting—along with his odd habit of using more postage than required—were recognizable. The extra postage was simply practical; he could just pop the envelopes into a mailbox somewhere without having to come in contact with a human who could later identify him, and he knew for sure his mail would be delivered. We would later see the Unabomber employ this same technique.

Although much attention was paid to the drawing and references to the Zodiac's bomb, I think other aspects of these communications, particularly the seven-page letter, are more significant. Consider the following:

> . . . I have grown
> rather angry with the police
> for their telling lies about me.
> So I shall change the way the
> collecting of slaves. I shall
> no longer announce to anyone.
> when I comitt my murders,
> they shall look like routine
> robberies, killings of anger, +
> a few fake accidents, etc. . . .

In numerous subsequent writings, the Zodiac would make reference to his new and improved body count. And after each of these, police would reevaluate unsolved murders in their jurisdictions, looking for potentially linked cases. In the early 1980s, some thought that the Zodiac and the Trailside Killer were one and the same. The conviction of David Carpenter in 1988 for those murders disproved this theory, as he was serving time for other crimes when several of the Zodiac killings occurred. Depending on whom you ask, though, today there are upwards of fifty possible victims of the Zodiac. In a sense, it's the opposite of linkage blindness, and we run into it with every large-scale unsolved serial case. To this day, people are still adding to the tally attributed to Seattle's Green River Killer, even though the first of those serial murders occurred in January of 1982.

Indeed, one of the reasons the Zodiac's crimes continue to haunt us is that he captured the imagination of psychopaths as well as law-abiding citizens, making him a favorite for copycat criminals not only in the Bay Area but even years later in New York City and Tokyo. For reasons too complex to get into here, police knew fairly quickly these cases were not the work of the Zodiac.

What the Zodiac had effectively done was create the illusion he was still active whether he truly was killing people or not. As long as he wrote to claim credit, the lore surrounding him would continue. He blamed the police and their lies for putting him in the position of having to keep his specific crimes secret, thus creating a face-saving scenario for himself. If he never kills again, people will still wonder. And if he does, he protects himself by not providing details that might lead police to his identity. Indeed, after this, he sent no more pieces of future victims' shirts, and no more detailed descriptions of crimes such as in the Jensen/Faraday and Ferrin/Mageau attacks.

One of the greatest mysteries of the Zodiac murders is why he stopped. Where did he go? We've discussed in chapter 1 how serial killers don't just move down south and retire. Since the Zodiac kept writing for years after Stine's murder, we know he wasn't dead or, presumably, incarcerated. Perhaps he got sick or suffered some physical degeneration that made it impossible for him to carry out more crimes, but I think he just plain got scared. You run into a couple of policemen minutes after you've killed a man and you're covered in blood, the adrenaline still pumping, that's not something you get over too quickly.

He'd shown in his crimes, communications, and ability to evade identification and capture that he was a sharp guy. He saw the writing on the wall. Offenders like this don't go down easy. To lose the high of being the lead story on the news for years, on and off, of having so many people fear you, to surrender all power and control and go to prison, that's when I advise a round-the-clock suicide watch, just as I did with the Unabomber, Theodore Kaczynski.

At the same time, I think the Zodiac resented being in what he considered a position of weakness. He couldn't admit the fear; that would have made him feel even more inadequate than he already was. So instead, he lashed out in page after page. And he didn't only sound angry, he had to overcompensate by providing lots of details that showed his superior intelligence.

> The police shall never catch me,
> because I have been too clever
> for them.
> 1 I look like the description
> passed out only when I do
> my thing, the rest of the time
> I look entirle different . . .
> 2 As of yet I have left no
> fingerprints behind me contrary
> to what the police say
> . . . I wear trans-
> parent finger tip guards. All it
> is is 2 coats of airplane cement
> coated on my finger tips—quite
> unnoticible & very effective . . .
> . . . If you
> wonder why I was wipeing the
> cab down I was leaving fake clews
> for the police to run all over town

with . . .
. . . I enjoy needling
the blue pigs. Hey blue pig I
was in the park—you were useing
fire trucks to mask the sound
of your cruzeing prowl cars . . .

p.s. 2 cops pulled a goof abot 3
min after I left the cab. I was
walking down the hill to the
park when this cop car pulled up
& one of them called me over
& asked if I saw any one
acting supicisous . . .
. . . & I said
yes there was this man who
was running by waveing a gun
& the cops peeled rubber &
went around the corner as
I directed them & I dissap
eared into the park . . .

Hey pig doesnt it rile you up
to have your noze rubed in your
booboos?

As the Son of Sam, David Berkowitz also wrote long letters to the
police, and by the end, we could see his degeneration pretty clearly, too.

In December, the Zodiac sent another letter, with another piece of Paul
Stine's shirt, this time to Melvin Belli. The message came in a Christmas
card, and its tone was strikingly different from that of the last diatribe. He
began by wishing Melvin a "happy Christmass," then moved on to ask for
help and expressed some insecurity.

Dear Melvin
This is the Zodiac speaking I
wish you a happy Christmass.
The one thing I ask of you is
this, please help me. I cannot
reach out for help because of
this thing in me wont let me . . .

The Zodiac warned that without help he might take his "nineth + possibly tenth victom," implying there had been more murders since Paul Stine's, although the killer provided no details. Then he stressed "Please help me I am drownding" and "Please help me I can not remain in control for much longer."

Now, Belli put a positive spin on this letter, publicly stating that he saw it as indicating that the Zodiac, realizing he would soon be caught, was getting ready to turn himself in and wanted the attorney to help him avoid the gas chamber. Belli even said someone claiming to be the Zodiac had called his home when he wasn't there and had had such a good conversation with the housekeeper that he expected to come home one day and find the two of them having a chat.

Years later, a vastly different interpretation was offered by my late esteemed colleague and valued friend Dr. Murray Miron. It was Murray's opinion that in this letter the Zodiac revealed his depression. Murray felt that waves of depression would pass over the subject, and that it was "not entirely unlikely that in one of these virulent depressions, such individuals could commit suicide." I would agree that the Zodiac might eventually commit suicide, but I also believe that, even in a depressed state, the Zodiac wrote letters with the goal of manipulating, dominating, and controlling their recipients and the larger audience he knew they would reach. So while this UNSUB likely did feel more alone and alienated from society around Christmastime, I believe this letter was a play for sympathy—one emotion the Zodiac hadn't yet tried to get from the public. To confirm this, I would note that despite Belli's assurances that he would protect the Zodiac from the gas chamber and do all he could to help him, the killer never contacted him again.

As I suggested earlier, one problem you confront when doing an analysis of this type of offender is there are so many potential Zodiac cases out there. Because we're dealing with a subject who at least predominantly killed strangers, who changed jurisdictions, who used different murder weapons and different MOs with different crimes, you can spend a lot of time getting hung up on cases that may not even be part of the picture. At the same time, you don't want to be guilty of linkage blindness.

LINKAGE BLINDNESS

I've culled through a lot of unsolved crimes that may have been related to the Zodiac's series, and so far in this chapter I've limited our discussion to cases for which the killer claimed responsibility and offered some details or material evidence to substantiate his claim. We will now look at a case that illustrates how difficult it can be to rule an unsolved crime in or out of this series.

Kathleen Johns, twenty-three years of age and seven months pregnant, had about four hundred miles to cover as she left her home in San Bernardino, California, headed for Petaluma. It was Sunday, March 22, 1970, and Johns was taking her ten-month-old daughter to visit her grandmother (Kathleen's mother), who was sick. Because of the length of the trip and the age of her baby, she planned to make most of the drive at night. She left in the late afternoon.

Around midnight on Highway 132, Johns noticed a car behind her, blinking its lights and honking its horn at her. The driver pulled up alongside her car and yelled that one of her back tires was loose. They pulled over and a clean-shaven, neat young man around thirty offered to tighten things up for her. She thanked him and stayed in the car while he ostensibly went back to fix it. When he was done and she tried to drive off, the tire fell off altogether. The young man returned to the side of the road and offered this time to take her to a nearby service station, which she could see up ahead of them. She and her baby got into his car as the man went to turn off her headlights and retrieve her car keys for her.

His kind acts stopped there, however, as he drove right by the gas station. They drove around for hours, with the man repeating to Johns that he would kill her and her baby. Finally, when he made a turn, she jumped out with her daughter and hid in a ditch. He tried to pursue her, but luckily for her, a truck happened on the scene and stopped, scaring the abductor off.

What makes many people think that Kathleen Johns and her children narrowly escaped becoming Zodiac victims is that her description of her abductor so closely resembles those of earlier cases. While she was being driven around, she put all her concentration into noticing details. She told police her abductor was a bit shorter than her five feet nine and weighed around 170 pounds. He wore thick-rimmed glasses held in place with an elastic band around his head. He wore well-polished black shoes, black bell-bottoms, a white shirt, and a dark nylon jacket. The shoes, coupled with his crew-cut brown hair, gave her the idea he was in the military.

Then, while giving her statement to police, she looked up and happened to see the composite sketch of the Zodiac circulated after Paul Stine's murder. She identified her abductor as the man in the drawing. The crime also took place on a weekend, like the others, and in a different jurisdiction, both aspects of Zodiac crimes. It is consistent with the overall presentation of the Zodiac as an organized offender, particularly since Kathleen Johns's car was later found moved from where it had been left and completely burned out, so as to eliminate any evidence that might have been left behind. It is also consistent with criminal progression and escalation that the Zodiac might want to experiment with spending more time with his victim. And he had announced his intention to kill Bryan Hartnell and Cecelia Shepard after conversing with them for a while. This is a perfect example of a crime that may or may not be linked to the Zodiac.

In late April of 1970, the Zodiac pulled out all the literary stops, sending a letter to the editor of the *San Francisco Chronicle* that included a teaser ("my name is" followed by thirteen symbols or characters), news that he'd killed ten people at that point (though the police couldn't identify any after Stine), an explanation of why he had not utilized his bus bomb (it had been damaged by recent rains), a schematic of a new bomb, and to top it all off, a dig at the police—the letter was signed with the crossed-circle symbol and the number ten alongside the initials SFPD and the number zero, written as a score.

As though to stress his importance and accomplishments far above those of law enforcement, he sent another communication just over a week later. In a humorous greeting card, he threatened again to bomb a school bus unless the police released details from his last letter and bomb diagram. He also suggested people start wearing "nice Zodiac buton . . . like . . . black power, melvin eats blubber, etc. . . . it would cheer me up considerbly if I saw a lot of people wearing my buton."

We've seen this shift in moods before. The Zodiac obviously wrote his latest missive when he was in one of his buoyant emotional periods. It no doubt fueled his needed sense of self-importance when the chief of police in San Francisco went before the press to inform the public of the Zodiac's latest bomb threat. But the diagram was not printed in the newspaper, and no one started wearing Zodiac buttons.

The summer of 1970 was a frustrating one for the Zodiac, if his letters are any indication of his emotional state. He wrote prolifically, sending three letters to the *Chronicle* in just a month. And one of these letters was the longest, and arguably the most creative, he'd sent thus far. At the end of June he mailed a brief letter expressing his anger at "the people of San Fran Bay Area. They have *not* complied with my wishes for them to wear some nice [Zodiac symbol] buttons." He noted that although he'd warned he'd retaliate for noncompliance by "anilating a full School Buss," school was out for summer vacation "so I punished them in an another way. I shot a man sitting in a parked car with a .38."

He drew another score, this time giving himself twelve [victims], SFPD still zero. With the letter, he included a Phillips 66 road map of the area around Mt. Diablo across the Bay from San Francisco, and a two-line cryptogram, which he asserted should be used in tandem to identify where he'd planted a bomb. The letter said authorities had until the fall to "dig it up."

As for his claim that he'd killed a man, while a police officer had been killed with a .38, there was a suspect in that case, and investigators found no evidence to suggest another Zodiac murder.

The next letter began, "This is the Zodiac speaking I am rather unhappy because you people will not wear some nice [Zodiac symbol] buttons." He then brings up:

> . . . the woeman & her baby that I
> gave a rather interesting ride
> for a coupple howers one
> evening a few months back that
> ended in my burning her
> car . . .

Since Kathleen Johns's abduction received only scant local press at the time, many interpreted this reference as proof that her abductor was, in fact, the Zodiac.

Just two days later, the next letter was received. It continued the tone of anger and frustration in the other two and upped the total of Zodiac victims to thirteen. It obviously greatly disturbed him that no one was wearing Zodiac buttons, and he wanted to let people know they would pay for this slight.

> I shall (on top of every
> thing else) torture all 13
> of my slaves that I have
> wateing for me in Paradice.
> Some I shall tie over ant hills
> and watch them scream & twich
> and squirm. Others shall have
> pine splinters driven under their
> nails & then burned . . .

And so on. The Zodiac then really revved up his creative talents, quoting from Gilbert and Sullivan's *The Mikado* and rewriting the lyrics.

As some day it may hapen
that a victom must be found.
I've got a little list. I've
got a little list, of society
offenders who might well be
underground who would never
be missed who would never be
missed. There is the pest-
ulentual nucences who whrite
for autographs, all people who
have flabby hands and irritat-
ing laughs . . .

It went on and on with examples of people he'd like to see done away with, quite incoherent in spots. But it's revealing of the Zodiac's nature. Line after line cited examples of people who "none of them be missed" when it was actually he who would not be missed. But this is a cross-section of society, a petty, detailed list of all the kinds of people whom he perceived as having scorned him. Most of us register a slight, deal with it or brush it off, and move on. But not the Zodiac. In his mind he was ever cataloging how society had wronged him. This letter was his opportunity to give some of that back. At the same time, he hoped he was impressing us with his talent.

Of course, his verse doesn't scan properly, his spelling is miserable, and the sections that do make sense are not even clever. At least the over-all metaphor works on some level, as the aria he embellishes is sung by the Lord High Executioner, which is doubtless a position he'd have liked to hold officially.

One more point needs to be made about this letter. A postscript reads, "PS. The Mt. Diablo Code concerns Radians & # inches along the radi-ans." Without getting too technical here (not that I could on this sub-ject), a radian is a mathematical term representing an angle of measure. One school of interpretation views the Zodiac crime scenes in relation to each other in time and space through mathematical analysis. As an exam-ple, the theory holds that Paul Stine's murder occurred one block farther than he'd written on his log sheet because the killer needed him to be at a precise point on the map. That's why the Zodiac switched his victim choice from couples to a cabdriver. Whom else could he get to a precise set of map coordinates so easily?

Of course, one could argue that the killer's new base of operations was

San Francisco and he needed a murder site that would afford him an easy getaway, so, being familiar with the Presidio and its environs, he figured that was the way to go. However you choose to look at it, the radian reference holds some meaning in that it is not something most citizens are aware of and it, along with the Gilbert and Sullivan rip-off, shows an offender who comes off as both well-educated and illiterate—a fascinating combination—which may help account for his occasional lapses into disorganization at the crime scenes (having the presence of mind to wipe off Paul Stine's cab, yet leaving fingerprints anyway, for example).

His exposure is wider than his expertise is deep, if you will. This is likely why one avenue of investigation pursued by Toschi and Armstrong in San Francisco came up empty. They investigated players with The Lamplighters, the city's Gilbert and Sullivan company. Interestingly, a run of *The Mikado* opened at Presentation Theatre one week after Paul Stine was shot, just a dozen or so blocks from the murder site. I would suggest that while this guy was reasonably sharp, he did not have the personality of a performer. You'd be looking for someone behind the scenes, someone with technical expertise. But this interest would stand out to the few who knew him well, since it would seem in direct contrast with his knack for such things as numbers and codes.

A LETTER TO THE PRESS

That fall there was a development that completely shook up the investigation. First, the Zodiac sent a Halloween card and a personal threat that proclaimed, "YOU ARE DOOMED!" to Paul Avery, the lead investigative reporter on the case at the *Chronicle*. Avery began carrying a gun, and he and fellow reporters started wearing buttons reading "I Am Not Paul Avery." The card got a lot of press from the *Chronicle* and elsewhere, and Avery received a bunch of tips, including one from southern California.

One letter (not from the Zodiac) encouraged Avery to check into whether the Zodiac had committed his first crime in Riverside, California. It was the unsolved murder of a young girl around Halloween. The anonymous tipster claimed he'd brought the possible connection to police but had been brushed off.

If you've been reading closely, you're probably returning to the murder of Cheri Jo Bates, the first case presented in this chapter. Recall the detailed letter, which, in retrospect, seems so similar to the Zodiac's painstaking descriptions of the Jensen/Faraday and Ferrin/Mageau crimes.

Remember how the letters to Joseph Bates, the police, and the press were signed with the letter *Z*. And I didn't even mention that the envelopes all contained extra postage, just like later Zodiac letters.

I've always said that in evaluating a series of crimes, you need to focus on the first one because that will show you where the inexperienced offender is comfortable. That crime is close to where he lives or works, and his behavior in the commission of that crime is most natural and revealing because he hasn't yet perfected his techniques.

What would the Bates UNSUB have learned from that crime? First, that a petite woman can still be hard to control. The next few blitz-style gun attacks eliminated that problem. Then, he really didn't get the credit he likely felt he deserved for such a crafty crime. After he'd gone to all the trouble to set the trap and kill his victim, and then got away with it, nobody paid attention to the letters he sent directly to police, the victim's father, and the press at the six-month anniversary of the crime. So he learned that if he wanted credit in the future, he had to supply the details, or tangible evidence.

But if Bates was "his," and this killer liked attention so much, why wouldn't he go for it once his credibility as the Zodiac had been established? For one, given his inferiority/superiority complex and his love/hate relationship with the police, I think he got off on what he saw as the ultimate "I know something you don't know." He must have relished every time he read the other murders referred to as the Zodiac's first. Also, if it truly was his first murder, it's possible he'd spent time around Bates and the library before. I'm not saying he necessarily knew her, but he'd seen her, because she and he had the same base of operations. He may have been afraid to let the investigation get too close to home, fearing that, if nothing else, someone might draw a connection with the dates of each change in venue. I believe the Bates killing is at least one more in the series, if not the first Zodiac crime. And this belief is backed up by the findings of experts such as California Bureau of Criminal Identification and Investigation handwriting expert Sherwood Morrill, who has connected the writings in the "BATES HAD TO DIE" messages and on the desktop with the later work of the Zodiac.

I also think it's more than a coincidence that after this link was made, communication with the killer dropped off. He sent a letter to the *Los Angeles Times* in March of 1971, the first time he'd ever contacted that publication. In it he boasted again that the "Blue Meannies" would never catch him and observed that "the longer they fiddle + fart around, the more slaves I will collect for my after life."

He did acknowledge the Bates murder as one of his doing, but scorned police, saying, "They are only finding the easy ones, there are a hell of a lot more down there." And this time, his score was seventeen-plus, while the SFPD stagnated at zero. Just about a week later, "Paul Averly" received a postcard featuring an advertisement for a condominium development in Lake Tahoe, the crossed-circle Zodiac symbol, and choice phrases cut out of newspapers. There was no obvious message, so investigators tried to interpret the meaning of the card, looking into unsolved crimes there to see if this was a veiled reference to another murder. Nothing could conclusively be linked to the Zodiac.

"THE BEST SATERICAL COMIDY"

And nothing was heard from the killer for nearly three years. Then, at the end of January 1974, another letter came in to the *San Francisco Chronicle*. In familiar handwriting, the letter read, "I saw + think "The Exorcist" was the best saterical comidy that I have ever seen," followed up with more misspelled references to *The Mikado*. By now, he'd raised his victim count to thirty-seven.

The next two letters came in to the *Chronicle* in May and July of that year. The May letter was full of anger, criticizing the paper for running ads for the movie *Badlands,* based on the Charles Starkweather–Caril Ann Fugate murder spree of the 1950s, which the Zodiac apparently found too violent for his refined tastes. The July letter was similarly critical of the newspaper's content, this time singling out a specific columnist. The man was spooked enough to leave the paper for a time.

Then, after a gap of nearly four years, the last verified Zodiac letter was received in April of 1978. It read simply:

Dear Editor
This is the Zodiac speaking I
am back with you. Tell herb caen
I am here, I have always been here.
That city pig toschi is good but
I am [crossed out letters] smarter and better he
will get tired then leave me
alone. I am waiting for a good
movie about me. Who will play
me. I am now in control of all
things.
Yours truly:

Where the signature would have appeared, there was yet another score: Zodiac—guess, SFPD zero.

I think the gaps of years between letters is significant. I wonder if our guy was in jail on some minor charge, frustrated but at the same time gloating that the criminal justice system had no idea whom they were holding. It's also possible that his silences coincided with trips out of the area, new military assignments if he'd been able to stay in, perhaps, or an illness. I also think it's significant that consciously or not, in this last letter he touches on all the major themes and motives operative in his life. He affirms his existence ("I am here") and his worth/superiority ("I am . . . smarter and better"). He reveals his desire to be left alone and his conflicting need for recognition ("I am waiting for a good movie about me"). Finally, he makes the ultimate claim of this type of offender: "I am now in control of all things." For a man with no murders left to claim, no real reason for continuing the dialogue, it reads like a suicide note.

It may well have been.

EPILOGUE

After all these years, it is safe to say that the Zodiac is not likely to resurface and continue his reign of terror in the San Francisco Bay area. But I am still asked if there was anything we could have done differently to get him.

By 1980, I'd been at Quantico a few years and had some research under my belt when I learned the FBI wanted to take another look at the body of Zodiac literature. I remember getting a file of letters to look at, and I had several conversations with Murray Miron over the finer points of our analytical approaches. Before we could get too deeply involved, however, the letters were pulled. I never did find out what prompted the renewed interest at the Bureau, or what caused our involvement to be canceled. And as usual, I was up to my ass in alligators already, so I didn't spend much time considering the matter.

I do believe that if we saw a case like this today, we'd have some success employing proactive techniques like those mentioned throughout this chapter. With this type of offender, a profile is much less important than the proactive techniques, and these should be designed to play off the subject's interests and weaknesses.

In the case of the Zodiac, some hot buttons might be his need to taunt and express superiority over police, his need to seek credit for his crimes, and his overwhelming need to establish credibility.

I would suggest that this last point would be one of his greatest weaknesses, because it is unusual for this type of subject to seek credit for his crimes. Guys like this are paranoid; they don't want all that attention. It strengthens the case for Cheri Jo Bates's murder to be a focal point for the investigation. He didn't want the recognition, then he did. There's something there.

What he would have in common with other killers is that he's always out looking for victims, as evidenced by all the reports of the suspect vehicle driving around the Lake Herman Road crime scene, and the witnesses who reported the strange man lurking around Lake Berryessa all afternoon on the day Cecelia Shepard and Bryan Hartnell were attacked. Like other subjects, the Zodiac could be influenced by his own press. Remember how quickly he responded to the challenge to provide details on the Ferrin/Mageau attacks? I think the Zodiac could be lured out to grave sites or memorial services on the anniversaries of the murders.

With the Zodiac, the signature element to his crimes is his taunting of the police. The murders themselves are merely symbolic of his superiority, designed to quash his overwhelming feelings of inferiority and inadequacy. Any technique that gave him the perception he was matching wits with the police would be a potentially good idea. So, for example, you could go back to the location of the first known case (Bates, Riverside) and announce a community meeting where the police would give a status update on the case presented by the lead investigator. To puff him up, you'd announce that the mayor and/or other community bigwigs would attend. The meeting should be held in a public arena such as a local school, but the site should be one people have to drive to. You want to videotape the audience, looking for the guy with the big smile on his face. You note license plate numbers for every car in the parking lot, knowing his is probably there. And you announce that you're looking for community involvement. Anyone interested in volunteering to assist us please sign up and register before you leave tonight. You could even skew the list of respondents to target your subject without making it too obvious. Say volunteers must be over eighteen, must have their own car, and must be familiar with the area. Knowledge of simple police procedure is helpful but not necessary. If five hundred people sign up, at least you have a working list. You eliminate all the women and go from there.

There was one idea that I think was good, although it wasn't designed to get enough, or the right kind of, information. When the movie *Zodiac* ran at the Golden Gate Theater in San Francisco, audience members were invited to fill in a slip with their guess as to why the Zodiac killer committed his crimes. A motorcycle was offered for the best entry. This would appeal to the killer's desire to be strong and macho and it offered opportunity for him to show how much he knows, or at least to get in another veiled jab at the police. And as we know from his later letters, the Zodiac followed popular movies and yearned to see one about himself.

So who was the Zodiac? Or a better and more meaningful question might be, what kind of personality is, or was, he?

A man once described by San Francisco homicide detective Dave Toschi as "a very, very good suspect," and who has been the subject of intense investigation by Robert Graysmith in his research, certainly fits the description I would put together: highly intelligent, IQ estimated around 135; spent much of his adult life living with his mother, with whom he had a difficult relationship at best; educated in chemistry and trained in codes; a hunter who once described man as the "most dangerous game" to a friend. And he could be placed in the different jurisdictions at the time each of the Zodiac crimes occurred. He had been a student at Riverside College, lived near other crime scenes, and received a speeding ticket near Lake Berryessa the very evening of the attacks there. He was also once observed by his sister-in-law to be holding a piece of paper upon which were written strange symbols. The day of the attack at Lake Berryessa, he was observed to have a bloody knife in his car, which he explained as having been used to kill chickens. And during one of the gaps in communication from the Zodiac, this man had been in prison serving time on a child molestation charge, although he told others he'd been arrested because he was the Zodiac. Despite these and many more circumstantially incriminating facts, the police had no direct evidence on which to arrest and formally charge him in connection with any of the Zodiac crimes. This suspect died of a heart attack in 1992 at age fifty-eight.

There are others, but my thought is that any good suspect in this case shares the qualities listed above, which is why I have not provided that man's name. None of them is likely to be brought to trial now. The important consideration here is to move forward in our understanding so that we can be as proactive with this type of offender as he is with us.

CHAPTER FIVE

American Dreams/ American Nightmares

There will always be cases that haunt us, the victims' stories so compelling, the nature of the crimes so heinous, that they will never be forgotten. But we hope that as advances are made in the forensic and behavioral sciences, fewer and fewer cases will have the power to haunt strictly because they have gone unsolved or had questionable outcomes. In the previous chapter, we saw how the traditional, tried-and-true investigative approaches that worked in the "old days" were not enough to solve a series of murders committed by a modern serial criminal. The Zodiac thwarted investigators in large measure because his motive was not recognizable among the classical motives of greed, jealousy, anger, revenge, and the like—something clear or, at least, identifiable that determined victim selection, MO, and ultimately, the course of the investigation.

Now we'll explore three cases that are particularly illustrative of how an offender's motive—or apparent lack thereof—can be instrumental in understanding a crime and directing an investigation. And to further make the point, we'll begin with a case from well before the days of criminal profiling or behavioral analysis: the murder of "the Black Dahlia."

"THE BLACK DAHLIA"

Elizabeth Short had big dreams, and her story is one of a young woman's quest to break out of the mold expected universally of her sex at the time, swapping the promise of husband and family for career and fame and the glamour of Hollywood. Ironically, her brutal death won her the fame she longed for, as her tragic and pathetic existence was transformed by the press into the romantic image of a beautiful starlet-to-be.

And as Stuart Swezey wrote in his publisher's preface to John Gilmore's study of the case, *Severed,* "The Black Dahlia murder—unlike such earlier headline-grabbing cases as the St. Valentine's Day Massacre and the Lindbergh kidnapping—was the first case to command the attention of postwar America with its stark carnality."

Around 10 A.M. on January 15, 1947, Betty Bersinger was out for a walk with her three-year-old daughter when she saw what she thought was a broken department-store mannequin lying in an overgrown vacant lot on Thirty-ninth Street near Norton Avenue in the Leimert Park section of Los Angeles, south of Hollywood. When she got closer, she realized it was the nude and dismembered body of a woman.

Although several witnesses had seen various cars in the vicinity, passersby had seen no body as late as 8:30.

Officers Frank Perkins and Will Fitzgerald responded to the police call. From what they could tell, the dead woman had been sexually posed, lying on her back with her arms raised over her shoulders, elbows bent, legs spread wide apart. The lower torso was angled upward at the hips, leading police to believe she had been in a semirecumbent position at the time of death. After death, she had been cut in half at the waist, and the severed sections had been placed in line, about ten inches apart. The liver was exposed. Her face and breasts had been badly slashed, including deep slashes from both sides of her mouth as though her killer were fashioning a grotesque extension of her smile. Ligature marks were visible on her ankles, wrists, and neck, and police surmised that she had been suspended by her ankles and tortured. A vertical incision that looked like a hysterectomy scar was between her pubic area and navel. Her pubic hair had been shaved or plucked.

The scene was soon thick with reporters, photographers, and onlookers. The body was taken to the LA County Morgue for fingerprinting. With the help of the *Los Angeles Examiner*'s facilities, the prints were sent to the FBI. They were identified as belonging to Elizabeth Short, twenty-two years of age, who had been printed when she'd held a government job at a military post exchange. She had also been arrested as a juvenile delinquent while out with men at a bar one night near Camp Cooke in Santa Barbara.

Autopsy findings suggested that the victim's body had initially been placed facedown in dew-wet grass, then turned over, and that she had been dead at least ten hours prior to disposal. There was some evidence though that she might have been refrigerated to aid preservation during that time. The cause of death was listed as "hemorrhage and shock due to concussion of the brain and lacerations of the face," but because of evidence of bleeding out through a severed artery in the abdomen, she might actually have been cut in half before death. No evidence of semen was in or on her body, but examination of her stomach revealed that she had been forced to swallow feces as part of her torture. The body and hair had been carefully washed after death.

As for victimology, Elizabeth Short had been born in Hyde Park, Massachusetts, on July 29, 1924, the third of five daughters of Cleo and Phoebe Short, moving at an early age to Medford, near Boston. Cleo abandoned the family when Elizabeth was young, faking suicide and leaving Phoebe on her own. When Cleo contacted Phoebe years later from California to seek reconciliation, she refused.

Young Elizabeth was often ill with asthma and tuberculosis and had to undergo serious lung surgery, so Phoebe sent her to Miami, Florida, in 1940 when she was sixteen. This allowed her to drop out of school and wait on tables. She stayed in Florida until she moved to California.

She was called Betty by her family and friends but changed that to Beth as a young adult. At five feet five and 115 pounds, with blue eyes and dark hair, she was described as a sweet, romantic, vulnerable girl who wanted to marry a handsome serviceman, preferably a pilot. Some people thought she resembled the actress Deanna Durbin, who was a role model for teenaged girls and often appeared dressed in black. Beth began to dress that way to create an image for herself.

In early 1943, while working at Camp Cooke, she had become involved with "a jealous marine," of whom she continued to be afraid. She repeated this story often and it became part of her personal myth. That summer, she found her father living in Vallejo, working at the Mare Island Naval Base. He allowed her to move in, but the relationship was strained. Cleo disapproved of what he considered Beth's obsession with men and her lazy and untidy ways. After her arrest at the bar near Camp Cooke, she was sent home to Medford. Her goal remained, however, to end up in Hollywood and become an actress.

She visited relatives in Miami Beach and on New Year's Eve, 1945, fell in love with a pilot named Matt Gordon, who was then sent overseas. One story has it that they became engaged, another that Gordon was already married and their engagement was only Beth's fantasy. At any rate, she confided to a friend that she was still a virgin when, back in Medford, she received a telegram from Gordon's mother saying he had been killed. The newspaper article announcing his death was in her belongings when she died less than two years later.

She went to Long Beach, California, to visit an old boyfriend, Gordon Fickling, also a serviceman. He put her up in a hotel miles from his base, but the relationship didn't seem to be going anywhere.

Just about that time, the Raymond Chandler movie *The Blue Dahlia,* came out, starring Veronica Lake and Alan Ladd. Some of her servicemen friends started calling Beth the Black Dahlia because of her shiny black hair and propensity for dressing in black, down to her sheer black underwear and black ring on her finger. Her red lipstick and nail polish and her constant talk about becoming an actress and movie star lent her a glamorous persona.

Beth liked the Hollywood nightlife and tried to be seen at the right places to be recognized and "discovered." Most of her hangouts were near the mythic intersection of Hollywood and Vine. But despite her glamorous dream, her life seemed aimless and somewhat tawdry, living on the edge, doing or saying whatever she needed to get people to take her in or do what she wanted. When she couldn't pay her share of the rent on an apartment she occupied with seven other young women, she went down to San Diego, where she was taken in by sympathetic Dorothy French, who found her sleeping in the movie theater where she worked. Beth lived with the Frenches without working or contributing to her upkeep until she was offered a ride back to Los Angeles by a pipe-clamp salesman named Robert Manley, nicknamed Red. They stayed together the night of January 8, 1947, then he dropped her off the next day at the Biltmore Hotel, where she said she was meeting her sister.

Red Manley became the chief suspect in her murder. LAPD put him through a grueling interrogation, twice administering polygraphs. Two days later he was released, but he collapsed in exhaustion and, sometime later, was given shock treatments for depression. When he was a psychiatric patient at Patton State Hospital in 1954, he rambled on about having committed a murder. But an administration of sodium pentothal revealed he knew nothing of the crime. He died in 1986, exactly thirty-nine years to the day from the date he had dropped off Beth at the Biltmore.

Police found luggage that Short had checked at the bus terminal. Inside were photos, clothing, and stacks of letters to and from men for whom she felt romantic attachment. The authorities were inundated with calls from people who had known her, but her own father refused to get involved, saying he had not seen her since 1943. Her mother—who first learned of her daughter's death from a reporter who'd managed to track her down faster than the police—made the trip to Los Angeles to claim her body. Then, after the inquest, Beth was buried in Oakland's Mountain View Cemetery. Police had hoped strange people might attend the memorial service and give them some leads, but none showed.

Not long afterward, a package was sent to the *Los Angeles Herald Examiner.* An accompanying note created from newspaper letters stated, "Here is Dahlia's Belongings" and "Letter to Follow." Enclosed were Short's social security card, birth certificate, a telegram, photographs with various servicemen, business cards, the newspaper clipping about Matt Gordon's death, and claim checks for the suitcases left at the bus station. There was also an address book with several pages torn out. A note to police near the end of January indicated the killer was going to turn himself in, but then another note arrived saying he had changed his mind and that the killing had been justified.

On January 26, a purse and black suede shoes were found at a garbage dump on East Twenty-fifth Street. Manley identified them as Short's. This suggested the killer was traveling north and may have been returning to the murder site. But nothing came of the discovery.

Some of the police and press theories about the Black Dahlia's killer mirrored the Jack the Ripper speculation. One faction believed that this was a first killing for the offender and that the dismemberment indicated medical knowledge and training.

Others thought they were dealing with a serial offender. In this vein, one suggested suspect was the "Mad Butcher of Kingsbury Run," who had killed, mutilated, and dismembered a dozen people in Cleveland between 1935 and 1938. He was believed to be a woman-hating homosexual sadist. The killings there had stopped after three years with no solution.

LAPD homicide captain John Donahoe and some of his detectives theorized from the viciousness of the injuries and that Short used to hang out with women that the killer was female, reminiscent of the "Jill the Ripper" theory. Short bore scratches on her arms said to be inflicted by a jealous woman friend.

Various suspects were investigated, picked up, and questioned, but none of them panned out. Others, both men and women, confessed to the crime; many, if not most, of them displayed psychiatric problems.

The press quickly seized on the image of the beautiful young starlet so tragically and viciously murdered, and their coverage captured the public imagination. Like many other high-profile cases before and after it, Short's killing sparked several copycat sex crimes in the area. Three days after Short's body was found, Mary Tate was savagely attacked and then strangled with a silk stocking. A month later, Jeanne French was found mutilated, with obscenities written on her corpse in lipstick. Another woman was mutilated, then throughout the summer three more suffered gruesome deaths through beating and/or strangulation. All bore some features that seemed to link them to Short's death—killed in one place then transported to another, several were barflies, some bodies were nude—and detectives worked hard to figure out if there were any direct connections.

As they investigated Short's death, police discovered a sharp contrast between the image and the reality. The Black Dahlia lived mostly at or below poverty level in California, essentially homeless. Police uncovered many rumors about Beth Short, one of the most prominent being that she had an underdeveloped vagina. There were stories that though she didn't have vaginal sex with her boyfriends, she performed oral sex in exchange for whatever she needed—shoes, clothing, a room for the night. Who she really was and what she really did or did not do is largely lost in myth.

The Black Dahlia case haunted the public because of its aura of seedy glamour and the easy irony of how quickly the American dream can turn into the American nightmare, but what I see here is so much more pathetic than that. Elizabeth Short longed for something that always eluded her. She had two goals: to become a movie star and to marry a serviceman; fame and fortune on the one hand and domestic stability and normalcy on the other. At that time, the movie stars had the image of being at the top, but the reality was that the servicemen were the true heroes; they had just saved the world. Either of those lives could have made her happy, but because of her background and personality, she was able to achieve neither. Like Hollywood itself, the image was hollow. In her early twenties, her beauty was already fading and her teeth were rotting because she had no access to dental care. She was never a movie star, never even a starlet. She was just a poor, sad girl who wanted something for herself.

Beth Short was young and emotionally vulnerable and needy, with a highly dependent personality. Because of the lifestyle she led (I hesitate to say "chose," but I suppose we have to acknowledge this), she was a high-risk victim. Like Tennessee Williams's Blanche DuBois, she relied on the kindness of strangers. She could easily be targeted by anyone who wanted to dominate or hurt women. And her killer would be the type who's always on the hunt. He could have spotted her a mile away.

The homicide falls under the heading of lust murder, as is clearly indicated by the torture to which the victim was subjected antemortem, but I would be hesitant to categorize this UNSUB as being in the same sort of crazed frenzy as we saw in Jack the Ripper's mutilations. The combination of the sawing in half—as opposed to frantic disembowelment—and the washing of the body indicates to me someone who knows he's got to get rid of his evidence. The washing is to eliminate forensic clues, and the severing of the body is for easier and less apparent transport. These are the actions of an organized offender, which combine with the more disorganized elements of the case for a mixed presentation.

Since the body was found in a vacant lot, we know it had to be physically carried at least some distance. We know people were in the area with some frequency before the body was found and that it was found shortly after it was dumped. From this we can conclude that the killer might have been seen by a witness, but did not arouse much suspicion. That speaks to the possibility that he carried the body in a bag, or even two bags. Transportation would have been a lot easier in two pieces.

Of course, if it could be shown forensically that the sawing of the body had taken place before death, I would have to reevaluate its meaning. I would still say that this was a lust murder, but then the offender becomes more of the disorganized type, more obviously mentally aberrational.

We can still conclude that the offender had an automobile because, frankly, there isn't any other way of getting the body to the dump site, and this is not the kind of thing you'd risk borrowing a friend's car for. Generally, the lust murderers we see don't drive vehicles. More times than not, they're disorganized types of personalities, often bordering on the psychotic. And in 1947, when fewer people had cars, it would be even more unusual for a disorganized personality to have one. This can tell us something about the killer. He's functional; he's not disorganized twenty-four hours a day. It may be that he's a chronic alcoholic, for example, who is able to hide or handle his problem well enough that he can still hold down a job. He has to have money to maintain his vehicle, keep it gassed up, etc. He probably worked with his hands, possibly in a job involving blood, such as at a slaughterhouse. Or, he could be a seasoned hunter.

To do what he did to the victim, both antemortem and postmortem, he also had to have a house or apartment of his own. It could be small and run-down as long as it was someplace private, with access to running water, where he knew he would not be interrupted. So now we know the UNSUB can't have been poor—at least, not compared to his victim. He had to have money for rent as well as car expenses. Even if he stole the car, he'd still need a private place to go.

The fact that the body was placed where people would quickly see it rather than where it would not be found for days or weeks tells us the killer wanted to shock and offend the community by what he'd done. And he communicated with the police, which was unusual for this type, again giving us a mixed presentation. This UNSUB wanted credibility, much like the Zodiac, although he was not nearly as organized, bright, nor detached.

In the Ripper examination we discussed general motives of the lust murderer. Here I would add that the sadistic elements, the degradation and humiliation inflicted upon this victim (forcing feces down her throat, for example), and the selection of the dump site for the body all indicate this killer's need to make a statement with his crime. It's not just this particular woman; his rage is directed at all women. And in selecting his dump site, he further shows his anger against humanity.

All of these points are important because as indicators of motive they tell us this was not the type of crime we'd expect a jealous boyfriend to commit in the heat of passion. Nor is it, to shoot down another theory suggested by some, the actions of a frustrated suitor who, in a drunken frenzy, went nuts when he learned that this girl was the ultimate tease— she didn't even have the proper equipment to have sex with him. These scenarios—and/or one involving a female offender—do not match the particular motive of this UNSUB as evidenced by the crime.

We would not see this level of degradation and mutilation from any of these other types. These are the actions of someone who fantasizes continually about hurting someone, who is on the hunt regularly for someone to dominate and to punish, and who knows just what he wants to do to that person once he gets her under his control.

While the washing and sawing appear to have been elements of modus operandi—performed to help him successfully commit and get away with the crime—the torture and carving of the smile into the victim's face were signature elements—those emotionally necessary and satisfying to the offender.

Doing all this took some time. We've already discussed the disorganized elements of this UNSUB's personality, yet he was able to fantasize, plan, and carry out this time-consuming, complicated crime. For this reason, we'd expect him to have some criminal history before his encounter with Beth Short. As we've shown repeatedly, you don't jump into this kind of thing without some criminal evolution and development.

I would also have advised police to try to link any of the so-called copycat murders that happened afterward. Someone this advanced in his murderous fantasies would not have been satisfied with one. Unless he was stopped, he'd continue. I'd even go so far as to say that if we saw this case today in isolation, we'd still know immediately that we were dealing with a serial killer.

As reported by John Gilmore in his book *Severed,* some indicators linked the Black Dahlia murder to an unsolved case from the year before, that of Georgette Bauerdorf, an oil heiress and beautiful L.A. socialite whose father, back in New York, worked with newspaper tycoon William Randolph Hearst. After Short's murder, Aggie Underwood, an aggressive crime reporter for Hearst's *Herald-Express,* wanted LAPD to reinvestigate the Bauerdorf case. Bauerdorf, who had known Beth Short through one of her hangouts, had been strangled before she was dumped facedown in her bathtub, a piece of towel wedged in her throat. Sheriff's investigators were unable to locate a six-foot-four, dark-complected soldier with a limp who had dated Georgette. She had been frightened of him and had broken off their relationship. A man of similar description was witnessed near her murder scene. I'd say we have to seriously consider the possibility that Short's killer also killed Georgette Bauerdorf. Both are lust murders, both involve bathtubs, and they were relatively close in time.

Gilmore has done extensive research into the Short case. In the early 1980s, he produced a tape recording of an interview he had done with a man named Arnold Smith. Smith was tall and thin, with a limp and a long rap sheet. He claimed to Gilmore that a character named Al Morrison killed Beth Short, and that Morrison had related the details to him. Gilmore went over his material with John St. John, the detective who had taken over the case in the 1960s. I actually met St. John once, when he had already achieved near legendary status. He held LAPD detective badge number one. He died in 1995 at age seventy-seven, having retired only two years previously.

According to Gilmore, St. John believed that Smith and Morrison were one and the same. At one point, Smith brought Gilmore a box of Short's belongings, including a handkerchief and a photo of her with a blond woman, Smith, and another man he identified as Morrison.

Smith gave a detailed account of Short's killer taking her to a Hollywood hotel, where it became evident that she hadn't realized he was planning to share the room with her. She reportedly refused liquor and was uninterested in a relationship with Morrison. He took her to another house and assaulted her when she wanted to leave. According to Smith's account to Gilmore, the killer threatened to rape Short, she screamed, and he hit her again and again until she stopped moving. Smith provided a full description of how the killer had tied her and stuffed her panties into her mouth before cutting, draining, and washing her body—including fairly convincing details such as how he laid boards across the bathtub to cut her in half and wrapped her in an oilskin tablecloth and shower curtain and carried her in the trunk of his car to the vacant lot where she was found.

According to Gilmore, Smith also made a veiled reference to "that other one" who had been found in "a bathtub"—possibly Bauerdorf. Smith had actually come to the attention of LA County Sheriff's detective Joel Lesnick in connection with that murder. Lesnick learned that Arnold Smith was one of many aliases for Jack Anderson Wilson, a tall, gaunt alcoholic with a bad leg and a history of robbery and sex offenses.

After hearing Gilmore's tape and his firsthand account of meeting with Smith, Detective St. John knew he had to get to Smith directly. A parallel investigation found no proof that Al Morrison, the violent sexual sadist, existed, bolstering St. John's belief that Arnold Smith/Jack Anderson Wilson was really the killer.

But in one of those eerie twists of fate, before a meeting between Gilmore and Smith at which the police planned to pick him up for questioning, Smith—an alcoholic and heavy smoker—passed out in his bed at the Holland Hotel and set the room on fire. He was burned to death in the flames, which apparently also consumed any photos or personal effects of Short's he had shown Gilmore.

In another book on the case, *Daddy Was the Black Dahlia Killer*, written with the respected crime writer Michael Newton, Janice Knowlton offers another theory. Knowlton claims that her late father, George Knowlton, was a child molester, serial killer of at least three, a baby-killer, satanist and necrophiliac—and Beth Short's murderer. Her understanding of the connection to the Dahlia case, she claims, emerged when deeply repressed memories surfaced while recovering from a hysterectomy. According to Janice Knowlton, Short called George from the Biltmore. In Janice's memory, after beating Short to death with a hammer, George Knowlton used a power saw to cut Short in two, then forced his daughter to accompany him as he took the body to dump it in the ocean at Seal Beach. When it floated back, he washed and gutted it, took it to a cemetery, then changed his mind and dumped it in the vacant lot.

In a *Los Angeles Times* story that ran two days after the murder, sources recalled Short saying she was engaged to an army pilot named George. At the end of January, someone named George visited a cafe on Santa Monica Boulevard several times, identified himself as an FBI agent but refused to show credentials, and asserted that he knew who killed Short. Knowlton believes from the description that this was her father. Newton concedes there is no proof of what she claims, but cites many coincidences in her father's life and the known facts of the Dahlia case. He also demonstrates striking similarities between the case and the unsolved murder of Frances Cochran in Lynn, Massachusetts, in July, 1941.

In an *Orange County Register* article in June 1991, John St. John declared, "The facts as she presents them to me are not compatible with the murder of the Black Dahlia." It remains unsolved to this date.

Other case devotees have claimed that the LAPD knew the identity of the Dahlia's killer, but covered it up to protect influential people. (Some of these sources claim the same thing about the death of Marilyn Monroe.)

Theories—conspiracy and otherwise—abound. But this much we can state with certainty: Elizabeth Short was a victim of opportunity. Her killer was the type who would project blame on the victim: she brought it on herself, or she had to be punished for the kind of life she led. He'd had an emotional need to find someone he considered lower than himself, then degraded her to drive home the point. He would be a risk-taker who showed a mixed presentation in his criminal work. After the crime, I wouldn't have been surprised to see some major emotional disintegration. If it was severe enough, it could have precluded him from committing and getting away with additional crimes of this nature, but then we'd expect him to have been picked up or identified. Either way, with modern techniques it should have been possible to recognize someone's postoffense behavior, whether that behavior involved another lust murder, a nervous breakdown, institutionalization, or suicide.

This crime was driven by fantasy, which would continue after the murder. So I would surveil the dump site to see if the UNSUB came back to relive it. I think checking the grave site would also be a good idea. He would be interested in the case, possibly hanging out in bars or coffee shops frequented by the police. He may have confided details of the crime to someone, although this person, too, would be someone who lived on the fringes of society, as this UNSUB wouldn't have a lot of "normal," successful friends. If he did confide in someone, it was likely at a moment of weakness—such as during a drinking binge—and he'd realize afterwards he'd made himself more vulnerable, putting his confidant in great personal danger.

We will probably never know for sure who killed the Black Dahlia. Had Detective St. John had the opportunity to interrogate Arnold Smith, the outcome might have been different. But figuring out what kind of person killed her is not that difficult. As in so many of the cases we've discussed, he told us through his crime.

LAWRENCIA BEMBENEK

If Elizabeth Short represents a rather feeble and somewhat antiquated version of an American icon, Lawrencia Bembenek represents a stronger, more modern one. In its own way, however, her story is equally poignant and sad.

Again, in Bembenek's life, the myth and reality played side by side. She called herself Laurie, but the public decided she would be better known as Bambi: a gorgeous, Midwestern, blond Playboy bunny who became a capable and tough career girl, breaking into the traditionally all-boy realm of police work. She engendered the romantic notion of a beauty horribly wronged, convicted of a violent crime she swore she didn't commit, and once imprisoned, saved by a handsome prince who helped her escape and offered her true love. Then there was the life on the lam, encapsulated by any PR man's dream of a tag line—"Run, Bambi, Run!"—in headlines, on T-shirts and talk shows. Even this phrase demonstrates the inherent contradictions in the story, hearkening back as it does to an archetypal Disney scene of innocence lost. The nickname was actually attached by male officers when she was a police recruit.

The reality of all of this was considerably different, yet no less haunting.

On May 28, 1981, shortly after 2:30 A.M., police officers responded to an emergency call at 1701 West Ramsey Street, on the south side of Milwaukee, Wisconsin. They were let in by Sean Schultz, age ten, and his eight-year-old brother, Shannon. In the bedroom officers found the boys' mother, Christine Jean Schultz, thirty years of age, evidently dead, lying on her right side in bed. She had dark brown hair and brown eyes and was wearing a yellow Adidas T-shirt and white panties. The shirt was torn around a large bullet entry wound in her right shoulder. A clothesline cord bound her hands in front of her, and a blue bandanna-type scarf was wrapped around her head, gagging her. There was no sign of a break-in, and the doors had heavy-duty dead-bolt locks. The home was on a well-lit street, in a safe neighborhood, near other houses. It did, however, back up onto a freeway overpass. The back door was secluded and shielded from view. The freeway could have therefore provided an intruder with an escape route.

It took two hours before the medical examiner was called, and an ambulance an hour later. When police wrapped the victim's body for transport, they removed a brown hair from her calf.

Sean told police he had awakened to the feeling of something like a rope tightening around his throat. A large gloved hand covered his face. He struggled and screamed, then heard his assailant utter a deep growling sound and run across the hall. Sean followed his brother into the hallway and saw a man in his mother's room.

Shannon described a large white male with a long ponytail, wearing a green jogging suit. He thought he held a pearl-handled gun. The younger boy heard a female voice from his mother's bedroom say, "God, please don't do that!" then a sound like a firecracker.

When the man ran out past them and scrambled down the stairs, both boys thought they noticed him wearing a green army jacket and low-cut black shoes, similar to the kind police officers wear. On this point the boys could be expected to know what they were talking about, since their father—Christine's ex-husband, Fred—and their mother's current boyfriend were both cops.

Sean raced back to his mother, who was still alive, and ripped open her shirt to try to tend to her wound. At around 2:30 A.M., he called his mother's boyfriend, forty-one-year-old Stewart George Honeck, for help. Sean would remember Honeck saying, "I knew this would happen. I think Freddie did it."

Honeck called the police emergency number, then immediately went to Christine Schultz's house, accompanied by his roommate, Kenneth Retkowski, another police officer. They arrived at virtually the same time as the patrol car Honeck had summoned. Once inside, Honeck went upstairs and rolled Christine's body over to check on her. Although this is a natural reaction on the part of a victim's boyfriend called in by her panicking children, technically he disturbed the crime scene. This would be just one in a series of investigative irregularities.

Elfred O. "Fred" Schultz, divorced from Christine the previous November after eleven years of marriage, was on duty that night when he was notified of the crime. He went to the crime scene while Christine was still in the house. Again, I can understand why he'd want to be there—especially with his sons in the house—but he should have been kept away. As the ex-husband, regardless of his alibi of being on duty, he would have to be considered a potential suspect. I know only too well, though, what must have transpired because we've seen it in so many cases where a cop's family is involved. These other officers know him, know these are his kids, this is his house, etc., and see him as a victim. It's a natural and common reaction.

Schultz called and awakened his twenty-one-year-old current wife, Lawrencia Bembenek, to let her know what had happened. Then he and his partner, Detective Michael Durfee, drove to his and Laurie's apartment, sixteen blocks from the crime scene. Fred felt the hood of her car, which he said was cold, and in Durfee's presence, examined his off-duty .38. Durfee smelled it and examined it himself. There was dust on the weapon and Durfee determined that it had not been fired that night nor recently cleaned. Fred asked Laurie to accompany him to identify the victim—his ex-wife—and took the off-duty pistol with him in a briefcase. In what would prove to be another investigative miscue, Fred failed to have his off-duty revolver—which would later be determined to be the murder weapon—properly registered with the crime lab. The serial number of the weapon was not recorded and the weapon remained in his possession for three weeks before he turned it in for examination.

Later in the morning, around 4 A.M., two detectives came to the Schultz-Bembenek apartment and asked Laurie if she owned a gun or a green jogging suit, then asked her some questions about her husband and

Stewart Honeck. In fact, the two men had once been roommates. Now, however, Fred was said to be unhappy about Honeck dating his ex, and they strongly disliked each other.

As for Laurie, she said that at the time of the murder she was home in the apartment alone and asleep. That evening, she'd been packing to move them into a smaller apartment. She had also planned to go out with a friend, but their date had been canceled.

Police reconstructed the events of what proved to be the last night of Christine Schultz's life. That evening, she had made dinner for Honeck and they had several drinks together, finishing around 9 P.M., when the boys went to bed. The two adults watched television, and then Christine drove Honeck home, about three minutes away by car. Another account has him leaving on his own with Christine requesting that he lock up behind him.

Twelve area residents, including two officers, had seen a man matching the boys' description jogging in the neighborhood a few weeks before the murder. He had reddish brown hair tied in a ponytail, wore a green jogging suit, and carried a blue bandanna similar to the one used to gag the victim. Two nurses at a facility a mile from the scene had noticed a man lying in the parking lot around 2:50 A.M. the morning of the crime. They called police and, when they returned, observed a man with reddish brown hair and a green jogging suit standing in the bushes. Ray Kujawa, a neighbor of the victim's, told police that on the night of the murder, when he was staying at a friend's house, someone had broken into his garage and stolen a .38 revolver and a green jogging suit.

The postmortem examination by Dr. Elaine Samuels indicated that, when fired, the gun had been held against the victim's back, touching the skin. It entered her right shoulder and cut a direct path to her heart. A contact gunshot of this nature would produce a "blow back" effect, in which blood and tissue would have exploded back from the wound into the gun barrel.

Christine's friends and relatives described her as a fine athlete, physically fit, and a lover of the outdoors. She also reportedly had a temper, and they felt it unlikely that she would have remained tied up in the kind of knot the killer used unless someone was holding a gun on her. Blood was found under her fingernails and on both walls near the head of the stairs.

From here, things start to get complicated.

Despite his partner's earlier assessment that Fred's service weapon hadn't been fired or cleaned recently, the regional crime lab's ballistics analysis indicated that the revolver, a Smith & Wesson .38 with a four-inch barrel, showed traces of type A blood, both Fred's and Christine's blood type, and that the slug that killed Christine matched markings inside the gun barrel. In the house after the murder, Fred discovered a box of 200-grain Speer bullets, which he said belonged to him. Speer bullets had been standard issue for Milwaukee PD service revolvers, and Monty Lutz, a nationally recognized firearms expert, stated that enough markings linked the off-duty gun with the fatal bullet to make a definitive match. Other analysts also declared that the bullet that killed Christine Schultz could only have come from her ex-husband's weapon. Both Fred and Laurie became suspects.

Ex-husbands are always suspect at least initially, and Fred Schultz could be seen to have a potential motive. Christine and the boys lived happily in the home that he himself had built, while he and Laurie lived in a small apartment. On top of that, to help control costs since he was paying alimony, child support, and the mortgage on the house, the newlyweds briefly shared an apartment with a friend, Judy Zess. According to Laurie, Fred was extremely bitter over the amount of money the divorce settlement was costing him. He complained that his ex-wife was getting everything. And Christine reportedly told her attorney that she was afraid of Fred, saying he had threatened her life and wanted to maintain control over her and the children. She also felt she was being followed. Of course, bad feelings and harsh words are common in divorce cases, and nothing indicated Fred had acted on his.

Laurie was viewed as a more likely suspect because, while it was Fred's off-duty revolver that was used to kill Christine, he had an alibi and Laurie had been home alone that night, with access to the murder weapon. And she refused to take a polygraph when Fred's attorney advised her against it, though Fred agreed to one. He passed, but the test was damaging: he admitted to having punched Christine in the past, to lying about a speeding ticket, and to holding back the truth about where he'd been the night of the murder.

In another departure from normal procedure, Fred Schultz's partner, Michael Durfee, could not produce his logbook from that night. It was later learned that although they said they had been investigating a burglary, two uniformed officers had actually conducted that investigation. Schultz and Durfee had been in a couple of bars the night of the shooting—while on duty. Schultz still had a solid alibi, but the revelation was embarrassing at the very least.

Circumstantial evidence piled up as people came forward to build the image of Laurie Bembenek as a conniving, greedy second wife. Judy Zess's mother, Frances, claimed she had heard Laurie talking at a dinner party a few months before the murder about having Christine "blown away." Judy confirmed this, and both said it was because of how much money Fred had to give his ex-wife. Judy also claimed Laurie had approached Judy's boyfriend, Thomas Gaertner, about finding someone who could have Fred's ex-wife "rubbed out." And according to Judy, Laurie had owned both a blue bandanna and a clothesline similar to those found at the crime scene. A number of people tied Laurie to a green jogging suit (including Judy Zess, who said there'd been one in the apartment she once shared with Laurie and Fred), though none was ever found.

But, as we've seen in other cases, accounts and leads went off in a variety of directions. Hairs found on the body and in the bandanna were consistent with those of the victim, according to Dr. Elaine Samuels. But then Diane Hanson, a hair analyst from a Madison, Wisconsin, crime lab, stated that two of the hairs were consistent with samples taken from Laurie Bembenek's hairbrush, seized by police.

This evidence is open to question, however, and could have been planted. In a 1983 letter quoted in the *Toronto Star* in 1991, Dr. Samuels reaffirmed, "I recovered no blonde or red hairs of any length or texture. . . . All of the hairs I recovered from the body were brown and were grossly identical to the hair of the victim."

Samuels continued, "I do not like to suggest that evidence was altered in any way, but I can find no logical explanation for what amounted to the mysterious appearance of blonde hair in an envelope that contained no such hair at the time it was sealed by me." Then she concluded, "These departures from standard procedure, coupled with the hostile attitude of police during the investigation . . . lead me to the conclusion that something may be amiss."

A reddish brown wig was found clogging the plumbing of the apartment where Laurie and Fred lived. Not only did the color match the description of the intruder's hair provided by the Schultz boys, the wig hair was also consistent with hairs found on the victim's body. But even this piece of evidence raises more questions than it answers: their apartment shared drainage with another apartment, and a woman who lived in that apartment said that Judy Zess had visited her and asked to use the rest room. The next person to use the bathroom found it clogged, occasioning the retrieval of the wig. Zess later admitted owning a brownish shoulder-length wig. And Laurie said that Judy's boyfriend, Thomas Gaertner, blamed Fred for the death of his best friend, an off-duty cop shot by Fred, and claimed he would get even.

Despite all of this, the bulk of the largely circumstantial evidence pointed to Lawrencia Bembenek. On June 26, 1981, she was charged with the first-degree murder of Christine Schultz, primarily because she had access to the murder weapon and lacked a confirmable alibi for the night in question. So, while she, Fred, Judy Zess, Thomas Gaertner, and the landlord all had keys to the apartment, Laurie was there alone around the time the murder occurred. It was believed that as a former police officer she'd know how to cover her tracks, and that since she was tall and strong, in disguise she could easily appear to be a man to Christine's two boys, despite the fact that Sean insisted he had seen a man and even testified that it couldn't have been Laurie.

Bembenek went to trial on February 24, 1982. Much was made in both the courtroom and the media of the defendant's beauty and feminist leanings, which led some to suggest Bambi was on trial as much for her image as for the murder of Christine Schultz. Circuit Judge Michael Skwierawski noted, "It was the most circumstantial case I've ever seen, with lots of individual pieces that would not have convicted her. But taken as a whole, the jury could reach only one conclusion."

An example of the kind of ambiguity Judge Skwierawski might have been thinking of concerned the murder weapon itself. In a July 31, 1990, article reviewing the Bembenek case, reporter Rogers Worthington wrote in the *Chicago Tribune,* "Ballistics tests showed the gun collected from Schultz and tested on June 21 was indeed the murder weapon. But at the trial, neither Schultz nor Durfee could say with certainty that the gun shown to them in the courtroom was the same one they had looked at the night of the murder."

The jury of five men and seven women took three and a half days to find Bembenek guilty and delivered their verdict on March 9. She was sentenced to life in prison. From Taycheedah Correctional Institution, Bembenek continued to protest her innocence, claiming she was framed by the Milwaukee Police Department to stop her from releasing evidence she had of drug use, debauchery, and improper use of government funds by members of the department. This was an important touchstone in the development of Bambi lore. To understand why so many people following the case at the time felt that she had been railroaded, we have to know something of her background.

Lawrencia Ann Bembenek was the youngest of three daughters born to Joseph and Virginia Bembenek in Milwaukee. Joseph had been a Milwaukee police officer, but left after three years because of what he saw as widespread corruption on the force. He then became a carpenter. Laurie, as she was called, grew up wanting to become a veterinarian but lacked the academic background. She took a two-year college course in fashion merchandising and earned money from a variety of brief jobs such as modeling and aerobics instruction, not surprising since she was tall, beautiful, and athletic. She once posed in a slinky dress as Miss March 1978, for a Schlitz Brewing Company calendar, which is where some of the mythology comes from.

But she also had strong feminist views and entered the Milwaukee Police Academy in March 1980. Right from the beginning, she felt harassed for being a woman in a man's world.

As Kris Radish recounts in her book *Run, Bambi, Run,* Laurie attended a concert in Milwaukee with then fellow recruit Judy Zess and three other friends. While Laurie was using the ladies' room, Judy was arrested by two plainclothes officers for marijuana possession. The following day, Bembenek's sergeant and another officer called her in and grilled her about every aspect of her life. Judy was fired when a small marijuana joint was found in a cup under her chair, and Laurie was once again hammered by her superiors, who tried to get her to confess to smoking pot, too. Laurie refused to confess to something she didn't do. It seemed to her that she was taking abuse for being a woman, but on July 25, 1980, she graduated sixth in her class from the Milwaukee Police Academy and got her badge.

She was assigned to the Second District, not a heavy crime area, and was almost instantly appalled by what she said she saw on the street and within the department: graft, corruption, drinking on duty, drug abuse, oral sex with prostitutes, mistreatment of suspects. Still, she took personal pride in being a cop and enjoyed the time out on patrol or working on her own.

On August 25, just a month after her graduation from the academy, Laurie got a call at home from a captain telling her she was being dismissed. She had no idea why. Two sergeants came by and took her badge, gun, and her uniforms. Chief Harold A. Breier axed three female officers that week, the other two black, all in their probationary period. The only explanation was that it was "for the good of the service."

According to the *Milwaukee Journal* a few days after this, Laurie "was charged with untruthfulness and making a false official report, but no details were given."

Weeks later, when she finally got to look at her personnel file, Bembenek found that Judy Zess had signed a statement saying that Laurie had also used marijuana at the concert. Judy admitted signing it but told Laurie it was done under duress, after hours of interrogation. Both women were appealing their dismissals and Laurie forgave Judy, agreeing that they should move in together.

Waiting out her appeal, desperate for money, Laurie got a job as a waitress at the Lake Geneva Playboy Club. She only kept the job a few weeks, but the bunny connection solidified the image she was to take on—the confusing combination of tough cop, ardent feminist, and beautiful sex object. As with Elizabeth Short, the public saw one thing and the individual herself lived quite another.

U.S. Attorney James Morrison began investigating allegations that the Milwaukee PD was misusing hundreds of thousands of dollars of affirmative-action funds and firing minorities on flimsy grounds. Laurie came forward to claim that women were being hired and quickly fired, just to satisfy federal quotas and take advantage of grants. She filed a lawsuit against the department, charging discrimination. In October of 1980, she obtained photographs of nude male officers dancing in a public park. After she handed them over to the internal affairs division, her car's tires were slashed, she found a dead rat deposited on her windshield, and she received repeated anonymous late-night calls. Perhaps significantly, when she was charged with murder, the federal investigation against the police, of which she was a key component, fell apart.

Bembenek met Fred Schultz in December of 1980, a month after he and Christine had divorced. Within a few weeks of their meeting, Fred proposed to Laurie, and they were married on January 30, 1981.

It's not difficult to see why some thought Laurie Bembenek may not have been treated as a normal murder suspect. I've said before that an individual doesn't just wake up one day and decide to become a murderer. In Bembenek's case, what we see is a history of going out on a limb to do the right thing. She seemed to believe cops should be held to a higher standard of behavior and she suffered because of her actions.

Does this mean it would be impossible for her to commit an illegal or violent act? No. But I think it makes it a hell of a lot less likely she's going to blow away the mother of two young children in cold blood.

To be fair in our assessment, though, let's begin with what we can learn from the crime itself, starting with victimology. What I've always said is that you start by looking at what was going on in and around the victim's life in the days and weeks leading up to the crime.

Christine Schultz was in her own home in a safe neighborhood, which would seem to place her at low risk to be the victim of such a violent crime. But she had worried she was being followed. If her ex-husband was as controlling as she said, and if, as has been reported, her current boyfriend had a drinking problem, a history of difficult relationships would raise her risk level.

The crime, as it unfolded, makes no sense. By this I mean that the chain of events is not logical. Why would an UNSUB start in the mother's room, then go for the children, then return to the mother to finish her off? It would be one thing if the boys were awakened by the shot and so the offender had to contend with them, but that's not what happened here. Let's say the offender surprised Christine in her bed and controlled her by threatening to kill her kids if she awakened them. He tied her up. Why would he then leave her alone—alive—and go into the boys' room? There's no motive or logic to that. Keeping those kids alive and asleep would be the best means the subject had for making Christine cooperate; it's much better control than any binding or weapon.

When the subject left Christine's room, this woman, described as athletic, would be like a mother bear with instincts to protect her cubs. At the very least, she'd scream out a warning to wake them before the intruder had a chance to start strangling one of them. This makes me wonder whether there wasn't a second subject, someone to keep an eye on the mother while the other went into the boys' room.

There has been speculation that the events were staged to unfold that way to make sure the children were awake and close enough to the intruder/murderer so they could get a good look at him and be able to state later who it *was not*. We can't be sure of this, of course, but it is a possible explanation for the otherwise bizarre chain of events leading up to the victim's murder. The bandanna ligature would seem to serve no real purpose in the crime and so might be considered an element of staging to try to throw off investigators.

This leads us to the greater question of motive for the crime. First, it seems unlikely this was a robbery, since the timing was high risk and everything indicates the intruder sought out the victim. If Christine Schultz had heard a noise, she would have been found someplace else in the house—where she'd gone to investigate—not still in her bed. There might even have been a call to the police. And we can rule out sexual assault as a motive, since there was no sign of it and the UNSUB actually left his victim to go to the boys' room.

It's not a criminal-enterprise homicide and it's not sexual homicide, so why did Christine Schultz die, and what kind of person would have killed her?

First off, it's pretty ballsy to enter a home when three people are there, which says to me that we're dealing with someone who's comfortable with breaking and entering, someone experienced. There was no sign of forced entry, so this UNSUB either had a key or knew how to get in unnoticed. And if he had a key and/or was that comfortable with the home, he likely knew the victim was the ex-wife of one police officer and girlfriend of another. He would have to consider that she herself might have a gun. Was he nuts? Between the risk level of the crime to the offender, and the way it was perpetrated (not the type of personal-cause homicide we see from female offenders—even strong, feminist ones), I am comfortable saying that Laurie Bembenek does not fit this profile.

I also have trouble with the case against Bembenek because I just don't see the motive as it was presented. Do I think she would have been happier with more money? Certainly. Who wouldn't? But if she were cold-blooded enough to kill for money, she would have taken out the kids, too. She didn't want to be the instant mother of two, no matter how much they may have gotten along during visits. She was a newlywed. And while it was a decent house, after the murder she and Fred fought over how she *did not* want to move there. We might expect her to protest a bit to throw off suspicion, but not to the point of risking damage to her relationship with her husband.

For me to see greed as a motive, it would have to have been affecting her relationship with Fred. There would have been reports from witnesses about how their previously great relationship had gone to seed because he was so upset over the loss of the house, or that their money troubles were ruining everything. But we didn't see this. To the contrary, instead of this being one of the world's great romances gone bad, Bembenek's relationship with Fred Schultz was really more of a rebound. He'd been married to Christine more than a decade and was only divorced a few months when he married Laurie. And they'd only known each other briefly when they married. No matter how sincere their affections, it was still a new, somewhat superficial relationship.

If we argue that she hadn't intended to kill her husband's ex-wife but merely scare her out of the house and then was forced to kill when Christine recognized her, this makes even less sense. First, it doesn't jibe with the chronology of the crime as outlined earlier. It's also terribly high risk—especially for a trained law officer—to assume that none of the three victims would recognize her. And then we might have expected to see some staging—such as a TV set taken or the victim's clothing pulled off—to make it look like something other than personal-cause homicide. Certainly, we wouldn't expect Bembenek—again, a trained police officer—to discard evidence (such as the wig) in such a way as to lead investigators right back to her doorstep, and to forget or to neglect to have an alibi.

So if Laurie Bembenek didn't kill Christine Schultz, who did? It's hard to answer that when the investigation could have gone off in so many different directions, with the conflicting leads generated. It is safe to say, though, that with this type of personal-cause homicide, the individual responsible would have been an obvious suspect and would have known this, so he or she would have gone out of the way to establish an alibi.

Laurie Bembenek's story didn't end with her trial, conviction, and incarceration. In 1983, the conviction was upheld by the Wisconsin Court of Appeals. Four months later, she and Fred filed for divorce, which was granted in June of 1984. During the trial, Fred had been supportive and later established a defense fund for her. But after the Court of Appeals decision, he said he had become convinced that she was guilty.

Bembenek fought unsuccessfully to get a new trial for several years. In the meantime, she continued to inspire passion. Several men reportedly became infatuated with her, or should we say, her image. One apparently even paid an imprisoned hit man to "confess" to the Schultz murder to get Laurie off the hook. But when prosecutors refused to grant the convict immunity, he refused to testify.

There was one positive aspect to her notoriety. As long as there was interest in her, new people were willing to work on her case. One such individual was Milwaukee private investigator Ira Robins, who spent years reinvestigating the Schultz murder. Before Robins and Bembenek's relationship soured over financial issues, Robins uncovered potentially exculpatory evidence attorneys would use in future bids to get Bembenek a new trial.

Then, on July 15, 1990, her story entered its next phase when she climbed out a small window in the prison laundry and escaped, fleeing with her handsome boyfriend, Dominic Gugliatto, brother of another inmate. While she may have be seeking a normal life, with this move she sealed her notorious celebrity status. Seventy-two percent of callers to a popular Wisconsin radio program said if they knew where she was, they wouldn't report it or turn her in. Coverage of her case, and the slogan "Run, Bambi, Run," grew well beyond the borders of the state.

The couple was arrested just three months later in Thunder Bay, Canada, following a segment on *America's Most Wanted,* which led to a tip that she was waiting tables at a local restaurant.

In an interesting move, Bembenek applied for refugee status under Geneva Convention rules, citing her inability to get a new trial in the face of mounting evidence of her innocence. After a number of legal maneuvers back and forth between Bembenek forces and U.S. and Canadian authorities, including an American judicial investigation into Bembenek's case, she was returned to Milwaukee.

Bembenek's attorneys prepared a motion for a new trial that included affidavits from witnesses who said a career criminal, Frederick Horenberger, told them that Fred Schultz had paid him $10,000 to kill Christine. Horenberger later recanted just before killing himself during a botched robbery and hostage situation in 1991.

The attorneys also secured affidavits from two forensic pathologists that the handgun used to convict Bembenek was not consistent with the muzzle imprints on the victim's body, eliminating it as the murder weapon. The following month a government lawyer produced a letter from a leading authority on gunshot wounds contradicting the affidavits of the pathologists. But at the very least, this exchange demonstrated that the issue was open to serious dispute.

Facing Horenberger's original story, the switched-gun theory, and other evidence developed by the defense, plus the loss of witnesses on their side over time, the DA's office was ready to deal. Laurie was afraid a new trial would come too late. She wanted to spend more time with her aging parents, so she agreed.

In a December 1992 arrangement, her prior conviction was set aside and she pleaded no contest to the lesser charge of second-degree murder in return for being released on parole, based on time already served. In recent years she has faced bankruptcy, lawsuits, and serious health problems, including hepatitis C.

We tried to interview her for this book, but she declined our request, which I have to say I can understand. Whether viewed as guilty or innocent, this woman has lived her entire adult life under the specter of this case and the image of her it created in the public eye. We'll close with words from an interview she did give years ago, when she summed up, "I'm tired of being Laurie Bembenek."

THE "BOSTON STRANGLER"

With the "Boston Strangler" murders, we get a different angle on myth versus reality and the quest for recognition and fulfillment: a man who gained lasting fame by holding himself out as the great American antihero and superman of serial crime, confessing to the brutal and sadistic killing of eleven women.

On the evening of June 14, 1962, Anna Slesers, a fifty-five-year-old seamstress, had just finished dinner in her small third-floor apartment in a converted townhouse at 77 Gainsborough Street in Boston's Back Bay. She had moved in only two weeks earlier. Most of her neighbors were students and retired people on limited budgets.

She drew the water for a quick bath before her twenty-five-year-old son, Juris, was to pick her up for the Latvian memorial service being held at their church.

Just before 7 P.M., Juris knocked at his mother's door and got no answer. He pounded on the locked door, first annoyed, then increasingly worried. She had sounded depressed on the phone the night before. Finally, he threw his weight against the door twice and broke it open.

Inside, he found Anna lying on her back on the bathroom floor with the blue silk cord of her robe tied in a tight, exaggeratedly large bow around her neck. He called the police, then his sister in Maryland, to say he believed their mother had committed suicide. It soon became clear, though, that this was not the case.

Boston PD homicide detectives James Mellon and John Driscoll arrived and found the victim in a blue taffeta housecoat with red lining, but it had been spread completely apart in front so that she was exposed from her shoulders down. She lay grotesquely, her head a few feet from the open bathroom door, her left leg stretched straight and the right spread wide, bent at the knee. There was blood on her right ear and a laceration on the back of her skull. Her neck was scratched and abraded, and a there was a contusion on her chin.

The apartment had been ransacked. Anna's purse was lying open and its contents strewn on the floor. Wastebaskets had been turned over and dresser drawers pulled open and messed around with, as if the killer just wanted to handle her personal items. A case of color slides had been carefully placed on the bedroom floor. The record player was on, but the sound had been turned off. Despite this attempt to make the scene look like a robbery, a gold watch and other pieces of jewelry had been left untouched.

The autopsy showed that Anna Slesers had died from strangulation, complicated by head injuries. Her vagina showed evidence of sexual assault with some hard object, possibly a bottle.

Victimology revealed a woman completely involved in her church, her children, her work, and her love of classical music. Divorced, she kept to herself and had few friends. There were no men in her life aside from her son. Police figured the crime had started out as a burglary, but when the burglar saw the woman in her robe, he was overcome by an urge to molest her, killing her afterward to avoid being identified.

Between that June 14, 1962, that Anna Slesers was murdered and January 4, 1964, thirteen single women in the Boston area became victims of one or more serial killers. At least eleven could be tied to the same UNSUB, who became known as the Phantom Fiend or the Boston

Strangler. Most were strangled with their own stockings or other items found on the premises, such as pillowcases, scarfs, bras, or other clothing.

Within ten weeks, six women had been murdered, the first four within twenty-seven days, then two more in August, nine days apart. All were older victims; Anna Slesers had been the youngest, by ten years, and the second victim, Mary Mullen, was eighty-five.

A second wave began in December 1962 with much younger victims—one just twenty-one—then a third wave ran from September 1963 to January 1964. These women were also younger. One of the complications with the Strangler case is found in the Zodiac murders, discussed in the last chapter. As the body count rises, there is a tendency to link future cases to a series—appropriately or not—and this certainly muddied the waters here.

In the crimes listed above, except for one woman who was killed in a hotel room, all of the victims were murdered in their apartments. All had been sexually molested. With no signs of forced entry, each victim apparently knew her assailant, voluntarily let him in, or failed to lock a door. Most of the women led quiet, modest lives.

The Boston community lived in terror. Warnings went out to all women to keep their doors locked and to be wary of strangers. For a time police commissioner and former FBI agent Edmund McNamara canceled all leave and transferred every available detective to homicide. A thorough investigation was conducted of all known sex offenders and violent former mental patients. More than thirty-six thousand people were examined and suspect lists ran into the thousands. Hundreds were fingerprinted and forty polygraphed. Six of them failed. But police were no closer to their killer.

Toward what would prove to be the end of the Strangler series in 1964, Massachusetts, Connecticut, Rhode Island, and New Hampshire were being terrorized by a rapist who became known as the Green Man, because he was generally dressed in dark green clothing of the type workmen might wear. He would either talk his way into a woman's home by claiming he was there to repair something or else break in. On one occasion, he raped four women in a single day. Police believed he might have been responsible for as many as three hundred sexual assaults, and the fear was so great that legitimate repairmen and deliverymen were being refused admittance.

The Green Man would threaten his victim with a knife, caress her, then rape her. But he conducted himself in a friendly, almost casual way and would often apologize before he left. In October of 1964, he broke into the bedroom of a twenty-year-old woman in Cambridge, Massachusetts, threatened her with the knife, tied her up, raped her, then asked for her forgiveness. He was about to leave when she complained that he had tied her painfully tight, so he loosened the binding.

This woman helped police produce a sketch good enough that it triggered a memory from one detective. The Green Man looked like the "Measuring Man."

The Measuring Man had worked the Cambridge area three years before, back in 1961. He would surveil attractive young women, then knock on their door, claiming to be from a modeling agency. Saying he was looking to sign up new talent, he would ask if he could take body measurements. That was all he would do, then he would leave. Most of the women didn't even realize there was anything strange about this until there was no follow-up from the agency.

In March 1961, Cambridge PD arrested a man attempting to break into a house. He fit the description and confessed to being the Measuring Man. Albert Henry DeSalvo was a twenty-nine-year-old factory worker and army veteran who lived in nearby Malden with his German-born wife and two small children. He had numerous arrests for breaking into apartments and stealing whatever money he could find.

When asked why he perpetrated this odd and distasteful measuring charade, he responded, "I'm not good-looking. I'm not educated, but I was able to put something over on high-class people. They were all college kids and I never had anything in my life and I outsmarted them."

He was sentenced to eighteen months in prison and released in April of 1962, two months before Anna Slesers was found strangled. He told his parole officer he required sex at least six times a day, but no one suggested he seek or receive psychiatric help.

DeSalvo was born on September 3, 1931, in Chelsea, Massachusetts, one of six children. His father, Frank, was a violently abusive man who regularly beat his wife and children. Frank also brought prostitutes home and had sex with them in front of his family. At five or six, Albert played sex games with his brothers, no great surprise in light of his father's example. Albert developed some sadistic compulsions, which manifested themselves in cruelty to small animals. Throughout his adolescence, he went through periods of delinquency and pretty criminality, interspersed with periods of good behavior and staying out of trouble. His relationship with his mother, Charlotte, was reasonably good.

Albert was in the army from 1948 through 1956 and stationed for a time in Germany, where he met his wife, Irmgard Beck, an attractive woman from a respected family. He'd been promoted to a specialist E-5, but was demoted back to private for failure to obey an order. In 1955, he was arrested for fondling a young girl, but the charge was dropped. That same year, his first child, Judy, was born with a congenital pelvic disease. This had a large impact on DeSalvo's home life. Irmgard, terrified she would have another child with a handicap, tried to avoid sex, while Albert had a voracious sexual appetite. He received an honorable discharge from the service. Between 1956 and 1960, he had several arrests for breaking and entering, but each time received a suspended sentence. In 1960, a son, Michael, was born without handicaps.

In spite of his brushes with the law, DeSalvo managed to stay employed. He was a press operator at a rubber factory, then worked in a shipyard, then as a construction worker. Most people who knew Albert DeSalvo liked him, and one boss characterized him as a decent family man and good worker. Unlike his own father, Albert treated his wife and children with love and consideration.

Police arrested DeSalvo at home for the Green Man crimes. He was mortified that Irmgard would see him in handcuffs, but she urged him to tell the truth. He admitted to breaking into four hundred apartments and to assaulting some three hundred women in the four-state area. Given his tendency to self-aggrandize, it was difficult to know if the number was actually anywhere near that high.

On February 4, 1965, DeSalvo was sent by the court to Bridgewater State Hospital for psychiatric evaluation. Shortly thereafter, George Nassar, charged with the vicious, execution-style murder of a gas station attendant, also came to Bridgewater. He had a high IQ and the ability to manipulate. The two men were placed in the same ward, and he became Albert's confidant. Around that time, a police detective had come to Bridgewater to take DeSalvo's handprint for the Boston Strangler investigation. Soon Albert was telling people that, indeed, he was the Strangler.

Nassar contacted his own attorney, the soon to be famous F. Lee Bailey, who met with DeSalvo in prison even though DeSalvo was at the time represented by another lawyer. Bailey was able to obtain unreleased information on the Strangler cases from Boston PD so he could learn what DeSalvo actually knew. He taped an interview, then played it for the police.

Bailey said he was convinced Albert DeSalvo was the Boston Strangler. Ultimately, the police came to the same conclusion. Now there was a larger issue to contend with: how to deal with a self-confessed killer and the people's demand for justice.

With Bailey as his counsel, DeSalvo went to trial on January 10, 1967, not for the Boston Strangler murders, but for the Green Man assaults and break-ins. During the trial, Bailey conceded that DeSalvo was the Strangler, so as to earn him a spot in a mental institution instead of a penitentiary. DeSalvo was found guilty of the Green Man crimes and sentenced to life in prison.

While he was awaiting transfer to Walpole State Prison, DeSalvo escaped from Bridgewater with two other inmates and stayed out for thirty-six hours before turning himself in. Though the entire area was terrified that the Boston Strangler was free, he said he just wanted to show his desire to go into a mental institution.

The Boston Strangler phenomenon was huge. A book by Gerold Frank became a best-seller. A movie starred Tony Curtis and Henry Fonda. F. Lee Bailey became a celebrity and legal star. And from prison, Albert DeSalvo, the Measuring Man and the Green Man, basked in his notoriety as an American nightmare.

On December 27, 1973, DeSalvo was stabbed to death in the infirmary at Walpole. The murder was believed to be related to his involvement in a prison drug operation. Three inmates were tried, but twice the trials ended in hung juries. The controversy over whether DeSalvo actually was the Boston Strangler lives on long after him.

From all of my study of serial sexual offenders, I believe it is virtually impossible that Albert DeSalvo was the Boston Strangler.

Why not? He was there at the time. He was mobile in the way the Strangler was. He'd already demonstrated his proficiency at breaking and entering, his voracious sexual appetite, and his willingness to rape. He certainly had the kind of abusive background you'd expect to see in a sexual predator. So what's missing?

Behavior.

Through a lot of research and case experience, we at the FBI's National Center for the Analysis of Violent Crime at Quantico have divided rapists into four major categories: the power-reassurance rapist, the exploitative rapist, the anger rapist, and the sadistic rapist. There can be some overlap and crossover, just as there is with organized and disorganized criminal behavior, but these categories hold up well in providing insight into the type of personality who commits a given sexual crime.

Simply stated, the power-reassurance rapist is someone who feels himself to be inadequate and compensates for this by forcing women to have sex with him. The exploitive rapist is an impulsive predator who seizes an opportunity when it comes along. He is very conscious of his body and ego and, unlike the power-reassurance rapist, will be unconcerned with the victim's feelings. The anger rapist, also known as the anger-retaliatory rapist, uses sexual assault as a displaced expression of the rage and anger within him. The victim might represent a mother, wife, girlfriend, or even a group of people whom the offender hates. The sadistic rapist attacks because of sexual fantasies involving dominating, controlling, and hurting other people. Depending on his fantasies and preferences, the victim might be subjected to normal vaginal intercourse or anything in the range of perversity—including torture and/or death. The only thing that really matters to him is dominating the victim and making her suffer for his own pleasure and satisfaction.

As should be clear, though all forms of sexual attack are horrible and heinous, the anger rapist and the sadistic rapist will tend to be the most dangerous.

All of the evidence in the Green Man crimes suggest that the perpetrator was a power-reassurance rapist. He threatened his victims to get his way, but did not attack them with his knife. He talked to them and was apologetic. In an admittedly weird and self-centered way, he seemed concerned for their welfare.

This type of behavior squares with DeSalvo's background as the Measuring Man. A power-reassurance rapist will generally start out with so-called "nuisance crimes," such as voyeurism, and, as he gets older and a little more confident, will evolve into less benign activities that are still nonviolent. The important consideration is that this type of personality does not evolve into an anger-retaliatory or sadistic offender. Even DeSalvo's background gives him away on this. He hated his father but had good relationships with his mother and wife. This is not the hallmark of an anger rapist. But with the precipitating stressor of the birth of a sick child and his wife's resultant antipathy to sex, we have all the motivation we need for the evolution into a power-reassurance rapist.

If we look at the Boston Stranger murders, we see clear evidence of a sadistic rapist at work. He not only targeted young women but older, more vulnerable ones. He not only raped but beat them. He strangled them with articles of their own clothing. He depersonalized them. He posed them in such a way as to degrade the victims and shock whoever came upon the crime scene.

From a behavioral perspective, everything about these two sets of crimes is different. Keep in mind that the Green Man was still operating after Anna Slesers was killed. There is no way DeSalvo or any other killer could have deescalated from such a brutal murder back to the kind of assaults the Green Man was committing. Albert DeSalvo was not an angry or sadistic guy. If he were, this behavior would have shown up in other aspects of his life, and it would certainly have shown up in his interactions in prison.

Though DeSalvo wouldn't have committed crimes as savage and sadistic as those of the Boston Strangler, it is understandable that, once the suggestion was made to him, he'd take credit for the crimes. If he's power-reassurance motivated, then anything that puts him into a more macho light can be appealing to him. If he's looking for status, he knows he's not going to find it as a brain surgeon, a movie star, or a pro athlete. And one way or another, he's not getting back out on the street anytime soon. But in the milieu in which he's used to operating, if he can be perceived as a celebrity criminal, well, at least he's a somebody.

If DeSalvo was taking credit for crimes he did not commit, it was not the first time. He had claimed responsibility for a robbery and assault in Rhode Island in 1964, though someone else was identified by the victim and arrested for the crime. As to how he could have gained specific information on the Strangler murders, he later said he was so fascinated by the press accounts that in some cases he used his burglary skills and broke into the victims' apartments just to look around.

Other than for George Nassar, we can't be sure whom DeSalvo had extensive contact with at Bridgewater, but it is clear that he easily could have been fed additional information on the Strangler crimes. It is also possible that Bailey might unintentionally have asked him leading questions. Much was published in the papers. And though DeSalvo wasn't the brightest guy in the world, he was known for his excellent memory. Not only that, Albert's own extensive experience as a burglar allowed him to intuit some of the right answers just because he knew how an intruder would have acted. Even so, DeSalvo still got a number of Strangler details wrong or didn't remember at all.

No witness ever identified DeSalvo in connection with any of the Strangler crime scenes, and no physical evidence connects him to any of the murders.

No one has ever been tried for the Boston Strangler murders. A number of accomplished detectives never believed DeSalvo was the Strangler and, in fact, thought there was more than one offender. A number of reasonable alternative suspects have emerged over the years, including George Nassar himself, a criminally sophisticated convicted murderer with a high IQ who has admitted to having killed for excitement. However, he has steadfastly denied that he was the Strangler, and no official attempt has been made to tie him to the crimes.

New York police lieutenant Thomas Cavanaugh believed he discovered the identity of the Strangler through a 1963 homicide he investigated: the strangling of a sixty-two-year-old woman tied to Charles A. Terry, twenty-three at the time and a native of Waterville, Maine. Terry had been in

Boston during the first six Strangler murders, and evidence from the New York crime scene matched many of the Boston details, including positioning of the body, strangulation with a scarf, and tying the bow. He had been diagnosed as a psychopath and sexual sadist and had a history of assaults against women. He died in prison of lung cancer in 1981.

After the August 20, 1962, murder of sixty-seven-year-old Jane Sullivan, the sixth Strangler victim, George Snubbs, a man with a deviant sexual history, committed suicide several blocks from Sullivan's apartment by tying a bow around his neck with a pair of stockings. After his death, the age range of the Strangler's targeted victims shifted from older women to younger ones.

A man whose stay at Bridgewater overlapped with DeSalvo's was a suspect in the deaths of Anna Slesers, Jane Sullivan, and three others of the first wave of murders, since he was missing from Boston State Hospital on those dates. A diagnosed psychotic with a low IQ, he had tried to kill his mother, whom he regularly punched and kicked. He reportedly told his sister that he was the Strangler.

And then there was another inmate at Bridgewater whose stay overlapped DeSalvo's by five weeks. He was a university student in the Boston area during the Strangler murders. Another diagnosed psychotic and possible schizophrenic, he had an extremely high IQ, as well as a history of drug-abuse and petty crime. He had been arrested for abusing his pregnant wife. Friends said he was subject to wild fits of anger and violence and claimed he said he would save the world by destroying its women. His move from Boston to the Midwest coincided with seven brutal sexual murders there, in two of which stockings were tied around the victims' neck.

There is no evidence that Albert DeSalvo had any knowledge or insight as to the true identity of the Boston Strangler or Stranglers. He acknowledged the mystery, at the same time adding to his own mythology and mystique, with a poem he composed in prison. It ends:

> *Today he sits in a prison cell,*
> *Deep inside only a secret he can tell.*
> *People everywhere are still in doubt,*
> *Is the Strangler in prison or roaming about?*

CHAPTER SIX

THE JONBENET RAMSEY MURDER

In the JonBenet Ramsey murder case, many of the themes we've been dealing with come together: family . . . celebrity . . . personality evaluation . . . the suffering of the most innocent among us . . . kidnapping . . . brutal, sustained-aggression killing . . . and the appearance of raw evil where we least expect to find it. It is also the one case in this book with which I have had extensive personal involvement.

And since I am personally involved, it's probably necessary to say a couple of things up front. My purpose here is neither to defend or condemn John or Patricia Ramsey, nor to justify the actions or positions for which, in certain circles, I have been roundly criticized and my motives challenged. My purpose is only to explain how I reached the conclusions I did through the use of the criminal investigative analysis that I helped develop over a quarter of a century.

As I've stated on many occasions, murder is the single most disturbing and devastating experience that can happen to any of us; because murder, unlike death by disease or accident, is an intentional act, one that turns our world upside down and robs us of all of our basic orientations to the world except, if we are very fortunate, our faith. And this particular murder is among the most horrifying of all: both because of its beautiful, six-year-old victim, and because of the horrendous evil it implies by raising the possibility that a father or a mother could be capable of killing his or her own child.

The case is also noteworthy—virtually unique—for other reasons as well. Many crimes are tried in the court of public opinion long before they reach a court of law—the Borden, Lindbergh, and Simpson-Goldman murders, to name just a few. But I know of no other case in which

267

the majority of people have decided the solution based on statistics. I know of no other case in which the public substantially believes what has been reported in the tabloids. I know of no other case in which the main-line media have let the tabloids take the lead and then reported on their reporting. And I know of no other case in which largely respectable television programs have so tried to outdo each other in sensationalism. I would not be so exercised except this is so clearly and fundamentally the enemy of fairness and justice.

Am I saying I alone have the inside track on those two ideals? By no means. Nobody knows for certain what happened on the night of December 25, 1996, that caused the unnatural and violent death of Jon-Benet Patricia Ramsey, except for the person or persons who perpetrated it. All that any of the rest of us can do is to make our best judgment based on our common sense, analysis, and whatever expertise and experience we can bring to bear.

If I am vilified for coming out and stating what I believe to be true, so be it. It won't be the first time and doubtless will not be the last. I had already experienced this reaction when I was called to Atlanta in 1980 during the horrifying string of child murders. I came away with the police pissed off at me for moving in on their territory and the public rejecting my suggestion that the killings of black children wasn't an organized conspiracy of hate by the Ku Klux Klan, but the work of a lone and inadequate young black man. That's the nature of the business.

But the important point I want to make here is that a criminal investigation is not a popularity contest. It is not, nor should it be, directed or determined by public opinion or media influence.

Some have called me a "hired gun" in this case, and it is true that I received a small fee early on, as I have in certain other cases in which I have consulted since leaving the Bureau. Some have called me a "publicity hound," and it is true that I have never been shy around a camera, particularly in the days when I was trying to get the FBI's profiling program off the ground and would seek publicity from just about anywhere, both to support the program and to elicit the public's help on individual cases. But I have *never ever* offered an opinion that wasn't deeply felt and fully supported by my own belief and the facts as I saw them.

A defense attorney has the responsibility of making a case for his client's innocence, whether he believes in that innocence or not. A criminal investigator has only one responsibility, and it is an extremely solemn one. It has to do neither with whom he or she works for, nor who is signing the paycheck. It should have nothing to do with personal glory or career advancement. It has only to do with the silent pledge made by the investigator to the victim, who can no longer speak for herself, that he or she will do everything within his or her power to uncover the truth of what happened and bring the offender to the gates of earthly justice. There is not enough money or fame in the entire world to lure me away from the enormity and seriousness of that pledge.

And I am far from alone in this. I believe in the sincerity of that pledge no less vehemently with regard to former detective Steve Thomas, with whose interpretation I disagree radically, than with detective Lou Smit, with whom I am in much more basic agreement, to name but two participants in this case. I believe both men to be of solid integrity and to want nothing more or less than justice for JonBenet. I hope they regard me the same way.

With that off my chest, let's look carefully at the Ramsey case and why it has haunted us so profoundly.

I don't think we can deny that we became obsessed with this one because the victim was so young, blond, and beautiful, the parents rich and prominent and intelligent, the neighborhood fashionable and safe, the community secure and self-satisfied, and the timing—Christmas. All these elements suggest a crime like this should not have occurred. If ever there was a "man bites dog" case, this is it. Even her unique name—a combination of her father's given names coupled with her mother's first name—added to the mystique.

And let us be plain: the first time we saw those beauty-pageant images of the mini Las Vegas showgirl—the pint-size cowboy sweetheart and the patriotic, red-white-and-blue-bedecked, tap-dancing tot, eyes always full of fun and mischief and hand resting confidently on a cocked hip—they were instantly and indelibly etched on our collective memory. District Attorney Alex Hunter offered the opinion that it was this pageant film that separates this case from two thousand other child homicides. In a bizarre and perverse mockery of our cult of celebrity, in death JonBenet became America's greatest cover girl.

DECEMBER 25–26, 1996

So how are we going to approach this case?

Regardless of who the killer is, we've got to deal with the facts as they were. We've got to be able to track a family from a morning of gifts and visiting and childish delight, through a happy and fun-filled Christmas dinner with good friends and the anticipation of an early-morning flight on their private plane to their vacation home, to the garroting, blunt-

269

force trauma, sexual assault, and fatal sustained aggression against a six-year-old last known to be asleep in her bed.

Those are the facts. Any participants and motives we attempt to plug into the scenario must work with those facts.

For law enforcement, the case began at 5:52 A.M. on December 26, 1996, when a Boulder, Colorado, police dispatcher took the following 911 emergency call from Patricia Ann Ramsey:

Ramsey: (inaudible) police.

Dispatcher: (inaudible)

Ramsey: Seven fifty-five Fifteenth Street.

Dispatcher: What's going on there, ma'am?

Ramsey: We have a kidnapping. Hurry, please.

D: Explain to me what's going on, okay?

R: There we have a . . . There's a note left and our daughter's gone.

D: A note was left and your daughter is gone?

R: Yes.

D: How old is your daughter?

R: She's six years old. . . . She's blond . . . six years old.

D: How long ago was this?

R: I don't know. I just found the note and my daughter's (inaudible).

D: Does it say who took her?

R: What?

D: Does it say who took her?

R: No. I don't know . . . it's there . . . there's a ransom note here.

D: It's a ransom note?

R: It says "S.B.T.C. Victory." Please . . .

D: Okay, what's your name? Are you . . .

R: Patsy Ramsey. I'm the mother. Oh my God, please . . .

D: I'm . . . Okay, I'm sending an officer over, okay?

R: Please.

D: Do you know how long she's been gone?

R: No, I don't. Please, we just got up and she's not here. Oh my God, please.

D: Okay.

R: Please send somebody.

D: I am, honey.

R: Please.

D: Take a deep breath (inaudible).

R: Hurry, hurry, hurry (inaudible).

D: Patsy? Patsy? Patsy? Patsy? Patsy?

Within a few minutes, Boulder PD officer Rick French arrived at 755 Fifteenth Street, a large, red-brick, Tudor-style house in the city's University Hill neighborhood. The exterior of the house was elaborately decorated for Christmas. He was met at the front door by the missing child's mother, Patricia Ramsey, three days short of her fortieth birthday, attired in a red sweater and black slacks. They were joined shortly by the father, John Bennett Ramsey, fifty-three years of age, dressed in a blue-and-white-striped shirt and khaki slacks. Patsy was John's second wife. His first marriage, to the former Lucinda Lou Pasch, had ended in divorce, and he and Patsy had been married for sixteen years. Officer French's impression was that Patsy appeared agitated and distraught, while John appeared tense but calm and controlled. Their nearly ten-year-old son, Burke, had not yet been awakened.

They told French that Patsy had come down from her third-floor bedroom around 5:45 A.M. to awaken six-year-old JonBenet and to begin getting everything ready for their flight to Charlevoix, Michigan, where their vacation home was located. From there, they had planned to fly to Florida to take Burke and JonBenet on a cruise on Disney's *Big Red Boat*.

JonBenet's bedroom was empty. Patsy then descended the back spiral staircase outside the child's room on the second floor. On one of the lower steps she noted three sheets of lined, white legal paper laid side by side. They showed French the communication, now laid out on the wooden floor of the hallway outside the kitchen:

Mr. Ramsey,
    Listen carefully! We are a
group of individuals that represent
a small foreign faction. We [cross-out]
respect your bussiness but not the
country that it serves. At this
time we have your daughter in our
posession. She is safe and un harmed
and if you want her to see 1997,
you must follow our instructions to
the letter.
    You will withdraw $118,000.00
from your account. $100,000 will be
in $100 bills and the remaining
$18,000 in $20 bills. Make sure
that you bring an adequate size
attache to the bank. When you

get home you will put the money
in a brown paper bag. I will
call you between 8 and 10 am
tomorrow to instruct you on delivery.
The delivery will be exhausting so
I advise you to be rested. If
we monitor you getting the money
early, we might call you early to
arrange an earlier delivery of the
[Page 2]
money and hence a earlier
[cross-out] pick-up of your daug hter.
Any deviation of my instructions
will result in the immediate
execution of your daughter. You
will also be denied her remains
for proper burial. The two
gentlemen watching over your daughter
do not particularly like you so I
advise you not to provoke them.
Speaking to anyone about your
situation, such as Police, F.B.I.,etc.,
will result in your daughter being
beheaded. If we catch you talking
to a stray dog, she dies. If you
alert bank authorities, she dies.
If the money is in any way
marked or tampered with, she
dies. You will be scanned for
electronic devices and if any are
found, she dies. You can try to
deceive us but be warned that
we are familiar with Law enforcement
countermeasures and tactics. You
stand a 99% chance of killing
your daughter if you try to out
smart us. Follow our instructions
[Page 3]
and you stand a 100% chance
of getting her back. You and
your family are under constant

scrutiny as well as the authorities.
Don't try to grow a brain
John. You are not the only
fat cat around so don't think
that killing will be difficult.
Don't underestimate us John.
Use that good southern common
sense of yours. It is up to
you now John!
Victory!
S.B.T.C

The note was written with a black, felt-tip marking pen, and the blocky handwriting appeared to belong to someone who was either extremely nervous or consciously attempting to disguise his or her normal style, possibly by writing with the nondominant hand.

Before long, the patrol supervisor, Sergeant Paul Reichenbach, came to the house. The note had warned against notifying the police—something just about any parent would do regardless of the threat—and if the house was under surveillance, or "scrutiny," as the note said, the presence of two marked patrol cars would have been quite obvious.

Along with Reichenbach, two sets of the Ramseys' close friends, Fleet and Priscilla White and John and Barbara Fernie, responded to Patsy's frantic phone calls and came over. The Whites had hosted the Christmas dinner the previous evening. It was the second year that the Ramseys and the Whites had spent Christmas together.

Reichenbach called for more personnel, including a crime scene evidence team, and someone from the victim-witness office. He instructed the telephone company to institute a trap-and-trace on the Ramseys' line, then notified the detective supervisor on call, Sergeant Robert Whitson. He directed that there be no further police radio traffic in case the kidnappers had access to a police scanner. Reichenbach conducted a quick survey of the house, including JonBenet's room. He found no obvious signs of forced entry. His observations were consistent with French's: Patsy was verging on hysteria while John was calm and composed. According to witnesses, they did not seem to interact much, especially once the Whites and Fernies arrived. The two women took Patsy into the sunroom off the living room to sit with her and comfort her.

Now, even at this early stage, we're already starting to see some problems with the investigation. The premises from which a victim has presumably been kidnapped are a crime scene and must be treated as such to preserve potential crucial clues. All investigators operate according to the "theory of transfer," which states that no one enters or exits a room without leaving something behind and taking something away. Therefore, the more people at a scene—and this includes police officers—the more corrupted the scene will be. It is perfectly understandable that the Ramseys would want their closest friends around them, and commendable that the police would want them to have this emotional support during their ordeal, but valuable evidence already could have been destroyed. The first choice would be to remove everyone from the house and take them to the police station or some other location, and to secure the house and grounds. If that was not deemed practical for whatever reason—such as the need to wait for a phone call from the kidnapper—and if everyone had to be there, then they needed to be contained in one place where they would not corrupt the entire scene. They should not have been allowed to wander the house freely, particularly in obviously critical areas such as JonBenet's bedroom. Unfortunately, these mistakes would be compounded as the morning wore on.

At one point Fleet White attempted to help out by conducting his own search. On the far wall of a storage room in the labyrinthine basement, a small broken window immediately caught his attention. In another part of the basement, White also walked through the small furnace room toward a door to another storage room the Ramseys referred to as the wine cellar, even though they were both very light drinkers. It was completely dark when White opened the door and he could not find a light switch, so he reclosed the door and returned upstairs. There, John Ramsey explained that he himself had broken the window Fleet had seen some months earlier when he'd returned to the empty house without his key.

By this time two victim advocates had arrived to offer emotional support for the Ramseys and to act as liaisons with the police. But this further complicated the scene. And as one officer left the house to bring the ransom note to police headquarters, the Ramseys' pastor, the Reverend Rol Hoverstock, of St. John's Episcopal Church, also arrived.

During this time Burke Ramsey was awakened and told that his sister was missing. He dressed and was taken from the house to the Whites'. John and Patsy wanted him removed from the tension and trauma as much as possible, but this action could be criticized. If JonBenet had (presumably) been kidnapped by unknown parties for unknown reasons, how much sense does it make to bring Burke to an unsecured location? Why did the police accede to it?

As with many aspects of this case, at least two explanations are possible. On the positive side, we could say that in times like this, under this incredible stress, you tend to think in a linear, immediate-result-oriented manner. John and Patsy didn't want Burke traumatized for life by what he might experience here, and so they wanted him taken to the place he felt most comfortable and safe. The police agreed to this because they were sensitive to the same things the Ramseys were.

The negative interpretation would hold that if one or both of the Ramseys had been the perpetrator, they would know that Burke was in no danger away from them. And the negative judgment on the police would be that they blew it: they never should have let a potential victim and/or material witness out of their protection. Yet, one (that is, the Ramseys or the police) could easily reason that if the kidnapper had wanted Burke, he would have taken him at the same time he took JonBenet. And at the Whites' house, Burke would be under constant visual supervision by people who genuinely cared for him, and no one is going to brazenly break in in broad daylight and grab him.

My decades of experience investigating kidnappings and murders tells me that the proper explanation cannot be determined in a vacuum. Each element must be fit into an overall pattern, which is what we'll attempt to do.

Sergeant Whitson put detectives on the case, then informed the Boulder County Sheriff's Department and the District Attorney's Office, in the person of Peter Hofstrom, chief of the felony division. According to Steve Thomas, the detective who was to play a major role in the investigation, a canine unit with a tracking dog was also put on standby, but for some reason was never used. Thomas considers this another mistake, and I agree. I have been impressed by the ability of tracking dogs to follow even a faint scent from a given point to where the victim was next taken.

John Ramsey called his friend Rod Westmoreland, an attorney and vice president of Merrill Lynch's Atlanta office, to arrange for the ransom money. John and Patsy had met in Atlanta and lived there until John's successful regional computer-distribution company, MicroSouth, merged with two others to form Access Graphics, with the central office to be located in Boulder. John moved there to become chief executive. Patsy and the children followed, after Patsy found the 1920s house on Fifteenth Street. Patsy's father, Donald Paugh, a former Union Carbide executive, worked for John's company in Atlanta and also moved to Boulder. Access, which topped $1 billion in annual sales, was then sold to Lockheed Martin, which kept John as chief executive.

In spite of the relocation of the family out West, the Ramseys still essentially considered themselves Atlantans, and Patsy, a native West Virginian who had represented the state in the Miss America pageant, missed many aspects of the Southern lifestyle.

Westmoreland, tracked down at his parents' home in Tupelo, Mississippi, quickly went to work on the money. He called back to tell John he had arranged for a $118,000 credit line on his Visa card, which would translate to a cash advance at any local bank. Needless to say, anytime the phone rang, the police immediately snapped to attention, expecting that it might be the kidnapper calling.

A little after 8 A.M., Sergeant Whitson contacted John Eller, commander of the Boulder PD detective division. Like so many other people at this time of year, Eller was out of town, vacationing with his family in Florida. Within a few minutes of this call, detectives Linda Arndt and Fred Patterson arrived on scene, having already seen the ransom note and been apprised of the situation thus far. From all accounts, Arndt treated the Ramseys with great compassion and consideration, trying to reassure Patsy as best she could. She instructed John on how to react when the kidnapper called, stressing that he should try to keep him on the line as long as possible.

John called Michael Archuleta, the private pilot who was to fly the Ramsey plane, a 1972, twin-engine Beechcraft King Air C-90, to Charlevoix, Michigan, and told him what had happened. Archuleta had worked extensively with John, and they considered each other good friends. John's two older children from his first marriage, Melinda and John Andrew, and Melinda's fiancé, Stewart Long, had planned to fly from Atlanta to Minneapolis where they would be picked up by the Ramsey plane, and then they'd all proceed to Charlevoix. John asked Mike to reach them at the Minneapolis Airport and have them divert to Denver. John's oldest daughter, Elizabeth, called Beth, had been killed in an automobile accident in Chicago with her friend Matt Darrington on January 8, 1992, when she was twenty-two. John had been devastated by the loss of Beth, going into an extended mourning, but by his own account had come out of the ordeal with his faith renewed and strengthened. The Beechcraft plane was named for Beth.

Police officers began questioning the Ramseys, trying to piece together an official version of the story. Both of them thought all doors had been locked the previous night. According to Steve Thomas's account, there was some discrepancy in Patsy's story as to whether she'd checked Jon-Benet's room and found it empty, which had prompted her to go downstairs looking for her and found the note, or whether she had found the note first and then gone to the bedroom to check. While this could be significant if Patsy was, in fact, still working on getting her story "straight,"

I have generally found that parents of child victims often don't remember details of their own actions during these times of fear and stress. I have seen parents block out the entire experience the way you hear of car-crash victims being unable to recall anything about the accident.

Both parents remembered leaving the Whites' house about 8:30 in the evening, making two brief stops to leave gifts at the houses of other friends, and returning home shortly after 9:00. JonBenet fell asleep in the car, and John carried her into the house and upstairs to her room, where Patsy got her ready for bed. They said she did not wake up during any of this. John then went to attend to Burke, but the boy insisted on completing assembly of a Christmas toy. By the time John put him to bed and came up to his own bedroom, a converted attic space on the third floor, Patsy was already in bed. John took a melatonin tablet to help him sleep and set the alarm clock for 5:30 A.M.

The detectives asked John if he could think of anyone who might have taken JonBenet or might wish him harm. The first person he thought of was Jeff Merrick, a longtime Access Graphics employee who had been let go and was apparently extremely bitter about it. He had filed a complaint with Lockheed Martin, and John was told by several people that Merrick had threatened to bring down both him and Access.

Patsy's first thought when asked a similar question was Linda Hoffmann-Pugh, their housekeeper. Patsy said Linda had been acting strangely and had asked to borrow $2,500 because she couldn't pay her rent. Patsy also recalled that her own mother, Nedra Paugh, had told her that Linda had once remarked, "JonBenet is so pretty; aren't you afraid that someone might kidnap her?"

The police sent officers out to interview Hoffmann-Pugh and her husband in nearby Fort Lupton. In the meantime, the 8:00–10:00 window in which the kidnapper had said he would call had come and gone, unless, John Ramsey recalled thinking, it referred to the next day. Since they didn't know exactly when the crime had taken place—before or after midnight—John could not be sure. At one point, John was seen going through the mail, and the rumor surfaced that he had left the house to go get it. In fact, the mail came into the house through a slot in the front door. Several people have commented on the apparent nonchalance and detachment this demonstrates, but John says that he was anxious to see if there was any communication from the kidnapper.

By lunchtime no word had come, and the various police officials began leaving the house and returning to the station to work the case. The two victim advocates had also gone. This left Detective Linda Arndt as the only police officer at the scene to supervise seven civilians: John and

Patsy Ramsey, Fleet and Priscilla White (who had returned after taking Burke to their house to be watched), John and Barbara Fernie, and the Reverend Rol Hoverstock. Arndt was clearly uncomfortable with this arrangement and called Detective Sergeant Larry Mason for backup. For whatever reason—possibly due to the holiday-thinned staffing roster—none came.

In what may have been an attempt to keep John occupied while she was dealing with everyone by herself, around 1:00 in the afternoon Arndt asked him to take one of the other men and look through the house to see if they could find anything new or possibly related to the crime. John asked Fleet White to accompany him and suggested that they begin in the basement and work their way up.

THE WINE CELLAR

John and Fleet went through the basement room by room. Past the table set up with Burke's electric trains, they came upon the broken window, where they found several small splinters of glass on the floor. John figured these were probably still from his unusual entry the previous summer. It certainly seems odd in retrospect not to have fixed the window in all those months, but this was a low-crime area. The Ramseys also had a burglar alarm, but had not used it for months because the children kept accidentally setting it off.

John and Fleet noticed a suitcase resting near the window. If there had been an intruder and the window was his point of exit, he could have used it as a step. But since the two men moved it in their search, it would be difficult to say. They looked through the crawl spaces under the dining room, then retraced their steps into the furnace room, coming to the wine-cellar door that Fleet had looked in earlier and found pitch-black.

But as soon as John opened the door, he saw something and, according to White, screamed, "Oh my God, oh my God!"

John raced in and found JonBenet lying on her back on the floor with a white blanket wrapped around her torso. Her hands were stretched over her head, tightly bound with thin cord. A piece of black duct tape covered her mouth. Next to her body was one of her favorite pink nightgowns.

Fleet touched JonBenet's ankle; it was cold. He turned and raced up the stairs for help. John knelt down over her, ripped the tape from her mouth, pulled off the blanket, and began trying to loosen the wrist binding. All the while he said he begged her to talk to him. Her eyes were closed.

He picked her up and carried her stiff body upright around the waist, up the stairs into the living room where Linda Arndt was. Fleet had already come upstairs and shouted for someone to call an ambulance. John laid JonBenet on the floor next to the Christmas tree, uttering words of comfort while Arndt checked for vital signs. But the detective could see that the child was in full rigor mortis and her lips were blue. Fleet then went back to the basement, where he picked up the piece of duct tape. That made two people who had now handled it.

Before Patsy came back into the room, John covered JonBenet's body with another blanket, as if he were tucking her into bed. The Reverend Rol Hoverstock saw what was happening and began praying out loud. When he completed his prayer, he informed John that he had performed the last rites of the Episcopal Church over JonBenet.

There are conflicting versions of what Patsy did at this point. According to Steve Thomas's account, which presumably came from his fellow police officers, as soon as Fleet came upstairs shouting, Priscilla White and Barbara Fernie hurried toward the sound, while Patsy did not move from the couch in the sunroom. She came in a few moments later supported by her friends. According to John Ramsey's account, Patsy essentially fought her way into the living room, rushing past him and falling onto JonBenet's body, screaming and crying hysterically. It is then generally agreed that she implored Hoverstock with something to the effect of "Jesus, you raised Lazarus from the dead. Raise my baby from the dead!"

Whatever the exact timing or sequence was, at one moment John Ramsey and Linda Arndt were face-to-face kneeling over JonBenet's body. It was right after Arndt had searched in vain for a pulse and John asked her if his daughter was still alive. She looked him in the eye and told him that JonBenet was dead. John emitted a low groan of anguish.

Now here the narrative gets strange. John and Patsy were both feeling that Arndt had been extremely solicitous and sensitive toward them and continued to feel so throughout that agonized afternoon and the days ahead. Other members of the police department apparently had the same impression. In fact, at some later point, certain other detectives were annoyed that Patsy would speak with Arndt but not with them.

But three years after these events, when she had left the Boulder police force, Arndt recalled the scene differently when she appeared on a nationally broadcast television program. "And as we looked at each other, I remember—and I wore a shoulder holster—tucking my gun right next to me and consciously counting, I've got eighteen bullets. . . . Because I didn't know if we'd all be alive when people showed up." She went on to say, "Everything made sense in that instance. And I knew what happened."

The implication, I think it's generally agreed, is that what she felt happened was that John had killed his daughter or had at least taken part in the killing or the cover-up.

To my way of thinking, this is an extremely peculiar statement on many levels. For one, none of it ever went into Arndt's reports. Second, she apparently continued to treat the Ramseys well, not giving any indication that she felt she was dealing with suspects rather than grieving parents. Third, even if John Ramsey was going to attack her right then and there, what's this about having to count eighteen bullets? There were only seven people in the house beside herself, and none of them was armed. I set great store in gathering impressions through face-to-face contact, but what kind of evidence is this—she saw murder in his eyes?

I would tend to chalk up this reaction to the profound stress of having to deal with the situation on her own without any support, having the dead child found right in the house after police searches had missed her, and realizing therefore that the crime scene was coming apart before her eyes. Even her former fellow officers found the statement curious.

FROM KIDNAPPING TO MURDER

As the case suddenly turned from kidnapping to murder, Linda Arndt directed John to call 911 again. When that didn't provide immediate results, she called twice more on her own. She would soon get the backup she'd been requesting: more police, an FBI special agent from the Denver Field Office, the fire department, and an ambulance with paramedics. Boulder police chief Thomas Koby called detective commander John Eller and told him his help was urgently needed.

Amidst the new clamor and turmoil, Detective Sergeant Larry Mason asked John Ramsey his plans. John's instincts were to get the family back to Atlanta, where their parents and his brother Jeff were, and where he already knew he wanted to bury his daughter, near Beth in the cemetery in Marietta, Georgia. Mason told him the family should stay in the area, at least for several days. According to John, he said they would. The police say they overheard a telephone conversation in which John told Mike to prepare the plane to fly to Atlanta and considered it suspicious that he'd want to get out of town so quickly. If, in fact, it did happen that way, I see nothing suspicious in it. This is a man used to being able to control things who wants to get to the comfort and relative safety of the place he considers his real home.

The police now wanted the house cleared. One of the Fernies suggested that the Ramseys go to the Fernies' house in South Boulder. Just as they were leaving through the front door around 2:15, a taxi pulled up with John Andrew and Melinda Ramsey and Stewart Long, who'd taken the first flight they could from Minnesota after getting the message from Mike Archuleta. John went to them and told them, "JonBenet is gone." Everyone erupted in a new flood of tears.

At about the same time, Detective Thomas Trujillo arrived with a consent-to-search form, which he handed to Larry Mason, who asked John to sign it. He did so, later saying he thought he was signing a consent form for an autopsy to be performed on JonBenet.

Then the Ramseys drove to the Fernies' home, where Fleet White would bring Burke, and where they would have a twenty-four-hour police guard. What they didn't know at the time was that those officers would be trying to listen to every word they said.

Though in retrospect the scene was already hopelessly compromised, detectives went about the collection of evidence. The most crucial piece was the ransom note itself, which fortunately had already been taken in and preserved. Sergeant Whitson had asked the Ramseys for handwriting exemplars to compare with the note, and John had quickly given him two white, lined legal tablets. One had been lying on the kitchen countertop and contained Patsy's notes, doodles, and shopping lists. The other was on a table in the hallway not far from the spiral staircase on which Patsy had found the note and contained John's writings. Whitson marked the top sheets "John" and "Patsy." The two pads were taken to the police department and given to Detective Jeff Kithcart, the forgery and fraud expert.

As he was going through Patsy's pad, Kithcart noticed something extraordinary. Toward the middle of the tablet, a few words were written on a page in black, felt-tip pen: "Mr. and Mrs.," along with a single downstroke that could easily have been the beginning of a capital *R*. The paper appeared the same as the one on which the ransom note was written. Apparently, this was a first draft, and after consideration, the writer had decided to address the note to Mr. Ramsey only.

What this meant, of course, is that police could now say with a fair degree of certainty that the three-page ransom note was written *in the Ramsey house,* using their own pad and paper. This narrowed the scenario considerably. Either an intruder (or intruders) had spent a fair amount of time in the house undiscovered, or JonBenet had been killed by one or more of the three individuals known to be in the house at the same time: John, Patsy, and Burke.

When a child is murdered in or near the home, the parents and close family members are always high on the initial suspect list. Statistics tell us that they are the likely killers. As a rule of thumb, the younger the child, the more probable a family member was involved. This was certainly well-known to Special Agent Ron Walker of the Bureau's Denver Field Office, who had been called in to consult on the case.

There are few people in law enforcement for whom I have higher regard than Ron. For one thing, I trained him in profiling and criminal investigative analysis at Quantico and found him to be a natural. For another, he saved my life. In December of 1983, when I had lapsed into a coma in my Seattle hotel room from viral encephalitis while working the Green River murders, it had been Ron and fellow agent Blaine McIlwain who'd gotten worried when they couldn't reach me and broken down the door and rescued me.

Ron advised the Boulder police to look closely at the parents; this was the highest-percentage shot in a case like this. He also pledged whatever assistance from the FBI the police would like. Similar offers would soon come from Denver PD and the Colorado Bureau of Investigation.

Just so we get this straight, since the passage of the Lindbergh law, the FBI has primary jurisdiction in a kidnapping case. But once a body is found, it becomes a local matter because homicide is a state crime. Then, the Bureau can do no more than offer whatever assistance the local agency wishes to have. The FBI can provide an evidence response team, profiling and criminal investigative analysis, lab facilities, legal advice, major-case computer management, cover out-of-state leads and liaison, whatever. But they have to be requested. Unfortunately, none of these services was used early on to an extent that could have made a difference in the investigation.

This is an important consideration in all of law enforcement. Just as in medicine, where doctors refer patients to other doctors with specialty training in a given field, no law enforcement official is going to be expert in everything. And the smaller and less experienced the department, the less specialized expertise they're going to have. This is completely understandable and there is no shame in it.

What is understandable but not acceptable is when a department refuses to accept assistance from another agency that does have the expertise and the experience. The Boulder PD was—and is—full of dedicated, hardworking officers. But it is also true (as well as fortunate) that the city has only suffered, on average, a single homicide a year. Regardless of their dedication, there's no way they could have the depth to work a homicide the way a major department such as New York or Denver could. Evidently, this one looked pretty straightforward to them, even though the crime scene itself was already a mess.

I've had it both ways, and I've often found that when a local department calls us in willingly and early, as opposed to when the investigation has already gone south and the media and the public are screaming for results, it means that the guy or woman in charge generally has a fair degree of self-confidence and therefore is not threatened by outsiders trying to help. Two out of many such individuals who come immediately to mind are Lexington County, South Carolina, sheriff Jim Metts, who asked for my unit's assistance when a young woman and a little girl were abducted from in front of their houses, and Rochester, New York, police captain Lynde Johnson, who asked us to help solve a series of prostitute murders. I personally worked the South Carolina case on scene, and my associate Gregg McCrary went up to Rochester. In both cases, a highly effective working relationship between local law enforcement and the FBI led to successful apprehensions and trials. I wish the same had happened in Boulder.

Linda Arndt and Larry Mason came back to the Fernies' house several times the following day to talk to the Ramseys. At one point Arndt asked John and Patsy to come down to the police station and answer questions more formally.

I don't mean to implicate either officer, but it was probably around this time that the antagonism and animosity between the Ramseys and Boulder Police really took root, and I don't think it was the conscious doing of either side.

Patsy was distraught, heavily sedated, and proclaiming she wanted to die. John didn't feel she was in any shape to leave the house and be subjected to the rigors of a police interview. The police had a high-profile murder investigation on their hands, the kind that often or usually ends up with parental involvement, and they wanted to lock the parents each into his or her own story.

The Ramseys' friend Michael Bynum was at the Fernies' paying a condolence call when Linda Arndt made the interview request of John. Bynum was an attorney who had been a prosecutor in the Boulder district attorney's office and was now in private practice with a large local firm. He told John he was wary of how they were now being treated by the police and asked if John and Patsy would trust him to make some decisions on their behalf. John said he was only too grateful to have the help of a close friend.

Bynum immediately told the police that the Ramseys would not be going down to the police station to be interviewed at this time because he didn't feel they were in shape for it. Then he contacted Bryan Morgan, a prominent Denver attorney and one of the name partners of Haddon,

Morgan and Foreman, and asked him to represent John. Bynum got another attorney, Patrick Burke, to represent Patsy. Bynum had enough experience with the criminal justice system to believe that anyone who became enmeshed with it needed to be personally represented by counsel.

POSTMORTEM

The postmortem exam was conducted by Dr. John E. Meyer, a pathologist and coroner of Boulder County. Meyer had been called to the Ramsey house around 8 P.M. on December 26 to conduct a brief examination and officially pronounce JonBenet dead. During that ten-minute look, he noted a ligature around the right wrist and, when the body was turned over, another around the neck, so tight it had dug a furrow into the skin. It was a garrote, knotted in the back and fastened to a broken four-inch stick that had been used to tighten it. JonBenet was wearing a gold cross and chain, which were tangled in the ligature. A small area of abrasion or contusion was on the cheek near the right ear, and a prominent dried abrasion was on the lower left side of the neck. The broken stick turned out to be part of a paintbrush handle from Patsy's painting kit in the basement. The kit itself was right outside the wine-cellar door, meaning it was the first handy implement the killer would have noticed.

JonBenet was wearing long underwear over floral print panties, both of which were stained with urine. A red stain consistent with blood was also in the crotch of her panties. At the time it was believed that semen deposits were found in the panties and on her leg. This report later turned out to be erroneous.

The actual autopsy took place in the coroner's lab in the basement of the Boulder Community Hospital. In addition to the observations he made at the house, Meyer noted tiny petechial hemorrhages on the eyelids. Further hemorrhaging appeared on either side of the ligature furrow around the neck.

Dried blood was found around the entrance to the vagina, as well as hyperemia, or engorged blood vessels, indicating possible trauma in the tissue around and just inside the vagina. The hymen was not intact, and abrasions along the vaginal wall were visible. The fingernails were clipped for lab analysis. Meyer reported occasional scattered petechial hemorrhaging on the surface of each lung and the anterior surface of the heart.

When he made an incision and pulled back the scalp, Meyer saw a large—seven-by-four-inch—area of hemorrhage on the right side. Underneath was an even larger skull fracture, approximately eight and a half inches long. A thin film of subarachnoid hemorrhage (that is, bleeding under the membrane covering the brain) overlay the entire right cerebral hemisphere. Underneath, the gray matter of the brain itself was bruised.

The small intestine contained fragmented pieces of semidigested fruit that Meyer believed might be pineapple. This detail became important in the investigation because neither John nor Patsy recalled JonBenet's eating anything after they left the Whites'. In fact, she fell asleep in the car and did not wake up when John carried her upstairs or when Patsy prepared her for bed. Yet the state of the pineapple in the intestines suggested it was eaten that day or evening, and a bowl with cut pineapple was noted in the Ramsey kitchen. The bowl was processed for prints; Patsy's and Burke's were found, but not JonBenet's. Police picked this out as an inconsistency in Patsy's story. Patsy and John said they were perplexed by the finding and had no explanation for it. I would expect guilty people to come up with some explanation.

The bottom line was that JonBenet had been strangled with a garrote-style ligature and had suffered massive blunt-force trauma to the right side of her head. Though there was and still is some question about which injury occurred first, either would have been sufficient to kill her. The petechial hemorrhages on the insides of the eyelids as well as other places, coupled with the lack of substantial bleeding from the head wound, suggest that the strangulation was first, so that by the time of the head injury her heart was no longer pumping or was pumping only weakly.

The official cause of death was listed as asphyxia by strangulation associated with craniocerebral trauma.

EVIDENCE

Everything that had touched JonBenet's body was collected—clothing, the blankets, even the silk blouse and jeans Linda Arndt was wearing when she had leaned over the dead child.

In the house, police technicians reviewed the scene in the basement where the body was discovered and the area around the broken window. There were pieces of glass outside the window and a scuff mark on the wall. During this search Detective Michael Everett found Patsy's painting box, from which the wooden stick used in the garrote had come. Splinters on the floor next to the box indicated that this was where it had been broken. It was then logical to surmise that here or near here was where the garroting had taken place, rather than upstairs in the bedroom.

On the second floor, in the bathroom off JonBenet's bedroom, investigators found a balled-up red turtleneck, which Patsy said JonBenet had been wearing when she went to bed. No one seemed to know how it ended up there. Next to the spiral staircase and opposite JonBenet's bedroom, there was a stacked washer/dryer unit and laundry-room-type wall cabinets. One of the cabinets was open with a package of pull-up diapers visible. This seemed odd in a household with a nine-year-old and a six-year-old, but JonBenet, advanced for her age in most other ways, had a fairly chronic problem with wetting the bed and, to a lesser extent, her pants. The bed-wetting was so common that Linda Hoffmann-Pugh reported that before she even got to work in the morning, Patsy would routinely strip JonBenet's bedsheets and put them into the washer/dryer.

The bed-wetting became critical in the investigation because it suggested a possible motive for one parent and hinted at possible behavior from the other. It would be suggested that Patsy had accidently fatally injured her daughter when she lost it with her over the bed-wetting. It would also be suggested that JonBenet's wetting and occasional soiling were a reaction to sexual advances and abuse by her father.

The police also searched the area surrounding the house.

WHAT KIND OF PEOPLE ARE THEY?

Several things happened in relatively quick succession that helped open a seemingly unbridgeable rift between the Ramseys and the police and ultimately created the enduring public perception of the couple.

First of all, the statistics pointed to them being involved in the murder, particularly in a house where they were the only known adults present and there was no clear-cut sign of forced entry. Second, they didn't appear to behave the way parents in this situation are "supposed" to behave. John was quiet, controlled, and stoic and Patsy often hysterical, but they didn't cling together and constantly comfort and reassure each other. They didn't make a big deal out of waiting for the ransom call that never came, and they didn't overwhelm the police with requests or demands that they find the killer or killers of their child—all of the things "normal" parents would be expected to do. Along with that, they refused to go into the police station the next day and submit to separate interviews. And finally, they "lawyered up" almost right away. If they were innocent and had nothing to hide, why would they decline to answer questions and why would they need an attorney, much less a separate one for each of them?

We can approach these issues in several ways, all of them inconclusive. As we noted in the Lindbergh kidnapping, each individual is going to react differently. Many people thought Charles Lindbergh might be involved in the disappearance of his toddler son because of his seeming coldness and emotional aloofness. In fact, this was a man who knew he reacted best to crises when he maintained complete control. The same could be said of John Ramsey, a self-made business executive, navy veteran, and pilot who had already experienced the devastating loss of one child and had gone through the emotional and spiritual journey of despair and renewal that entailed. Much like John, Anne Morrow Lindbergh had been publically stoic during the crisis and its aftermath, doing her crying strictly in private. And like the Ramseys, Charles and Anne were never seen comforting each other or even having much to do with each other. Anne's subsequently published journals, though, made clear the depths of both parents' despair. So on this first point, remember that each person reacts differently. This is important not so much to defend the Ramseys as to give due consideration and compassion to any individual who suffers such a loss to violent crime.

That they took on lawyers so quickly could be interpreted as a sign that they knew they "needed" them. Or it could be because their friend Mike Bynum realized the perils of going into the criminal justice system unprotected, especially when Bynum believed—rightly, as it turned out—that the Ramseys had already become the focus of the police investigation. He has since confirmed that the lawyering was his idea. The Ramseys were wealthy, sophisticated people and were totally used to working through attorneys and other professionals in many aspects of their lives, much like Charles Lindbergh, who called Henry Breckinridge as soon as he discovered his son's abduction. And being such types to begin with, they quickly became "good clients," letting their attorneys call the shots and following their advice. The attorneys would have no real way of knowing whether their new clients were innocent or guilty, and their task would be to limit potentially jeopardizing exposure. This, in turn, might easily reinforce the message the cops already thought they'd received.

If I were still with the FBI and had been called in on this case, my first instinct, even before I'd seen any of the evidence, would be to look seriously at the parents. This, of course, was just the advice that Ron Walker gave.

But another factor that had been brewing long before the murder, of which the Ramseys had no knowledge or control, contributed to the investigative nightmare this case became: the Boulder Police Department, under chief Thomas Koby, and the Boulder County District Attorney's Office, under longtime elected DA Alex Hunter, were enemy camps. They did not see eye to eye on how the law should be administered in this well-off, very liberal, freethinking community that was often referred to as "the People's Republic of Boulder." The crime rate was low, and what crime there was, the DA's office was usually able to keep out of court with what the police considered absurdly generous and inappropriate plea bargains. This is an oversimplification of the issue, but rather than working together, the two agencies were often at cross-purposes.

This antagonism reached a boiling point within a few days of the murder and contributed incredibly to the mutual mistrust between the police department and the Ramseys.

Once Dr. Meyer completed the autopsy, Commander Eller and Chief Koby still had questions, mainly relating to the actual cause of death, the weapon used in the blunt-force trauma, and the meaning and significance of the vaginal abrasions. On the other side, the Ramseys wanted their daughter's body returned to them for burial. This message came to the police through the district attorney's office via assistant DA and felony division chief Pete Hofstrom.

According to Steve Thomas's account, Hofstrom informed John Eller that the Ramseys wanted the remains back. The police were already annoyed because direct communication between the Ramseys and the DA's office, rather than the PD, meant they were dealing through lawyers rather than directly. They particularly didn't like the fact that Haddon, Morgan had close ties with several members of Alex Hunter's staff. Eller told Hofstrom that he, the police chief, and the coroner had decided to hold the body for further tests. Eller was also irritated by his inability to get the Ramseys in for individual formal interviews.

Hofstrom then told Eller that the police could not "ransom" the body in exchange for an interview. Eller didn't see it this way. Mike Bynum did, and the consequent bad blood between the police and the Ramseys on one hand, and the police and the district attorney on the other, would never go away.

The Ramseys "won" this round when, through their attorneys' and Hofstrom's insistence, the police did release the body, which the Ramseys brought back to Georgia for burial next to Beth. But unquestionably, the battle was joined.

GOING GLOBAL

A memorial service was held for JonBenet on Sunday, December 29, at St. John's Episcopal Church, not far from John's office at the Pearl Street

Mall in downtown Boulder. It was Patsy's fortieth birthday. The family then flew to Atlanta for the funeral and burial on Tuesday, December 31.

On Saturday morning, the day before the memorial service, Linda Arndt and Larry Mason had gone to the Fernies' home wanting to set up formal questioning with the Ramseys. John spent about forty minutes with them there, with two lawyers in attendance, but said Patsy was still highly medicated and in no condition to speak. In giving the officers some family background, he told them something about Patsy that, apparently, they had not known.

In June of 1993, after complaining of severe back and shoulder pains and a progressively distending belly on her normally trim and well-cared-for figure, Patsy was diagnosed with ovarian cancer. Originally labeled as stage III, she was soon downgraded to stage IV, the worst and most ominous designation, when it was found how far the cancer had spread. The Ramseys were once again devastated, so soon after Beth's death, to be facing death yet again. Patsy said she questioned why God would give her two beautiful young children, only to take her away from them when they would most need her.

She was enrolled in a rigorous experimental program at the National Institutes of Health's National Cancer Institute in Bethesda, Maryland. The protocol called for a week of chemotherapy treatment in Bethesda every month, followed by recovery and a battery of tests in Boulder, before returning for another depleting treatment in Bethesda. She lost her hair and was often too weak to get out of bed, the specter of death always close. This routine went on for many months, during which she saw many of her new friends and fellow cancer battlers in the program weaken and die.

She eventually made it, attributing her miraculous cure (if such a word can be used with regard to cancer) to a combination of first-rate medical care, emotional support from her husband and children, and God's grace and intervention.

The detectives left the Fernies' house disappointed that they had not been able to secure the interview they sought. And with the Ramseys leaving town for the funeral and burial in Georgia, they felt the pair was slipping out of their grasp.

By the time of the memorial service, this unusual and tantalizing case had already aroused great public attention. The Ramsey attorneys hired Washington, D.C., media consultant and former reporter Patrick Korten to handle television and press and keep them one step removed from John and Patsy, as well as the attorneys themselves. This was yet another move that brought on a flood tide of criticism: the Ramseys were trying to manage the news. Fleet White was apparently troubled by their girding themselves with lawyers and suggested the best way to get their story out was to go on national television and just tell it.

They addressed this by agreeing to appear on CNN in Atlanta the day after the burial: January 1, 1997. They would be interviewed by veteran reporter Brian Cabell, who, coincidentally, went to college with Mark Olshaker.

Toward the end of the interview, Cabell homed in on the question everyone wanted to ask. "The police said there is no killer on the loose. Do you believe it's someone outside your home?"

"There is a killer on the loose," Patsy responded.

"Absolutely," added John.

She went on, "I don't know who it is. I don't know if it's a he or a she. But if I was a resident of Boulder, I would tell my friends to keep . . ." At this she broke down. John tried to comfort her, then she continued, "Keep your babies close to you. There's someone out there."

The story had gone global, so much so that Boulder mayor Leslie Durgin, who knew the Ramseys personally, would call a news conference on January 3 and proclaim, "People have no need to fear that there is someone wandering the streets of Boulder, as has been portrayed by some people, looking for young children to attack. Boulder is safe, it's always been a safe community. It continues to be a safe community."

The day before, the second thrust of the globalization of the Ramsey murder story had taken place. ABC's Denver affiliate ran videos taken officially (for sale to parents and friends) at the All Star Pageant in which JonBenet had competed on December 17. Then there was an amateur video of a Royal Miss competition at a shopping center. Finally, an official video from the National Sunburst Pageant held in Atlanta during the summer of 1996 was shown in which JonBenet was wearing the sparkly white Vegas or Ziegfeld Follies–style outfit. These images brought most of the public into a world they hadn't even known existed and made them wonder what kind of parents would allow or encourage their children to enter these pageants where little girls imitate big girls.

The Ramseys would be quick to point out that many little girls and their families participated in them, particularly in the South where they came from. It was JonBenet's own choice, she wanted to get involved, had loved dressing up and performing since she was three, and had begged her mother to let her do it. At home, she even made her mother pretend to be the emcee and announce JonBenet walking down the runway. It was no different, they said, from parents and children involved in Little League, Cub Scouts, or Brownies, skating or any other type of performing. Anyone who saw anything suggestive or inappropriately sexual was reading into it. The pageants developed confidence, talent, and poise, and many of the participants dreamed of growing up and going on to Miss America, in which Patsy and her sister Pam had both competed.

But regardless of any explanation or decidedly unapologetic statements John or Patsy would make, to countless millions of viewers around the world, the images spoke for themselves. These were rich, arrogant parents who were alone in the house the night their daughter was killed, they refused to cooperate with police, they surrounded themselves with lawyers, and they dressed up their little six-year-old girl with lipstick and rouge and tinted hair and glittery makeup in suggestive outfits that made her look like a Vegas showgirl. What kind of people were these?

Meanwhile, Boulder PD had geared up for the most challenging and public case they had ever faced. Among the detectives John Eller assigned was Steve Thomas, who had been working undercover narcotics.

WHERE I CAME IN

On Monday, January 6, I was in Provo, Utah, preparing a training seminar for police officers with Greg Cooper, a former FBI special agent and one of the stars in my unit who was now the chief of police in Provo. When I called in to check my voice mail, I had a message from a private investigator named H. Ellis Armistead from Denver, who said he had been hired by the Ramsey family. He wanted to know if I was available to provide assistance regarding the homicide of their daughter. In return I left a message that I would be tied up in Utah for several days, but looking at my calendar, if they still wanted my assistance later in the week, I could probably meet them in Denver. I had heard about the Ramsey murder through the media, but between traveling and planning the seminar, I hadn't thought much about it and didn't know many details.

The next day Armistead got in touch with me at the Provo Park Hotel where I was staying. He said my expenses and a consultation fee would be paid, though the rate was not discussed. He indicated that attorney Lee Foreman, a partner of Hal Haddon and Bryan Morgan's, the attorneys for John Ramsey, would be contacting me.

Foreman called around 9:00 that night and said he would like me to come to Denver and Boulder and conduct an analysis for them. He continued by saying that he had researched pedophiles and that John Ramsey did not fit the profile. John was successful in business, financially well-off, and married to a former beauty queen. I listened to Foreman's evaluation without comment. It seemed clear to me that he was looking for someone "objective" to come up with the same analysis and evaluation.

I gave Foreman the standard rap I'd given all potential clients since I'd left the Bureau, whether they were private citizens or police agencies: You can buy my time if I have it to give, but my analysis is completely independent, and you can't influence it. I will give you my report verbally. You may or may not like or agree with what I have to say, and it's up to you whether you use it or not. If you wish, I will then produce a written report, which, since I am not an attorney, may be subject to subpoena. I won't reveal any privileged or protected information you give me or say anything based on it. But if I'm asked for my opinion based on public information, I reserve the right to give it. Foreman agreed to the terms.

I flew to Denver on Wednesday, January 8, 1997. During the flight I made notes for myself of things I felt I needed to know and understand:

I. Facts of Case
   Day, date, time. When was child determined to be missing? What did they do? Who did they call? Did they call police? What time? What time was child located? Where? By who? Describe location and position of child, crime scene, how dressed, cause of death. Blood? Where? Sexually assaulted? How do you know?

II. Note
   Where found? By who? Paper—where obtained? Review letter.

III. Background of Family
   —Business
   —Who lives in house?
   —Prior marriages
   —How long married?

IV. Access to House
   —Who?
   —Security systems

V. Modeling Career [I was under the impression the victim was a child model.]
   —Who sponsors?
   —Who photographs?
   —Family photographs?

When I got to Denver, I met with Lee Foreman and Bryan Morgan in their law office, which had been converted from an historic downtown building. We met in a glass-enclosed conference room they called "the bubble."

I prefaced my conversation by saying I understood that they might have an opinion relative to the Ramseys' involvement based upon their experience and research with pedophiles. However, I told them, at this stage they should not necessarily assume we were dealing with a pedophile. I explained the differences between preferential and situational child molesters, going through the steps necessary to do an analysis and noting that they would not have the autopsy reports, crime scene photos, and toxicology results, all of which I routinely use in making a determination about the type of offender.

I said that based on the limited media reports I'd read, it didn't look good for their clients. Whether the information I'd seen was fact or fiction or a combination of both, the perception of the general public seemed to be that the Ramseys were responsible. For example, it was my understanding that they did not immediately contact the police department after finding their daughter. You can see that my factual knowledge at this point was still very limited.

I said I had heard that the Ramseys had never cooperated with the police, which sounded problematic to me.

The lawyers responded by saying that the Ramseys had been very cooperative with the PD since day one. Even though the extortion note had advised them not to contact the police or FBI, they had immediately notified the police. The police had searched the house along with some of John and Patsy's friends but did not locate the victim. The Ramseys were so visibly upset that a friend of theirs had suggested getting John to search the house with a neighbor to keep him occupied. John and his friend Fleet White searched the house, ending up at a ten-foot-square wine cellar used for storage. The friend noticed that a window in the basement was broken and that glass fragments were on the floor. Ramsey remarked at the time that he was responsible for the broken window because he had locked himself out on several occasions and had broken the basement window to gain access. A window well outside the window was covered by a grate. You would have had to know about the broken window underneath to have attempted entry from that point.

As you can see, there were even some minor discrepancies in the attorneys' version of events. The story was still being pieced together.

They continued by saying that Ramsey and White had searched the basement, and that it was Mr. Ramsey who went into the wine cellar room, then screamed, "Oh, my baby!"

This was an important point to me. From our experience with staged domestic homicides—that is, murders committed by a family member and made to look like something else, such as a rape or burglary gone bad—the killer will generally maneuver and manipulate to have someone else find the body. It is much easier for him to "react" and to maintain some distance from the crime.

For example, I had a case in which a man had killed his wife in their bedroom, then gone to work. But before he left, he moved the body to a storage cellar with access from the outside, then made the body look as if she had been sexually assaulted. He did this because he didn't want his son to find the body when he came home from school, and so that, when it was found, it would appear to have been a rape gone bad. At his office, he called home several times to establish a phone company record, then, in the afternoon, called a neighbor who had a key to the house, telling her in a worried voice that he had been unable to reach his wife and would she please go over and check. The neighbor looked through the house without finding her, called back and told him his wife wasn't home but that the car was there and the bedroom was pretty messed up (the wife had been a meticulous housekeeper). The husband then called the police, relating the entire story told to him by the neighbor, and when they came over to investigate, they found her in the storage cellar. After this, my unit was called in.

You'll recall that in the Borden murders, Lizzie couldn't avoid reporting the death of her father, but she went to some complicated lengths not to find the body of her stepmother herself. She orchestrated it so that Bridget Sullivan would be the one, and when Bridget refused to go upstairs alone, Lizzie still wouldn't go and had Adelaide Churchill accompany the maid.

So the fact that John Ramsey was the one who found his daughter aroused my attention. From the scenario the attorneys had laid out, it would have been so easy for him to have said to Fleet White, "I'll check the laundry room, you check the furnace room and wine cellar, then we'll meet back here." But he didn't.

I was told that when JonBenet was found, a blanket was wrapped around her torso. Just her torso, I inquired.

Yes, the attorneys replied, her arms and legs were sticking out.

This was another important consideration. As we noted in the Lindbergh case, the way the body is left often tells us a lot about the relationship between the victim and the offender. Charlie Lindbergh's body was casually tossed into the woods when it was no longer of any use to the kidnappers. No attempt was made to protect it from the elements or animals, and nothing caring or gentle was evident.

In the case of the man who killed his wife, on the other hand, the body was carefully wrapped in the blanket from their bed, so that nothing but her head was exposed. It was a protective, "considerate" presentation. We say that this shows a "proprietary interest" in the victim. Sometimes, it even demonstrates remorse on the part of a parent.

At first, I had been under the impression that such proprietary interest and consideration had been evident when JonBenet's body was found, but this seemed to be a case of covering the body for convenience rather than any kind of protection or nurturing instinct.

When John Ramsey found JonBenet, a piece of black duct tape was across her mouth, her hands were tied, and a rope ligature was around her throat, tied from the rear. What interested me here was that John's first instinct—the first thing he did—was to rip the tape from her mouth and attempt to untie the wrist ligature. He succeeded in loosening it but not removing it. Then he carried his daughter upstairs.

The first thing I had to ask myself was, if John Ramsey had killed his daughter or been involved in her death and had subsequently staged the scene to look like the work of a sadistic intruder, why would he *unstage* the crime to the extent of removing the duct tape and loosening the wrist ligature before anyone else, particularly the cops, got to see it? It didn't make sense.

The lawyers told me there was a small amount of blood, apparently from her vagina, in JonBenet's panties, and another stain that appeared to be semen. This, of course, suggested a male offender, and if the sample turned out to match John Ramsey's DNA, that was going to be a pretty easy case to make. It turned out that one of the prime reasons I had been brought to Denver was to evaluate Ramsey for the benefit of the attorneys. Though they could not come right out and say so, I had the strong feeling they wanted me to let them know if I thought their client was guilty.

Before I met with John Ramsey, though, I predicted to the lawyers that the police lab analysis would eventually determine there was no semen on JonBenet's body or in her underwear. From my experience with sexually motivated crimes, particularly crimes against children, I didn't think this offender was the kind of guy to rape a little girl. Anyone who could kill with that degree of force and aggression—either from the strangulation or the blunt-force trauma—would not spend his time on traditional penile intercourse. He might abuse her in some other way, such as by inserting his fingers or an object to demonstrate his control and contempt, and in fact, we soon learned of the vaginal abrasions and bruising. But I was really skeptical about the semen report.

According to the lawyers, there were obvious signs of bruising around the child's head, which the minister (I didn't know his name at the time) attempted to cover so that Patsy would not see the extent of the wound. It was clear to me at that point, though, just as it was clear to Lee Foreman and Bryan Morgan, that the crime scene was not only in a state of bedlam, but had been severely contaminated. I knew that this would present the police and prosecutors with severe problems if a suspect was charged and sent to trial.

Foreman told me that the Ramseys had taken part in a two-hour-plus preliminary interview and that their nine-year-old son (whose name I also didn't yet know) had been interviewed by police without his parents' knowledge or consent. I was informed that the boy did not really understand what had happened or that he would not be able to see his sister again. In addition to the interviews, the Ramseys had willingly given whatever hair, blood, and handwriting samples the police had asked for. They did the same for their son.

In the evening on January 8, Bryan Morgan and Ellis Armistead, the investigator hired by the Ramseys, took me to the Ramsey home. Armistead was tall and blond, a former homicide detective with an easygoing manner that contrasted with Morgan's friendly but authoritative, take-charge attitude. The purpose of the visit was for me to get an understanding of the layout of the house and the circumstances and chronology of events on the night and morning of the murder.

According to newspaper accounts I'd recently read, the brick Tudor was about five thousand square feet on four floors, including the converted attic, and was valued at $1.3 million. It had two additions built on by the Ramseys. From everything I could gather as we approached the house, the neighborhood lived up to its published reputation. It seemed upscale and prosperous, the type local police would take care to watch over and where the only kind of serious crime you'd routinely expect would be breaking and entering for cash, jewelry, and other valuables. Thieves hitting houses in this neighborhood would probably know a good deal about what they were looking for. I was given to understand that several of the houses, including the Ramseys', had been on recent charity open-house tours, which, unfortunately, are often a good way of gaining inside intelligence about a prospective target.

Inside, I observed that because of the inherent design of the house and the additions the Ramseys had made, the flow from one part of the home to another was choppy. You couldn't walk from one room to another without coming to a dead end. The home was well-furnished with both contemporary pieces and antiques. Two staircases led from the first to the second floors, one being the spiral set where Patsy had found the ransom note. You would need some agility to carry a large package or something the size of a six-year-old up or even down those stairs. The master bedroom, converted from the attic on the third floor, seemed tucked away, removed from the rest of the house. John had work space up there, and he and Patsy had elaborate separate bathrooms and closets.

JonBenet's bedroom was typical for a six-year-old in a middle or upper-middle-class family. I noted quite a few dolls and memorabilia of her pageants. Any sound coming out of this room, even a rather loud one, would be difficult to hear upstairs and over in the other wing in the Ramseys' bedroom. A noise from the first floor would be even more difficult, and anything coming from the basement would be virtually impossible to hear up on the third floor.

As a test, I had one of Armistead's investigators go into JonBenet's room and count to ten, gradually increasing his volume as he counted. We stayed up in the master bedroom. We could not hear him clearly until he reached number five. The residence had no intercom system or any other monitoring system between the upper floor and the children's bedrooms.

I also noted that the house had about a half dozen entry doors on the first floor and that JonBenet's room had a balcony that you could reach with a small stepladder or by standing on a garbage can.

My overall impression was that the perpetrator had to have some pretty good knowledge of the layout of the Ramsey home and the family's comings and goings on that night, possibly through surveillance. In addition to the residents, one immediately considers maids or other service personnel, construction workers, friends and business associates who had been invited over on repeat occasions.

This was a high-risk crime on the part of an intruder. However, that did not necessarily mean he was an experienced criminal. I felt in looking around the house that if the perpetrator were an outsider, it would be someone dedicated to his "mission" to cause harm to the Ramsey family. We couldn't tell from the crime scene if JonBenet was attacked initially in her bed. The police had taken all the bedding and cut sections of carpet that I figured must have contained either potential blood or body-fluid stains or dirt or other evidence. I surmised that the child may have been awakened and initially immobilized in her room before being taken down to the basement.

The basement would be a dangerous place for an intruder if the Ramseys were to awaken and go downstairs. He would be trapped.

MEETING THE RAMSEYS

Around 9 A.M. on Thursday, January 9, I met with the Ramseys at the Haddon, Morgan and Foreman law offices. The key meeting was with John, since the attorneys believed that semen deposits had been found on the body and/or at the scene, which would give the primary exposure to him. Bryan Morgan was there. Patsy was not present for my initial meeting with John.

Upon meeting John Ramsey, I informed him who I was, shook his hand, and expressed my sorrow for his loss. As it turned out, there was some significance to the fact that neither he nor Patsy knew who I was. Subsequent to this, several sources, including Detective Steve Thomas, reported that *Mindhunter,* the first book I wrote with Mark, was on John Ramsey's nightstand. In this book we deal with staging crime scenes, and some speculated that one or both of the Ramseys had read it and "learned" how to outwit investigators to make it look as if someone from outside had killed their child. First, I have to say that they—or anyone else—would not have learned this from reading the book. We didn't write a how-to course, and any good investigator would see right through such a primitive attempt. Morever, much as we would like to think that everyone has read our books and knows who we are, *Mindhunter* was *not* there on John's nightstand or elsewhere in the house, and I looked through the place pretty carefully. Believe me, as an author you learn to spot your books anywhere and everywhere. And it was not on the long police list of items removed from the house, although a "Dave Barry book about cyberspace" was. This is just one small example of the mountain of erroneous information that has come out about this case. While I understand that John read *Mindhunter* after meeting me, he was completely unfamiliar with my work at the time of the crime.

I said to him this was not an easy thing to do, but I had been asked by his attorney to do an analysis of the crime and to provide an opinion as to who or what kind of individual was responsible. I prefaced the conversation by saying something similar to what I'd told Morgan and Foreman the day before: Based on the public source information, I didn't feel it looked good for him. Family members are always the first suspects in cases such as this, and information in the public domain suggested that he and his wife were being uncooperative with the police.

He replied rather bristly that this could not be further from the truth, that he and Patsy had furnished everything they'd been asked to and had answered many questions. However, he acknowledged that they had not yet participated in an in-depth interview with the police.

John was depressed and sad-looking. The day before had been the fifth anniversary of his daughter Beth's death. I had him take me through Christmas day and evening and then the next morning, leading up to the time he and Patsy said they had discovered that JonBenet was missing.

Christmas morning had been typical for them, with the two children delightedly opening presents from Santa Claus and both parents taking pictures. I was informed that Boulder PD had the photos. At around 4 they went to Fleet and Priscilla White's house for a Christmas celebration dinner, just as they'd done the year before. The Whites lived about six blocks away. John and Patsy were both social drinkers and each had a glass of wine at the Whites'. The Whites had children around the same ages as Burke and JonBenet. They all played together, and shortly before 9 P.M. the Ramseys returned home, after making two brief stops to exchange gifts. John said that he had carried his daughter to her bedroom asleep and was going to finish getting her ready for bed himself, but Burke wanted him to help him with something, so he let Patsy finish putting JonBenet to bed.

When he'd gotten Burke in bed, he went upstairs to the master bedroom, setting his alarm clock for 6:30 the next morning to be on time for their flight to Michigan, with a stop to pick up his two older children and prospective son-in-law. The Ramsey Jeep was in the garage, already packed with presents for their friends in Michigan.

I paid close attention to what he said, concentrating on his inflection, breathing, body language, word choice—matching him up against the experience I'd gained through thousands of interviews with both violent offenders and victims and their families. I took John through the entire morning and afternoon of December 26, up to when he said he discovered his daughter in the wine cellar. When he talked about carrying her upstairs, he started blinking, as if revisualizing the scene. Then he began to sob.

After I had spent about two hours with Ramsey, he excused himself to go to the rest room. I turned to Bryan Morgan, who'd been in the room the entire time, and said simply, "I believe him."

"Oh, God, what a relief!" Morgan replied. He was in his sixties, passionate and charming when he wanted to be. I had the distinct impression that he sincerely believed his client was innocent but was eager for some guidance or reassurance about that instinct.

When Ramsey returned, I told him that I had sat across the table from hundreds of criminals. Some have been so convincing that I went back to the files and looked up the case materials to make sure that the evidence was, indeed, solid against them.

I then said, "Mr. Ramsey, you are either one hell of a liar or you're innocent. I believe what you're telling me."

He seemed pleased by my reaction. I said, "Why don't we go to the police and have you tell them the story as you've just told me?"

He said he wanted to be on their side and cooperate. Morgan commented that at some point they would sit down with the police and that he was going to try to meet with them that afternoon around 4:00.

I told Morgan that I was ready to speak with Mrs. Ramsey, but that I'd changed my mind about having to do it without Mr. Ramsey present. He could be present during the interview. I didn't tell him and Morgan why I had shifted strategy. They may have assumed that I was now so trusting of John that I had no need of Patsy's unadorned version. The truth of the matter, though, was that since John was the prime focus of my analysis, I was most concerned with gauging his reactions. Now that I had had him alone, I wanted to see what he would be like as Patsy was telling her side of the story. I wanted to see if I could pick up any tension in him as she spoke, or any friction between the two of them about reactions or specific details.

Patsy Ramsey appeared, wearing a black sweater and skirt outfit. I paid special attention to the large pewter cross around her neck. I have often seen accused people suddenly "get religion" and make a big, obvious deal about it, and I made a mental note to go through their family snapshots to see if she had ever worn this cross or anything like it before. I had been told that she had been under sedation, and it was apparent that she had been crying and was in need of rest.

I introduced myself to her, but rather than ask specific questions I told both Ramseys about how I would go about analyzing the case, though I said that I didn't have all of the case materials I would normally have for such an analysis. I described the *Crime Classification Manual,* produced and published when I was with the Bureau and of which I was the lead author, and how it sought to classify criminal behavior for the benefit of law enforcement professionals in the same way that the *DSM,* the *Diagnostic and Statistical Manual of Mental Disorders,* did with mental diseases for health care professionals.

Four major categories of homicide were listed in *CCM*—criminal enterprise, personal cause, sexual, and group cause—with subcategories within them. This case had a demand for ransom (criminal enterprise), an apparent sexual assault (sexual), and a reference to a foreign group taking responsibility for the abduction (group cause). My opinion was that while this case had certain markers for the three other categories, I believed this was primarily a personal cause homicide, particularly with regard to the elements of revenge or retaliation.

As soon as I said this, John Ramsey once again began to cry. He said he felt it was his fault that his daughter had been killed, that someone had been trying to get back at him. Patsy then became very emotional herself and asked why someone would do this.

"I believe you have had the killer in your home before," I said. "I believe Mr. Ramsey is familiar or has had contact with this person, and that the subject has been harboring ill feelings toward him."

I asked if either of them had observed any unusual behavior from anyone since the murder. Patsy commented that the Whites had been "acting odd" toward them. I responded that people sometimes do act strangely in these situations, not because they are guilty or have something to hide, but because they don't know what to do or say. I related my illness and coma and long recovery in 1983, when people who I'd thought were close friends never came to see me in the hospital or later at home. Patsy said that she had had similar experiences with her cancer. A number of her close friends had never come to see her. She told me she had survived that illness because of her strong faith and by placing herself in God's hands.

At several points during my conversation with both Ramseys, I glanced at Bryan Morgan and found him moved to tears. This confirmed for me that he did really believe in his clients' innocence and was full of compassion for the incredible loss they'd suffered. One time, he asked John to show me a photo of Beth. John took the picture from his wallet and began crying. Morgan put his hand on John's shoulder, began crying himself, and said, "John, I'm so sorry."

Could this have been more staging for my benefit? I quickly concluded it was not. I think after interviewing hundreds of offenders and victims, I'm experienced enough to recognize genuine tears when I see them.

MEETING WITH THE PD

When we finished talking, Morgan asked the Ramseys to go into another office while I briefed Ellis Armistead and media consultant Pat Korten on my impressions. Morgan wanted to discuss the upcoming meeting that afternoon with Boulder police. He said he wanted to be able to offer them my consultative services and to get Chief Tom Koby to make some public statements that would neutralize the large amount of misinformation Morgan felt was out before the public.

At police headquarters, about a ten-minute drive away, scores of media people surrounded the front steps, so we were escorted in through a side door and into the commander's conference room. I was introduced to Chief Koby, Commander Eller, and a police legal adviser. Accompanied by the media adviser and three attorneys—Morgan, Hal Haddon, and Patsy's attorney, Patrick Burke—I saw immediately that Koby had not been expecting this large a group.

Koby said he was prepared to discuss leaks, but did not want to discuss material details of the case under these circumstances. He was scheduled for a 7 P.M. press conference and was anticipating heat from the media regarding the commonly held belief that the police had botched the search for the victim by not looking through the entire basement, had lost control of the people in the house, and had therefore critically damaged the crime scene.

The chief came across to me as soft-spoken and professional. On the other hand, Eller's facial and physical cues communicated an attitude of "Don't bother me." Koby left for a meeting with his own people, then returned about ten minutes later to tell me that they wanted to hear what I had to say. I was told the police had been given a copy of my CV beforehand.

Koby then left to prepare for the press conference, leaving Eller in charge of the meeting. He looked indifferent and gave the impression that this wasn't a productive use of his time.

He began by saying they were going to treat me as a witness. During the conversation it came out that I had spoken with the Ramseys that morning.

His eyebrows rose, and in a voice that seemed to me dripping with sarcasm, he said, "Oh, so you interviewed the Ramseys!"

I finally got fed up with his attitude and said, "Look, I'm here to try to help. If you're not interested, so be it. I've got other things to do and I'll be on my way." It was almost the exact same thing I'd said to Atlanta police sixteen years earlier when I was down there for the child murders investigation.

No, they were interested, Eller countered, and they would set up an interview with me the next day with two of their detectives. He asked me if I was part of the Academy Group, a consulting firm made up primarily of former and retired agents from Quantico. I said I wasn't but that I had trained many of their people. I had heard the police might have contacted Pete Smerick, one of the agents who'd been in my unit and subsequently worked with the group to take a look at the ransom note for content analysis.

About this time I started hearing that when I'd first been contacted by Ellis Armistead, the Ramsey attorneys had also contacted Gregg McCrary, whom I had brought into the unit and who had distinguished himself on many important cases while he was at Quantico. Morgan told me they never actually got to talk to McCrary personally, but Gregg had announced publicly that he did not and would not accept an assignment in this case because such situations usually turn out to be a parent or someone close to the family, that that was the way this one looked to him, and that he did not want to risk being in the camp of the killer.

Neither do I, but I was disappointed and somewhat distressed by the way Gregg approached this. It was as if he had made a prediagnosis of disease without first examining the patient, going on the statistical likelihood that the patient was sick. Gregg has since become a frequent media commentator on the case. I certainly don't question his motives in making the decisions he did. But I have to say that when I was heading the Investigative Support Unit at Quantico, I would have been very concerned if I felt that any of my agents had evaluated a case beforehand or were leaning in a certain direction to try to please the local investigative agency. I always wanted our consultations and opinions to be as unaffected by outside influence as possible. That's why, when a local department would send us all of the facts and case materials for a given crime, the standing rule was that the one thing they were not to provide us with was their suspect list. We didn't want to be influenced.

As the case progressed, Gregg offered his opinions. At the same time, he criticized me for coming to my conclusion without having complete information. Since he didn't have anything but public sources, I kept wondering where *his* analysis came from. Like Gregg, I went into the case believing there was a strong possibility that one of the Ramseys could be involved based on the statistics of this sort of crime. But I reserved judgment until I saw the evidence.

Contrary to what has been reported, I was not called upon to do a profile of the killer and have never done so. I never had all of the material I would need for that. I saw it as my role with the attorneys to do an assessment of whether their clients were involved, and with the police to give them the benefit of my experience in analyzing and researching thousands of homicide investigations. I made a point of telling Eller that if they hadn't done so already, they should get in touch with Ron Walker in the FBI's Denver Field Office. Eller remained poker-faced, not letting on whether he had contacted Ron or not. I had the impression he wasn't too keen on bringing in the Bureau on any greater level than he had to.

Let me mention here that I had not been in touch with Ron on this case. In fact, my recommendation that Boulder PD contact him was the extent of my "contact" with the FBI on this case. I have spoken to no one in the Bureau about it, have not asked for, wanted, nor have any "inside" information from the FBI.

The meeting lasted no more than forty-five minutes, and when it was over, we were escorted out the side door, as far as possible from the media.

That evening, Chief Koby surprised the Ramsey team by really taking the media to task for unfair and misleading reporting. He went off on one particularly aggressive reporter, lecturing him that he could not imagine what it was like to lose a child to crime. The chief said they were looking at a number of potential suspects and that the public had a need to know some information, but not all. He added that the results of forensic tests would be coming in in pieces over the next several weeks. What no one could predict was that by the time some of the important results came back, relations would be so poor between the police and DA Alex Hunter's office that the police would not even tell the prosecutors what they had.

THE DETECTIVES

On Friday morning, January 10, accompanied by Bryan Morgan, I met at police headquarters with Detectives Steve Thomas and Thomas Trujillo. They were both well-groomed, good-looking guys who appeared to be in their late twenties or early thirties. They were cordial in their introductions. We went to an interview room furnished with a table and four chairs.

Morgan laid out the ground rules, which were that I would answer any specific questions regarding the Ramseys and that I would talk generally about what I did, how I did it, and what my impressions were. The detectives said they had no trouble with this. They asked if either of us had any recording devices on our persons, and we told them we did not.

For the record, they asked me my full name, date and place of birth, home address and phone number, etc. When I said I was born in Brooklyn, one of them commented that he could detect a little bit of an accent. I described my background and experience for about fifteen minutes, after which both men said they were impressed. Morgan added, "John's the best at what he does and that's why you have to listen to what he has to say." I was somewhat embarrassed by this testimonial but let it pass.

I gave them my analysis thus far and why I believed the Ramseys' stories. The nonverbal cues Thomas and Trujillo were giving off indicated that they were interested in what I was telling them. I said it was my belief at this point that the motive of the crime was personal and directed at Mr. Ramsey. I thought the $118,000 figure demanded in the note had to be significant, as that was virtually the exact net amount of his bonus from the company ($118,117.50), deposited electronically into his retirement plan account. His paycheck stubs for the entire year would have reflected that amount. Though I couldn't be sure, I didn't sense that they knew that.

I told them it was my opinion that the writer of the note was a white male in his thirties or forties with some business background. (Once I had the opportunity to study the note in more detail, I revised my age prediction somewhat downward. Age is one of the most difficult factors in criminal investigative analysis because chronological age and behavioral age do not always match.)

I said the letter was written in a businesslike fashion and at some points the extortionist could not fully disguise himself. They wanted to know if I thought the crime was perpetrated by one individual. I said I thought so, and it had to be someone who was either intentionally or inadvertently given the information on the bonus amount. If it was inadvertent, the UNSUB could have seen a pay stub or retirement plan printout on John Ramsey's desk in his office or a desk, counter, or dresser top at home.

This crime and crime scene was a mixed presentation, with elements of both organization and disorganization, which strongly suggested a criminally unsophisticated individual. However, even though not a professional criminal, the subject had to have the boldness to enter a home and kill a child with the parents inside. Even the letter itself showed mixed organization. Very long for a ransom note, it had all kinds of extraneous stuff in it, which took some planning and organization to put together. On the other hand, the paper and writing implement came from inside the house. This either suggested lack of planning or superplanning—using only materials inside the house so as not to leave additional clues. But if that was the case, then the subject had to know that the family would be out long enough for him to take the time to write the note.

I said that regardless of who committed the murder, a family member or intruder, I did not believe the note could have been written after the fact; it had to have been written before the murder. In my entire career, I had never seen anyone with that kind of control and presence of mind to write out so long and involved a letter. It just didn't make any sense.

I had found nothing to suggest that the parents had any reason or motive to kill their child. From what I'd been able to gather, JonBenet was everything to Mrs. Ramsey. And after losing one daughter, if anything, Mr. Ramsey would be overprotective of this one.

I have to say that whatever either detective has said since then, I sensed that they were paying close attention and giving serious consideration to my analysis. I said that to catch this subject, the public comments made by the police and DA's office should be positive and confident. I took them step-by-step through proactive measures I'd employed in the past. A profile per se would not necessarily be that valuable, but what could be effective was to try to get the media's cooperation in publicizing likely pre- and postoffense behavior patterns that someone close to this individual might recognize. This ought to be done as soon as possible before memories faded.

"Look at the Unabomber case," I said. "The downfall of the Unabomber was when he wrote the communiqués. Then we had something to assess. We could begin to understand what his motive was." And now we had the opportunity to make this writing public in the hopes that someone would recognize it and come up with a name for us. Had the "manifesto" not been published by the *New York Times* and the *Washington Post,* I believe Theodore Kaczynski could well still be living in a cabin in Montana terrorizing the country.

One technique that could produce immediate results would be to use newspapers and billboards to reproduce the actual ransom note. In 1989, Special Agent Jana Monroe (now assistant special agent-in-charge of the Denver Field Office) had worked a case for my unit down in Tampa, Florida, in which a woman and her two teenaged daughters visiting the area had been found dead in Tampa Bay. They were obviously the victims of sexual murder. The only tangible piece of forensic evidence was a scribbled note found in the woman's car, giving directions from her motel to the spot where the car was found. When other leads didn't pan out, Jana got the local police to blow up the note and put it on local billboards to see if anyone recognized the handwriting. Within a couple of days, three separate individuals who had never met each other called the police and identified the handwriting as belonging to an unlicensed aluminum-siding installer who'd produced unsatisfactory work for all three of them. He was arrested, tried, and found guilty of first-degree murder.

The Boulder detectives seemed to like this idea.

I asked them if they wanted any advice from me on how to interrogate a subject once an arrest was made. They said yes. This was a strange situation. Here I was with John Ramsey's attorney, telling the cops what techniques to use, knowing there was an excellent chance they'd be used against this attorney's client. I suggested dressing the interview room with props and artifacts from the crime and scene, saying that the killer would inevitably be drawn to them and would help give himself away with his nonverbal cues. It was awkward because this is how I really felt it should be done, but I knew that if Bryan Morgan went back and told John and Patsy what I'd said, and they were called in for questioning and were guilty, then they'd have even more trouble avoiding the "props" than if they knew nothing of the technique. Anyway, the chips were going to fall wherever they fell.

I added that the Ramseys genuinely seemed to want to talk extensively to the police, but the attorneys were concerned that the chief wanted them polygraphed, even though polygraphs were not admissible in court in Colorado. I explained that my unit and I had never set much store in polygraphs and considered them more in the realm of interrogation techniques than anything else. I said there were too many inconclusive results, and anyone who feels guilty about not sufficiently protecting his child, as John Ramsey clearly did, would likely show a false positive so soon after the event. The other side of the coin was that sociopaths often did well on lie detector tests. If you have no conscience and can lie to other people without a problem, lying to a box isn't any big deal. And even when they were "effective," polygraphs indicated belief more than truth. I said I was reasonably convinced O. J. Simpson could pass such a test this far after the fact when he had convinced himself that he was justified in what he did. In fact, when I consulted with attorney Daniel Petrocelli on the Goldman family's civil suit, I advised Petrocelli not to push for a lie detector test.

In early spring of 2000, another round of controversy on this subject occurred when the Ramseys declared on national television that they had never formally been asked to take lie detector tests and were perfectly willing to under fair circumstances. I believe what happened here is that, trying to prove their innocence, they "got out front" of their attorneys without understanding as much as the attorneys and I know about the nature of polygraphs. Once the declaration was made, the lawyers couldn't pull them back from it without another public relations fiasco, so they ended up with a solution that didn't really satisfy anyone: a privately administered test that they passed, but which was done without the FBI's participation. I believe enough time had gone by that John Ramsey would have some perspective on the case and so would not fail for misleading reasons, but I don't think it changed many opinions positively or negatively.

Altogether, on that first trip to Boulder, I spent about two hours with the detectives, and when we were done, Bryan Morgan and I both thought it had been a productive meeting.

I left Boulder that afternoon, with Morgan saying he'd probably want to call on me again.

THE CASE MATURES

Despite a massive investigative effort in the ensuing months and years, the outlines and contours of the case remained pretty much what they had been almost from the start: a police concentration on John and Patsy Ramsey as the prime suspects in the homicide of their daughter, and ever-mounting tension between the police and the district attorney's office. The police could reasonably say that their prime focus remained on the Ramseys because that was who they believed did it, just as the focus of the LAPD in the murders of Nicole Brown Simpson and Ronald Goldman remained on O. J. Simpson—there was no evidentiary reason to look elsewhere. The police certainly believed this. It has been reported that my former unit at Quantico believed this. And certainly that is what the tabloid press, most of legitimate journalism, and the vast majority of the public believed. But as the case matured, a number of people—myself included—became increasingly troubled that it just wasn't adding up the way it should if the identity of the UNSUB were as clear-cut as Boulder PD supposed.

The disarray of the investigation was pretty clear. Before I even got to Boulder, Sergeant Larry Mason had been removed by Eller as lead investigator for leaking inside information to the media. He was later cleared. By May of 1997, detectives Linda Arndt and Melissa Hickman had also been removed from the case.

One of the issues with the police and the Ramseys was that, despite the belief that either John or Patsy did it, the investigators disagreed about which one. The initial report had been that semen was found on the victim, which would suggest a male offender. But that report was not panning out, and by March handwriting analysts brought in by the police had eliminated John Ramsey as the writer of the note, but said they could not eliminate Patsy. So a lot of the speculation shifted to her.

In September, a search of the Ramsey home uncovered fibers that appeared to match the cord used to bind JonBenet. But the roll the duct tape had come from and the remainder of the cord were not found, which suggested to me that, unlike the notepad and pen from the ransom note and the broken paintbrush handle from the neck ligature, the cord and duct tape originated outside the house.

Only weeks after this search, lead investigator John Eller was replaced by Commander Mark Beckner. A little over a month after that, the police union passed a no-confidence motion against Chief Tom Koby, who later announced he would resign. Within a few days, Eller also announced that he planned to resign. Ultimately, Koby was replaced by Beckner. But by the one-year anniversary of the murder, despite the focus on the Ramseys, no suspects had been named and no arrests had been made.

While a murder always has horrible and long-term fallout for the family and friends of the victim, I have never seen another case that became so devastating and destructive to the investigating agency itself.

Alex Hunter brought in famed forensic scientist Dr. Henry Lee and attorney and DNA legal specialist Barry Scheck as consultants. So far as I can tell, neither has been able to advance the case. And rather than narrowing the focus, new pieces of potential evidence often raised more questions than they answered. Detective Steve Thomas placed great store in the fact that JonBenet had apparently ingested pineapple the evening of her death, contrary to what the Ramseys said, yet seemed to discount what I consider to be a major finding: that DNA, definitely not belonging to Jon-Benet and definitely not belonging to either of her parents (or anyone else tested, for that matter), was found in her panties and under her fingernails.

To me, the relative weight given to these two possible clues says a lot about the unbalanced nature of the Ramsey murder investigation. What are the implications of Patsy saying that she did not feed her daughter, nor did she see JonBenet eat, cut pineapple on the night she died? Why would Patsy lie about something like that? What is the strategic advantage?

How about "JonBenet woke up and she was hungry so I gave her some pineapple"? That's completely innocent; it doesn't imply, "Oh, and while she was awake, I killed her." It would be too easy for Patsy to explain it away to bother lying about it. And yet she stuck and continues to stick to her story. Maybe the child got up and had some pineapple on her own. Maybe Patsy or John gave it to her and forgot. Maybe an intruder gave it to her. If this advances the case in any way, it is only likely to be a minor one.

Yet what about that DNA? Foreign DNA found under the victim's fingernails and in her underpants certainly suggests at least *the strong possibility* of another participant. Maybe the material under the nails came from her digging in the dirt (in the Colorado winter) and coming into contact with some organic material. Maybe at some recent point another little girl had worn her underwear and it was her genetic material.

A pubic hair of unknown origin was also found on her blanket. Again, maybe there is a completely natural explanation for it, such as someone else having slept in her bed and the hair never having been cleaned away. Evidence can come from some strange and off-the-wall places. But we're jumping through hoops to come up with alternative explanations for some very strong points of evidence.

And yet the police and public continued to believe the Ramseys did it, largely for the simple reason that no solid outside suspect had surfaced. This is remarkably similar to the events of the Sheppard murder case in Cleveland in 1954. Dr. Sam Sheppard, an osteopath, was accused, tried, and convicted of murdering his wife, Marilyn, on the Fourth of July. Sheppard claimed a mysterious stranger broke into the house, knocked him unconscious, and killed his wife. He eventually received a second trial and was released from prison, but the prevailing attitude has always been that he did it. Only recently has evidence surfaced that strongly indicates that the late Dr. Sheppard was innocent and his life ruined by false allegation. If nothing else, the Sheppard case is a cautionary tale about assuming something simply because you don't have evidence to the contrary.

One of the avenues of investigation was for an indication of any kind of child sexual abuse or inappropriate behavior in John Ramsey's background. Absolutely nothing surfaced. Not with his first set of children, not with his second set of children, not from his first wife or anyone else. Nothing. This is a very, very important point, because as I've found throughout my career and as my colleague Dr. Stanton Samenow has so articulately stated, people don't act out of character. If they appear to, it is only because you don't understand the character well enough.

No one suddenly becomes a child abuser . . . or anything else. There is always evolutionary behavior, a pattern of thought and act. Not only did the police scrutinize Ramsey's life and every relationship, so did the tabloid press, which has a lot less in the way of scruples. And this is not the kind of guy he was.

So what did happen? None of us knows, but let's look at some of the possibilities that have been considered or implied.

WHAT-IFS?

None of the scenarios makes perfect sense or is without loose ends, either those involving the Ramseys or one or more intruders. If one did, the case would have been solved long ago, the Boulder PD's relative inexperience with homicide notwithstanding. The only thing we're going to say definitively to begin is that the little girl did not write the ransom note herself, then commit suicide by garroting herself, and she didn't die as the result of a botched alien abduction, though some of the theories are nearly as bizarre. We are going to try to follow Sherlock Holmes's dictum that "when you have eliminated the impossible, whatever remains, *however improbable,* must be the truth." Let's see how far we can get with this approach.

First scenario: Patsy accidentally kills JonBenet in a fit of anger. Why? Well, maybe Patsy was completely fed up with the bed-wetting. She smacked the little girl across the face, JonBenet lost her footing and maybe hit her head on something hard. Or, same scenario, except the motive is a little deeper: JonBenet gets ornery and sassy and tells her mom she's tired of the beauty pageants and doesn't want to do them anymore. Patsy gets hysterical because now she's living her own fantasies vicariously through JonBenet. Patsy snaps, strikes out at the child in a momentary loss of reason and control. JonBenet hits her head just as we've described above; it's one of those fluke things and she dies or is severely injured.

So now what? Patsy's got to do something in her panic. She races up to the bedroom and awakens John. "Honey, I accidentally killed JonBenet in a fit of anger. I don't know what came over me. What should we do?"

John pulls himself together enough to ask how it happened. Patsy describes how JonBenet was sent flying across the room and struck her head on the edge of her dresser. "Okay," John says. "We'd better take her to the emergency room and say she had an accident."

"No," Patsy disagrees. "What if they see my handprint across her face [or shoulder, back, bottom, whatever] and realize what really happened?"

"Okay, you're right. We'd better make it look like a botched kidnapping."

"How do we do that?"

"We'll need a ransom note, and we need to make it look like the kidnapper killed her. Let's tie her hands together and fashion a garrote tightly around her neck to strangle her."

"Just in case the kidnapping isn't believable enough, I guess we'd better make it look like she was sexually molested."

And it could have gone on from there.

Now as you read this, I hope you felt it sounded at least slightly absurd. And if it did, why? We'll analyze what doesn't work here and see if it tells us anything about the case itself.

Let's begin with the basic premise. Was Patsy capable of killing her six-year-old daughter, and if so, why and how?

We'll set aside the motive question for a moment. For now, we need to deal with the forensic findings.

As we noted earlier, the coroner's report describes a seven-by-four-inch temporoparietal hemorrhage over an eight-and-a-half-inch skull fracture, over an eight-by-one-and-three-quarter-inch contusion of the brain itself. This is a severe blunt-force trauma. It was estimated for me that a blow this hard could bring down a three-hundred-pound man. And this was a forty-five-pound, six-year-old girl.

So if Patsy caused the fatal blow, albeit accidentally, how did she do it? Was it with her open hand? Her fist? There is no evidence or testimony to suggest that John or Patsy even spanked JonBenet. What would suddenly cause Patsy to lash out forcefully enough to deck a three-hundred-pounder? But let's say she did hit her daughter. Presumably JonBenet would have been facing her. Did the blow send her sprawling and she just happened to hit her head on an edge or hard surface sufficient to cause the hemorrhaging, fracture, and gray matter contusion the coroner reported? Yes, it's possible, but the description of JonBenet's head wound is much more consistent with a direct blow to the head *with an object* than it is with an injury caused by secondary impact after being struck with a hand or fist.

And that's a scenario that is pretty tough to work out. We have to assume that the events that led to JonBenet's death began in her bedroom. If Patsy was suddenly angry with her, we can therefore say that her reaction would have taken place in the bedroom, or possibly the adjoining bathroom if the anger was over a bed- or pants-wetting incident.

Then what? Does Patsy pick up the nearest heavy object she can find and bean her kid with it across the skull? It doesn't make any sense. And what was the object in question? Though it has never been positively identified, police speculated (with good reason, I think) that it might have been a heavy flashlight, either the one found in the kitchen or one like it. Was the flashlight in JonBenet's bedroom? Why? If not, where did it come from? Did Patsy say, "You just wait here, young lady, and when I come back, you're really going to get it!" then go downstairs to bring it up to punish her daughter with? Or maybe she was so angry she dragged JonBenet down to the kitchen or basement to mete out this uncharacteristically harsh discipline and hit her even harder than she'd planned to.

I don't buy it. A mother who doesn't even swat her six-year-old's behind doesn't suddenly have the impulse to bash her brains in. I've never seen a spontaneous display of violence against a child when there was no preconditioning behavior in that direction.

But let's say Patsy did hit her that hard. Where did it happen? In the bedroom? The bathroom? The kitchen? The wine cellar in the basement? Well, where did police find a lot of blood?

Nowhere!

I have investigated a fair number of blunt-force head-trauma assaults in my career, and one feature that is pretty consistent among them is blood. When police have a suspect in a blunt-force head-trauma murder, the first thing I advise in interrogation strategy is to see how the suspect reacts when you tell him you've got blood evidence on him, on his clothing, in his car, whatever. Because the overwhelming odds are that the victim's blood did end up somewhere incriminating to the offender.

But at the Ramsey crime scene there was very little blood. Was it because the killer had time to clean it all up? I don't think so. That kind of evidence is really difficult to get rid of. You pretty much have to get it out of the house, as we believe O. J. Simpson did. And his house wasn't even the murder scene. It is completely unlikely that any killer—an insider or an intruder—could have cleaned up the scene well enough to erase large amounts of blood evidence.

Which gets us back to the cause of death. While the blow to the head was certainly forceful enough to have caused death, the coroner's report only speaks of it as an associated cause. The specific cause, as we've noted, is listed as "asphyxia by strangulation." And with good reason. The most reasonable scenario under which the victim would not suffer massive head bleeding would be that her heart was no longer pumping, or pumping only faintly. In other words, she'd already been garroted. The petechial hemorrhages under the eyelids are consistent with this finding.

Now, if that was the case, how can we work in an accidental, sudden-rage-provoked injury on Patsy's part? You can suddenly lash out and hit someone with your hand or fist (though the evidence is not good that this is what happened), but you don't accidentally garrote your child, or anyone else, to death. That is very much an intentional act, and to my knowledge, no one has suggested that this mother did that to this child.

Okay, then, maybe John did it. Maybe this ligature was part of some horribly perverse sex game. My esteemed colleague Roy Hazelwood has done a lot of research on autoerotic asphyxiation and why it so often ends in death. The scenario would have John choking his daughter to the point of passing out, then reviving her, all the while performing some kind of sex act on her.

Possible? Physically, yes. But again, not one iota, not one scintilla, of evidence suggests he practiced or was capable of this kind of behavior, and an overwhelming amount of evidence suggests he was not. People do not act in a vacuum. Every action is tied to every other action. John

Ramsey is not and was not a sex offender and has none of the characteristics.

Another problem with this scenario is, if John killed JonBenet, then even if the death was accidental, the sexual abuse that accompanied it would not be. Under this circumstance, John could not have counted on his wife to stand by him. Yes, maybe if she were particularly crazy she might have perceived a sexually abused child as a rival and been satisfied that she was eliminated. Maybe she would have considered that John was her ticket to the good life, so no matter what she thought of his actions, she had to stand by him. But those are pretty bizarre possibilities for people who gave no indication of any aberration of this nature, and a reasonable, calculating executive such as John would have known he couldn't count on his wife not to give him up, especially over time.

I almost feel as if I am dignifying John Ramsey's accusers by going over this, but we have to make very, very clear that he could not have done this to his daughter.

So if we go back to our made-up scene, we see that no part of it makes any sense.

I said we would get back to the issue of motive. Let's look at a possible scenario suggested by Detective Steve Thomas in his book, *JonBenet: Inside the Ramsey Murder Investigation.* I'm not going to present it in the level of detail that Thomas does, but I want to represent it accurately, because though he and I disagree, I believe we're both after the same thing.

Thomas believes there was already tension between Patsy and JonBenet on Christmas Day, based on the child's willfully refusing to wear the dress her mother had selected for her. After dinner at the Whites', the Ramseys came home and before long put the two children to bed. Patsy was frazzled with the hecticness of the holidays and preparations for the trip to Michigan, which Thomas says she did not want to make.

Thomas speculates that JonBenet wet the bed and woke up. The red turtleneck shirt found balled up in the bathroom must have been what she wore to bed, then Patsy stripped it off her when it became wet and redressed her in the clothing in which she was found.

The detective goes on to say, "I never believed the child was sexually abused for the gratification of the offender but that the vaginal trauma was some sort of corporal punishment. The dark fibers found in her pubic region could have come from the violent wiping of a wet child."

I have to say here that I find this part of the theory, particularly, bizarre. The abrasions around and on the inner wall of the child's vagina certainly seemed to be the result of some form of digital sexual penetration, but the suggestion that they actually resulted from Patsy forcefully wiping her there brutally enough to do that is hard to imagine.

In any event, Thomas then postulates "some sort of explosive encounter in the child's bathroom," in which JonBenet was slammed against a hard surface. At that point, Patsy was overtaken by panic at what she'd done, quickly decided she couldn't risk the emergency room route, so she moved her daughter's body down to the basement room. She then went back upstairs to the kitchen and wrote the ransom note from her own tablet to make the crime appear to be a kidnapping.

After that, she returned to the basement and realized that though JonBenet was mortally wounded, she wasn't actually dead. Thomas allows for the possibility that JonBenet was already dead at this point and that Patsy realized it. In her desperation, Patsy seized the closest items available to her, the handle from the paintbrush in her painting box and a length of cord, with which she fashioned a garrote around the child's neck and tied her wrists in front of her.

For the next several hours, she fine-tuned the staging, placing the three-page note where it was later found and putting a piece of duct tape over JonBenet's mouth. The rest of the roll and the remainder of the cord were either deposited in a neighbor's trash can or perhaps down a nearby storm sewer.

Then she "discovered" the note, screamed, alerted her husband, and set the events of the morning into motion. When Officer Rick French responded to the 911 call shortly before 6 A.M., Patsy was still wearing the outfit she'd had on the evening before; she'd never gone to bed. Evidently, she'd been too busy.

Thomas speculates that John Ramsey first grew suspicious while reading the ransom note, more so when no kidnapper called, and probably found JonBenet's body on his own sometime during the morning when Detective Arndt noticed him missing. Then John faced his own dilemma: whether to give up his wife or stand by her. JonBenet was gone and he'd already lost another beloved daughter. If he turned on Patsy, the family would effectively be destroyed. So he became part of the cover-up and used Arndt's suggestion that he and Fleet White look through the house as an opportunity to officially "find" the body. And the Ramseys have stood together, hidden behind their lawyers, and stonewalled the police ever since.

I have trouble with this scenario on many levels, all of them based on my two and a half decades studying violent crime, particularly the behavioral aspects. First, if Patsy took such time to set up the scene to make it look like something other than what it was, why didn't she do the one truly obvious and mandatory thing: make it look as if someone had broken in and then left again? If you're going to go to all the trouble of writing a ransom note and staging the body, how do you forget to make it look like a break-in? The Ramseys actually said they thought they'd locked all the doors. Okay, maybe Patsy was panicked and not thinking clearly. But it defies logic that she would think of all these arcane, sadistic things to establish credibility, then not do something so simple. Possible, but highly unlikely. The same is true with the legal pad that the ransom note came from. If Patsy wrote the note herself, she knew where the paper came from, she knew it would be evidence, she knew it would help tie her to the crime. And she's going to leave it out in plain sight? Totally illogical. If you're going to do that, you're going to leave the duct tape roll and the cord out in plain sight, too. If you dispose of one, you dispose of all of them.

Thomas believes that when John carried JonBenet's body upstairs, he had already previously discovered it. Having seen John's reaction when he was describing finding the body to me, I am certain that his reaction was genuine. I also believe that if either John or Patsy knew that JonBenet's body was in the house, they'd be itching to get the ordeal over with rather than let it drag on for hours. One of them would have innocently said, "Has anyone checked the basement?" "Has anyone looked downstairs?" or "I thought I heard some noise downstairs."

I also think the condition in which the body was found suggests Patsy wasn't the perpetrator. Many commentators have mentioned JonBenet's being wrapped in the blanket and cited my frequent observation that parents or others with proprietary interest in the victim will leave her in some kind of loving or protected state. In his book, Steve Thomas went so far as to state, "John Douglas was almost denying his own writings in order to give the Ramseys a pass."

Well, I can't help it if readers, particularly law enforcement professionals, misunderstand or misinterpret what I say, or only look at the surface material. This is a problem I run into again and again. It's as if there is a Profiling 101 course that can easily be applied to fit every case. Unfortunately, that's not the way it is. It's not easy to become an experienced profiler, and even if you get to that stage, all profilers are not created equal. In this case, if Thomas had ever asked me about this detail, I would have been happy to clarify it for him.

For one thing, the body was not protectively wrapped as I would expect to find in a parental murder. It was haphazardly draped, with the arms and feet sticking out. In all probability, the intruder intended to use the blanket to carry JonBenet out of the house. This is in no way similar to the almost hermetic wrapping or sealing I have often seen. But much more to the point, I cannot conceive that a loving mother with a profound proprietary interest in the victim could possibly insert her fingers into her little girl's vagina to punish her, let alone make it look as if an intruder had molested her, and then stage her dead six-year-old's body with a garrote tightly around her neck. If that were the case, we would have seen profound evidence of psychopathology from Patsy by now, and we have not. And with Beth's death and her own cancer, not to mention a prostate cancer scare with John, this woman has experienced precipitating stressors in her life.

Then there is the issue of motive, the one we deferred a little earlier because this is the most fruitful context in which to discuss it.

To react in a certain way requires precursive behavior. As mentioned previously, we are told that JonBenet had a chronic problem with bed-wetting to the point that Patsy had a morning washing routine for dealing with it. So why would one more incident make her snap? With the excitement of Christmas, the late nights and parties, preparing to go away and generally being off schedule, if anything, a mother would expect it to be more likely for an accident to occur and would take it in stride.

It's not enough to suggest that she was tense because of the upcoming trip; that's not enough of a reason. It's not enough to make Patsy say something to the effect of "JonBenet, you've wet your bed five hundred eighty-two times already and I'm not going to take it any longer," then slam her across the room. Mothers don't suddenly act that way. No one does.

And, of course, a bed-wetting confrontation would much more likely occur in the morning than the middle of the night. You have to jump through too many of those hoops to make it work.

This goes as well for the other possible motive some have suggested: that JonBenet suddenly wanted out of the pageant world and Patsy couldn't deal with that. This is another scenario you have to jump through hoops to achieve. All indications are that JonBenet loved performing, in fact pushed her parents to let her do more. The family had enjoyed a happy day, and even coming up with such a notion at bedtime when all she was thinking about was going to Michigan and then on the Disney boat would have been completely out of context. And it is not the kind of thing that would have come up in the middle of the night. If it did, JonBenet would have to have gone up to her parents' bedroom and made her announcement, thereby involving John as well as Patsy, which means that one person couldn't have flown off the handle without the other intervening. And if such a mother-daughter confrontation had occurred at bedtime, both John and Burke would have heard it. It doesn't work.

When my unit consulted on a potential domestic case or when I was teaching criminal investigative analysis at Quantico or for any other police agency, I used to stress that it is absolutely critical to look closely at what was going on in and around the victim's family in the days or weeks before the crime.

The 1996 Christmas season was a happy time for the Ramsey family. They loved Christmas anyway, particularly the excitement of the kids, and this was one of the best times of their lives. John's company had topped a billion dollars in annual sales. Patsy had recovered from a terrifying and deadly cancer. The children were happy. JonBenet charmed everyone, and she and Patsy loved going to the pageants together, despite whatever judgments any of us might have about their value. The family was looking forward to the vacation in Michigan and then the cruise on the Disney ship.

Now fast-forward several hours to this beautiful little girl, strangled to death with a garrote, bashed in the side of her head, tied up, and left in the basement wine cellar. How do you get from point A to point B?

One of the first things we look for in profiling is a precipitating stressor: something that made the offender act or react the way he did. We don't have any here. There's nothing going on. No matter how badly JonBenet messed the bed (if she did at all; the urine stains in her panties and long johns could easily have come about when her bladder tension released at death), I don't believe that Patsy would suddenly lose every instinct and inhibition she'd ever had and strike out violently at the being she clearly loved as much as anyone else in the entire world. And God knows she wouldn't strangle her daughter to death. It just doesn't happen that way. There would have to have been some previous behavior to suggest this was possible, and there simply was not.

I mentioned that when I first met Patsy, she was wearing a large cross around her neck. I've often seen people accused of crimes suddenly get religion, and I was wondering if the stress of what she was undergoing had occasioned this necklace. But then when I had the opportunity to examine many of the Ramsey family snapshots, I saw that she had been wearing this same cross for several years. I learned it had been given to her by her minister during her cancer treatments. I saw nothing to imply to me that her religious faith and her belief in her miraculous salvation from cancer were anything but genuine. And I have trouble believing that she could have been so cynical as to assert that her baby's killer would get his just desserts from God even if he eluded temporal justice if she were the killer. This is not to say that I have been taken in or influenced one way or another by her religiousness. I am only pointing out a belief structure on her part that seemed to be internally consistent.

LOU SMIT'S SCENARIO

I was not alone in my analysis. In March 1997, Alex Hunter hired a retired El Paso County Sheriff's Department homicide detective named Lou Smit to conduct an investigation on behalf of the DA's office. El Paso County is due south of Denver and encompasses Colorado Springs and the U.S. Air Force Academy. Smit, a gentle and soft-spoken man in his sixties, had acquired legendary status in Colorado as a brilliant investigator with an astounding 90 percent clearance rate on more than two hundred homicides. In his wallet he kept a plastic photo folder with pictures of some of the victims for whom he'd obtained justice.

Smit's legend was solidified with his working of the 1991 murder of Heather Dawn Church, a little girl who was killed in her house near Colorado Springs. The case went nowhere for four years with the prevailing attitude being that someone in the family had done it, and the police were not aggressively seeking other potential suspects. With dogged determination and an obsessive attention to detail, Smit found a print at the scene that had pretty much been overlooked. He was able to match it to a suspect who was subsequently arrested in Florida. Smit had pulled the proverbial rabbit out of the hat.

Shortly after Smit came on the Ramsey case, he examined all the evidence and, unlike the Boulder PD, concluded that, as in the Heather Church case, an intruder had killed JonBenet. He believed that a pedophile who had seen JonBenet in public decided to go after her that night and broke into the house while the Ramseys were celebrating with the Whites.

The offender probably went in through the grate and window well to the basement, then explored the entire house. He used Patsy's pad and pen to write the ransom note. Then, before the family returned home, he hid and waited for them. Once he was convinced they were all asleep, he went into JonBenet's bedroom and immobilized her with a stun gun applied twice directly to her skin. He taped over her mouth with duct tape he had brought in with him and carried her unconscious down to the basement, where he could remove her from the house without disturbing the parents on the third floor.

He found Patsy's paint box and broke off the brush handle to fashion into a garrote with the cord he'd brought. As he choked the child as part of his erotic fantasy, he simultaneously penetrated her with his fingers. The unidentified DNA under JonBenet's nails and in her underpants, the unidentified pubic hair, an unidentified palm print on the door, a Hi-Tec brand bootprint on the floor, and a scuff mark on the wall below the win-

319

dow all came from the UNSUB, according to Smit's theory. The finger-nail deposits occurred when JonBenet awakened and tried to fight him off. That was when he panicked and struck her hard in the head, possibly with a flashlight. Believing he'd killed her, he left the body and escaped from the house, taking with him the articles he'd brought in—the cord, the duct tape, and the stun gun.

Smit also had an interesting alternative theory to the $118,000 figure. If the intruder was planning to flee to Mexico, at the exchange rate in effect at the time, $118,000 would have yielded 1 million pesos.

After he left the DA's office, Smit went through his presentation on the case for me. I didn't necessarily agree with all of his interpretations, but his overall approach made a lot of sense, much more than the twisted logic of the bed-wetting scenario. Many of the other investigators, including, according to Steve Thomas, some from Quantico, objected to Smit's assertion that an intruder would be bold enough to break in and then hang around a house full of sleeping people. But there is much precedent for this. You can be fearless or mission-oriented without being particularly criminally sophisticated.

THE STUN GUN THEORY

Lou Smit pursued the Ramsey investigation with every bit of the dedicated meticulousness with which he had worked the Church case and all the others. His theory took shape when, studying photographs of JonBenet's body, he noticed two sets of small red welts on her skin. Each set was the same, with the two marks in the same relationship to each other. He thought it highly unlikely that two such regular marks could be coincidental. He pursued this with several people, eventually ending up with Michael Dobersen, the coroner of Arapahoe County, Colorado. Dobersen had worked on a case involving a stun gun. After studying the photographs Smit showed him, he said that they did seem to be consistent with a stun gun, but he couldn't say for sure without examining the body itself.

Smit pursued the stun gun possibility and narrowed down the type of weapon that could have produced the telltale marks to an Air Taser brand. According to Steve Thomas, the police discounted the possibility of a stun gun being used in the crime, but I do not know why. I am not an expert on such weaponry, but when Smit showed me his evidence, it looked compelling to me.

Like the attic floorboard in the Lindbergh kidnapping, this is one of those elements upon which the entire case can hinge. If, in fact, a stun gun was used by the offender, that would virtually rule out the parents by itself, in my view.

A stun gun could be used on a six-year-old child with only two possible intentions in mind: to torture her for sexual pleasure or to immobilize her. Neither of these fits into any reasonable scenario involving the Ramseys. The presence of a stun gun would show planning and intent, not accident. If the marks on JonBenet's body did come from a stun gun (and it would be unlikely to have two sets that so match up to an Air Taser that did not), it is interesting to note that while the notepad and the possible head-blow weapon were in plain view in the house, the items intended to *control*—the duct tape, the cord, and the possible stun gun—were not found, suggesting the offender probably brought them with him. This is also probably true of the flashlight, which would be another natural implement for an intruder to bring. When he found he needed a blunt-force weapon, then, he had it right there.

THE RANSOM NOTE

Few would disagree that the three-page ransom note is as important a piece of evidence as exists in this case. Anyone hoping to come up with a theory of who killed JonBenet Ramsey has to come to grips with the significance and meaning of this communication.

When I saw the note, how long and bizarre it was, my first thought was that, regardless of who wrote it, it had to have been written before the killing, not afterward. No one—family member or intruder—would have had the presence of mind, the mental concentration, to sit down in the house and write this out with the body lying there in the basement. For this reason, I don't believe the note was part of a staging in the same way that the police and some members of the FBI seem to believe. This does not mean I think monetary gain was necessarily the prime motivator in the case, although it could have been. It just means that the note was written deliberately, not as a hasty cover-up after the fact.

With very few exceptions, the spelling is correct and the syntax consistent, leading me to believe the note was written by an educated individual. Compare this to the Lindbergh communications or the Jack the Ripper "From hell" note. But it is so strange and the amount of the ransom demand is so small relative to the Ramseys' wealth and what we would expect an extortionist to ask for that we can rule out sophisticated or professional criminals. If this is a criminal-enterprise homicide, it was perpetrated by an amateur.

For the sake of convenience, I will use the masculine pronoun in this analysis.

To begin with, the phrase "Listen carefully!" implies an offender unsure of himself who therefore feels the need to secure attention. Using the plural "we" lends him more strength and credence, as does the suggestion that they are foreign terrorists with a political agenda. However, the silliness and awkwardness of the sentences "We are a group of individuals that represent a small foreign faction. We respect your bussiness [*sic*] but not the country that it serves" gives him away. What occurs to me is the construction of a teenager or young adult who watches a lot of movies. I can imagine a movie character saying, "They represent a small foreign faction . . ."

Even the phrase "At this time we have your daughter in our posession" is awkward and unsophisticated. And interestingly, though there are repeated references throughout the note to "your daughter," she is never mentioned by name. Is it possible the writer of the note did not know her name or, even more likely, did not know how to spell it?

On the second page, the writer says, "Any deviation of my instructions will result in the immediate execution of your daughter. You will also be denied her remains for proper burial." This also speaks to the writer's insecurity. And I don't believe a mother would refer to her daughter's death as an execution. In the same way that Patsy wouldn't physically abuse the body, I don't believe she would talk about withholding the remains. This would be too painful for the mother to countenance.

Anyone trying to make up a ransom note as staging would write something as short and to the point as possible. You'd be careful not to give any unnecessary clues.

I find it equally interesting that the note instructs Ramsey to "withdraw $118,000.00 from your account." It doesn't merely demand the money, it gives specific instructions, as if the writer knew that this precise amount of money was available in the account. I therefore think it likely that the writer had been in the house before and seen some documentation, possibly a pay stub, that this amount had been deposited in John Ramsey's account. To a young adult, this might have seemed like a lot of money and a good amount to ask for.

Many have suggested that the $118,000 figure was such an inside piece of information that the note had to have been written by one of the Ramseys. I must admit, I don't get this at all. If one or both of the Ramseys were using this note to stage an apparent kidnapping, why would they purposely point the finger at themselves by using inside information? If John Ramsey knew he wasn't going to have to pay the ransom anyway, why not ask for $5 million and make it look more legitimate?

The only scenario that might make some logical sense in which one of the Ramseys came up with the figure would be if Patsy wanted to stick it to John through the note; that is, if she were trying to give him a message. This could also account for such phrases as "You are not the only fat cat around so don't think that killing will be difficult," "Don't underestimate us John," and "Use that good southern common sense of yours. It is up to you now John!"

But if that were the case, Patsy would have found ways to continue revealing herself and sticking it to John after the fact, and she did not. In fact, the police were monitoring all of their interactions with each other that first day at the Fernies' house, and there was no evidence of her trying to get back at him or punish him in any way. To me, the $118,000 figure points away from the Ramseys but toward someone who knew them or had observed personal details of their lives.

There are quite a few movie references in the note. "You and your family are under constant scrutiny as well as the authorities. Don't try to grow a brain, John" corresponds to "You know that I'm on top of you. Do not attempt to grow a brain," lines delivered by the Dennis Hopper extortionist character in *Speed,* which was out on video at the time of the murder.

"Speaking to anyone about your situation, such as Police, F.B.I., etc., will result in your daughter being beheaded" corresponds to "Do not involve the police or the FBI. If you do, I will kill him," from *Ransom.*

"If we catch you talking to a stray dog, she dies. If you alert bank authorities, she dies. If the money is in any way marked or tampered with, she dies" sounds like "If I even think you're being followed, the girl dies," and "That's the end of the game. The girl dies," from the Clint Eastwood hit *Dirty Harry.*

The phrases "Now listen to me carefully" and "Now listen. Listen very carefully" also come from *Dirty Harry,* as does "It sounds like you had a good rest. You'll need it." Compare that to the note's "The delivery will be exhausting so I advise you to be rested."

That's a lot of very similar material to be merely coincidental, and it is difficult to conceive of Patsy sitting alone in the kitchen writing out a fake ransom note after she's killed her daughter and coming up with all these movie phrases. If Patsy could recall any movie lines, they'd likely either be favorites from her childhood or current children's movies. Even John would not know the kinds of references found in the note. To me, that sounds more like the conception of a teenager or young adult.

So does the phrase "we are familiar with Law enforcement countermeasures and tactics." So does "will result in your daughter being beheaded." Who uses words like *beheaded* these days? People who play Dungeons & Dragons type games and watch *Hercules* or *Xena: Warrior Princess* on television, I should think. I was told that beheadings were a key element of the *Highlander* TV series.

The point is, I can't be certain from the note who wrote it and who killed JonBenet, but from the psycholinguistic analysis, it does not appear to have been written by a forty-year-old woman panic-stricken over having just accidentally killed her daughter.

The transcript of Patsy's 911 call is also instructive here. Toward the end of the conversation, the dispatcher asks, "Does it say who took her?" At first Patsy doesn't understand the question and it has to be repeated.

Finally, she says, "It says 'S.B.T.C. Victory.' Please . . ." If she had written the note herself, I think she would have answered with something like "No, it doesn't say. But someone's got my baby . . ." Instead, I visualize her leafing through the note looking for the answer to the question. The only thing she can find is what is written at the end. So she mentions "S.B.T.C.," which in itself doesn't really answer the question, so she moves one line up, to "Victory," which also doesn't help. But this strikes me as someone who is unfamiliar with the note and desperate to find out who has taken her daughter.

What does "S.B.T.C." mean? Who knows? We've heard everything from "Saved by the Cross" to "Santa Barbara Tennis Club." One of the early interpretations was "Subic Bay Training Center," since John Ramsey had served at Subic Bay in the Philippines while in the service. The problem with that one is that there was no such training center there. I have often found when interviewing violent offenders after they've been convicted and incarcerated that they come up with obscure references that mean something only to them. This was certainly the case with the interlocking circles and punched holes in the Lindbergh notes.

With respect to the Ramsey ransom note, an inevitable question arises: If this really was a kidnapping or an attempt to extort money or get back at John Ramsey for some reason, why wouldn't the offender bring the note with him, rather than count on being able to write it at the house?

I don't know.

I can suggest several possibilities: he was disorganized enough that he forgot the note at home or didn't think about it until he got there; he didn't want to risk leaving a note on his own paper for fear of being linked; he had enough time alone in the house to write a "better" one than the one he brought with him or intended to send after taking the child; and he wanted to implicate the Ramseys by tying the note to them. But these are only possibilities. There are almost always aspects of a case you can't work out, such as the absence of fingerprints in the Lindbergh nursery or why the Ripper used a different weapon in the first killing on the night of the "double event," or the odd costume the Zodiac wore at Lake Berryessa. But I don't have an explanation I'm completely satisfied with.

A lot of information has come out about how the experts have not been able to "rule out" Patsy Ramsey as the writer of the note. While this is apparently true, it is misleading, like so much of the reporting of this case. At least four highly reputable handwriting experts were called both by the police and the defense (probably a lot more), and the consensus was that while Patsy's handwriting could not be ruled out, the similarities were at the very lowest end of the spectrum. In other words, many, many people would "qualify" or fail to be ruled out under this criterion.

From a behavioral perspective, I have to question whether, if Patsy had written the note, she would have so willingly submitted to so many handwriting tests and given up so many previous handwriting exemplars. Even if she were purposely trying to disguise her penmanship, handwriting analysis was a field she knew nothing about, so would she have believed she could fool the experts, particularly with three pages of evidence?

One of the most interesting analyses of the ransom note came from Vassar literature professor Donald Foster, who has made quite a reputation for himself as a literary sleuth. He stunned the academic world by proving through textual analysis that a 578-line poem he had found on microfilm in the archives of the UCLA library had actually been written by William Shakespeare. This was the first discovery of a previously unknown Shakespearean work in 112 years. Using a similar technique, comparing the work to known examples of the author's writings, he unmasked *Newsweek* columnist Joe Klein as the anonymous author of the best-selling political novel *Primary Colors*.

In 1998, Foster announced he had determined that Patsy Ramsey had written the ransom note, which sounded pretty compelling coming from such an established expert, and Steve Thomas has written that he placed great weight on Foster's analysis. But then it came out that in the spring of 1997, he had written to Patsy Ramsey at the Charlevoix, Michigan, house to offer his condolences, encouragement, and the statement "I know you are innocent—know it, absolutely and unequivocally. I will stake my professional reputation on it."

He had also stated that he believed John Ramsey's son John Andrew had been posting on the Internet under the code name "jameson," and that this jameson was the actual killer. When it turned out that jameson was, in fact, not a twenty-year-old male college student named John

Andrew Ramsey but a forty-five-year-old North Carolina housewife named Susan Bennett who had merely developed a tremendous fascination with the case, Foster's analyses with regard to the Ramsey case were severely called into question.

The fact is, no one has, or will, come by the whole truth from a single clue or piece of evidence.

POSTOFFENSE BEHAVIOR

A significant aspect of the consulting services we provided at Quantico was to describe an UNSUB's expected pre- and postoffense behavior. In this way, it might be possible for someone who recognizes this behavior to come forward and aid the investigation. Likewise, we can use analysis of pre- and postoffense behavior to help rule out suspects. We've already talked about the behavior of the Ramseys leading up to JonBenet's murder. Now let's look briefly at their behavior afterward.

One of the greatest raps against them is that they didn't behave like people who were innocently bereaved. One component of this was their supposed emotional reaction to their daughter's death, and I think we have effectively dealt with that. Another is the fact that they lawyered up right afterward, though saying they did not cooperate with the police is another entire area of misleading reporting.

We have shown how they did answer all police questions on the day of the discovery of JonBenet's body. We have shown how they agreed to give all the physical and handwriting samples they were asked for. And it is well documented that their attorneys made numerous offers to have them speak with the police, but the two sides could never get together over the rules until June of 1998, when they submitted to three days of interviews.

One reason for the Ramseys' attitude toward the police was the police's attitude toward them, and this can be explained whether they are innocent or guilty. As I travel around the country giving presentations, one of the laments I hear over and over again from members of victims' rights groups is that the police were not forthcoming with information, did not keep them in the loop, did not make them part of the search for the killer of their loved one. Some departments are sensitive on this issue and some are not. But the problem is certainly compounded if the cops come in with the attitude that the bereaved are also the criminals.

Once the Ramseys realized the police were holding up turning over their daughter's body for burial until the Ramseys agreed to the interrogation under the conditions the police dictated, they realized they were in an adversarial relationship with the investigators and had to protect themselves. I don't find this behaviorally indicative of guilt.

More to the point, both John and Patsy spoke regularly with law enforcement officials they trusted. In the first several weeks, Patsy communicated repeatedly with Linda Arndt, they both communicated with members of the district attorney's staff, and once he came onto the case, they communicated regularly with Lou Smit.

They cooperated with the people they trusted. This is totally consistent behavior.

They also allowed me to fly to Atlanta at my own expense (I had long since stopped being paid on this case at my own request) and talk to them extensively over a three-day period in March 1999. There were no ground rules and no lawyers present.

Did they agree to speak with Smit and me because we believed they were innocent? Sure. But they also knew that each of us had been roundly criticized for our opinions and for being taken in by this couple. And they were smart enough to know that Smit and I would each jump at the chance to solve the case, and who the perpetrator was would be immaterial. We would give either of them up in a heartbeat if we could show he or she had killed their daughter.

Did they think they were so clever that they could go *mano a mano* with either of us and not slip up? That shows incredible arrogance or incredible criminal sophistication. And here lies the crux of the postoffense behavioral issue.

My analysis is that though there were organized and planned elements, this crime was basically criminally unsophisticated in its conception and perpetration. If the Ramseys were involved, then their postoffense behavior has been criminally sophisticated in the extreme. They are both master criminals and sociopaths who sprang full-blown into that position without any preparation or practice. They were so confident that they felt they could take on their accusers such as Steve Thomas on live national television (*Larry King Live,* CNN, May 31, 2000) where one slipup would give them away.

If John thought Patsy had done it and that she was mentally unbalanced, would he let her out of his sight? Would he let her make numerous trips on her own without fear she would inadvertently spill the beans and sink them both? Most important, would he let her continue to care for his son?

If they both thought their son Burke knew or suspected anything or had ever overheard them saying one word about having been involved in JonBenet's death, would they let him go off to school on his own, let alone sending him off to the Whites the very morning after the crime? Who would trust a ten-year-old never to say anything he knew? Not me, and I've had three of them.

Most people have been looking at the surface behavior, but not thinking about the truly indicative stuff.

THE GRAND JURY

Moving into 1998, little demonstrable progress was being made on the case. Trying to move forward, Boulder PD had been lobbying for a grand jury investigation, figuring that such an entity could compel testimony that they could not. On March 22, a grand jury of four women and eight men was impaneled. It began its work on September 15. By that time, though the case had not progressed, there was a major development on the personnel front.

On August 6, Steve Thomas submitted a letter of resignation to Chief Beckner, complaining about the handling of the investigation by the police and the interference by the DA's office in not charging the Ramseys. He doubted that justice would ever be done for JonBenet.

On September 20, Lou Smit submitted his own letter of resignation to District Attorney Hunter, stating, "I cannot in good conscience be a part of the persecution of innocent people. It would be highly improper and unethical for me to stay when I so strongly believe this."

The second anniversary of the murder came and went without any suspects being identified. John Ramsey had lost his job with Access Graphics. He believed it was because he was perceived as a corporate liability because of all the negative publicity. He was probably right.

On March 19, 1999, Detective Linda Arndt resigned from the department. To me, this represented just one more example of an investigation in disarray. Arndt described how she had looked into John Ramsey's eyes and knew what had happened. The inference most people drew from her statement was that John was the killer. Steve Thomas, having access to the same evidence that Arndt had available, concluded that Patsy had been the killer and that John wasn't involved until the cover-up.

The grand jury's term was scheduled to expire on April 21, 1999. But on April 7, it was extended for another six months since its work was far from complete.

I testified before the grand jury on April 26 and 27, 1999. Since their proceedings are secret, I'm not at liberty to reveal what I said. But some in the press have speculated that my testimony and Lou Smit's created serious doubts in the grand jurors' minds. I don't know if this is true and I don't know what Smit testified. I only know I told them what I believed and I'm sure he did the same.

Prior to my testimony, Detective Sergeant Tom Wickman, who was now heading up the investigation for Boulder PD, introduced himself and told me he'd read all of my books and particularly admired the *Crime Classification Manual*. He thanked me for the work I'd done in the area of criminal profiling and what he considered its significant contribution to law enforcement. I was very appreciative of all of Wickman's comments.

On October 13, 1999, Alex Hunter and the grand jury announced that it had found insufficient evidence to indict anyone in the JonBenet Ramsey case. Some speculated that the final decision might have been Hunter's, because under Colorado law, both the grand jury foreman and the district attorney must sign a true bill of indictment for it to take effect.

Steve Thomas condemned Hunter for not indicting the Ramseys and letting a jury decide the truth. Attorney and Harvard law professor Alan Dershowitz declared Hunter a "constitutional hero" for taking all the barbs and not bringing a case to trial that he did not feel could be supported. This was just one more example of the huge and seemingly unbridgeable divisions this case has engendered.

LOOSE ENDS

There is no way to be exhaustive on a case of this scope, and anyone who studies it will have his own crucial element or piece of evidence. I've tried to present what I considered to be the important points. But items are always left over in any discussion, and we'll try to deal with some of them here.

1. If there was an intruder, why didn't his footprints show up in the snow around the house?

This is another of those greatly misreported "facts." Contrary to what was originally reported, only a light dusting of snow was on the ground on the night in question, plus the walk had been shoveled. So even if the intruder had left through the window well, he would not necessarily have left tracks.

2. How would an intruder get in?

Smit believed he got in through the window well to the basement. This may well be the case. It is also possible that he gained access by using a key. At least twenty keys to the house were floating around that were not in the Ramseys' possession. If the offender was someone who knew them well, or knew someone who had worked for them or had a key through some other legitimate reason, this is a likely possibility.

It is also possible that one or more doors had been left unlocked. This was a low-crime area, and the Ramseys sometimes did leave doors unlocked when they were not at home. This was also true of ground-floor windows. During a search on the morning of December 26, a police officer reportedly found the door on the south side of the house unlocked.

3. If neither of the Ramseys killed JonBenet and the real killer is still out there, why hasn't he been caught and why hasn't there been any evidence of his subsequent work?

First of all, this was not the work of a serial killer. This is not someone who killed for the fulfillment and satisfaction of exerting manipulation, domination, and control over a victim of opportunity. This was an inexperienced, mission-oriented offender. So there is no particular reason to believe he would repeat the same signature crime over and over.

And it is unfortunately true that many homicides go unsolved, particularly in jurisdictions without a lot of experience working them. On December 21, 1997, almost exactly a year after JonBenet's murder, Susannah Chase, a University of Colorado student, was murdered in downtown Boulder. Like the Ramsey murder, Boulder PD has been unable to solve this one. Where is that killer?

4. If JonBenet's body was discovered on December 26, 1996, but the Ramseys chose to mark the date of death on her tombstone as December 25, doesn't that imply specific knowledge that only the killer would have?

That's apparently what the police believed. Having dealt with many bereaved families of murder victims, I think the use of this date as a "clue" is ridiculous.

Parents will always search for some meaning or significance out of the tragedy of their child's death. Christmas Day had a happy and symbolic significance to the Ramseys. If they didn't actually know whether JonBenet died before or after midnight, it was perfectly natural that they would choose the date that had the most meaning to them. On one level, I believe choosing this date was an attempt to remind people of the presence of evil in the midst of innocence and joy.

5. Would an intruder risk this much time in the house?

Certain types of intruders would. In 1988, my unit worked a kidnapping case in Jackson, Mississippi. On July 26, Annie Laurie Hearin, seventy-two years of age, in poor health and the wife of Robert M. Hearin, one of the state's wealthiest men, was abducted from their elegant Georgian home in a well-to-do neighborhood in broad daylight. Only about an hour window of opportunity existed between the time Mrs. Hearin's brunch guests left at 3:30 P.M. and her husband returned home at 4:30. Nothing in Annie Hearin's background or lifestyle suggested her as a target, yet the UNSUB was willing to go to great risk to get to her. Clearly, this was not a victim of opportunity.

There was a ransom note, as bizarre in its way as the Ramsey note. It was typed on an old typewriter and referenced School Pictures, a company that Robert Hearin had controlled, although it was only a small part of his holdings. The note also listed twelve individuals who had been franchise owners of the company and directed Hearin to "Put these people back in the shape they was in before they got mixed up with School Pictures." So the UNSUB was someone who felt he, and School Pictures, had been wronged by Robert Hearin.

Bill Hagmaier, who, by the time of the Ramsey case, headed up CASKU, the FBI's Child Abduction and Serial Killer Unit, the successor to my Investigative Support Unit, took on the profile of the UNSUB and put in his usual first-rate effort. As I recall from our case consultation discussions, he defined Mrs. Hearin as a symbolic victim and the offender as mission-oriented, with a strong commitment, even though the crime was crudely planned and somewhat impulsive and high risk. He believed the residence was probably surveilled ahead of time and that the UNSUB had most likely been inside before, either through legitimate or illegitimate means. Despite the ransom note, Hagmaier believed the motive was primarily anger rather than material gain.

Working from the profile, the ransom note, and such leads as the fact that a white van with Florida plates had been observed on several occasions near the crime scene, investigators identified a prime suspect. Newton Alfred Winn, one of the individuals listed in the ransom note, lived in Florida and was losing virtually everything he had as the result of a lawsuit over School Pictures. At Winn's home, police found a typewriter that appeared to be linked to the note, and a map of Jackson, with the Hearins' neighborhood circled. Winn was convicted of extortion, conspiracy to kidnap, and perjury and sentenced to nineteen years.

But like the Ramsey case, this one continues to haunt me. Annie Laurie Hearin was never found and no one has ever been charged with her murder. Her husband, Robert, died two years after her disappearance of a heart attack. But there are enough similarities between the two cases, particularly in the astuteness of Bill's profile, to open our minds to the possibilities in the Ramsey case.

SUMMING UP

Actually, there is no way to sum up a case like this. I don't claim to know who did it; I only think I have a pretty good idea who didn't do it, and that is what I've tried to present.

Having said that, though, it would be ducking the issue if I did not at least present a theory of what might have happened.

The behavioral evidence I have discerned and the forensic evidence I have seen and read, plus what has been conveyed to me by Lou Smit, lead me to believe that JonBenet Ramsey's killer was a white male, relatively young, who had a personal grudge against John Ramsey and intended to carry it out by defiling and robbing him of the most valuable thing in the world to him.

I believe he entered the house while the family was out, either through the basement window well or with a key, bringing with him a stun gun, a roll of duct tape, and a spool of cord. His intention was to incapacitate JonBenet, abduct her, and molest her. This was a personal-cause crime rather than a criminal enterprise. The ransom consideration was secondary and may not even have occurred to the UNSUB until he was in the house. This could account for the note's being written on Patsy's pad, and this could account for the $118,000 figure. That is, he had no real intention of collecting so low a sum; he was just trying to make a point.

Or maybe he brought a briefer ransom note with him, but when he had the time, he altered his plan and wrote a note on the Ramseys' own paper that was lying out on the counter, getting out more of his anger and resentment. How bad or insulting would this look for the Ramseys?

The high risk for the intruder would have been mitigated by the complexity of the physical layout of the house. He could have hidden out in the basement, which he would have illuminated with the flashlight he brought, getting familiar with the warren of rooms.

The UNSUB stole up to JonBenet's bedroom after her parents were upstairs asleep, incapacitated her with an Air Taser stun gun, which would not make a loud noise when fired, taped her mouth, and carried her down to the basement, which he had already checked out, and where he used Patsy's paintbrush handle and his own cord to form a garrote around the child's neck. He also bound her hands tightly. Whether he intended to or not, his tightening of the neck ligature either killed her or nearly did so.

When he realized what he had done, he panicked and finished off the job with a blow to her head. Then, instead of removing her from the house, he fled in panic.

This is only one possibility. Another would be that this actually was an intended kidnapping, planned by one or more teens or young adults who had been inside the Ramsey house and had seen John's pay stubs. Maybe they were friends of one of JonBenet's baby-sitters, workmen, or friends of friends; that's just a guess. But to a teen, $118,000 would be a lot of money. He would also be so unsophisticated as to have no idea how difficult it is to pull off a kidnapping, even the kidnapping of a six-year-old girl.

He would be bold and foolhardy enough to enter the house and wait there, during which time he could have written the ransom note he forgot to bring with him. In this case, both the stun gun and the garrote may have been instruments of control rather than torture. The digital penetration of the child's vagina would have represented the young man's casual sexual experimentation while he had the opportunity. This type of behavior would not be rare. Again, when he realized he had killed or nearly killed his victim, he would have panicked and fled.

Normally, a teen or group of teens will fold like a house of cards when confronted by investigators. But if the heat was never on him because of the focus on the Ramseys, he may have been able to slide under the radar.

The fact remains, I'm not sure who killed JonBenet Ramsey, and the fact that her killer has not been found and charged represents a terrible injustice. That injustice will only be compounded if the wrong people are accused.

I always said that having a child murdered was the worst possible thing that could happen to a person. I guess I was wrong. Having that happen and then being blamed for it is even worse.

CHAPTER SEVEN

PERSPECTIVES

In examining the themes these cases share to figure out what continues to haunt us about them, one idea that comes to mind is that of "archetype" or "icon." From lurking evil to the inner workings of family, from celebrity and its implications to the mystical and arcane, from sexual obsession to the corruption of innocence, each of these cases, as we've seen, represents an archetype we can all understand. Each of these cases represents the dark side of something potent and elemental. That's why they're fascinating.

But they're also important and instructive. Because while they give us a window onto the human condition, these cases also show us what can happen when we're not prepared to deal with them.

Each of these cases suffered from serious investigative difficulties, errors, irregularities, or other problems. In the Whitechapel murders, the investigators didn't yet understand what they were dealing with. In the Borden slayings, they were hamstrung by societal stereotypes about women and class. In the Lindbergh baby kidnapping, well-meaning and sympathetic officials lost control and let the connection to the kidnapper slip away from them. In the Christine Schultz and JonBenet Ramsey murders, the crime scenes and evidence were compromised from the get-go and the investigations stymied by departments with questionable agendas. With the Boston Strangler, a confession provided a simple, quick "solution" that ultimately proved unsatisfying and unconvincing.

These cases are also representative of much larger issues in crime solving and criminal justice. So what can be done?

Several things, I think.

We've made a lot of progress in the century-plus that this book spans, and as we've said, we think we could help solve some of these cases that haunt us if they were presented to us today. We have techniques, abilities, and understanding we didn't have back then, whether we're talking about the 1880s or the 1980s. DNA analysis, medical examination, computers, preservation of evidence, laser enhancement, modern psychology, profiling, interview techniques, threat assessment, and other fundamentals of investigation are just a few of these. And yet even as you read this, several thousand unidentified dead are lying in the nation's morgues. In 1960, the clearance rate for homicide was around 91 percent. Now, due to factors such as proliferation of "stranger" murders (that is, offenders and victims unknown to one another), it's around 65 percent.

Unless we actually use what we've got and learn how to consistently manage investigations in a uniform and competent way, all of the modern developments and improvements are going to be meaningless. If you have excellent techniques for hair and fiber analysis but adulterate the crime scene before the evidence team arrives, you've got nothing. If you can identify murder weapons from bullet markings but don't determine who was in possession of the weapon, you've got nothing. If DNA evidence can determine which specific individual in the entire world was at a scene but your chain of custody is called into question, you've got nothing. We could go on and on with examples.

I speak all over the country on criminology and related subjects. When I address and meet with victims' groups, people always come up to me and describe absolutely heinous crimes that I've never heard of. And if I haven't, who else has outside the immediate circle of those affected? With such serial killers as John Wayne Gacy, Jeffrey Dahmer, and Joel Rifkin, the dead had piled up before authorities even knew there was a problem. There are not only more violent crimes than there used to be, but increasingly they're committed by "strangers"—someone who doesn't know and has no personal grudge against the victim . . . the victim of opportunity. And that kind of homicide gives us big problems.

The point is, we've got to use what we've got, better and more efficiently than we're doing now.

In 1985, I attended a ribbon-cutting ceremony at Quantico for the FBI's new VICAP: the Violent Criminal Apprehension Program. Attorney General William French Smith and Bureau director William Webster attended. VICAP is a computer database listing in-depth particulars of predatory crimes. It was intended that when one of the more than seventeen thousand law enforcement agencies in this country had a violent predatory case—a potential serial murder or rape, for example—the case would be entered into the computer by filling out a carefully constructed questionnaire, and then VICAP would be able to provide them with the experience of anyone else in the country who had similar evidence or clues. It was a tremendous idea, coming originally from former LAPD homicide detective Pierce Brooks.

But while the profiling program quickly got on its feet and established itself, VICAP faltered and stumbled. By the time I retired from the Bureau in 1995, only a few thousand cases had been entered. The local agencies just didn't want to go through the trouble, particularly if not everyone else was doing it. Meanwhile, the Canadians have studied our system, instituted their own, and run with it. The difference? Participation by Canadian forces is mandated. Anyone who doesn't use it risks losing government funding. It does no good to have a sophisticated national resource like this unless everyone participates.

As anyone who's read Mark's and my recent novel, *Broken Wings*, knows, for a long time I've been advocating the creation of a "flying squad." This would be a team of specialists in all areas of criminal investigation—detectives, profilers, medical examiners, crime scene technicians, ballistics, hair, fiber, and blood-spatter experts, forensic anthropologists and entomologists, whatever is needed—who could quickly get to a major crime scene anywhere in the United States in their own well-equipped plane and work the case while it is still fresh and uncorrupted. They wouldn't all have to be Bureau people, either. I would make it like the military's Delta Force, taking the best people from whichever agency or service could provide them.

I also advocate the establishment of an independent national laboratory for processing evidence, separate from the FBI and other federal agencies, whose scientists would be the best and whose reports would be reliable and unassailable. One of the issues we've seen in some of our haunting cases is that we really don't know whose facts or whose evidence to believe. For example, was rail sixteen a legitimate piece of the Lindbergh kidnapping ladder or was it planted by overeager police officers? Was Elizabeth Short cut in two while she was still alive or after death? This lab could go a long way toward restoring the credibility of evidence in criminal investigations and prosecutions.

In the meantime, states can do some things on their own. A lot of times, a local police department's or prosecutor's office's chief problem is that it can't or won't communicate, either with the victims of a crime, the public in general, or other departments. I think this could be greatly ameliorated if each state would set up a major-crimes task force. Some have already done so, and the results have been impressive.

Such a group would hold regular meetings with representatives of individual police and sheriff's departments and state investigative and lab facilities. They'd hear formal presentations on various aspects of forensic science and discuss both hot and cold cases. The critical consideration is that each official, detective, or investigator anywhere in the state would know what resources were available and how they could be used. This would avoid a Ramsey-type situation in that a local department without necessary resources or experience would have both the means and, just as important, the self-assurance to quickly call on the best help available.

While the FBI hasn't enjoyed the success I would have liked to see on VICAP, a major, nearly incalculable contribution has been made with the National Academy program. Chiefs, division heads, and senior officers and detectives of local and regional agencies are brought to Quantico for intensive training, orientation, and familiarity with the latest trends and techniques of law enforcement. Not only does the National Academy give its graduate fellows a deeper understanding and wider perspective, it also creates an informal network of people around the country and the world who know each other and can call on each other when the need arises.

Some of my greatest successes have come about because the local officials who called in my unit had become familiar with us through participation in the National Academy. The 1985 investigation of the Shari Faye Smith and Debra May Helmick murders in South Carolina I alluded to in the previous chapter were examples of what can happen when profiling and related services are married to superior local police work to catch a serial killer before he can go any further in his devastation. And I've often said that one of the key reasons for this was because the two outstanding officers in charge, Sheriff Jim Metts and Undersheriff Lew McCarty, were both National Academy graduates. Metts understood that by calling us in, he was not displaying weakness or uncertainty, but strength and commitment to putting together the best team he could to protect his community. And for that reason he, McCarty, Rochester police captain Lynde Johnson, and so many others like them will always be heroes and role models in my book.

There are other lessons and commonalities in these cases that I hope come through.

Borden, Bembenek, and Ramsey demonstrate that you don't just wake up one morning and decide to become a murderer. There is always some predictive behavior. If there isn't or you can't find it, then you've really got to wonder about your suspect. And the Boston Strangler case shows that a criminal can't suddenly and for no reason change his personality.

The Ripper, Zodiac, Dahlia, and Ramsey cases all teach us that there is no such thing as a motiveless crime. It just means you don't fully understand it.

Lindbergh, Borden, and Ramsey—particularly Ramsey—can warn us of the danger of jumping to a conclusion without knowing or understanding critical facts, because of preconceived notions. If we do, we play right into the hands of the tabloid and sensationalistic media and are no better than they are. In the Ramsey case, even the mainstream media came under their influence to the detriment of all . . . except the person who got away with murder. If there is a feeding frenzy to be the first, truth is the likely casualty, as we saw in the unfair accusations against security guard Richard Jewell in the Atlanta Olympic Park bombing case, a perfect example of the perversion of profiling by people who didn't really understand what it was all about.

Conventional wisdom is often based on mythology, and each time and place is going to have its own set of standards.

Lizzie Borden couldn't have killed her parents because that's not the way well-off, well-brought-up ladies behave.

It must have been someone like Bruno Hauptmann who killed Lucky Lindy's baby because a true American wouldn't have done that.

Bambi Bembenek must have killed Christine Schultz because she was an aggressive, conniving second wife.

The Ramseys must be responsible for their daughter's death or else they would have cooperated with the police.

These are not statements of truth or fact. They are myths of conventional wisdom.

And finally, I think of these cases like statues on a war memorial: a few specific images that represent all of the thousands upon thousands of soldiers who cannot be named but who gave and suffered just as much.

Two weeks after JonBenet Ramsey's murder, a nine-year-old child, known only as Girl X to protect her identity and privacy, was beaten, raped, poisoned, and left for dead in a corridor of Chicago's notorious Cabrini Green public housing project. She was found by a janitor with her own T-shirt tied around her neck and gang symbols scrawled on her body. She wasn't a child beauty queen and she didn't come from a prominent or wealthy family. But she suffered unspeakably, and she and her family deserved not only our sympathy, but our attention and outrage, just as every victim does.

The same year that JonBenet died, 804 children aged twelve and under were murdered in the United States, according to the FBI's 1996 Uniform Crime Report. Yet there is only one name among them that we know. I don't want to take anything from the enormity of what happened to JonBenet, I only want the same emotions extended to all the others.

Like those fallen soldiers, there are thousands upon thousands of cases that you will never hear about that will never be given sufficient attention or resources to be solved. And those cases haunt me just as much.

INDEX